SEDUCED
BY THE
SEA

SEDUCED
BY THE
SEA

MORE STORIES FROM
SEAFARING KIWIS

EDITED BY
TESSA DUDER

HarperCollins_Publishers_

National Library of New Zealand Cataloguing-in-Publication Data

Seduced by the sea / edited by Tessa Duder.
ISBN 1-86950-446-1
1. Seafaring life—Anecdotes. 2. Sailors—New Zealand-Anecdotes.
I. Duder, Tessa.
910.45—dc 21

First published 2002
Reprinted 2003
HarperCollins*Publishers (New Zealand) Limited*
P.O. Box 1, Auckland

ISBN 1 86950 446 1

Designed and typeset by Janine Brougham
Set in Times New Roman
Printed by Griffin Press, South Australia on 80 gsm Bulky Book Ivory

Contents

Preface

Salt Beneath the Skin, an anthology of true sea stories, was published in late 1999 as the 2000 America's Cup challenge got under way on Auckland's Hauraki Gulf.

The success of the book proved two things: that there was no shortage of readers eager for stories written by seafaring Kiwis, and second, that there was no shortage of fine writers about the sea.

Seduced by the Sea is a second collection, appearing as New Zealand prepares to defend the Cup for a second time in its home waters of the Hauraki Gulf. Two years after the first successful defence, there is less need to shout New Zealand's rich maritime heritage from the rooftops, to demonstrate to an incredulous world how a small, remote country of almost four million people could take on the giants of international yachting and win the America's Cup — twice, the only country besides America to do so. Even if a mighty challenger emerges from the rough and tumble of the Louis Vuitton Cup series and takes the Cup back to the northern hemisphere, the point will have been well made.

As an Aucklander who travels quite regularly around the country, I see clear evidence of a growing awareness and pride in our maritime activities and heritage. A growing number of port areas and heritage buildings — in Auckland, Whangarei, Napier, Wellington, Wanganui, Timaru, Hokitika and Oamaru — are being revitalised and returned to public use. Cruise ships, among the world's biggest, now regularly berth at major ports: over forty ship visits to Auckland during the 2001–2 summer alone. The superyacht industry in Auckland and Whangarei goes from strength to strength.

Most dramatically, a four-part television documentary *Captain's Log*, screened in 2001, took stunned viewers on a circumnavigation replicating James Cook's historic chart-making voyage of 1769–70 — stunned because they had little knowledge of Cook's achievement, and no idea that our varied coastline, its working vessels and their stories could make such riveting high-rating television. From that came *Captain's Log: New Zealand's Maritime History* written by the country's leading maritime historian, Dr Gavin McLean, among a general surge of books on maritime matters.

Seduced by the Sea presents a second collection of Kiwis' sea stories. About half are from published books or magazines by some of the great names, Dr David Lewis, Dame Naomi James, Johnny Wray, Gerry Clark, Rob Hamill, with a few surprises like merchant sailors Hank Cavendish and Peter Taylor; rock star turned solo voyager Andrew Fagan; Freddy Ladd learning to land on water; and Pippa, Lady Blake, writing of her honeymoon voyage with the late Sir Peter from England to New Zealand in 1980.

For the other half I am indebted to the *Sunday Star-Times*. From an appeal for stories by contemporary writers, ten were selected. They spin tales as graphic as Gordon Mann's nearly fatal encounter with a rogue wave off the coast of Sydney; as amusing as Gwen Skinner's violin recital in a Greek harbour; as insightful as J. Edward Brown's first run as a newly qualified radio operator to the Chathams.

There are four parts. The longest section is 'Passages', celebrating those who crossed oceans for reasons of challenge, pleasure, or simply, in the days before air travel, to get to another country. Thus Englishman Charles Wycherley and his family of eleven emigrate to New Zealand via the longest passage of them all, non-stop from England to New Zealand. Four cross the Tasman east-about: settler Sarah Mathew in 1840, Andrew Keyworth on *Pamir*'s last such voyage, Neil Arrow and Andrew Fagan in small yachts. Jenny Webster sails her catamaran from Alaska to Canada, and Stephen Prinselaar travels from Las Palmas to the Cape. Graeme Dixon's family weathers a tough cruise to Stewart Island. Rob Hamill rows the Atlantic, west-about.

'Running Free' emphasises the meditative, lyrical or plain funny aspects of seafaring. Anthony Swainston lands two record fish — or are they? Sarah Ell goes racing with a bunch of hard-sailing, hard-partying mates in the Hauraki Gulf. The young Andrew Fagan learns to capsize in Wellington harbour, and terrified adult novice Barbara Newburgh takes a swim in the Christchurch Estuary. For Ted Dawe, it all happened on a beach. Anne French meditates that being skipper means you never get a good night's sleep.

By contrast, 'Working on Water' takes us into the world of professional sailors, fishermen, divers and explorers: the merchant seamen, naval shiphandler Jack Welch, Pacific navigator David Lewis, pioneering seaplane pilot Freddy Ladd, Antarctic ornithologist Gerry Clark, radio operator J. Edward Brown, *Pamir* mate Andrew Keyworth.

'Drama at Sea' tells of those who came through Tasman and Pacific storms, Grand Banks fog, shipwreck on a sub-Antarctic island, rescuing a castaway Barry Crump — and survived to share their fear, despair, strength and courage.

8

Finally, there are the poets, those whose works frequently draw on images and metaphors of the sea: Denis Glover, Hone Tuwhare and Anne French.

To all the writers contributing their experiences at sea and their narrative skills to a memorable new collection, sincerest thanks.

Tessa Duder
Auckland, April 2002

Acknowledgements

Warm thanks go to deputy editor Donna Chisholm and literary editor Iain Sharp at the *Sunday Star-Times* for their help in calling for contributions, resulting in eleven memorable and unpublished pieces from all corners of New Zealand; to others who wrote original pieces, Anne French, Sarah Ell and Jack Welch; to the former editor of *Sea Spray*, Shane Kelly, for his invaluable help in tracking down Ian Walker and Jenny Webster; and to the ever-helpful librarians at the Auckland Central and Takapuna Public Libraries.

Measurements (of distances, boat length, etc) have been given in metres or retained as the more traditional miles, yards and feet, as appropriate to the extract.

Contributors

The publishers are grateful to the following authors, publishers and copyright holders for their permission to reproduce copyright material:

Part One:

Anne French, 'Going Aboard', from *Cabin Fever*, (Auckland University Press, 1990); Andrew Fagan, *Swirly World in Perpetuity*, (HarperCollins Publishers (New Zealand), 2001); Pippa Blake, *Sea Spray*, (Slice Publications, December 1980); Brian Clifford and Neil Illingworth, *The Voyage of the Golden Lotus*, (A H & A W Reed, 1962); Bill Wycherley for Charles Wycherley, *Leaving England, from The Diary of Charles Wycherley, Voyage on the* Jessie Readman, *London to New Zealand, 1885*; Jenny Webster, *Sea Spray*, (Slice Publications, November 1988); Graeme Dixon, *Close Hauled to Stewart Island (and Back!)*, (previously unpublished); Stephen Prinselaar, *Las Palmas to the Cape*, (previously unpublished); Robin Grigg, *Under Squares off Akaroa*, (previously unpublished); Rob Hamill, *The Naked Rower*, (Hodder Moa Beckett, 2000); Tessa Duder, *Travelling by Sea*, (previously unpublished)

Part Two:

Anne French, 'So Many Days', (previously unpublished); Sarah Ell, *The Adventures of the Good Ship* Whimaway, (previously unpublished); Andrew Fagan, *Learning to Capsize*, (previously unpublished); Barbara Newburgh, *Caul of the Sea*, (previously unpublished); Ted Dawe, *It All Happened at the Beach*, (previously unpublished); Gwen Skinner, *Making Music in the Adriatic*, (previously unpublished); Anthony Swainson, *Two Records before Breakfast*, (previously unpublished); Anne French, *On Being the Skipper*, (previously unpublished); Gretchen Brassington, *Stoney's Story*, (previously unpublished)

Part Three:

Hone Tuwhare, 'Sea Call', from *No Ordinary Son*, (Random House New Zealand, 1964); Jack Welch, *Ship-Handling*, (previously unpublished); Jane Taylor, *From Rudders to Udders – and back again*, (Col-Com Press, 1996); Peter Taylor, *Wet Behind the Ears*, (HarperCollins Publishers (New Zealand), 2001); David Lewis, *Shapes on the Wind*, (HarperCollins Publishers (Australia), 2000); Sid Marsh, *Divers Tales*, (Reed Publishing, 1991); Fred Ladd with Ross Annabell, *A Shower of Spray and We're Away*, (A H & A W Reed, Wellington, 1971); Jeanette Churchouse for Andrew Keyworth in Jack Churchouse, *The* Pamir *Under the New Zealand Flag*, (Millwood Press, 1978); Marjorie Clark for Gerry Clark, *The* Totorore *Voyage*, (Century Hutchinson, 1988); J. Edward Brown, *To the Chathams on Matai*, (previously unpublished)

Part Four:

Rupert Glover for Denis Glover, 'Cross-Tides', from *The Wind in the Sands*, (Caxton Press, 1945); New Zealand Red Cross Incorporated for John Wray, *South Sea Vagabonds*, (Herbert Jenkins Ltd, 1939); Naomi James, *At Sea on Land*, (Hutchinson, 1981; used by permission of The Random House Group Limited); Ian Walker, *Sea Spray*, Slice Publications, March 1990; Jack Crooks, *Rescuing Crumpy*, (previously unpublished); Gordon Mann, *Rogue Wave*, (previously unpublished)

PART ONE
PASSAGES

Going Aboard

Here we are ashore with the metaphors.
Here is my small cabin trunk, from which I
may not unpack certain items. Nor, if at all
possible, allude to them, even on an afternoon
when the wind is spanking through the channel

between Nelson Island and Kaikoura Island
and the sun is shining on the waves as though sun
and waves will not cease. And your large sailing-
bag, whose mysteries are neatly stowed where all
the sea's rolling will never shift them.

Now it is time to go aboard, to risk a foot slipping
on the lines. Look, there you go, stepping so lightly
without looking, the improbable left foot below the
knot,
right on the stemhead, left over the rail; and you are
aboard, leaning over the pulpit, one hand stretched out.

Anne French

Swirly World in Perpetuity

ANDREW FAGAN, better known as a member of the 1980s rock band The Mockers, took part in the 1994 Solo Tasman Yacht Race from New Plymouth. Eventually he was to set a record for the smallest boat to complete a Tasman return crossing.

He was no blue-water novice. In his beloved 5.2 metre *Swirly World in Perpetuity*, inspired by his hero Johnny Wray, he had built up some impressive blue-water experience: a voyage to Sunday Island in the Pacific and back; a coastal voyage to Wellington and back. Despite a controversy surrounding her size (significantly less than the 7.62m required minimum length), *Swirly World* was eventually allowed to enter the Tasman race. She finished long after bigger, faster competitors, to win her division ('there was no one else in it') and her rock star skipper much public acclaim.

But Fagan had a problem: to get his little ship back to New Zealand. *Swirly World* was laid up at the Moreton Bay Yacht Club for six months while her owner went back to his music in New Zealand. But it was never far from his thoughts that sooner or later he had to get *Swirly World* home.

*S*ix months were gone. I had to get *Swirly World* out of Australia. It had been inevitable, a sentence hanging over me. I had to get the boat back before the cyclone season.

This time I would be without the support and psychological security blanket the race and the New Plymouth Yacht Club had provided. It had been a good warm up . . . for the return voyage. We were only halfway there. On making it back to New Zealand, *Swirly World* would become the smallest boat to have sailed both ways across the Tasman. That was a partial incentive. I wasn't sure I wanted to go, but it was obvious I had to.

The weather had changed, something I'd been counting on. Hard westerlies had been howling across the sea to New Zealand for the past couple of months, just the direction I was hoping for. The wind never sounds good at night. Blowing in the trees, hearing all that motion, the wind letting you know it's there.

The Tasman Sea beneath us was covered in cloud and kept from view. It didn't matter as I had no window seat and from that height there wasn't much to see. I arrived at Brisbane Airport with a limited budget (two hundred dollars Australian) and seven pieces of luggage. David Manzi from De Amalfi was true to his word and I was gratefully loaded down with the GPS, EPIRB, etc. The life raft, and a pile of freeze-dried and boil-in-the-bag rations were to follow on later in the week. In packhorse mode I staggered from bus to train then to the Sandgate taxi rank and finally, just before another humid Queensland dusk, I was deposited at the Moreton Bay Boat Club.

Turning down past the tree-clad reserve next to the motor camp I spied *Swirly World*'s radar reflector on top of the mast. A mast high enough to need a hull floating on the surface. A good start. There were no other competitors about. No one I knew. The club was swinging into full action mode with lots of social members coming to the end of their 'happy hour', with a busy bar, food on tables, corner solo entertainer. Everyone having a reasonable time. The enormity of having to sail back to Auckland sullied my impression of things. I'd felt this way before.

John and Joy, from the steel replica of Slocum's Spray *Ada Jane*, had been aboard a few weeks earlier to mop out rainwater and I borrowed their dinghy to reach the pile mooring. Dave Walker, my Redcliffe-New Zealander storer of sails, sextant, SSB and folding dinghy turned up simultaneously and I ferried all the bits out to *Swirly World*.

Jim had warned me about cockroaches or 'cockies' as the locals fondly called them. Each item moved was intensely scrutinised but two still managed to make it onto *Swirly World*'s deck. They were more creatures than insects and equipped with wings. I expected a fight on my hands. They fought bravely, almost tactically, but somehow fell into the sea. Apart from the large pelicans having obviously enjoyed *Swirly World* as a defecation perch, all was as we had left it. Only the wind indicator was missing from the top of the mast. Pelicans . . .

I'd allowed seven days before leaving but it stretched to eleven while waiting for the life raft to arrive from Auckland. Each day the boat systems went back together, a new expensive carburettor for the engine, GPS wired in, secure stowage and plastic bags for everything and screwable bungs on the offending drainage holes in the main hatch. New antifouling, new log cable crimped in, weathercloths and self-steering, batteries charged on the marina. Sleeping aboard and slipping back into the rhythms of single narrow bunk living, one burner Primus — life in the *Swirly World* space capsule. The weather was unsettled, hard westerly one day, fresh sea breeze the next, light southeasterly, thunder and lightning storms. Each day more suitably subtropical than Auckland.

The Commodore gave me a temporary member's pass to use their clean and tidy facilities and to spend as much as I dared on Australian-made brown liquid. After the rapid loss of sunlight each evening I'd row back to get a weak portion of beer, empathise with the corner entertainment, and possibly do a conversation or two.

They were turning over forty thousand dollars a month in the bar. A lot of people are practised at standing around talking, interspersed with standing around drinking. Time goes by. Long periods of time. People enjoy it. I could have enjoyed it more, but something was worrying me. It had something to do with 1200 miles of sea to the southeast. In the company of others I didn't know, I felt left out and misplaced. 'New Zealand in what? How long? Have you thought about selling her?'

The party was over but I'd hung around too long. Now I was on my own. The only way home was *Swirly World*, the sooner the better. Stop hanging around. You'll envy them the security of their bar in a few days' time . . . I couldn't underestimate the mileage to come. Walking pace across the sea. We had to get out of Australia but what would the wind bring?

Dave Reid, another friend of Jim Williamson, gave me rides about Brisbane, foraging for the overdue life raft and eventually retrieved it for me. A few days prior to leaving, a Friday-night barbecue was held at his place in honour of *Swirly World*'s departure. We dined outdoors amongst the foreign chatter of exotic wild parakeets and caged canaries.

'So you're off then, can't say I envy you.' Someone mentioned Ross River fever, a localised neighbourhood thing.

'Which neighbourhood?'

'This one.' Mosquitoes carried it. There had been a lot of little things flying around all evening. They should have said something earlier, I didn't want to go to sea with a subtropical disease on the boil.

Dave had wanted to hear some of my 'new stuff', so I brought a copy of the single 'Exciting' over for him. As the evening progressed Dave monopolised the sound system. 'Exciting' got its chance and quickly became anything but, as we all had many opportunities to hear it even louder next time. High on grog he invaded a teenage party next door. No one followed as reinforcements. Soon 'Exciting' was very audible across the back gardens. Dave was scouting for a fresh audience for me. Above and beyond the gardens, the ever-present wind waited patiently in the tall trees. No escaping it, soon we'd be with it.

In eleven brief days confined to the Redcliffe Peninsula, I locked in with shopkeeper faces and the rhythms of north suburban Brisbane. Sunny Queensland was rapidly running out of water and the farmers inland were feeling it bad. Parched earth and too much solar radiation, sunlight overload. A huge patch of the Indian Ocean, the size of Australia itself, had a surface sea temperature two degrees colder than usual and some believed it was responsible for the lack of precipitation.

Rain came by night, one particularly sticky, humid one. A fresh northeasterly and cloudless sky had given no warning of a cloudbank rising out of the south. On the verge of sleep and thinking not particularly productive thoughts, I noticed the wind suddenly drop, cloud racing up through the starry sky then lightning and thunder tones, heavy rain driving horizontal on an instant southeasterly squall shift. The palms on Oyster Point bent to the onslaught and the thunderstorm raced through off to the north. I slept fitfully with nightmares of savage possibilities. Over as it began, a mere fifteen minutes, and the next day was dry and sunny once more.

The survival gear arrived on Friday afternoon but wasn't to be cleared by Customs until Monday. Weekend off. Monday afternoon it was aboard *Swirly World*, a gloriously compact four-man Beauport life raft tucked securely inside aft of the mast support post. Thunderbirds were definitely go. At nine-thirty on the Tuesday morning the pre-booked customs officer arrived at the Club pontoon and with a minimum of fuss gave us clearance. On his identifying form the customs officer who met us at Mooloolaba had described *Swirly World* as 'looking like half the boat's been cut off.'

I'd collected fresh onions, oranges, pineapples, lemons, bread and cheese earlier that morning when the shops had opened, and after a cursory peer inside from the slightly bewildered customs man, it was time to start the engine and glide out alone, the wind to be our everything once more.

Two hands were shaken and once again *Swirly World* moved away, leaving two mildly unsure people in her wake. She had a habit of it. It was a quiet, sunny, calm weekday morning and no crowds had gathered on the breakwater to wish us well . . . No expectations from others, nor any expected.

Departure. Motoring out through the breakwaters, a school of large dolphins swam near to let me know I wouldn't be totally alone. The customs man beeped the horn on his expensive government Holden parked out on the breakwater arm (making sure we left). Three hours there, how many back?

A light northerly on the nose (surprise) with the promise of a northeasterly sea breeze freshening in Moreton Bay had me motivated to get the most out of the outgoing tide and move up beside Bribie Island before all the elements opposed us. Before heading southeast for New Zealand we had to go north round the top of Moreton Island, 20 miles to windward. We motored up to Bongaree on Bribie Island, giving the batteries a final decent charge until the breeze began filling in and *Swirly World* could sail hard on the wind on port tack for Gilligan's Island. A large motorised gin palace roared past heading for the Caboolture River. Someone on the bridgedeck bellowed the obvious question. 'New Zealand' sounded ambitious and probably wasn't heard.

Mathew Flinders would have approved. At the end of the eighteenth century he put in a lot of isolated miles around the coast of Australia. He'd charted the Pumicestone Passage dividing Bribie Island from the mainland, by sails and oars in a little undecked boat. He'd done many perilous coastal miles in the same vulnerable craft. *Swirly World*'s decked in, heavy-keeled, auxiliary-motored, GPS and self-steering splendour would have impressed him. And the batteries were fully charged for all those future conversations with Penta Comstat on the Australian coast and hopefully Kerikeri Radio in the Bay of Islands. With the passage of time the mariner's lot has undoubtedly improved.

Loaded down again with food and water for at least thirty-five days, *Swirly World* ploughed enthusiastically along, full main and genoa getting the best out of the breeze. The tide sucked us up to windward through the gap between Gilligan's and Bribie, a shallow patch kicking up short, awkward, breaking wind against tide wavelets. *Swirly World* was hindered more in such conditions than in offshore-scaled waves. Water-line length has a lot to do with it. Slam, crash, short slamming crash. Spray, spume, call it what you like, wetness everywhere.

On the nose back up Skirmish Passage the other way this time, the far distant skyline of the Caloundra buildings looked a dauntingly long way. If we'd needed the depth of water the huge ships racing past required, we would have been obliged to carry on all the way up to windward and Caloundra before being free of the shoals and able to head eastward. But as there was no significant swell or sea running in the bay, I picked an early moment to hang a right on to port again and tack out over the welcoming Wild Banks, setting us on course for the northern tip of Moreton Island. The Wild Banks were fortunately anything but, and the outgoing tide set us nicely to windward. We sailed over various shallow shades of blue suspicious sea and reached the less intimidating east channel exit to clear deeper water as the tide turned. Late thunderstorms had been forecast for Brisbane. The sea breeze eased to leave us wallowing maudlin with the prospect of seasickness and the reality of a long way to go, near the north end of Moreton.

Feeling unwell, I clung to the Perspex dodger on a lumpy swell. I watched the southerly cloud and associated thunder and lightning gradually work its way up the coast to eclipse Bribie, from where we had come, then Caloundra, and the distant peak of Mooloolaba's Point Cartwright, in violent black rain squalls. Ours was a parking spot with a view; the wind and wet stuff confined to the land behind. From there on the wind was going to be very important to me, and I didn't like the look of what it could bring.

I got our first GPS fix to check its accuracy before leaving land. The huge amount of application required in turning it on, holding it up and pressing a button was too much for me and I dry-retched my feeble self about the cockpit coaming. That windless sloppy sea had got the better of me. Grasping an immediate sense of purpose — progress, I resorted to motoring once more, direct for the Cape Morton light to pass close in near to cliffs under cover of darkness. The front hatch had to be open to cool the engine and a fair bit of wave toppings found their wet way inside. I was feeling too poorly to pay proper attention.

We rounded the corner in the company of a large motor sailer, spreader lights revealing its decks. It looked big, fast and comfortable inside. They turned south close in to the shore and followed the coast down. I steered *Swirly World* out further away from the immediate traffic lanes and onto the convenient conveyor belt known as the East Australian Current. The further out the better. Convenient if you want to go south at 3 knots without even trying. A few miles offshore I turned the engine off, resigned to a dark, windless night, feeling wretchedly ill and watching out for the lights of nearby shrimp boats. Setting the egg-timer alarm for the first of a series of deeply relaxing and refreshing (not) 20-minute mental disengagements. A catnap. Poor cat, never enough sleep.

On a confused sea *Swirly World* lurched and rolled vindictively. Leaving a headsail up and sheeted in hard steadied her a bit, but generally a despondent night was had by all. The current setting south revived my spirits when it became obvious we were being carried down to higher latitudes at wonderful speed. Without sailing or motoring, new shore lights were appearing on the coast, Stradbroke Island, old ones receding.

When it got light *Swirly World* was still becalmed and had done 20 miles south in seven effortless hours. Another sea-breezed afternoon arrived and with main and genoa poled out, we sledged south to reach Cape Byron by seven that evening. From being out of sight of land that morning, we'd edged back towards the coast all day to maintain maximum current thrust. With the even, rhythmic roll of running before the wind under self-steering my interest in existence picked up and I started functioning again.

The bright night-lights of the settlement cluster near Cape Byron glowed hospitable and secure. Let's go there, sell the boat, have a good time. The low flash of dim red ahead warned of lights unlisted on my large-scale chart so we gybed over to head offshore in a freshening northerly with a falling barometer, on course more or less for the top of New Zealand, 1100 miles southeast. Goodbye Australia. Offshore we must inevitably go.

Patches of fine drizzle set in and the barometer kept falling. Penta Comstat's morning weather forecast on 4483 confirmed that a depression was forming off the New South Wales coast. Coff's Harbour AM Radio began forecasting severe thunderstorms and strong to gale force northerlies. Great, just what I came for . . . what was I there for? Necessity. You've got to get the boat back, nowhere else to go. Don't remind me.

All day the wind increased as we reached away from the invisible land and south-setting current, under reefed main and working jib. Superb sailing was had by all, surfing down the growing seas at up to 9 knots. The low was going to bring the inevitable southerly change and southeasterly quarter blow right on the nose so the further southeast we tracked the better. Broad reaching in 35 knots I changed down gears to accommodate any further increases while I went below for a wind of the egg-timer alarm and a bit of a lie down. Going to bed before the gale . . .Warnings about huge hailstones and getting your car under cover not to mention hiding humans indoors had me eyeing the horizon for improbable shelter. Australian radio was doing its best to unsettle me.

Clouds of malevolent intent had been gathering all day on the western horizon. Gradually they reached out to engulf *Swirly World* in a downpour of cold, fresh water accompanied by the dreaded sight of forked lightning darting, unpredictable and impressive, to the surface of the sea — all over the place. Places nearby. I'd already deposited a couple of metres of battery cable bolted to a copper plate over the stern — clipped to the uninsulated backstay, but held little faith in it conducting the electricity harmlessly away from us. I'd seen the full fury of the discharges up close.

Cowering like a wee doggie on the foam quarterberth mattress, careful to avoid touching anything metallic, I listened in awe to the tones of destruction zapping down outside with simultaneous thunderclaps. How far away? I stopped looking. Fortunately all things come to pass and it did, taking much of the wind with it. No safe seat in the house — Australian thunderstorms. A couple of repeat performances, then the sky settled down. I elected to stay indoors for the evening, content to let the self-steering sail us gradually further southeast under working jib alone at 4 knots, 100 miles true east of Coff's Harbour, fatigued and disenchanted with the prospect of things to come.

While sleeping in the flash of the strobe light mounted on the cockpit dodger, the wind shifted to the southwest sometime near midnight and I awoke heading unhappily north. Going the wrong way for more than an hour without noticing a wind shift was tantamount to elemental deception. I would have to tune in more if we were going to get to New Zealand.

The sky was clear and cold, an audience of stars disinterested in our long overdue return to the right magnetic course. Sleepily re-aligned, we tight reached south as far as the wind would let us, before going hard on the wind against the inevitable southeasterly. Two reefs in the mainsail and the No.2 jib balanced well enough for the self-steering to cope with 30 knots.

Back indoors, strapped in the lee cloth and suspended in midair above the dirty dishes clanging about on the swinging Primus stove, it was life on an angle. The kind of conditions anticipated but not appreciated. A 4-metre swell built up quickly with a rough sea on top making progress for *Swirly World*'s water-line length slow — minimal even. Suffer the little children who grew into adults and wanted to go sailing on the deep, serious sea.

In the coming week *Swirly World*'s deck leaks were thoroughly detected. I knew where they were and the water knew how to get to where I was. The main offenders — air vents of course, keeping me mopping a bucket of water from the bouncing bilge every evening and morning, evening, morning . . . It was an uncomfortable start and my stomach agreed. Life in a lurching wet bed. Twice consumed by spasms of sicky expulsion when drawing up our position. Throwing up all remnants of application and enthusiasm into one small bucket. Appetite remained a distant memory. Plenty of food on board, but no one to put it in — yet.

Derek at Penta Comstat spoke of rough seas round Lord Howe Island and a heavy ground swell. The sky had begun to look friendly so things had to eventually ease. Rain squalls came and went, *Swirly World* ploughing faithfully on to windward over a very disorganised surface. The SSB roll calls made good listening with 'tremendous' being the most compelling adjective associated with one motor sailer's experiences off the coast. Appropriate that we'd got so far away from the wind versus current showdown before involuntarily hardening up onto the wind. The fresh southeasterly was there to stay due to a slow-moving high sitting south of us. We were destined to seven days on the wind slowly tracking east-northeast up and away, at a hearty 3 to 4 knots, away from beloved Aotearoa and towards Norfolk and fuelless enough to be confined to working the wind as the sea ancestors did. The reality of actually coming to a halt when the wind deems it so made *Swirly World* privileged in a purist way. But there was nothing privileged about being subjected to hours of perpetual unpredictable motion. The endless noise of wave-slapping sounds, water rushing, crashing, pouring, dripping all about. Patience, perseverance, endurance. Things to willingly manifest, I tried to convince myself. As Joe Davison said in a later letter, 'conditions sent to test a sailor's resolve.' A hard-work way to see it. Application was needed. Round-the-clock wind fluctuation called for sheets to be retrimmed, self-steering realigned. A constant sensitivity to balancing the wind's influence. And the rest of the time? Something's happening in your mind. Isolated environment immersion (IEI) makes you think differently. Or perhaps you think you're thinking differently? I'm not sure. Why aren't you sure? Haven't had enough sleep. Are you sure?

In the face of perpetual nonstimulus from outside distractions, emotions sift through memories. Encouraging or discouraging, made all the more poignant by sleep deprivation to an almost hallucinogenic degree. The things we've thunk about over the years.

The frequencies of sea colour and water movement sounds affect you physiologically. They tone up the etheric body and all the while you're immersed in one huge negative ion bath called salt water. All a bit natural.

As wind and sea moderated more sail came out until the deck was festooned with damp, smelly fabrics. *Swirly World* drifting becalmed 280 miles almost true west of Norfolk Island. There was nothing to see . . . other than sea and sky. The anticyclone had decided to set us free and was heading slowly north over the top of us. *Swirly World*'s deck resembled a chemistry experiment. Salt crystals covered all, the residue of our wetness.

All alone here, but entertaining elsewhere, when I went into sleep consciousness I made contact with otherworldly entities. Called dreams on land, at sea they took on a greater significance. I'd meet with unidentified presences, most often encountered on rocks beside a still sea and twilight sky, and experience calm moments of conversation. My mind was keeping me occupied.

On a sloping, pastoral hillside, set in tall pockets of secondary manuka growth, a shantytown of scattered eccentric dwellings stretched down to mud flats in a sheltered tidal bay. A hard wind blew and handpainted flags with unorthodox motifs flew spectacularly from the ridges. Ancient vehicles, boats, watertanks and tent-like structures had been hauled up the hillside to provide accommodation of an unconventional kind. Perched in surrounding gullies, large hydroponic growing rooms soaked up sunlight. Large wind generators blurred energy-generating blades and solar panels absorbed the sun's silent radiation.

In a separate gully a large barn-like structure emanated live music and in smaller similar units it sounded like theatre groups and amateur bands were rehearsing. A network of flying foxes criss-crossed the slopes and gullies and people were travelling through the air.

Down on the mud flats a huge sailing catamaran — 75 metres long, sat high and dry, three tall masts devoid of sail. A large flying fox terminated beside it and people were loading bales of food. Not the kind of nourishment New Zealand is usually known for— mutton, beef and beer — it was concentrated protein, durable, long-lasting, just add water and you're in business. Beans. No refrigeration or rapid transit required. The hillsides were dedicated to legume production. On closer inspection even the odd dwellings were wrapped in the green tendrils of bean growth. Intensive horticulture and everything engineless. Winch and tackle, pulleys and hemp rope. Manual effort and a completely different concept of time replaced oil-based mechanical exertion.

Where was the dehydrated protein going? It sounded like a long-term Red Cross nutrition mission, transporting fresh water from isolated rivers, and grains and pulses from the growing regions to the overpopulated deprived zones. Wind-driven food and water carriers riding the timeless trade winds and Southern Ocean conveyor belts and currents of the globe to the under-resourced Old World. Only a drop in the ocean but not a bad sense of purpose.

Were they survivors of some human catastrophe or a voluntary branch of separated consciousness? A Spielberg post-meteorite thriller or parallel eco-universe? It was hard to tell. The sloping hillside looked good for launching a hang-glider, then I found myself running off the ridge and leaping faithfully out into empty air. The wind held me up and it was real, the sensation of flying unaided. With a few leg movements I could clumsily direct my airborne path and with a little effort I managed to lift up above the circle of hills to see the ocean stretching away up the coast. Down and out over the wave tops, using the breeze like a seabird, effortlessly controlling my elevation. The sound of the sea beneath became louder and the flight a little turbulent then I slowly seeped back into the all-consuming noise and motion. A sailing boat journeying on the surface of the ocean and I was in it. Alone again, hundreds of miles from land. For a moment I'd forgotten.

Then I remembered, it was my final segment of the Messiah World Championships. Your messianic vision of the future in less than 30 seconds. Keep it simple. The plan for the sons of man. The advertising agency's video representation of 'how your life could do more for you'. I needed a good night's sleep.

Technically asleep, I often had visitors. One lectured on the vitality of triangles and the triangular relevance of sails. I awoke with the name Vito Dumas in mind. An Argentinean solo sailor, since deceased, who circumnavigated the globe engineless in high latitudes in the 1940s.

Elderly, imposing entities were back the next night scrutinising my emotional attitudes and sorting out amongst themselves whether *Swirly World* should make it back to Cape Reinga. Penetrating and disconcerting, I can still remember their eyes. Otherworldly gatekeepers. Are you worth it? Did we deserve it? Pass on that one. A question of self-belief to a certain extent. Faith in oneself manifested in resolve. Mind was taking me where body could not. Most encounters would end with having to politely inform those in my company that I had to be elsewhere and would have to get back to my body hundreds of miles out to sea. Sensing the motion of the sea movement and sound of water noise returning, fully present in the *Swirly World* space capsule again.

Food finally resurfaced as a source of interest. Funny how a flat calm surface always did that. De Amalfi were the agents for the 'Freddy Chef' and 'Harvest Foodworks' brands of freeze-dried and boil-in-the-bag meals. Not quite what you'd seek out at the supermarket weekly shop but very convenient out at sea, when the only effort required was adding boiling water. An extra 'sauce' sachet gave more taste than expected; my one-pot extravaganzas became worth looking forward to.

Our pause, 600 miles short of New Zealand, was followed by a benevolent warm northerly blowing down from tropical latitudes and freshening to allow us the pleasure of pointing the bows finally towards the Promised Land.

For three days and nights *Swirly World* ran before the wind, clocking 115-mile runs in consecutive 24-hour periods. It appeared we weren't going to be out there forever so I took the opportunity to hand steer during the day as much as possible. Breakfast at dawn (muesli and water — dull but chewable) followed by the making of a packed lunch, then goodbye inside, hello outdoor living, hand on the stainless tiller instinctively keeping sails powered up with the thrust of forward motion, the invisible wind always urging us on. Steering away the day, the sun slowly moved through the sky, subtly changing the look of the seascape with its travels up, across and down. By dark the self-steering kept us going southeast, a slightly reduced sail maintaining the appropriate balance. Keep her moving, sliding southeast, home over the horizon . . . keep moving.

Typical low dark frontal cloud descended as we crossed the shallow Wanganella Banks and the agitated current induced a confused sea state. Bigger than before, gullies of water careered about. A shoal patch to be avoided in heavy weather. A serious place where freighters could founder. Not enough wind this time. Rain brought the southerly change and with two reefs and the No.2 jib, *Swirly World* hardened up onto another tight reach, on course more or less for North Cape, southeast and unseen. Successfully dodging cold harsh rain squalls on top of impolite seas, it was back to life on an uncomfortable angle, undoubtedly down in colder latitudes. It couldn't last and didn't, the gradual improvement in weather welcomed with more sail, an even sea and increased boat speed.

The shallow low responsible for our southerly wind direction paused over the upper North Island, kindly maintaining a convenient air flow compared with the impending southeasterly forecast. No more southeasterlies please. Not another contrary forecast.

Pointing where we wanted to go, even if the horizon ahead remained endlessly empty, was a more fulfilling way of travelling. The wind spirits agreed with me and on the wind we stayed, heeled over for another few days and nights, pointing the right way.

To get the best out of *Swirly World* and maintain concentration over long periods of time I stuck Chris Dickson, and when he got tired, Russell Coutts, down to leeward in an identical boat to *Swirly World*. Hour after hour I kept a loose cover on them, *SWI* keeping *SWII* and her furious champions pinned down to leeward. Maybe if we got Kevlar sails and changed the keel shape we'd get a bit more out of her . . .

Inner Dunedin Harbour is shaped a lot like Evans Bay. Wind blowing up or down it. Coutts stood behind me in the queue at the P Class nationals while we waited to have our centreboards measured. It was what competitive teenage males did in their weekends. Even Russell had to stand in line at the Nationals. 'I remember you.'

'I remember you too.' That's because I beat you. I beat him twice again in similar conditions in the Tauranga Cup. Sixty-something little boats behind us . . . If the wind picked up I usually ended up further back in the fleet, crossing tacks with an also-ran from Nelson or Bucklands Beach, heroically battling it out for the honour of ourselves primarily, and our sailing clubs sometimes. I didn't know that would be the pinnacle of my fleet competitiveness.

On our sixteenth day out from Scarborough the horizon renewed my interest with the Three Kings appearing ahead to starboard at dawn, just as the GPS predicted. Land ho. It looked great, all grey and permanent. A distant solid something. All day watching the shape of Great Island gradually close and change as we sailed slowly past towards the top of the North Island. After another tireless circuit of the sky the sun plunged down to silhouette Cape Reinga and Spirits Bay where it's said the released souls of Maori dead soar north. I didn't see any in the daylight but I kept looking. *Swirly World* was close in under North Cape, having tight reached at 6 knots for 12 hours, relatively secure with the proximity of land.

Being so close to New Zealand that I could see it was a pleasure. I was too pleased, and at 3 a.m. a close encounter with a steel ship got me rethinking my application to lookout duties. We saw each other. They looked close enough to disturb my sleepy startled self.

Close to the coast on the route from the rest of New Zealand to North Cape there are lots of those things motoring around. Big steel mobile islands. In 20 minutes one can come over an empty horizon and be on top of you. Out in the Tasman the chances are slight, but you never know, they might. I only saw one coming back. How many saw me?

While sleeping in the more frequented areas I enlisted the support of a strobe light designed 'for when you need to be seen', a description appropriate for on-stage performances. It ended up seeing more indoor activity than out. But there in the watery darkness it flashed with reassuring conspicuousness. Egg-timer catnaps were brief. No one's going to run us over now we're this close. Just stay awake, go on, it's fun.

Next day the wind left us to savour the primary scent, colour and contrast of land close at hand off the Cavalli Islands. Eighteen hours worth. I did a little becalmed battery charging, motoring towards a hazy, distant Cape Brett but it seemed hardly worth it at 3 uneconomical knots. Too much noise, vibration and heat. Let's wait for the wind.

There was an old Cavallis chart on board, all brown and heavily stained, more like a treasure map. When I first found it years previous, the Cavallis looked a very long way from Auckland. At that time I hadn't sailed alone past Waiheke. Having done 1100 miles to get there, the way I viewed distances had changed considerably.

An obliging northerly crept up unseen by dark and sent us on our way gurgling downwind once more. Whales off Whangarei checked us out in a big way. Lots of them at rest and play, launching thin chins and bluff profiles lackadaisically skyward. It was their gig. I'd write the review if they let me off the stage. Large smooth pools of disturbed sea water, where coy monsters had recently surfaced then sunk, all around us. We were outnumbered and outsized. While waiting for the wind we stayed surrounded. They weren't that interested in us. I couldn't say the same and I had no choice. The wind eventually allowed an escape, running flat off with the spinnaker drawing us south for the gap between Leigh and Little Barrier Island. None of them bothered to follow.

The spinnaker. Nasty little spinnaker that had humiliated me at the start of the Tasman race. I'd left it sodden and twisted into a disgusting snarly ball in its sail bag for some time after that. Now near the end of the voyage I retrieved it from exile and gave it another chance. Without an audience the kite filled out with an air of redemption. I let it off. Could it really have been my fault? Not enough practice.

Swirly World tracked past familiar landmarks and into the outer Hauraki Gulf at her maximum 6 to 7 knots, surging to 9 on the right piece of liquid slope. Moonless, the phosphorescence made its presence known in no uncertain terms and dolphins joined us as *Swirly World* surfed into the Hauraki Gulf, their phosphorescence-lit bodies looking like benign torpedoes. For 2 hours we shared the closing miles of our voyage with an entourage of streamlined naturals. Apart from them, I was the only one watching.

A 12-metre American cruising yacht identified on the Kerikeri roll call was a couple of miles east of *Swirly World* and motoring for Auckland, giving an ETA of around 3 a.m. Overhearing them on the radio, they only had a 5-knot following northerly, hence their motoring. *Swirly World* on the same piece of sea most definitely had 15 glorious knots behind her and it was obvious by the respective progress of navigation lights that we were holding our own against them.

Precarious but successful, the kite was gybed under self-steering off Flat Rock light, then we ran down against a swiftly departing spring tide to Tiri Island. There they were again, opening up from behind the Whangaparaoa Peninsula, the bright lights of Auckland's East Coast Bays. After nineteen days and nights of sailing I'd come a long way to see Auckland with a more appreciative gaze.

Onto a broad reach that tightened all the way, we were finally aiming for the lit-up Auckland City buildings suspended over the Takapuna skyline. I'd done this run many late nights before. This time we were coming in out of the darkness beyond New Zealand without having stopped since being sick in the company of Moreton Island, almost three weeks before.

Now that we had become a part of the dark, the lights of the city looked spectacular. Free from the mid-sea worries of windworld it should be a pleasure to readjust to the land. At this point in my life it was hard to feel glum in paradise.

The motoring yacht had gradually pulled ahead of us but *Swirly World* had done admirably, holding 6 to 7 knots by wind alone. At 3 a.m. on 5 November, the spinnaker came down on top of me, all over the foredeck, and we gybed off North Head to ghost up the flat harbour on the beginning of the incoming tide. The batteries went flat in the handheld VHF as I was talking to the customs representative so I was left guessing where, and if, a welcoming committee of officialdom would greet us.

Johnny Wray in the *Ngataki* had always returned to Admiralty Steps but that had been in the 1930s. I aimed there, and discovered the American had already parked up. He was conspicuous, big and seaworthy. No sign of life on deck. There was no welcoming party, no finishing gun. I rafted *Swirly World* up to the pilot boat and paused to fill in a final log entry. Three hours there, 432 back. We'd doubled the Tasman. Good morning Auckland.

At 6 a.m. with the seeping of dawn into a sky of many office buildings above the open hatchway, Customs and MAF personnel arrived, camera clicking lest their colleagues didn't believe such a tiny craft had actually come in direct from Brisbane. 'You've been living in here for how long?'
'Long enough to want to get out now.'

After swift and friendly formalities I pulled down the inside-out yellow sweatshirt that had once again doubled as the quarantine flag, then motored round to Hobson Wharf and the Rangitoto Sailing Centre. There wasn't much traffic on the Waitemata at that hour.

I intended to take David Ingram by surprise, placing *Swirly World* in beside the Soling moorings. With the sun, the wind had picked up from the north sending a sloppy little sea onto the exposed pontoons. It was a man-made leeshore of exceedingly minor proportions. My sleep-deprived mind made a lot of it and I became apprehensive about stopping. I didn't stop for another reason. No matter how grand a voyage I conjured up for *Swirly World* to have sailed, the security man on the pontoon with a walkie talkie in his hand wasn't buying any of it. 'You have to have permission to berth here.' I'd seen his grim face before. He knew me, and I knew him, sailing Solings in and out, we'd seen each other. 'You can't stay here.'

While I was being made to feel unwelcome in no uncertain way, the wind picked up and set a little sea jostling *Swirly World* against the pontoon. It was time to clear out. I didn't hold it personally against him, although I suppose I did.

We motored under the Harbour Bridge against a swiftly exiting spring tide, revving hard. 'Don't stop now little engine, can't be bothered sailing anymore, lost interest.' *Swirly World* found her way to a neglected-looking mooring, our own, all weedy and marooned without boat. Secure once more to the harbour floor it seemed like all those miles had never really happened. Had they?

Andrew Fagan, Swirly World, 2001

Voyage to New Zealand, March 1840

SARAH MATHEW first came to New Zealand in March 1840, aged 35 and travelling alone from Sydney on the *Westminster* to join her husband Felton. He was already in Kororareka in the Bay of Islands, having been appointed by Governor William Hobson as first Surveyor-general of the fledgling colony.

We owe Mrs Mathew a huge debt for her lively, keenly observed account of the founding of the modern city of Auckland on the Tamaki-makau-rau isthmus on 18 September that same year. Her skills as a diarist and her interest in people, clearly evident in her narrative of the Tasman crossing six months earlier, were to be similarly displayed in her account of the two winter months she spent sailing with Felton down the coast from the Bay of Islands to the Waitemata Harbour, searching for the best place to site a capital town.

But in March 1840, shortly after the signing of the Treaty of Waitangi, this adventurous English gentlewoman was about to set off across the Tasman. Contrary winds would make it a tiresome and unusually long passage of fifteen days . . .

March 2nd, Monday—Came on board the good ship *Westminster*, Captain Mollison, amidst the greatest noise and confusion I ever beheld; the vessel so crowded and lumbered that there is nothing but quarrelling and fighting among all the deck passengers: men, women, children, pigs, fowls, goats, sheep and horses are all trying which shall make the most noise . . . It is a calm, pleasant evening and the vessel perfectly still; she is anchored off Pinchgut . . .

March 3rd, Tuesday—In the course of this day all my companions have come on board; one or two among them I think will prove valuable acquaintances. I am quite prepossessed in Mrs Freeman's favour; I begin to think and hope that she has been cruelly calumniated; it is hard to believe that depravity can lurk under so sweet, and simple, and gentle an exterior. She is extremely fascinating; her manners so quiet, so artless, and so winning, that it is impossible to believe that she can ever have erred beyond perhaps some imprudences which, considering her youth, are almost pardonable. She appears to be much younger than I had thought her, she can scarcely be more than twenty, I imagine. Mrs Burrowes seems a most agreeable person, one whom, you may at once feel, it is allowable to like without hesitation. She is a quiet, ladylike person, very preferable in my opinion, to her husband. Mrs Grimstone looks a genteel little woman, Mrs Hayes so so, but I have not heard either speak yet. I think this is all the lady passengers. I went on shore to try and get a servant, but was unsuccessful; both my neighbours have offered me theirs for the voyage. I had no sleep last night for the heat and mosquitoes and noise, so I must try to get some tonight. It has been a beautiful day, but is close and warm down here. Thermometer 77 degrees.

March 4th, Wednesday—This morning, about 8 o'clock, Mr Jeffrey and Mr Lord came on board, and took Mary back with them. We had weighed anchor and were moving slowly through the water with the help of the tide, there being scarcely any wind; however, we made some progress, and by about 11 o'clock were between the Heads when the pilot left us, and I was very soon after compelled to leave the Deck. Three days of utter misery follow, which make a blank in my journal. Mrs Freeman and Mrs Burrowes, who suffered but little, were very kind to me, and their servants most attentive. During all this time we made but little progress, the winds being very light and generally contrary.

March 7th, Saturday—This day being a little better I had my mattress taken up on deck and have been lying there all day, reading at intervals 'Nicholas Nickleby', and listening to Mrs Freeman's conversation. She seems to attach herself almost exclusively to me and Dr Johnson, who is very kind to us both; I like him very much. I like Mrs Burrowes more and more, and hope we shall be neighbours in our new country. She has a sister married to a surgeon at Paihia, who is anxiously expecting her, so I suppose we shall lose them for a time when we get to the Bay. The winds are still so light we get on very slowly, and the heaving and rolling of the vessel is very trying. Dr Johnson, however, insisted on my trying to walk a little this evening, and with his assistance I managed to do so for a short time, but I am very weak and often feel nearly fainting, which last is a new accomplishment for me. We suffer much from heat, which I did not expect, but this evening being very cool and pleasant I remained on deck till near 9 o'clock partly employed with Mrs Freeman and Dr Johnson in discussing the merits of Scott, Bulwer and James (the author of 'Darnley'); this last Mrs Freeman supported against me and the Doctor, as equal to Scott; it seems she was personally acquainted with him in Paris, and I have observed that an acquaintance with any writer very often enhances your opinion of his merits, which I attribute to a little feeling of vanity as if a sort of reflected honour devolved on you from personal association with an author of celebrity, and you are thus inclined to laud his works and look on them with as much pride as if they were your own. Mrs Freeman is a woman of cultivated mind and talents, I think ill-directed; she reads Latin authors with apparent pleasure and writes very passable poetry with ease. She read me yesterday some pretty lines she had composed, which I criticised unmercifully, but which were in reality superior to the usual run of *Annual* poetry, both in subject and versification. The only thing I do not like about her is a sort of perpetual representation as it seems, but so natural, that you feel doubt whether it is display or not: her every action and every attitude is a picture, and I cannot yet satisfy myself whether all her grace, simplicity and innocence and artlessness is not in fact most exquisite acting, a thought which most ungratefully crossed my mind, while I was nearly fainting on deck, and extended on my mattress with her kneeling beside me, fanning me most kindly, her dress most tastefully arranged, a white veil surrounding her face, and her whole form a beautiful picture. I was vexed that the thought would intrude, for it may be unjust as well as most ungrateful. She has enjoyed the advantage of long travel; France, Germany, Italy she knows well. At this time four years ago she was in the Bay of Naples; I have no such reminiscences to contrast with the Bay of Islands.

Sunday, March 8th—The weather is fine and wind moderate; if I were but tolerably well I should almost enjoy the voyage, for my companions are all very pleasant; there are two or three equivocal looking men who form part of the cabin circle, but they do not at all interfere with our coterie. We sometimes amuse ourselves with fancying what our arrangements shall be at our new settlement. Dr Johnson says we must, for some time at least, form a sort of mess, and have a large tent exclusively for a saloon or dining-room and so meet as at a *table d'hote*. I think this would be pleasant enough, and save an infinity of trouble and difficulty in domestic arrangements. I was too ill this morning to hear all Mr Burrowes' discourse; it was indeed much too long. I was displeased, too, that he curtailed the beautiful prayers of our church, omitted the Litany, and yet kept us with his own inane nonsense till nearly noon; he is, I believe, a good man though, and I forgave him for his wife's sake, she seems such a very kind, nice creature.

In the afternoon we had a slight alarm. One of the mechanics, a hard, stern-looking Highlander, refused to take his turn in handing water out of the hold for the horses. The Sergeant and Kendall appealed to Mr Smart, he to the Captain. The recusant, who was backed by half a dozen of his companions, was obstinate in his refusal and extremely insolent to the captain, who, at length, ordered him up on the poop as the ringleader, and as he still continued most violent in his manner and language, he was put in irons and an armed sentry placed over him. The man is a stonemason and has a very sinister countenance. He has a wife and children, who all came screaming and rushing across the poop, but were speedily sent down again. The Captain showed the greatest firmness and decision; but still without violence or harshness, which I was much pleased to see, as he certainly endured great provocation: meantime the confusion increased on the quarter deck, and I fully expected a general rush was preparing to rescue the culprit; but Mr Smart ordered his men to their arms and a sentry paraded the quarter deck, the malcontents withdrew forwards, still in great excitement, and then poor Mr Galloway, who has been too ill to leave his cabin before, appeared; he had been sent for, by the wife of the prisoner, in expectation that he would be wrought upon to request from the captain her husband's release; they all flocked round him. 'We were placed under your charge, we will not obey anyone else,' was the universal cry, or words to that effect; while his voice, weak from illness, was almost inaudible, seemed to be endeavouring to convince them that the Captain on board his ship must be obeyed by everyone there. After some altercation, and several conferences between Mr Galloway, Mr Smart and the Captain order and quiet was restored, poor Mr Galloway returned quite exhausted to his bed. He looks quite the ghost of himself, and I much fear his health is very precarious. The prisoner still remaining on the poop, Dr Johnson, who boasts himself half a Highlander, endeavoured to reason with him and convince him of the folly of his conduct, as also did the Captain, a proceeding which I thought extremely injudicious, as making the man believe himself of much too great consequence; and it proved quite unsuccessful, for the man, being the more exasperated, only repeated his insolence, and obliged the Captain to declare that he should now apologise to him before he was released. We left the poor creature sitting by the Taffrail with his hands behind him in handcuffs, no very pleasant situation to pass a cold night in.

Monday, March 9th—Still contrary winds and a strong current rolling us about unmercifully. I still continue very sick and miserable, but contrive to crawl on deck by about noon, and if tolerably fine usually get better towards the afternoon and evening. I found the prisoner of yesterday released: it seems he was subdued before midnight, and so escaped the night's captivity. The fact is they are very poorly supplied with provisions, some are almost starving, and that naturally makes them discontented. I was discussing French writers with Mrs Freeman today; our mattresses are always side by side, and we pass the greater part of the day in conversation, varied sometimes with Mrs Burrowes joining us with her work, or Dr Johnson helping our discussions: we form a very pleasant little coterie.

Tuesday, March 10th—The same monotony pervades which all journalists on board ship complain of. The wind has been for the last twenty-four hours freshening every hour, but still quite against us; it has blown from N.N.E. and N.W. ever since we left the Heads. Towards night it became half a gale, and I was, of course, very ill. Mrs Freeman, who enjoys excellent spirits, strove to amuse me and Dr Johnson with her wild Welsh Melodies, and very sweet and plaintive they are. She has a rich, splendid voice, but totally uncultivated, and she seems quite ignorant of the power she possesses. The words of her songs were also original, and her own arrangement; yet she knows not a note of music, it seems a natural gift. Poor Mrs Burrowes had a terrible fall; in passing to her own cabin, which is the stern cabin next to mine, she attempted to support herself by one of the other cabin doors, which suddenly gave way, and precipitated her under a couch in the cabin, bruising her head and side terribly, and in her very delicate situation may produce, I fear, much worse mischief. The Doctor gave her some red lavender drops first and afterwards some port wine and water, with a good dose of laudanum, and we left her asleep quietly.

Wednesday, March 11th—Still contrary winds, but more moderate; the land of promise seems flying from us. The same unvarying round of listless idleness pervades us all, we recline all day on our mattresses on deck, reading light works, or in desultory conversation, all seem too languid for better occupation. Mrs Burrowes very ill, we all entertain great apprehension that a premature accouchement may be the effect of her fall.

Thursday, March 12th—As usual, very ill in the morning, but better towards evening; a beautiful calm evening, but almost without wind, but what there is against us. Mrs Burrowes wonderfully better, and took her seat among us again. In the evening there was such a heavy dew that the doctor advised our going below earlier than usual, and as he considers us specially entrusted to his care (Mrs Freeman and I) we always obey his behests. For want of better amusement, we made a party of whist, I and Mr Galloway against Dr Davies and Mrs Freeman, Dr Johnson occasionally assisting me, notwithstanding which we lost: I have not memory or observation enough for whist.

Friday, March 13th—The wind today still contrary, with showers and cold, disagreeable weather; I, however, kept on deck as long as possible, feeling so much worse when below. Towards the afternoon the wind increased and changed considerably for the better: but accompanied with cold, drizzling rain, which compelled us to remain below. We again tried to beguile the long evening with Whist, Dr Johnson and I against Mrs Freeman and Mr Galloway, and this time I played better; but the ship becoming more and more uneasy, I was obliged to retire to my cabin, where I passed a miserable night, alternately sick and tossed almost out of my bed with the violent rolling and pitching of the vessel. About midnight it blew a heavy gale, which continued with unabated fury all day on.

Saturday, 14th—The noise and confusion was absolutely deafening. I am quite sure there are not half the number of sailors necessary for a ship of this size; and I heard that the Captain depended on the assistance of some of the emigrants we have on board, but they are all such a lazy, idle set that they would never move from their berths at all if Mr Galloway and Dr Johnson did not go below and insist on their coming on deck. However, the weather was so bad all this day that it was quite excusable for landsmen to be glad to hide themselves anywhere. I never was in a vessel that rolled so tremendously as she does. I was twice forcibly ejected from my bed and only escaped being very much hurt by throwing my feet first, and so alighting on them, instead of my head. Everything in my cabin was disarranged, and every small article kept alternately running from side to side, my water jug was jerked out of the hole in which it seemed to ride secure, and rolled up and down the floor till broken to pieces; and every instant I watched with dread some of my larger and heavier lumber, expecting that every violent roll would loosen the fastenings and send them pell mell upon me and my devoted piano. It was without exception the most terrible day I ever spent at sea; and the Captain acknowledged that he has seldom seen such a sea, for he says it was not so much the violence of the gale, as the swell and strong contrary current which made the vessel roll so heavily. The poor horses on the Lee side suffered terribly; they all fell down and were kicking and biting each other in the most dreadful manner, until Mr Smart and Mr Galloway went down and insisted on the men doing their duty and getting the poor creatures up: they are some of them very much injured. My poor beauty was fortunately on the weather side and is, I am told, quite well and saucy as ever. About ten o'clock Dr Johnson came to my cabin door with the comforting news that the wind was fair, and the sea going down a little, and promised me a quiet night, but about midnight it again blew very hard, accompanied with very heavy rain, which, however, did not last very long, and soon after I forgot my miseries in sleep, being perfectly worn out with sickness and watching.

Sunday, March 15th—Still miserably ill, but as the weather was finer made an effort to get on deck, where I lay all the morning extended on my mattress. It was too rough to attempt anything like reading the service publicly: but Mrs Freeman lay by me, and we read it together: poor Mr Burrowes suffers terribly, and was unable to appear all day. Towards the afternoon the weather improved, and all our spirits rose accordingly, as we learned at twelve o'clock the progress we had made, and that probably we should see land before sunset. Accordingly, soon after dinner the first of the Three Kings appeared, and afterwards we sighted them, all three presenting an exact resemblance to my sketch. It was a very beautiful evening, and we remained till nearly ten o'clock on the poop. We soon lost sight of the islands, but the wind falling light we did not see the mainland, but promised ourselves to rise very early in the morning for the purpose.

Monday, March 16th—We must have passed the North Cape in the night, for we saw no land till after breakfast this morning, then it was at considerable distance. The wind, however, freshened and a tide setting us also towards land, we rapidly neared it. It was a very beautiful morning, and I, having enjoyed a quiet night's rest, felt so much refreshed and so much better that I could feel pleasure in watching these new shores. A bold and rugged coast it seems, but not very high; the sides of the mountains seem thickly wooded, but vast patches of white sand or perhaps cliffs intervene. Off the coast we have passed numerous islets, but we keep at a very respectful distance, for our Captain, who has never been here before, is exceedingly cautious, and is so dissatisfied with his imperfect sailing directions, and the very imperfect state of the charts in these latitudes, that he will not keep so close as he might with this wind. The weather, too, has been so thick since the gale of Friday and Saturday that they have not had a good observation for some days. At noon, however, we found with delight that we must be very near our destination, and all heads were anxiously watching each opening in the coast, and we came closer in, the shores becoming more and more beautiful as we advanced. The outline is extremely rugged and broken, the sides of the mountains seem riven into deep ravines and wooded glens; the rocks and cliffs assume most romantic and picturesque forms, which imagination may easily fancy to be walls and castles, towers, turrets, houses, churches, all the works of art and all the appearances of civilised life. Many doubts were now expressed respecting a large inlet, very open; all seemed to expect this must be the long sought Bay of Islands. It fell almost calm, however, and we watched anxiously as we drifted towards the opening. At length a sail appeared in sight, evidently tacking out of this Bay, but for a long time her movements were so inexplicable, that her course was the subject of much discussion and various opinions. The wind freshened, however, this strange ship brought it up with her, and our Captain resolved to speak her. Joyfully, our vessel was put about for the purpose, and in a short time we closed to, Captain Mollison, armed with a speaking trumpet, commenced with asking her name, where from, where to, and we found to our great satisfaction that the Bay we saw her working out of was the 'Bay of Islands'. She was the *Victoria*, had left the anchorage that morning, was on her way to Sydney; and that the *Herald* had come in from her cruise the day before. Still our knowledge was of little use, for the wind freshened, blew directly out of the Bay, and there was not the least chance of our getting any nearer our destination. All we could do was to stand off and on, keeping the curious perforated rock which rises on the left of the entrance, in sight, and wait for a fair wind to run in.

Tuesday, 17th March—This morning at daylight I was on the Poop, but alas, we had drifted during the night far to sea, and our watch tower, the Perforated rock, was dimly visible through the morning mist. The wind, however, was getting up, and before breakfast we had worked up to nearly our former position, then came the land breeze, which kept us off again and now it is a calm, eheu!! A beautiful day, but very warm, our progress very, very slow, but with the assistance of the tide, we were, about noon, within the heads, which are bold and rugged, and full ten miles across. Our course was soon very interesting, every half-hour opening new points, the shores are rugged and picturesque beyond description, and by dinner time several neat houses, and patches of cultivated ground were visible. Our chart was so doubtful that Captain Mollison was evidently very uneasy, and we proceeded very slowly, the Lead going all the time. At length, about 4 o'clock, the town of Kororarika, Mr Busby's House with the Flag-staff near it, the pretty little Village of Paihia, all opened upon us. Soon after, several boats were seen approaching and in one of them I had the supreme delight of seeing my precious husband; he was accompanied by Mr Freeman, and soon after they got on board we anchored in the harbour of Kororarika.

Wednesday, 18th March—This morning the gentlemen returned on shore, and I amused myself almost all the morning in watching the various points and shores of the Bay, all so broken, so rugged, yet so green in places, as to seem to be perfectly beautiful. The weather was fine, the sea a beautiful green, not blue, like the waters of the shores of Australia. The town of Kororarika is a few scattered cottages extending along the shore, the hills rising abruptly at the back, high and precipitous, and generally clothed with some sort of vegetation, apparently fern or brushwood. In the course of the day we received a visit from Mr Shortland and Captain Clendon, who acts as American consul and looks like a Yankee. He has a very beau-tiful property here, extensive stores by the waterside, and a pretty cottage residence on the rising ground behind: there are also appearances of a garden, the first I have seen. He kindly gave Mrs Freeman and me an invitation to his house; we are to go tomorrow. In the afternoon everyone was employed getting the horses for the Mounted Police landed. The ves-sel lay as close as she could to a sand bank, which extended to the shore. The poor horses were lowered over the side of the ship into the water, and towed or hauled by boats through the deep water, and then they easily walked or swam to the shore: it was a cruel operation, though necessary, and they all reached the shore in safety. A tent and some men were sent to remain with them.

The gentlemen returned in the evening, and I enjoyed a lovely moon-light walk on deck till half past 10 o'clock. The report from Waimate was favourable, the Governor was much better. Mr Shortland and Dr Johnson are to ride up there tomorrow.

Professor J.C. Rutherford (editor),
The Founding of New Zealand:
The Journals of Felton Mathew, First Surveyor-General
of New Zealand, and his Wife, 1840–1847, 1940

With the Blakes to New Zealand

PIPPA AND PETER BLAKE were a newly married couple when they sailed from the Hamble River in England in September 1979 aboard one of the world's most famous ocean racers, *Condor of Bermuda*, bound for New Zealand.

Peter was 33 and the regular skipper of *Condor* at the time. Ahead, until he was tragically killed by Amazon River pirates at the end of 2001, lay a marriage of twenty-three tremendous years: two children, a knighthood for Peter's successful campaigns to set round-world non-stop records and win the Whitbread race and America's Cup twice. By the time of his death, having developed a new focus on conservation, Sir Peter Blake was renowned internationally as one of the greatest blue water sailors of the age.

Too often we read only those accounts of ocean passages where things go disastrously wrong. Pippa Blake's first ocean voyage via Gibraltar, Suez and Fremantle was nearer the more usual experience of crew enjoying five months aboard a well-found and skilfully sailed yacht. They did, however, have their share of storms, in the Red Sea and approaching Fremantle, and a full-on cyclone in the infamous Tasman Sea . . .

'Yes, eight men for a hundred days!' and watched the incredulous stare on the supermarket salesman's face turn to a welcoming smile as we re-affirmed our lengthy shopping list. We were in the final busy stages of stocking up with enough food to last eight of us on a 15,000-mile voyage to the other side of the world.

This was not to be a leisurely island-hopping cruise to the Antipodes but a routine delivery trip for the mahogany 78ft (23.7m) ocean-racer *Condor of Bermuda*. She would be affronted to have the word 'cruising' attached to her! We had a tight schedule to meet which meant arriving in Sydney early in December ready for a pre-Sydney–Hobart tune-up and to pick up our full quota of 24 crewmen.

The voyage was to be a race against time as we planned to leave England on 12 September, having had only a quick breather since racing during August in Cowes week. In fact when the day for departure arrived it had only been a month earlier that *Condor* had sailed victoriously into Millbay Docks, Plymouth, having broken the Fastnet Race record by seven hours — a triumph sadly marred by the other events of that now well-documented race.

In the short space of time since the end of the Fastnet we had attended a memorial service for those lost in the race, delivered *Condor* back up the Hamble River and had been to church again, this time for our own wedding! Then, after a three-day honeymoon in a Scottish castle, we plunged into last-minute preparations for the trip down-under.

Having emptied the supermarket's supplies of crates and tins, and miraculously stowed them below, we were ready to leave the fast-approaching English winter. The blustery day of the 12th had arrived, our gear was stowed, the bonded booze on board and all that remained to do was to say goodbye to family and friends assembling on the marina pier.

One important last detail to see to was for the local customs agent to return to us the ship's armoury. He seemed clearly relieved to have the responsibility taken off his hands. A .38 calibre pistol, two shotguns, a .303 rifle and two semi-automatic machine guns used by Nato forces would be enough to scare off most marauders.

So now we were ready to head out into the ever-grey Solent and English Channel, having had our photographs taken for the local press who had strangely latched onto the idea that this was to be a 'Honeymoon cruise in a floating hotel'. (If only they knew!) I was leaving behind a family still somewhat bemused by their daughter's elevation into the ocean-racing world, having previously scorned their sailing adventures in an 18-foot lugger around Chichester Harbour. Still I felt safer to be in a 78-footer as we motored down the Hamble until the last waving arms were lost to view. The only thoughts now were on regaining our sea-legs and of the oceans ahead.

Two days at sea found us in an unusually calm Bay of Biscay where we ended up motoring most of the way to the first port of call, Gibraltar. This first short leg of the journey proved uneventful apart from a stop for the first swim of the season in warmer waters and a visit from a Spanish bat in the rigging. By now all were accustomed to the watch system of three hours on and nine off which were taken by two at a time, with one day out of four in the galley. I may have been the only girl on board but all duties were shared regardless of sex and anyway a long sea voyage such as this calls for varied and inventive cooking.

On board were four New Zealanders, three British and one Australian who was only ever known as Okka.

Six days out from the Hamble we arrived at the murky waters of Gibraltar's harbour, greeted by dolphins who surprisingly thrive in the polluted port. *Ondine* was also in harbour on her way back to the States after racing in Sardinia. We stayed for only two days, refuelling, watering and buying fresh provisions to replenish our already adequate supplies.

Glad to leave Gibraltar we sailed into a fresh westerly and made fast progress in leaving the Rock behind. The Mediterranean by no means lived up to its reputation of blue seas and azure skies as advertised in the glossy travel brochures. The weather was among the worst of the trip with either gale-force winds and short, steep seas, or no wind and huge swells. At one point we hove-to for 12 hours, as, though pressed for time, we had no intention of damaging any gear and *Condor* had to be in tip-top condition for the Southern Cross racing ahead.

One night of this leg was particularly memorable. Early in the evening during our watch we had passed through a severe electrical storm preceding pitch black cloud and thunderous rain. Peter and I felt glad to hand over to the next watch, leaving them to the dark night and poor visibility while we clambered into our aft state-room berth. I fell to sleep dreaming of those nice sunny Mediterranean holidays of previous years when — whoosh! I awoke with the cold brine actually swirling around inside my sleeping bag, 20 gallons of the stuff having been deposited down our hatch by some misguided helmsman on deck. Some mysterious premonition had promoted Peter to step out of the bunk only seconds earlier so, with the helmsman, he shared my wet fury.

The aft hatch seemed to attract such mishaps and in warmer climes one airless night a stray flying fish found its way down our windchute only this time to land on Peter's side. He was not amused by this wet awakening and found fish scales in his sleeping bag for days. As a small matter of interest, anyone who presumes that an aft cabin state-room is the height of first-class opulence is sadly mistaken. It was one of the more vulnerable areas of *Condor* under bad weather conditions and at times we were literally strapped in with lee-cloths and ropes at all angles to make sleeping comfortable.

The rain and gloom didn't last for ever and the day before approaching the long breakwater out from Port Said the skies cleared and the day warmed. This was well-timed as it was 1 October, Peter's birthday, and a party was called for. This time, a 'drag' occasion, preparations were made well in advance so for days beforehand I had numerous requests for lipsticks and sequinned ballgowns. The boys seemed surprised that I didn't carry suitcases of such things.

Our arrival in Port Said was again heralded by dolphins, and brightly-painted fishing boats, as we motored into the harbour, passing sad old relics from past wars heeling in the shallows. This was the furthest east I had been in my life and I felt keen anticipation to be in such foreign lands.

Using the *Pilot* we located the Port Said Yacht Club, though it was hard to find as the title was all that existed, the club having suffered badly in the Six-Day War. Still, the site boasted an old rusty shower and a lively custodian, not surprisingly named Ali!

We had been forewarned about Suez Canal procedures in that unless prepared to pay agents' fees and heavy bribes it could mean waiting for weeks before making the Canal trip. The only other private yacht in Port Said was a charter boat on her way to the Maldives and she had been waiting for at least three weeks.

Not having time to spare, nor the inclination to stay as the temperature was high and shore visits were curfewed, we went ahead and found as reliable an agent as possible. With the aid of a few bottles of whisky and some stale Benson and Hedges he did a marvellous job in getting all the correct documents and passes stamped for us.

All formal procedures taken care of and we were in the fortunate position of being able to make the Canal trip three days after arrival. Needless to say we were held up for another day, for the ludicrous reason that it was the one day in the year the Canal was closed — for the annual swimming regatta! Having seen several dead rats floating past nothing would have enticed me into the water!

It was only a day's delay and we were woken early next morning by the agent who eagerly pointed his finger at the long convoy of ships heading towards the Canal entrance. We assumed we should join the long queue and after taking aboard an obligatory Egyptian pilot manoeuvred into position.

The pilot didn't speak a word of English nor we Egyptian, but by using sign language and pidgin French he gave us our orders. The canal passage is not difficult, being basically a straight line, but at intervals huge dredgers are swung across the canal by means of large wire hawsers which, if hit, would cause a fair amount of damage to our 3.8-metre draft keel. Fortunately the pilot knew when they would occur.

After the first fascination had worn off, motoring in the heat became tedious and we looked forward to getting under sail again. Though our pilot had been working on the canal for 20 years this was his first trip on a yacht and he kept insisting we keep top speed up, unaware of possible overheating problems to the engine.

The Suez Canal is 100 miles long from Port Said to Suez, approximately 12 motoring hours, but we stopped overnight at Ishmalia on the Great Bitter Lakes. There was a change of pilots here, a noisy procedure as the one disembarking would not leave without a bottle of whisky and cans of beer, on top of his already high fees.

By chance, that night was the anniversary of the end of the Six-Day War and there were great fireworks and explosions from ashore. We were keen to join in the festivities but were thwarted by two armed soldiers who had moored astern of us in a small coracle. I think they were there more to protect us from the locals rather than the other way round. It wasn't long before they were asking if we had any drink on board to see them through their vigil, so Dennis began to mix a potent brew. Consisting of Pimms, Vodka, Kahlua and various dregs he handed it over along with a large King Edwards cigar — and that was the last we saw of them.

At daybreak we set off again down the canal, passing a northbound convoy and waved to the crewmen towering above us on the ships' decks. We stopped in Suez only to drop off the pilot and were then free to carry on as we wished. As if in defiance of all the motoring we'd done we immediately set a small spinnaker to speed us down the Gulf of Suez.

The Gulf is a busy shipping lane so we were on a constant lookout, especially for oil-rigs which are numerous in this area. At night it was easy to spot the rigs from miles away with their bright lights and flames leaping high into the air.

The next port of call was to be Jeddah, halfway down the Red Sea and one of the main ports for Saudi Arabia. An English friend, the Major, who had sailed on *Condor* in the previous Whitbread Race, was expecting us for a three-day visit, which apparently had been no small headache to arrange. Private yachts are not welcome in Saudi Arabia (the Saudis in general have no conception of yachting, particularly as a sport) and there are stories of visiting yachtsmen being held in jail for months and their yachts impounded.

The Major had spent days filling in forms and visiting consulates before he'd been given the go-ahead for our visit. Fortunately he was helped by the fact that *Condor*'s victory in the Fastnet had made front-page news, even in Saudi Arabia, so they were aware that we were not just any old yacht.

Sailing down the Red Sea the air and sea temperatures began to rise and we soon found we were consuming about two to three gallons of liquid per day each as well as having to take salt tablets. The sea temperature eventually rose to 37°C so no chance of even a cooling douse of water from a bucket.

Making radio contact with the Major we arranged that he could come out to greet us by tug, as we had no charts of the narrow harbour channel which is dotted with coral reefs around its entrance. The Major also sent firm instructions that by no means should we take cameras ashore and to lock up any alcohol aboard.

Of most interest to me was that I should be well clothed from top to toe so as not to offend Moslem laws. In the stifling heat this seemed more like a punishment!

However, we carried out these procedures with great care as it was quite an honour to be even allowed into Jeddah. The port is vast and still under construction in some areas, but it already shows off the extreme Arabian wealth.

There was a strict curfew on crews of all visiting ships but the Major had managed to get the hour of six o'clock waived so that we could meet some of the European community in the evenings. Our hosts one night were the Red Sea Sailing Association who had a strong Laser and Hobie Cat following. They were keen for a glimpse of *Condor* and next day evaded the officious port guards to come aboard.

One chap, however, had his car searched at the gates which led to his precious yachting magazines being confiscated. To strict Moslems, even ladies modelling full wet-weather gear are seen to be offensive! Females are certainly very much third-class citizens and I felt highly conspicuous with blonde hair and in the company of seven men. The Saudi customs men seemed relieved to learn that not only was I a married lady, but married to the skipper!

Provisions were hard to come by in Jeddah so the only supplies renewed were tinned soft drinks and fresh fruit and vegetables. The tinned drink was to help out with the heavy intake of fresh water in the heat.

Buying the fruit and vegetables was an experience. We wandered around a large market consisting of tented stalls which at dusk were lit up with oil lamps — a scene resembling Belshazzar's feast with all the strange-looking and brightly coloured fruits. The Major did the interpreting and bartering for us but then to my chagrin, the boys loaded me up with our goods and insisted that I walk six paces behind in true Arabian style! The local menfolk wore a few large grins.

Another interesting visit in Jeddah was to a sacred area still used for building dhows in the traditional method, relying solely on the eye for hull shape, with no plans and using naturally shaped boughs of wood.

We were sorry to leave Jeddah after such a fascinating stay but time was pressing and though on schedule, there were still thousands of miles to go. After a last-minute shopping expedition to the 'Souk' for presents and Arabian outfits for the crew, we headed out early one morning once more into the Red Sea.

The sailing now was the worst of the trip and we were soon battling ferocious headwinds and steep seas. This in itself wasn't so bad but to keep dry all hatches were closed and conditions below became unbearably hot and muggy. Tempers frayed and it was hard to muster energy even for our strongly competitive games of Scrabble and cards, let alone a sail change up on deck! At last we beat out of the Red Sea setting an easterly course into the Gulf of Aden, but as we did, so too changed the wind to an easterly. More beating.

We kept to the northern side of the Gulf, always on a lookout for ships and at one time we counted 16 vessels in sight. Passing close to Aden, a dark shape of scorched rock in the evening light, we then crossed over to the North African coast. By this time the wind had died and dawn found us motoring along the barren coast of Somalia, towards the Horn of Africa and the Indian Ocean.

We hugged the African coast as we headed south again, to steer clear of the island of Sokatra, north east of the African Horn. The island is ruled by a sultan who condones piracy and we had no wish to put our rifle training into practice. The guns were kept loaded during this time and we had a day's refresher course, aiming at balloons thrown overboard and passing driftwood. In a bikini I felt like a terrorist.

The Indian Ocean was the first major ocean I was to cross and I felt excited at the prospect of clearing land and sailing away from the regular shipping lanes. However, it didn't contain all the starry skies and balmy nights I'd somehow imagined. We had one day of true doldrum weather and the rest consisted of tight reaching into lumpy seas.

Four of us had never crossed the Equator before and the line-crossing ceremony was approaching rather too quickly for our liking! Throughout the voyage any bad habits we'd formed or wrongs done had been marked down as to the severity of the punishment. The actual crossing was on the morning of 28 October but as the seas were bad no one felt in the party spirit so we just let off a flare and forced down a stiff drink.

Next day was calm and blue and the ceremony began. We were given one hour to hide while King Neptune and his servants finished off their preparations of making a cat-o'-nine-tails and adding more ingredients to an evil-smelling brew which had been bubbling for days!

Our time up, we were dragged or winched up to the foredeck and tied down. Now the suffering began and we were stripped, spattered with grease, raw eggs, shaving foam and then forced to taste the foul brew. To be fair my punishment was not as severe as the boys, who were accosted with a razor and 'Emma' lost half the treasured moustache he'd been nurturing to show his girl-friend in Sydney. To clean off the mess we jumped overboard but we still stank of rotten eggs for days.

Having been initiated into Neptune's Kingdom we sailed on, towards our fourth stop, Diego Garcia, a British-owned lagoon in the Chagos Archipelago. Four days after the Equator crossing we were anchored off tiny Danger Island, roughly 45 miles north west of Diego Garcia. This was an unplanned stop, but as the mile long by half-mile wide island is uninhabited, we decided it would be well worth a visit. We anchored off a sandy beach on the western side, the rest of the island being surrounded by coral reefs, hence its name.

We made two expeditions ashore, the first landing party tumbling over and over in the surf so those in the second group made sure of wrapping camera gear in plastic bags! There was not a sign of humanity on the island, apart from a lost shipment of plastic sandals littering the shore. However, it was home for thousands of hermit crabs, booby birds and gannets, and we must have been the first humans these birds had seen as, unafraid and like the Hitchcock film, they made alarmingly low swoops over our heads.

Hermit crabs I don't mind, but as we clambered into the undergrowth and thick creepers, suddenly we were stopped in our tracks by an enormous coconut crab waving its claws in the air. Worse than that was its friend who, lurking beneath an old palm trunk, must have been at least two feet wide. We later learnt that it would probably have been 20 to 30 years old.

We returned to *Condor* with a feeling of the true explorer and with booty of shells, spongy red coral and the odd glass Japanese fishing float. On arrival we'd set a fishing line over the stern but any fish we might have caught had been snapped up by the sharks which are notorious around Danger Island.

It took a day of unpleasant sailing into 40-knot winds before reaching the peaceful haven of Diego Garcia's lagoon. Although British-owned, the island is leased to the American Forces who have built a large airstrip there, which is in the process of being enlarged, as the island is strategically placed. The population at the time of our visit was 26 British naval personnel, 1400 Americans and no ladies!

Before arrival we made radio contact with the island and were instructed to anchor halfway down the lagoon on the eastern side where there is a government reserve. Instructed not to go ashore, it was not until we met the British commander next day that we realised how unwelcome yachts are to the lagoon. The main reasons for this are that, being a Forces base and a major satellite tracking station, strangers are treated with the utmost suspicion. There are also no facilities for provisioning or watering, which is stated in the pilot book. Apparently many yachts have abused this information and aggressively insisted on being given supplies, so marring prospects for future yachtsmen.

We were lucky to have a good contact in that the previous commander had been a tenant of mine in London — little knowing I'd ever be visiting the island. Once the present commander realised we weren't clamouring for provisions he seemed to warm to us and even supplied some Navy flour and fresh vegetables, flown from Singapore.

Eight years earlier there had been a copra plantation but the natives were ousted from their homes and sent elsewhere. Under supervision of the naval officer we were shown round their old village and finding an old rusty tap in one of the decaying cottages were able to fill our water tanks — a complicated ferrying operation by dinghy.

Apart from the fearsome coconut crabs the only animals on the island were a herd of donkeys and three horses left from a biological expedition. The horseshoe-shaped lagoon is six miles wide with palm-fringed beaches and turquoise waters. The pilot book claims it is shark-infested, though we were told that there had been no deaths for 28 years. Nevertheless we kept close to the boat when swimming!

The lagoon's calm was idyllic, though its beauty at times was shattered by aircraft circling overhead, and the day we left we saw a large fleet of American warships accumulating outside.

Time to go. We had had three days in Diego Garcia and when Jaws had filled the aft lazarette with coconuts and fresh palm hearts we sailed out into the southern Indian Ocean. This was to be our second-longest leg at sea, and needless to say the first 10 days were spent heading into the South East Trades. However, we made good progress, necessary as the cyclone season was approaching. The whole journey had consisted of so much beating to windward in strong winds that we'd almost given up hope of any decent sailing.

Dropping into the Southern Ocean the seas and winds began to build up and at last the sailing really came into its own. Up to this point the trip had been most memorable for its different stops. On this leg it was the elements. It was hard to fathom at first the enormity of the Southern Ocean seas. We dropped south to pick up the westerlies of the Roaring 40s before turning east to our next destination of Fremantle. With the winds at last behind us the sailing was exhilarating, sliding at speed down the immense seas.

Soon the first albatross and stormy petrels began to follow our wake and we came to expect the birds daily. Many hours were spent watching the roaming albatross soaring and wheeling up and down the wave troughs. Any rubbish thrown overboard, though, revealed a latent clumsiness as they scrabbled around in the water searching for the best pickings.

At sea for many weeks at a time we used to think up sources of amusement other than the usual games of cards, Scrabble, reading and listening to music. On this leg Peter and I thought up an inter-watch kite flying competition, with prizes for design, ingenuity and the highest flight. The ingenuity prize definitely fell to Dennis who went to the extremes of chopping up his guitar to perfect his kite struts! I'll have to admit that his kite design was a great improvement on his guitar playing. Sadly his first air trials turned rapidly to sea trials and his painstaking effort was last sighted sinking astern. Happily our tinfoil construction achieved the highest flight, though the crew reckoned it was a biased win since we were the judges as well.

The wide gap to Western Australia was closing and as it did the air temperature dropped and the winds rose. We would clamber out on watch wearing several layers of polar and wet-weather gear, having taken far longer to dress.

I had my first real experience of helming downhill in a gale during this time which, even though short of sail, on *Condor* is an overwhelming sensation. When it suited, Peter would announce he had to go below for a 'spot of navigation', leaving me fiercely gripping the wheel with a sense of power not to be forgotten.

Three days from Fremantle we kept a sharp lookout for yachts in the Parmelia Race from Plymouth to Perth, which had started a week before we left England. We arrived the same night as the Australian maxi *Siska* who we'd been racing against in Cowes Week. She had just been pipped at the mark by *Independent Endeavour*, a Swan 65 who, like *Siska*, had her hometown in Perth. We lay outside Fremantle that night, anchored off Rottnest Island, neither wishing to steal the limelight from the Parmelia Race yachts nor get caught up in their celebrations. *Condor* was given a tremendous reception in Perth both by the race officials and the locals and we found ourselves included in celebrations marking the 150th anniversary of Western Australia.

Our main job here was to haul out on the travel lift for repairs. The hull needed revarnishing in patches which had peeled off in the Red Sea heat, plus a minor repair to the keel which had possibly suffered a knock in the Suez Canal. One welcome aspect of Fremantle was being able to eat more varied meals, which had been getting somewhat limited in the last few weeks. *Condor* had a large deep-freeze so we had eaten fresh meat until the southern Indian Ocean, apart from a large turkey and leg of pork which hadn't coped with the Red Sea temperatures. Potatoes and onions had lasted the 75 days to Perth with careful sorting procedures each day, as did the Vaselined eggs, though these were fit only for scrambling by this stage.

Having had an extremely social time in Perth, after a six-day stop we once again headed out to the open seas and straight into a fierce headwind gale. Our mainsail was badly ripped, leaving us powered by storm jib and trisail for a day until the main was repaired. The weather can be notoriously bad around Cape Leeuwin and true to form we were beating into the storm until well around the corner.

We kept well south across the Great Australian Bight to catch favourable winds, which never materialised and until safely past Bass Strait we were constantly battling into strong winds and high seas. The seas again were awe-inspiring as we sailed along the most southern latitudes of the journey. Past Bass Strait we began the first north-bound passage since leaving England. From then on the winds died and we motored the rest of the way to Sydney.

Keeping close to the coast we passed many basking seals and heard the first sound of a blue-backed penguin barking. It was an exciting moment to at last reach our major destination of Sydney. We sailed through the Heads with the battle-flag flying, feeling highly satisfied that after a voyage of 74 days at sea and 15 in port we'd arrived on the day originally planned and only two hours late. No time, though, for respite or relaxation and after a good night's sleep we were out sailing again next day in Sydney Harbour with the new crew and racing sails.

Then followed a hectic few weeks of the Southern Cross series, culminating in the Sydney–Hobart which began on Boxing Day. I welcomed the sunshine, having spent all previous Christmases in my life in the snow and frosts of Europe.

The start of the Sydney–Hobart was one of the most exhilarating moments of my life. *Condor* led the fleet out of Sydney Heads, which were lined with thousands of spectators while hundreds of small craft followed our wake. The tension and excitement from 25 of us was unparalleled. However the start of the race was for us its climax and sadly as the wind died we ran up the river to Hobart, lying second to the Australian *Bumblebee*.

After the race Hobart is a story in itself and after four days of exhausting celebrations we felt it high time to leave for the final stage of the journey — to Auckland. There were 17 on board for the Tasman crossing, some having joined us for a quiet holiday cruise home. This could hardly have been further from the truth, as the weather progressively turned from bad to worse.

We sailed from Hobart on the afternoon straight into north-easterly winds gusting 60–70 knots, and after the excesses of Hobart there were few takers for dinner that night. I'd heard many stories about the Tasman Sea, which certainly seemed to be living up to its reputation.

We then had two relatively good days sailing before beginning to feel the first effects of Cyclone David, which was to pass close by to the west of us. At the height of the storm, as *Condor* experienced it, the winds were screaming at gusts of about 80 knots, with seas which made those we'd encountered in the southern Indian Ocean seem like sheltered waters. We hove-to for approximately 30 hours, under storm trisail. On a yacht the size of *Condor* life below carried on as usual, but few people slept that night and we were all anxious to hear news of the yachts crossing the Tasman with us.

On deck it was a different story. Two at a time kept watch, crouched low in the cockpit, harnessed in and with the wheel lashed hard over. It was an awesome experience as the waves crashed over the decks, swilling into the cockpit, and though jokes were made about drinks being ruined by salt-water dilution, I think some people were more than a bit apprehensive.

It was hard to fathom the size of the waves, they were just mammoth and we timed one climb out of a trough upwards as lasting five to six seconds. As we neared the tops it often seemed that we would slide down backwards, but *Condor* always just managed to get there before sliding into the next trough. It seemed the incessant shrieking wind and spume-laden air would never die away but suddenly, within 12 hours, the winds dropped to nothing and we were left slopping about in huge uncomfortable seas, with, however, a warming sense of relief.

Sadly it was during this storm that the Auckland yacht *Smackwater Jack* was lost, having been part of the Hobart–Auckland Race.

The sloppy seas stayed for a few days, serving as a reminder of what we'd been through, and we were all glad when we drew near the north coast of New Zealand. I was disappointed that we sailed past Cape Reinga in dense fog and I had to be content with the smell of the land as my first taste of New Zealand. Our first stop was the Bay of Islands where we cleared customs, tidied up and relaxed for two days before the final sail to Auckland.

In a fresh south-westerly and rain squalls it took us two hours next day to reach North Head and we beat up the harbour before finally lowering sails and seeking a berth at Westhaven. Waiting to greet us were various friends and relations, particularly Peter's family eager to see for the first time what kind of person would sail 15,000 miles to her first married home.

We arrived in Auckland on 17 January, almost five months after leaving England and having had a fascinating and memorable voyage. I cannot say, though, that it was the voyage of a lifetime, only because I've a funny inkling that it's not the last time we're going to cross from one side of the world to the other under sail.

Pippa Blake, 'With *Condor* to New Zealand', 1981

Painted Ocean

NEIL ARROW had owned the 30ft *Taihoa* for twelve months when he followed up an advertisement for an unpaid crew on the *Miru*, bound for Boston via Panama. On board would be the owner, heading to the USA to take up a medical scholarship, with his wife and two sons.

Five months, 100,000 miles and many adventures later, *Miru* sailed into Boston Harbour. Arrow returned to Christchurch, where his old sailing mate Sam and *Taihoa* were waiting. He was fit and fired up for another challenge. The 1954 Trans Tasman race from Auckland to Hobart, then the Southern Hemisphere's longest race, and the subsequent passage back to Lyttelton, a round trip of 4000 miles, seemed just the ticket.

With his crew of four, Arrow took *Taihoa* to sea off Lyttelton for thirty-two consecutive weekends' training. Then came the 800-mile pre-race run to Auckland . . .

January 14th 1954: '*Scorpio* (*Mars*) Monday provides good aspects for mental work, science and research. The rest of the week promises unusual interests. Remember that work, hopes and ambitions may be linked with friends in some strange way. Get off the beaten track when on holiday.'

Even for a cynic this pertinent piece of advice was too much to ignore. I cut my horoscope from the local paper, pasted it in the log book and showed it to Sam.

'Humph!' he said.

Into a confined space, thirty feet long, four feet deep and ten feet wide, we had crammed 1½ tons of stores. Lashed to the deck were cans containing 100 gallons of petrol, and a few minutes before we departed, Lyttelton friends arrived with gifts. The bunks sagged beneath weighty parcels of fruit cake. Owen searched hopelessly for a place to stow two sacks of fresh vegetables. My pockets bulged with the offerings of three small children; a jar of jam, a bottle of ginger pop and a hand worked tea towel. Jimpey grasped a hastily proffered lucky button and Sam's ears burned with the opinion of a local yachtsman who considered us a bunch of playboys that would never get past the heads.

With *Taihoa* well below her marks we cleared Lyttelton harbour to spread her ketch rig wing and wing before a breeze from the South. The first watch was mine and with the joy of it I sang for an hour until a chorus of abuse from the cabin ruined my concert. Sam said,

'If you are so keen on lifting dat bale and toting dat barge come down here and use some muscle on nine fruit cakes, five tarts, two plum puddings and some bloody thing that looks like a sodden time bomb. If we've got to eat our way through this lot before I get to use my bunk I'll not sleep for a month!'

A loud pop and a hiss set Jimpey wailing — 'That bottle of ginger pop has just erupted in my bunk!'

Owen appeared in the hatchway brandishing an enormous cabbage —

'If you think that three hours at sea is enough to make me want to sleep with this, you're crazy . . . there's enough unmentionable food on this unmentionable barge to feed an equally unmentionable army!'

'Once upon a time there were three bears!' I told him and he disappeared. From below deck a muffled conversation was followed by peals of laughter. They solved the problem neatly. Everything had been shifted onto my bunk.

By late afternoon the wind deserted us. The sea slept as *Taihoa*'s motor drank deep into our petrol. For seventy-six hours the only movement on the ocean was the ketch, clouds of feeding sea birds and a school of blackfish wallowing north. Our log registered the 361st mile as we powered through the Gisborne roadstead towards its diminutive harbour.

Following the time-honoured custom I reported to the harbour master and requested permission to moor my ship.

'What ship?' he said.

'The ketch over there!' I pointed out.

'That thing . . . it looks like a life boat!'

'To me it's a ship!' I said testily.

'Granted boy, granted . . . where you from?'

'Lyttelton, bound for Auckland then Hobart, Tasmania.'

'My dear sainted aunt and flaming Highlanders . . . and you do this for pleasure I suppose!'

'Sport! Do I get your permission to lay alongside?'

'Certainly boy, certainly!'

'What will it cost?'

'Not a brass skerrick boy, the water is free also and if you care to use the ablutions here, you're welcome.'

'Thank you, Captain!'

'Don't mention it, Captain; would you care to take tea with me?'

'Thank you no, I'll tend to my ship if you don't mind.'

'Proceed boy, proceed,' he said and as I walked out of his office he remarked to no one in particular:

'Hobart indeed . . . there's hope for this world yet!'

'How did you get on?' asked Sam when I climbed on board.

'Everything is free,' I told him. 'There's hope for this world yet!'

The intention to leave Gisborne as soon as our petrol cans were refilled was thwarted by a raging north-easter. *Taihoa* spent the day happily nudging the wharf and seemed a little smug at having reached shelter just in time. Next morning the gale had added weight.

'What do you think?' I asked Sam.

'Let's reef her down and go out for a look see!'

'We haven't a hope in hell of making any headway.'

'I know,' said Sam. 'But the experience wouldn't hurt us and if *Taihoa* has any weaknesses now is the time to find out!'

'When do we go?' asked Owen.

'Now!'

'Could you wait ten minutes?' he enquired.

'Sure, why?'

'I'll rush up town and buy a bag of can openers!'

'What does he mean by that?' asked Sam after the cook had departed.

'It's his way of saying that in this weather we eat out of a can.'

For six hours *Taihoa* bucked, rolled, thumped, and porpoised her way out to sea. All night the phosphorus-laden spray shot like comet tails through the rigging. By midnight we put about to porpoise, thump, roll, and buck our way back to Gisborne. Riding lights gleamed on the salt-scrubbed paintwork. Below decks cook sang to Stove, 'Ah, Ha, Ha, Ha.'

At 7 a.m. we tied up to the wharf and greeted the harbour master.

'Where have you been?' he demanded.

'We spent the night at sea for practice,' I told him.

'My dear sainted aunt . . . practice . . . practice he says . . . absolutely mad . . . practising in a gale . . . no hope at all!' he muttered and stalked off.

'He's lost his faith in the world,' I told Sam.

Late in the afternoon the gale paused, switched to the south and re-gained its anger. We took *Taihoa* to sea again under storm canvas and ran north through the night towing warps to make our roller-coaster progress less dangerous.

At dawn the ketch surfed round East Cape and into the shelter of Hicks Bay to anchor and sleep for five hours. Before retiring Sam had something to say.

'Sam!' he said.

'Yes?'

'She's a stout wee ship!'

'None better!'

'Sam!'

'Yes?'

'No one was seasick.'

'Nobody will be now!' I said.

'Abso-bloody-lutely marvellous,' sighed Sam and settled into his bunk with a grunt of satisfaction.

Sleep took care of ravelled sleeves and turned the gale into a calm that lasted long enough to motor for 100 hours across the Bay of Plenty and into Auckland harbour — nine days out from Lyttelton. 800 miles of pre-race experience.

Saturday January 30th: Boom! and a pint-sized cannon announced the Southern Hemisphere's longest ocean race. Trans Tasman 1954. Time 10.30 a.m. Six yachts with wind-starved sails showed no inclination to cross the line. Sun-sparkled wakes of dozens of motor boats gave life to an other-wise immobile scene. From slack water the tide came sneaking back car-rying competitors in the wrong direction. *Taihoa* was first to drop anchor and so lead the field for 20 minutes. A zephyr from the south produced a flock of balloon spinnakers, then we were last. The wind moved the fleet seven miles and deserted them. It came back for us and worked until we caught the leaders then deserted again. *Ghost* drifted alongside *Black Rose*.

'Do come aboard for tea,' said the Skipper.

'Tea?' came the reply, 'my God, if this keeps up I'll be opening the bottle marked medicinal purposes only!'

Taihoa inched near *Te Rapunga*. The girls were wearing jeans. Because of the heat we wore pareus. The prerogative to whistle was theirs.

'That little one's not too bad,' announced Jimpey.

'Get to the mast head and look for wind!' I ordered.

Dusk assisted a feeble south-easter and sent opposition riding lights ahead into a star-filled night.

Sunday, January 31st

The dawn watch was mine. To welcome the morning I sang *For those in peril on the sea.*

'Hardly an appropriate ditty for these light conditions,' complained Sam as he appeared in the hatchway.

'I think it is!' I told him. 'Three miles to starboard are some rocks known as the Poor Knights . . . twenty-five feet to port is fifty feet of whale!'

Sam looked to port, blinked and gasped a rude word. Whales fill me with fear. This one had been doing just that for half an hour. His barnacle-covered bulk rose and fell, sometimes in towards the ketch then away. By way of saying 'Good morning' he slammed the water with his tail and spouted with a deafening hiss.

'Pooh!' said Jimpey coming on deck. 'That blighter stinks . . . somebody ought to tell him about tooth paste!'

As though offended with the mention of halitosis, our whale dived and departed.

'Just as well, too!' declared the cook. 'I won't have those things round when I'm cooking!'

Away on the horizon tiny white sails indicated an increasing lead. The anaemic breeze sent hopes plunging.

Monday, February 1st

It came with the strength the radio had promised. Twenty knots of chilling north-east precisely at 1.30 a.m. With full sail *Taihoa* beat towards Cape Brett. On through the night and into the path of a home running trawler that swept past our bow with inches to spare.

We rounded Cape Brett at breakfast time. Free sheeted, hoisted the Genoa and leapt ahead, six full knots. The chase was on and the weather *Taihoa*'s, but not the navigator's.

'It's all dead reckoning,' he said, 'with this low cloud I'll not get a sight . . . would like to know exactly where North Cape is before we take on the Tasman.'

'How about a direct course from here to 3 miles off North Cape? . . . at this speed we should reach there early tomorrow morning.'

'Mmm . . . it's close . . . 3 miles . . . but we need a positive departure point . . . I'll have ulcers before this is over!'

'I like mine fried in batter!' said Jimpey.

'I said ulcers not oysters you clot . . . you're always thinking of your stomach and what . . . Oh! what's the use!'

'Ah. Ha, Ha, Ha,' said someone.

Tuesday, February 2nd

They run in threes it's said. A whale, a trawler and early in the morning, rocks.

Owen called me at 3.30 a.m., half an hour earlier than usual.

'There's a freighter two miles to starboard, she's signalling!'

I clambered on deck with a torch and clung to the rigging trying to decipher the message. Our call sign during the race was A. I flashed it three times. On this occasion I didn't realise that three A's is the international code for asking 'What ship are you?' A reply came back with confusing speed. I tried again and painfully spelt out Y-A-C-H-T — T-A-I-H-O-A. This time the answer was slower — U-U-U — U-U-U.

'What the hell does three U's mean?' I asked Owen. Then it suddenly struck me: 'You are standing into danger'! I looked ahead. Faintly but positively there it was, Land!

'Put her about, quick!' Owen threw the tiller over.

'Sam! Jimpey! on deck, quick!' We adjusted sheets as *Taihoa* changed course and nonchalantly sailed out to sea. I sent a nervous T-H-A-N-K-S to the freighter. It replied.

'What did they say?' asked Owen.

'I would like to think it was Y-O-U-R-E W-E-L-C-O-M-E, but I've a suspicion they said B-L-O-O-D-Y A-M-A-T-E-U-R'!

Wednesday, February 3rd

'Position 36° 11´ South. 170° 52´ East. Day's run 109 miles,' murmured Sam.

'The wind is about 35 knots from N.W. Seas rough but I think we can hold the full reefed main and jib for a while yet. I wish it would stop raining,' I said.

Jimpey dripped his way down into the cabin.

'I've looked and looked,' he complained, 'but there's not another yacht in sight . . . I wonder where they are?'

Owen called from the cockpit.

'Hey, you fellows!'

'Yes?'

'Do you want to know what's on the menu tonight?'

'Yes!'

'Vegetable soup . . . steak and kidney pie . . . potatoes, peas and cabbage . . . pineapple and cream . . . coffee.'

'Any returns?' enquired Jimpey.

'You're a pot-bellied guts!' roared the cook.

'Ah, Ha, Ha, Ha', was the mimicked reply.

Thursday, February 4th

Five times in the night we tended the sails. By morning she wallowed along under small jib and reefed mizzen. She shouldered into the crests which retaliated by slapping her stern and occasionally frothing into the cockpit. The wind settled for a westerly origin and gusted either side of 35 knots. Damp clothes were draped round Stove who assumed a bland oriental expression. We stood watches, dozed, pored over charts, disbelieved the radio report of calmer weather and pondered on the whereabouts of the other yachts. The navigator caught the sun once, which indicated a day's run of seventy slow and sloppy miles.

Friday, February 5th

'Are you feeling poorly?' I asked Owen.

'Not bad,' he said.

'This lousy weather upsetting you?'

'In a manner of speaking it is,' he admitted. 'It's all very well having the bowsprit as a toilet in fair weather . . . Look old man, it's just not natural having to struggle out to bow in this weather, drop your tweeds and bare your nether end to the element across that bowsprit!'

'I've done it!'

'No doubt,' he replied, 'but when I try it, this ruddy ship bounces and buries her bow and my stern deep in the Tasman . . . as for handling a toilet roll in a gale . . . it's sheer lunacy.'

'It sounds screamingly funny . . . I must watch next time.'

'Please do, Jimpey does and gets convulsed every time!'

'Have a look at this,' said Sam indicating his chart. 'Our position is 35° 14′ South 168° 48′ East, that means we've covered another 81 miles. That's mighty slow progress but I don't think the others will be doing much better . . . Wonder where they are?'

'Wonder if they've got toilets?' said Owen wistfully.

'A ship! A ship!' cried Jimpey from the cockpit.

In the distance a liner hurried on her way.

'I wonder if they would give us some fresh bread,' said the helmsman.

'Let's throw that boy overboard,' suggested the cook.

Saturday, February 6th

Our seventh day at sea was calm and hot. *Taihoa* waddled 46 measly miles. Sam took sight after sight. I listened constantly hoping to hear from the fleet. Jimpey swung in and out of the rigging checking and rechecking. Owen spent the morning on the bowsprit and the afternoon preparing a banquet.

Sunday, February 7th

Another day of rest. In a pleasant breeze from the South we hung all *Taihoa*'s wardrobe aloft. She preened herself and gurgled off 80 lackadaisical miles.

'Why didn't you sing this morning?' asked Sam.

'Too busy figuring the location of the others,' I said.

'I bet they would like to know where we are!' he said.

'They are behind us!' stated Owen.

'A clever cook . . . a wise cook,' quoted Jimpey.

Monday, February 8th

For three days all sail had stayed aloft. Another 93 miles in 24 hours and a constant desire to break 100.

Tuesday, February 9th

Sam and I came to an exciting conclusion. We had kept *Taihoa* edging west in the hope that soon the prevailing N.W. winds off the coast of Australia would reach us. Then we could free sheets and follow our prescribed semicircular course. We were certain the other yachts would work on a straight course for Hobart. If that was so they would be approximately 100 miles to the S.W. of us, in the very place our weather report had promised strong head winds up to 40 knots with heavy seas. Our weather was fair and for the day *Taihoa* marked up 94 miles. I sang again as Sam marked our position 34° South, 163° 11′ East.

Wednesday, February 10th

Sam sat beside me as I struggled with the tiller.

'If we don't reduce sail soon we'll pull the sticks out!' he said.

'Get the boys on deck and take in the mizzen.'

From the north swooshed 40 knots of welcomed wind. *Taihoa* planed off the long steep seas like a thoroughbred, hard and fast down hill toward Tasmania. The crew's team work was magnificent and I spurred them on with the old school song *Altiora Peto*.

'My God this bitch can go!' said cook, and go she did. 126 glorious, sweeping, surging miles in one unforgettable day.

Thursday, February 11th

The north wind joined with the west and screamed. Under the one straining genoa *Taihoa* flew from tops to troughs through surf and spume. This was what we came for and this was why we trained.

Owen slid back the hatch and bellowed at me

'Stop singing!'

'Why?'

'Down here it sounds like you're calling for assistance!'

'More wind is what we need!'

'You're just like Stove,' he said.

'How's that?'

'She's pink with excitement!'

The watches through the night were tough but exciting. None of us had ever driven a ship so hard.

When I took the helm at dawn *Taihoa* was going like an express train. I settled in the cockpit and looked ahead where a dozen whales were crossing our path. *Taihoa* was almost on them. There was nothing I could do. I shut my eyes and she found her own way through. Never have I felt disaster so close. It was worth it, in 24 hours we covered 146 miles.

Friday, February 12th

Those wonderful winds from the north and west continued to speed *Taihoa*. They had eased a little and, as though caught by this kindly spirit, the ocean made less of throwing its weight around. Tricks at the tiller were easier. Excitement mounted. Tasmania was only 500 miles away.

I joined Sam at his plotting table.

'How goes it?'

'Sam,' he said, 'I just don't know . . . theoretically our navigation is working well . . . this will be my first landfall . . . we could miss Tasmania altogether!'

'I don't think so, nor do you!'

'We will see . . . the old girl is astounding . . . even if we are last it's all been worth while!'

'We'll be first!' I said.

'You really think so?'

'Well no, but I'm certain we can't be far behind . . . we've a few hours' handicap up our sleeves . . . I think we will get a place!'

'You know, there's one thing that worries me,' said Sam.

'What?'

'The kitty. Thirty-nine and six is a miserable sum to celebrate on!'

'There's an Australian magazine that owes me £45, I'll telegraph for it when we arrive . . . let's hope they pay out!'

'Mmm . . . the payout for *Taihoa* is 117 miles for the day, not bad eh?'

A terrific caterwauling broke out on deck.

'What the hell is that?' asked Sam.

'It's Jimpey teaching the cook to sing!'

Saturday, February 13th

Position 38° 47′ South 153° 35′ East. Day's run 106 miles. A little overcast. Wind moved from north to east-south-east, the wind change made seas lumpy.

Lumpy. When a sea is lumpy a small ship becomes skittish. A skittish ship makes it difficult for the navigator.

At mid-day I was steering. From the cockpit I could see into the cabin where Sam was gently removing his sextant from its box. *Taihoa* lurched to port and sent Sam flying. He fell hugging his precious sextant to his chest. The box shattered to pieces against Stove. Sam sat for a moment looking at the damage then crawled over to the wreckage and out of my sight. A few minutes later he came on deck.

'Sam,' he said, 'Sam . . . My God . . . Sam!'

'Is the sextant all right?' I asked, getting alarmed.

'Yes! Yes! but . . . Hell's teeth I can't believe it!' He was white.

'What's wrong?' I demanded.

'In the box,' he stammered, 'hidden in the bottom . . . look, nine five pound notes and five half sovereigns!'

Sunday, February 14th

The wind favoured the north. Its constant 10 knots called for more sail. We crowded it on. Owen and Jimpey took the day watches between them while Sam and I checked and rechecked the navigation.

An animated conversation from the cockpit eased the tension of those below.

Jimpey: 'Do you think we'll win?'

Owen: 'If those two crazy types have anything to do with it we will!'

Jimpey: 'They are not crazy!'

Owen: 'Yes they are . . . if they hadn't been I would not have come!'

Jimpey: 'Oh . . . what are you going to do when we get to Hobart?'

Owen: 'What do you think?'

Jimpey: 'Go to the pub!'

Owen: 'Right! . . . thank God you won't be allowed in!'

Jimpey: 'Humph . . . I wouldn't want to go . . . I'm going to see a girl I know . . . she's got a sister too!'

Owen: 'Would you like an extra large dinner tonight?'

Jimpey: 'You bet!'

Owen: 'What's the name of the sister?'

Monday, February 15th

Raining. 109 miles with gusting north-easter. The strain was showing in bloodshot eyes. *Taihoa* felt the urgency and boiled her ten tons through increasing seas. There were 200-odd miles to go.

Tuesday, February 16th

'It's becoming a gale . . . can she stand this amount of sail?'

'She's got to!'

'The mast is beginning to shudder!'

'What's our position?'

'42° 08′ South 149° 31′ East . . . 136 miles for the day!'

'I've got Radio Hobart . . . but all they're talking about is rich red tomato sauce.'

'We'll give her one more hour then drop the main.'

'You guys eat out of a can tonight!'

'We better double up the night watches . . . if *Taihoa* hit another yacht at this speed she would cut it in half!'

'Ah, Ha, Ha, Ha!'

Wednesday, February 17th

'It's 2 a.m.,' said the navigator. 'In half an hour we should see Tasman lighthouse at the entrance to Stormy Bay . . . its visibility is 18 miles.'

'The wind is dropping . . . she's hardly making two knots . . . if only we had a gale for the next six hours.'

'You're gale happy!' Sam told me and climbed into his bunk.

'Is breakfast ready?' called Jimpey from the forward cabin.

Thirty-eight minutes later Tasman light loomed dead ahead. I went below and woke Sam with the good news.

'Abso-bloody-lutely wonderful!' he sighed and went back to sleep.

By six in the morning *Taihoa* was just inside Stormy Bay and a few miles away from the finishing line. In a glassy calm she was going nowhere. A painted ship upon a painted ocean. At 9 a.m. the rubbish thrown overboard at breakfast time still lay alongside. At 10 a.m. we tidied up the ketch. At 11 a.m. Sam warned about blood pressure as I paced around the deck. At mid-day I broke out the brandy, poured three block busters and told Jimpey to help himself to the ship's lime juice.

With tantalisingly weak zephyrs the wind arrived, *Taihoa* moved sedately up the Bay, paused before the entrance to the Derwent River, fluttered her sails daintily at Hobart, then drifted sideways and waited for dusk before making up her mind and crossing the line.

Boom! a pint-sized cannon marked our finishing time across the line. Auckland to Hobart in 18 days 9 hours 2 minutes and 7 seconds. Weariness closed in like a fog.

A small power boat towed us into Constitution Dock, where we moored. An official came on board and made a statement.

'The *Black Rose*, *Hope* and *Ghost* are in. *Ranganui* retired from the race on the second day out. *Te Rapunga* has not arrived yet. We cannot make an official statement about the placing until she arrives . . . even though we've worked out the handicaps!' He moved towards the hatch.

'The winner of the race won by 4 hours 33 minutes 43 seconds,' he said.

'Who won?' I asked.

'It's not official until all yachts are accounted for . . . *Te Rapunga* must arrive before we make a statement!'

'Unofficially, who won?' I pleaded.

'*Taihoa*!' he said and left.

Sam sat down suddenly. Owen hung on to Stove. I looked blankly at Sam.

'Whoopee!' bellowed Jimpey.

And all hell let loose.

Neil Arrow, *Painted Ocean*, 1961

By Junk to New Zealand

BRIAN CLIFFORD was an apprentice officer with the Union Steam Ship Company, on ships plying the Pacific and Indian oceans, when he saw his first Calcutta river boats, Ceylon dhows, Indian river boats, Singapore junks. Why not satisfy his urge for ocean cruising in something a bit different from the conventional yacht?

Eventually, he had the 35ft junk *Golden Lotus* built in a Hong Kong shipyard. Intrepid but inexperienced mates were found in his home town of Kaitaia. Brian had his merchant navy training; his brother Graham had sailed as an able seaman, but neither had much small-boat cruising experience. The other two, Ray and Max, were farmers; the oldest of the four was Max, who was 25. They fitted out their unusual craft, provisioned her, accepted the gift of a tiny chow puppy they called Choy, and in December 1961 set sail for Singapore, the first major port on their 8500-mile journey to New Zealand.

As they sailed south into the shipping lanes of the China Sea, the weather worsened. Brian, as skipper and sole navigator, was really on his own.

*F*or two hours that afternoon we ran before the gentle breeze toward the western entrance of the Hong Kong harbour. I was in command and the others were sprawling round the cockpit in the cool of the late afternoon taking their last look at the city receding astern. It was a wonderful feeling to be on our way after the exhausting turmoil of the past few days. We were in our own little ship at last, independent from the rest of the world and feeling more free than we had ever done before.

Land over to port? Land meant nothing to us. We had food for a month or more and water for a good two months. We were at sea and that was where we wanted to be. The sooner we lost sight of land the better. We were heading for Singapore, fourteen hundred miles away to the south-south-west, and we did not want to see anything or anybody until we got there. Like the famous actress, we wanted to be alone . . . and little did we realise then how in the next two weeks we would long for land and civilisation . . .

At midnight the light of Wang Lan Island was fading on the starboard quarter and we were back on the course we had held for just ten seconds until the batten broke seven hours before. Graham and Max turned in and Ray and I settled down for the first four-hour watch of the voyage proper.

The wind, moderate to fresh from the north-east, was on our port quarter, our pace was brisk but I was not easy in my mind.

This was the first time I had taken my shipmates out of reach of land and the weight of my responsibility came home fully to me. Their fate depended on my skill as sole navigator and I knew that the seas ahead were scattered with reefs and shoals, some of them not charted. I had done plenty of navigating on big cargo ships, but there had always been somebody to confer with if I was in any doubt. Now I was really on my own.

As the land fell away astern the swells began to get unpleasant. Ray and I squirmed uneasily and took deep breaths from the eye of the wind to try to settle our stomachs and clear our heads. We both admitted that we regretted the big stew Graham had made for dinner as we plugged out from Aberdeen against the wind. At least the engine was not running and there was no smell of diesel fumes to add to our discomfort.

I was aware that Graham and Max were tossing in their bunks and I knew that we were all suffering. Well before four in the morning they were both on deck, eager to take their turn on watch.

We were all feeling miserable and I felt it was my job as leader of the crew to try to keep the spirit up right from the start. We knew the boat well by day, but we had done little sailing at night and none in such a lively sea. Every time we moved we bumped into things and fell over things and I realised that none of us felt really at home.

In the dark young gale at four o'clock that morning I even felt that the *Golden Lotus* was slightly hostile to us, as though she resented leaving her homeland for foreign parts.

'Hell, you look miserable,' I said to Max. 'How about a nice fat greasy pork chop?'

He did not answer for a while. 'Not too best,' he said in his interpretation of Pidgin English, 'but give me those tiller tackles and you get down below into that — concrete mixer.'

Ray and I did go below a few minutes later, after giving Graham and Max the course, but that night I did not sleep.

The next day was even more miserable. The wind grew fresher and the swells increased. Early in the morning Graham and Max reefed the mainsail right down until only the canvas between the top two spreaders was pulling. The foresail was reefed down to half and the mizzen still had not been set.

We boiled eggs for breakfast and drank hot soup from heavy mugs for lunch. I felt too ill to bother taking a midday sight to check our position. We were barely out of sight of land and in clear waters, so it did not matter much.

There were some sarcastic comments about the staff of the Hong Kong weather office, who had told us that we could expect nice fresh sailing winds of about fifteen knots. They were not far from right — I suppose the wind was not more than twenty knots — but they had not told us it had been blowing this way for weeks, setting up the heavy swell that was throwing us around so uncomfortably.

Right through the afternoon the deck was the most popular place to be. We were all still subconsciously fighting the motion. Even our previous sea experience did not enable Graham and me to adjust to this, an entirely different motion to that we had grown used to on big ships.

And for Max and Ray it was a nightmare of three-dimensional movement such as they had never experienced. We were rolling, pitching, tossing and at the same time yawing about on the swells like an idiot corkscrew.

When we changed watches at four o'clock we held a worried conference round the tiller. The weight of the skewball following seas was throwing a great strain on the rudder and it was difficult to hold course, even though the steering tackles reduced the weight transmitted to the helmsman to a quarter of that thrown on the tiller itself. The rudder was taking a constant thrashing because our course was angling across the direction of the seas and when particularly heavy seas struck our stern at an angle we could hear creaks of protest as the tiller worked slightly in the rudder stock.

My concern was increased by the fact that our tiller was not made from the wood the Chinese usually use. Wung Kee had taken it into his head to make ours from Borneo yacal, which, although it is very strong, is brittle because it will not flex. He had assured us that it would be 'more better', but I had insisted on having a spare tiller made in case he was wrong.

That afternoon I laid the spare ready in the cockpit, but I feared that if the one in use broke we would not get time to change it before we lost control of the *Golden Lotus* and got into serious difficulties.

At seven that evening there was a sharp brittle crunch from the tiller and when we rushed to inspect it we saw a big crack deep into the wood where it entered the stock.

Graham and Max immediately dropped the mainsail to take the way off the boat and I altered course to run directly before the sea. Ray hammered the butt of the heavy tiller out of the rudder stock while Graham unshackled the tackles and began to change them on to the spare tiller.

Max and I tried to steady the wild thrashing of the rudder by grasping the stock in a bear hug, but our efforts were futile.

Before the tackles were on the new tiller we jammed it in the stock and Ray, Max and I held on for dear life while Graham completed the task of shackling on the tackles.

Even three of us hanging on could not hold the tiller still, but at least we stopped it thrashing right from one side of the cockpit to the other and kept it sufficiently steady for Graham to screw in the tiny shackle pins.

The drama was all over in a few minutes and we returned to our course, but left the mainsail down and sailed under only the reefed foresail to try to reduce the strain on the tiller.

First job was to trim off the cracked end of the broken tiller and shape the end roughly to fit the stock in case the spare smashed. We were very thankful for the basic kit of carpentry tools we had bought in Hong Kong. With the saw, chisel and axe Ray quickly completed the job and I realised that without the tools we would have been helpless.

I silently thanked Max, who had insisted on the tools and even offered to pay for them himself when our funds were dwindling and the rest of us were toying with the idea of sailing without them. It was one of the many times I was glad of Max's practical, down-to-earth attitude.

At eleven o'clock that night a swell heavier than the rest caught us under the stern and slewed us heavily off course. The foresail gybed and the spare tiller broke off clean at the rudder stock. The original tiller was shipped in its place within minutes, but half an hour later it smashed again.

Fumbling in the dark we trimmed and refitted the spare, but it was a bad fit and while one of the men on watch steered the other had to hammer it back every two or three minutes as it worked from the stock.

We hove to with our bow up slightly into the wind. The foresail was sheeted in flat and the rudder was held to leeward, locking the *Golden Lotus* in this direction while she drifted slowly down wind. This took a lot of the strain off the rudder, but right through the night the helmsman had to fight to prevent further damage. The technique was to ease the tackle on the weather side whenever the strain became heavy, then to heave it back gently as the swell passed under our stern.

We were all very tired by this time because our watch system had been disrupted by the emergencies. All we got was occasional snatches of sleep between the calls: 'All hands on deck.' And when we could get below it was not easy to sleep because of the combination of the crazy motion and the worry about our position.

The wind had increased considerably and it was moaning softly through the rigging. This noise was like the traditional water-torture, gentle but insistent, and it played havoc with our nerves. It was not our ship singing to us, she was growling at us with fangs bared.

Hove to we felt quite helpless. There was nothing else we could do but wait out the long wild night until daylight gave us a chance to repair the tiller properly.

It would have been hopeless to try under the dim light of the swinging hurricane lamp and we realised anyway that the tiller would need strengthening. There was no point in making a further makeshift repair as we had done earlier in the night.

Each time the tiller snapped about ten inches was lost from its length and we could not afford to lose much more or there would be nothing left. Each time it was shortened the helmsman lost some of the mechanical advantage that its length had given and steering became harder as more strain was felt through the tiller tackles.

It was one of the longest nights we can remember. Graham was not quite so seasick as the rest of us and he kept us supplied with hot soup at intervals. But more he could not do. Ten minutes at a time was all he could stand in the heaving galley with the kerosene fumes from the primus stove.

Sleep was impossible for those off watch. The clunking of the back of the hatchet being used to keep the tiller in place was transmitted through every timber of the boat and amplified by the enclosed space of the cabin, which acted like the soundbox of a violin.

At six-thirty next morning it was all hands on deck to repair the tiller. We trimmed the tiller that was not in use, then swapped them over. The new tiller was a better fit in the stock but we realised that it was only a question of time before it would break again. We cut two three-foot lengths from a stout board we had in case of emergencies, placed one each side of the tiller, secured them to the tiller with two bolts and then drove screws and nails through the after end into the stock.

Round the splint we lashed three-quarter inch manila rope and then wet it with sea water to shrink it tight.

The result was a much more robust tiller and half an hour after the work began we were back on course, still sailing only under the reefed foresail but at least we felt we were in control again and we were heading where we wanted to go.

We debated whether we should try to return to Hong Kong, but we realised it would be all but impossible to battle our way back against the strong wind and rough seas. If we had tried it would probably have taken longer than to proceed to Singapore and it would have been much harder on both us and the junk . . .

That night — the third out from Hong Kong — we were hove to again. The boat lay fairly quietly most of the time but when she rolled she rolled heavily. It was at this time that we decided to lash the men on deck watch to the mizzen mast. This was not only to keep them in one place with reasonable comfort but also to avert the very real danger of a man being thrown over the side. I ordered life jackets to be worn at all times on deck, but the thought of what would happen if a man went overboard chilled me. In that sea we had no hope at all of turning the boat back.

We reached the lowest ebb of our despair the next day. The wind had increased to between twenty-five and thirty knots — verging on gale force — and the swell had become shorter but still very heavy with foaming crests. To add to the confusion the wind whipped up steep breaking seas on the backs of the swells.

That afternoon I got another sight and found that we had made sixty miles in twenty-four hours. We were still steering south-south-east to make due south into the shipping lane across the China Sea but we were not really sailing, we were surfboarding.

I was sprawled on my bunk below after my watch when one of my shipmates came to me and began a roundabout conversation. No names no pack-drill, because it could have been any of us and the thought he expressed had even crossed my mind.

Hesitantly, he asked: 'What would be the chances of signalling a ship if one came past?'

'Possible but not very good,' I said. 'Not likely to see us in this swell. Why?'

'If we do see one would you consider abandoning ship?'

My first reaction was anger. 'Pull yourself together for goodness sake,' I said. 'Even if a ship saw us no one could take us off safely in this sea. We've got to stick with this whether we like it or not and belly-aching won't help.'

Then my anger turned to sympathy as I realised that he had expressed what everybody on board must be thinking, even poor Chow. I took from the chart drawer the bottle of Chinese whisky we had bought in Saikung for four shillings and sixpence.

Uncorking it, I handed it to my companion.

'Here,' I said, 'what we all need is a damned good swig of this.'

He took a deep gulp and thanked me with a sheepish grin. Then I took a big pull on the bottle myself and we both went up on deck to minister to the others.

The whisky was part of our medicine chest, but I felt it could never be needed more than it was now. The bottle went down by about one-third and our spirits went up in proportion. Chow missed out.

That night we were once more hove to without a stitch of sail. The loneliness of the open sea was upon us and we were weary from lack of decent sleep. The log book tells the story. In writing made childish by the vicious motion of the boat I entered: 'All hands very weary and nearly done in.'

Through the night we were rolling lee rail under with every second swell. Green seas were scooped into the cockpit as wind and swell caught the bottom of the *Golden Lotus* and hurled us bodily sideways. The draining scuppers in the cockpit could not cope with the flooding and a lot of water found its way below. It was two men on watch, and one of those supposed to be resting was constantly pumping the bilges to keep the junk from foundering.

The tiller groaned ominously throughout the night and when we inspected it with an electric torch we could see that the nails and screws with which we had secured the splints were working loose. Obviously it could not last much longer.

We managed to nurse it until just after dawn; then it snapped with a dry crunching noise.

The warp we were trailing saved the day by keeping our stern into the seas while we struggled with the repair. Realising that we needed something stronger than the splints we had used in the last repair, we pirated the two hardwood bunkboards from the upper berths in the main cabin. Ray was our carpenter. He cut the boards roughly to size while the rest of us shipped the spare tiller. Then Ray fitted the new splints as they had been on the broken tiller, which had lasted two days almost to the minute.

As the heavy bolts and nails went in we said a silent prayer. The bunkboards were the last suitable material for the job we had on board and if they broke we might literally be sunk.

Most of the morning was gone before we got under way and with the courage of despair we decided we had had enough of drifting helplessly. We would sail.

Graham and Max took off the lashings we had put on three days before to secure the furled mainsail and for the first time since losing sight of land we raised two sections.

It was a defiant gesture and probably not very sensible, but it steadied our boat and made us feel that at last we were making some progress.

Instead of sitting deep in the sea and wallowing heavily the *Golden Lotus* began to cream over the tops of the swells with an easier motion. We found we were making four knots but the increase in our speed brought us into conflict with the rhythm of the seas. One moment we would be surging along smoothly and the next we would sail right off the top of a sea and drop with a chilling shudder into the trough beyond.

When this happened the ship shook as though we had struck a submerged mountain. The mast seemed to be trying to smash its way through the keel like a pile-driver and the standing rigging twanged like a guitar.

After half an hour of this heady but frightening progress I took my noon sight. We had covered seventy miles in the day and we were well to the west of our plotted course.

I realised that we must be in the grip of the strong current that sets south-west across the China Sea at this time of the year. Its effect on our small boat was far greater than I had expected.

I had a bit of a shock when I plotted our position on the chart. In the night we had sailed within a few miles of a treacherous little shoal. It was clearly marked on the chart but the previous day I had been too sick to notice it.

Seventy or eighty miles south of our present position were the Paracel Islands and Reefs, a dirty area of foul ground dotted with jagged hazards. It half registered in my mind at the time that a line drawn through our last three positions showed that in spite of the fact that we were steering south-south-east we were being swept south-west directly on to them.

But it only half registered and the smell of the detergent remaining in the bilges was again making me feel sick. I went up on deck to take my trick at the helm.

Only minutes later I got my biggest fright of the whole voyage. I heard a roar like an express train in a tunnel, turned and saw right behind us a swell far bigger than any we had experienced. It seemed to tower thirty feet above our stern and as it raced toward us the crest was breaking.

By the time I saw it the crest had broken to within fifty yards of the *Golden Lotus* and the top was curling over down the length of the swell with such frightening speed that there was nothing I could do.

I watched horrified as hundreds of tons of water crashed off the top in seconds. It seemed that it was going to engulf my little ship completely but as the roaring wall of water raced down the swell diagonally across our stern the *Golden Lotus* seemed to sense the danger and surged forward a yard or so.

It saved us, but even so the thundering white breaker burst right under our stern quarter, picked us up at a crazy angle and slammed the boat round through half a circle.

The drama was over in seconds and we were left facing the way we had come with the sails flapping wildly about while the vicious swell roared on to look for other prey. The tiller tackles had been torn from my hand and if I had not been lashed to the mast I would have been thrown over.

As we spun I had bellowed 'on deck,' fearing that we must founder and that my three companions would be trapped below. By the time they reached the deck it was all over. They were bruised and very white-faced, but there was no time to assess the damage.

We had to get back on to course fast because with our bow into the sea and being forced backwards our rudder would have been carried away in no time. Anyway, we had no control in that position and my unconscious reaction was to resume course.

Graham rushed for'ard and backed the foresail to bring our head round while I took up the tiller tackles and steadied the thrashing rudder.

The junk was rearing and pitching wildly and taking green seas over the bow. I was very anxious about Graham on the foredeck, but I could see he was hanging on for his life as the seas surged almost to his waist.

Max and Ray grabbed the thrashing mainsail and tried to steady it as the *Golden Lotus* slowly paid off and I brought her back on to her course.

This was the trial; the moment the head began to pay off we were committed to going through with the manoeuvre. As she came round she wallowed for an instant broadside on to the seas and another big one like the last would have surely rolled us right over.

But luck was with us and we got round safely. We decided that there was too much risk with the mainsail set so we furled it again and sailed, as we had been doing, with only a corner of reefed foresail. I was relieved to see that the warp came clear and trailed astern again; it could have been tangled in the rudder. And surprisingly, after the pounding it had taken, the tiller was still intact.

The shock of our close escape from tragedy snapped me out of the lethargy I had sunk into during the previous three or four days and I told my crew we must seek shelter. Manila in the Philippines was the nearest port where we could hope to make shelter safely. Hainan Island was much closer, only a hundred and eighty miles to the west, but we had no coastal chart of the area and besides it was Chinese Communist territory.

We all agreed that we would rather take our chance with the seas than with what might happen to us there, so Manila it was, four hundred and fifty miles away due south-east. Pirates there were on the Philippines coast, but Manila itself should be safe and we thought that any pirates who were at sea off the coast in this weather deserved all they could find. We might even have been glad to see them!

I changed course to head for Manila and as I did so I felt relieved. I realised that the new course was carrying us away from the dangerous Paracel Islands, and it was only then that it came home to me that on our old course we would certainly have ended up among them, where no sensible skipper would go even in the best weather, never mind a gale.

Through the rest of the day and right through the night we continued on this course, logging about one and a half knots. Our spirits were better at the thought of heading for shelter out of this purgatory, but our hands were painfully raw from the constant chaffing of the tiller tackles. We all had broken blisters and calluses and the salt water made them agonising.

We tried putting socks over our hands and that helped a little, but the coarse Chinese ropes still cut into our tender flesh.

To add to our discomfort, we were all living in the same clothes we had been wearing when the gale first struck. We were too tired and dispirited to be continually changing and by this time our clothes were soggy and sticky with salt. Anyway, there would have been no point in changing because the salt in the atmosphere had pervaded everything and the spare clothes were sticky, too.

One other problem that almost became too much for us at this time was the constant changing of the tiller tackles. The poor Chinese rope was chafing rapidly on the sheaves and the cheeks of the blocks, and the tackles had to be renewed every day. Graham was a wizard at this and he could reeve new ropes on each side in a couple of minutes.

But it meant that the rest of us had to fight the thrashing tiller while he did so.

And that meant broken watches for the two who were supposed to be resting. I considered changing the tackles regularly at the time the watches changed, but we were going through our spare rope rapidly and I realised we would have to make each set of tackles last as long as possible.

The system was to wait until they had chafed right through or were obviously going to do so, then call all hands on deck. This always seemed to happen just as those below had got to sleep.

At this nightmare stage of the voyage I realised that we could never have managed without the fourth member of the crew. We could have done with a couple more hands and I kicked myself for ever having toyed with the idea of setting off with only two companions, let alone by myself, as I had vowed I would do if I could not get a crew.

At noon the next day — the sixth out from Hong Kong — my sight showed that we had covered eighty miles in the past twenty-four hours but although we were sailing as close into the wind as we could we were still being swept so strongly by the current that our actual course was well to the south of the course we were steering. We were trying to make a course just east of south-east, but we were travelling south-south-east.

Again the log tells the story for me: 'All hands feeling the strain of watch-keeping and the broken sleep. Our hands are very sore now from the steering tackles. The weather is the same and none of us are very happy.'

In the afternoon we again risked two sections of the mainsail to get more speed, but after a harrowing night when the wind increased we had to take it down in the morning.

Ray was the only one showing signs of cheerfulness and Graham was still the only cook who could face the galley. I have no memory of anything that morning except heavy grey-green seas with white foaming crests and the constant irritating drone of the wind in the rigging.

But my noon sight gave me a new interest — literally an interest in life. We were right on the edge of the Macclesfield Bank and being swept directly towards the centre of it.

I calculated that just four miles further on that course and we would have been right in the heaving holocaust of seas breaking on the bank. It was certain death. The bank rose to within five fathoms of the surface and with the huge swells that were running we would have been smashed to matchwood on the rocks.

My sight the day before had indicated that we would clear the north-east corner of the bank with plenty of searoom, but in the past twenty-four hours we had not been making east at all; we had been swept even west of south.

Immediate action was called for. I warned the others to hold on and told Ray to gybe the *Golden Lotus* round to steer north-west. We came around with a crash of sails and headed away from the bank with the wind hard on our starboard beam. Through the afternoon we sailed along the length of the hair-raising swells. It was like being on an insane roller-coaster and time after time only the tremendous beam of the junk saved us from being rolled right over.

I was sweating a cold sweat for another reason. We were heading straight back for the Paracel Islands and the problem was to sail far enough toward them to clear the western end of the Macclesfield Bank, then alter course to head south-west down the narrow passage between the bank and the islands.

Too far before we changed course and we would be swept on to the south-eastern corner of the islands and their outlying reefs; not far enough and we would be wrecked on the south-west corner of the bank.

There was no other way out of the danger. We could not head up wind any more than we had been doing to clear the northern side of the bank. And it was also impossible to clear the northern side of the islands and sail right round them.

Right through the afternoon we kept a weather eye open for signs of breaking water that might indicate the bank. It was an almost hopeless task; the water was breaking everywhere in the gale anyway and if we had seen signs of the bank it would probably have been too late.

I was praying that my navigation was right. If the noon position had been wrong — and it was taken under the worst of conditions — I might be sailing us into danger, not away from it.

The responsibility was all mine and my shipmates had to trust my navigation. I, in my turn, had to trust my wristwatch and the time signals we had received on our portable radio to check it by. I also had to trust that my sight that day had been accurate.

We ran off on this course until seven-thirty that evening. Then the reading from the mechanical log towed astern told me that we had covered thirty miles and I estimated that it was time to alter course and run the gauntlet down the narrow passage.

The wind was directly astern when I pointed her head south-west and we had to take the scrap of mainsail down. It was dark and there was only forty miles between the eastern reef of the island group and the western point of the bank. There were no navigation lights.

The tension was high but there was nothing we could do so we kept to our watches. We were logging four knots under the reefed foresail.

The night dragged through slowly and although I took my turns below I never slept. I was on watch at dawn and as the sea lightened I looked around anxiously but there was no sign of danger.

For the first time that night I relaxed my tense grip on the tiller tackles a little — and realised that my hands were even more painful than they had been.

There was not much conversation as the morning wore on toward the crucial noon sight. The weather began to moderate and this raised our spirits a little, but nobody was in a mood for celebration until we knew exactly where we were.

Noon came and everybody pretended it was just another sighting as I took my sextant on deck, lashed myself to the mizzen mast and carefully took my reading.

Down below again at the chart table I anxiously worked out our latitude and crossed it on the chart with my morning position line.

We were clear of the danger. I shouted the good news to my companions in the cockpit and when I climbed back up the companionway I was delighted to see that they were all grinning widely.

It was the first time for a week.

Brian Clifford and Neil Illingworth,
The Voyage of the Golden Lotus, 1962

What Would Cook Have Thought?

IN MID-NOVEMBER 1966, some two hundred years after Captain James Cook's famous circumnavigation of New Zealand, Dr Philip Houghton sailed his 40ft cutter *Murihiku* out of Auckland harbour with 'the vague hope' of completing a similar voyage. This was a decade or two before the 'in the wake of' voyages became fashionable.

The voyage lasted 'a long, rich summer' of five months, and the resulting book bears witness to Houghton's accomplishment, his extensive research into Cook's and others' coastal explorations, and the changes wrought to the coastline over two hundred years.

Despite Admiralty charts, *New Zealand Pilot* and echo sounder, none of which were available to Cook's *Endeavour*, Houghton and his crew, Mike Hutchins, had some anxious moments taking *Murihiku* in and out of Stewart Island's narrow bays. The wind blew hard and southerly until finally, anchored in desolate Port Pegasus, they heard a forecast that 'for the first time since reaching Stewart Island was vaguely encouraging'. They got up at dawn, planning to round South Cape and turn north for the coastline that had so captivated Cook — the spectacular fiordland sounds of Dusky and Doubtful.

*W*e left by the south entrance of Pegasus as dawn came, and thought ourselves cunning; calculating to catch the last two hours of the ebb down to South Cape, and then the flood, which sets strongly up the west coast of the main island for a way, inside a cluster of smaller islands.

The first bit worked perfectly. A light, chill south-easterly, the first for a long time, came in over the grey ocean, and from the south-west a tremendous swell marked the end of the land. This swell to those on the

79

Endeavour marked the victory of the anti-continentalists. On March 10th 1770 Cook wrote: 'I began now to think that this was the Southernmost land and that we should be able to get round it by the west, for we have had a large hollow swell from the S.W. ever since we had the last gale of wind from that direction.' Banks, on the same day: 'The land appeared barren and seemed to End in a Point to which the hills gradually declined much to the regret of us continent-mongers . . .' The next day he added: 'Blew fresh all Day, but carried us round the point to the total demolition of our aerial fabrick called Continent.'

It was a sunless, overcast morning and the sea was dark, with the surface of the great swell fretted by eddies and cross-currents. The inevitable mutton birds floated or flew around *Murihiku* as she bent to the wind and climbed up and down over the sea, and we kept her a mile or more offshore to avoid some sunken rocks. Not that there was much enticing about the land. It had a blasted look, the scrub flattened to a uniform carpet with a liberal exposure of rock and not a suggestion of a clearing or a habitation, or, as Stokes remarked, 'Soil enough to nourish a potato.'

Murihiku kept on with the tide and the wind and soon lay abeam of the last point of land, South Cape, no very impressive thing, a minor tongue of rock protruding from low hills which very soon could hardly be seen, for mist formed thickly between the overcast sky and the sea, and the land was only a blur. We turned her bow northward for the first time in months and at that moment thought we might have been the southernmost boat on the coast; then, out to sea, where the mist was thinner, made out the shape of a fishing boat, rising and falling as she drifted, catching blue cod.

'The southernmost yacht anyway,' said Mike, and there could have been no argument on that, for our only possible competitor, Francis Chichester, having been forced to lower latitudes by a cyclone, was at that time a hundred miles off North Cape, and not to the south as planned.

Murihiku entered the stretch of water between the offlying mutton bird islands and the main island. 'Can be dangerous to small craft,' says the *Pilot*, and the chart, for what it is worth, indicates a current of from two to five knots. 'It's after low water,' I said. 'We'll catch the flood now.'

But we didn't. Something had gone wrong. We entered a tumult of waves, and for the next four hours plugged the four-knot current that had kicked these up. At the end of this time we were exactly five miles further on, still among the smaller islands but out of the main channel where the current ran most swiftly. By then it may have been with us. Weary of such dismal progress, not at all sure where we'd erred, and somewhat humbler, we bore westward to less distracted waters. It was mid-day . . .

We were promised a few more hours of southerly wind, then a return to the usual nor'westerly stuff. But in the meantime the wind at our backs was fresh, and in Halfmoon Bay I had asked one of the islanders: 'How often do you get an easterly here? We want an easterly to reach the fiords.' He had laughed and said: 'You might wait six months for an easterly.' And we had seen large fishing boats waiting and waiting for a break in the westerlies, waiting to get round the infamous Puysegur Point where night after night on the radio we heard report of gales when the rest of the coast was calm.

We fetched up the chart and looked at the distance, at the final part of this difficult curve round the southern end of the land, the crossing of the western entrance of Foveaux Strait. The *Acheron* once made four attempts to reach Preservation Inlet from Stewart Island before being successful, and we were resigned to being blown back any number of times.

'Shall we try? We need twelve hours of this wind.'

The matter of dinghy and outboard came to mind, but this was too painful a subject and we suppressed the thought. We plotted a course for Puysegur.

I took the first watch and Mike went below to sleep. The last of the small islands, with its rocky shores and windtorn scrub, and a few semiderelict shacks for the mutton-birders in the autumn, dropped astern. Then I had an unhappy halfhour for the wind turned abruptly to the northwest, mist descended and drizzle began to fall, classical beginnings to a nor'wester, and if it arrived a few hours earlier than prophesied, I'd put us on a long lee shore for the night. There were harbours we could still run back for and reach before then, but when I turned to look for them — and I actually turned *Murihiku* herself downwind, sure this was the wise thing to do — Stewart Island was immersed in mist. Unhappy, I returned to the course of 360 degrees, trimmed the sails and gazed at the log with the words 'lee shore' drumming in my head. Twenty miles were essential, thirty miles safe and anything more luxury if a nor'west gale blew up during the night.

The change didn't last. After not much more than half an hour the wind returned to the sou'west, quite vigorously, and the air cleared a bit. Not weather I understood, but I clung to the course through the long afternoon hours and hoped the wind stayed in place. At dusk the Solanders came up ahead, where they should have been, and I complimented the compass.

The Great Solander, a sort of long-humped immense rock about twelve hundred feet high, stands two miles off its western and smaller outlier. 'This then,' wrote Bullen, 'was the famous and dreaded Solander whaling ground. Almost in the centre of the wide stretch of sea between Preservation Inlet on the Middle Island, and the western end of Stewart's Island, rose a majestic mass of wave-beaten rock some two thousand feet high, like a grim sentinel guarding the Straits.'

His heights were a bit exaggerated but the rest is accurate, and it is hard to believe that men could survive five years on that barren place as one marooned party did in the early sealing days, living in a cave and eating seal-meat and seabird eggs. Not surprisingly one went mad. The rest were at last taken off.

Low in the west the sun came briefly into a clearing sky and the Solanders were splashed with sunset, there was red across the clouds and the sea and the Solanders themselves — a soft sort of red for all its vigour and something that made me think the wind and sea abeam might remain there, for there was no menace in that sky. *Murihiku* smoked along under staysail and reefed main, the log read thirty-five miles, and I'd forgotten about lee shores. Now it was all hope that we could get round that horrific corner so unexpectedly.

Mike called up, 'Fifteen knots south-east at Puysegur.'

I'd never heard of a south-east wind at Puysegur. Abeam of the Solanders and outside them, and that meant thirty-five miles to run. I read the log and altered course. It was getting dark. Away to starboard, out of the corner of my eye I saw a plume of spray and thought, that's good, I haven't seen a whale for ages, and turned to watch.

I saw one plume continually rising and then two, and they were moving very quickly, much more quickly than I'd ever seen whales move before, coming on directly abeam to *Murihiku*. Then they were closer, perhaps a hundred and fifty yards off, black masses surging in the water, and I realized these were like no whales I'd ever seen before. In the last light I saw them, square-headed things of the glossiest black above, with rounded dorsal fins, and mouths very distinctly open and eyes — now they were close — very distinctly watching and calculating, and I knew that for the first time I was looking on the undisputed master of the sea, the killer whale.

These leading two came close abeam of *Murihiku* before turning astern and following, perhaps fifty yards off. Smaller than a right whale, they still looked ominously too big and I wondered what they made of this strange fish with the great white dorsal fin, and of size not much more than themselves. Having read of them tipping icefloes to slide seals or men into the water, I sat down on the floor of the cockpit and peered astern. Then I saw the rest of the pack or school or whatever they come in, crossing *Murihiku*'s track further back, many of them, all smaller than the leaders, cows and young, and, unlike these formidable two, leaping clear from the water like dolphins to display the hideous yellow of their bellies. They passed away to the west and then the two guardians turned and followed. But I can still see them very clearly, those great mouths agape, and those eyes watching, the brain behind reasoning — there is a claim that, considering the size and convolutions of its brain, give the whale a thumb, an opposable digit, and it would rule the world.

Mike came up and viewed with puzzlement the helmsman sitting on the cockpit floor. I left him gladly and went below, out of the chill and the damp, and where, surrounded by the polished woodwork of the saloon and with, if I remember correctly, Turina's *Canto a Sevilla* coming over the radio, such creatures became unreal and far away.

I must have slept for a long time. When I woke and poked my head out of the doghouse, there was a wet mist everywhere and the light on Puysegur was flashing once every fifteen seconds over the starboard bow. I made some cocoa and we sat on deck and watched the light. In the mist its distance was impossible to judge. I checked the log and when I had finished my cocoa went below and paced the chart with the dividers.

'Ten miles short. We'll be off the light before dawn. Long before.'

I sat below and read. After a time Mike called, 'There's a lot of white water over to starboard.'

'Waves,' I said. 'There's nothing near.'

He was silent for a minute or two and then said, 'You're wrong, you know.'

I went up, and certainly something was breaking to starboard. The echo-sounder read ten fathoms, which it shouldn't have. We cleared off to the west, and then the mist seemed to thin a little and we saw ourselves to be close under the lighthouse, having nearly encountered the Marshall Rocks a couple of miles south.

'This is silly,' I said, 'because we're not there yet.' We retrieved the log rotator. One fin was missing and another loose. It may have been suffering an 'inveterate sea-scurvy' as Cook would say and its teeth were dropping out, but more likely one of our visitors of the previous evening nuzzled it. Whatever, it had caused the log to under-read by about fifteen per cent. But we were not sorry to be where we were, despite a dropping wind and a lumpy sea. Until dawn we rolled around. Then in the light, we saw the dreaded point, an innocuous-looking, long low finger of land, nothing as we had imagined it.

We entered Preservation Inlet, passing several fishing boats coming out for the day. Some came alongside to see if we were happy. We were. In the anchorage we ate a breakfast of crayfish and blue-cod fillets someone had tossed aboard. Then slept.

I woke with a vague awareness of being somewhere unexpected and delightful, but in the first sluggish stirrings of consciousness could not orientate myself. Rectangles of sunlight lay across the cabin and swung from floor to lockers as *Murihiku* rolled slightly. A mess of clothing lay scattered around the floor and on the ends of the bunks. Mike, his head shoved in the shadow of a corner, snored gently. It was mid-day. Rather blearily I went up on deck, and Fiordland was there.

Not a cloud crossed the sky, and the sea breeze came in quite strongly to the anchorage. The broad expanse of the sound ran back between hills of the richest green, rising steeply from the water for two or three thousand feet before flattening and turning brown with tussock. The sun was warm, and I hadn't felt real sun for weeks.

I lit the Primus and poached some crayfish, then woke Mike. We sat in the sun on the hot deck and ate the white flesh. Afterwards, with difficulty, for our sense of lethargy was great, we weighed anchor and ran into the sound with the sea breeze. Like the others northward — a dozen of them — it runs well inland, more than twenty miles. After two hours' fair sailing between islands and close under bush slopes we came to a deep bay where a long beach of white sand fronted a flat-floored valley that promised an evening stalk. As happens commonly in the fiords, the soundings came up rapidly, from fifteen fathoms to nothing in a matter of yards, and after nearly putting *Murihiku* on the bank we pulled her back to fifteen fathoms where she lay out of the wind and with the chain vertical. Bush, hills and the calm of the late afternoon were liberal reward for any number of endured westerlies.

Driftwood littered the beach. In the evening we lit a great fire and baked bread, and Mike floundered back into the bush, through masses of waisthigh fern, and shot a couple of deer. This solved the meat problem for a while, but there were lots of others, for our abrupt departure from the island had left us short of provisions. There was wholemeal enough to bake a vast number of loaves and a mere pound of butter to coat them all. We had no vegetables beyond a cabbage that was starting to look like a mouldy football. But as long as we possessed a fish-hook there was no chance of starvation, for all the tall stories about fishing in the fiords turned out to be short of the truth. It simply came down to the fact that if a hook lowered over the side didn't have a fish on it in ten seconds, the bait had come off. In point of fact the time interval is nearer five seconds, but one mustn't stretch people's credulity.

In the morning we went back down the sound on the same sort of day, cloudless and hot, with a light sea breeze . . .

The weather office maintained faith in their imminent nor'wester. We, at the fringe of the western ocean, couldn't see it, but wanting to enter Dusky Sound on a clear day, made out of Preservation, across the mouth of Chalky Inlet and inside the rough tops of the Balleny Reef. Captain John Balleny of the *Eliza Scott*, a sealing vessel in the 1830s, named it, but Cook himself saw the danger much earlier. In the *Resolution* on his second voyage he made his landfall a little far south, intending to fetch Dusky but finding Chalky. It was misty: 'Fearing to run, in thick weather, into a place to which we were all strangers, and seeing some breakers and broken ground ahead, I tacked in twenty-five fathoms of water and stood out to sea, with the wind at N.W. This bay lies on the S.E. side of Cape West, and may be known by a white cliff on one of the isles which lies in the entrance of the bay.' The breakers and broken ground would have been the Balleny Reef, and Cook added, with customary frankness: 'This part of the coast I did not see but at a great distance, in my former voyage: and we now saw it under so many disadvantageous circumstances, that the less I say about it the fewer mistakes I shall make.'

We lost the wind and motored in an uncomfortable fashion across all manner of confused waves and currents at the entrance to Chalky. Beyond the white-cliffed islands which identify it we found a light southerly and made northward up the Fiordland coast. It is not really characteristic here, in the 20 miles between Chalky and Dusky, running in nearly a straight line without any worthwhile indentation and coming in low cliffs to the water. Even beyond the coast the land rises only slowly, and without the usual chasms and summits. Only about halfway to Dusky does any sort of headland protrude, and this is Cape West. Again, no very significant thing, but it did mean that *Murihiku* had rounded the four extremities of the land. It is a curious thing that the two capes of the south, which by and large has a more formidable coast, should be less remarkable than the two of the north.

A couple of hours beyond the cape we lay opposite Dusky and if, in retrospect, we had to say that any one moment of the cruise stood out above all others — in truth, that would be a hard question — it was this moment. Dusky lay before us. It is immense. We were lost in the width of the vast entrance and the sound seemed as wide as deep; but not of course in fact, for the sea cuts deeply beyond the concealing islands. Within the farspaced entrance points we saw a calm expanse of water strewn with dozens of islands, large and small. Behind rose the sharp peaks of Resolution Island and the mainland. The nearer greens of the land changed to brown and purple with distance and at this season only a few scraps of snow lingered around the highest summits. Not a habitation, not a boat, and the white standard of the light on the southern entrance point must have been the only addition, the only thing changed in the scene since the *Resolution* had entered nearly two centuries before. The *Resolution* and not the *Endeavour*, for Dusky was only viewed and named on the first voyage. Night came as the *Endeavour* approached the land, and she had been blown northward by morning. But from its position, in the track of the westerlies, Cook perceived its potential as a harbour for sailing vessels: 'It is about three or four miles broad at the Entrance, and seems to be as full as deep. In it are several islands, behind which there must be shelter from all winds, provided there is a sufficient depth of water.' And of course this last is no problem. Rather, there is too much water; a hundred fathoms will not find bottom in places within the sound, and it is necessary to moor close in, with a warp ashore. Making the bay from southward on the second voyage the *Resolution* found water enough, forty fathoms at the entrance and then no bottom at sixty: 'We were, however, too far advanced to return; and therefore stood on, not doubting but that we should find anchorage. For in this bay we were all strangers; in my former voyage having done no more than discover and name it.'

Five miles within the entrance the *Resolution* brought-to and came to anchor off the eastern end of one of the larger islands, for this reason subsequently named Anchor Island; but the place was clearly unsuitable for any prolonged stay, and Cook himself went in one of the ship's boats to reconnoitre the northern part of the bay, discovering Facile Harbour, while Lieutenant Pickersgill investigated to the south. Preferring Pickersgill's report to his own, Cook made to the south in the *Resolution* after a calm night: 'On the 27th, at nine o'clock in the morning, we got under sail with a light breeze at S.W. and working over to Pickersgill Harbour, entered it by a channel scarcely twice the width of the ship; and in a small creek moored head and stern, so near the shore as to reach it with a brow or stage, which nature had in a manner prepared for us in a large tree, whose end or top reached our gunwale. Wood, for fuel and other purposes, was here so convenient, that our yards were locked in the branches of the trees; and about 100 yards from our stern, was a fine stream of fresh water.'

Inside the entrance points we lost all wind and started an untraditional engine. A small black fishing boat resolved from the shore and came alongside. On the bow was written *Chappie*. 'Going to Pickersgill?' called the solitary man aboard, and we nodded. A bag of crayfish came thudding on the deck and *Chappie* headed off for the islands across the bay. Later we more formally met Billy Maquarie, a descendant of the famed Gilroy, and possessed, I would think, of an unsurpassed knowledge of this coast and its fishing. He once spent a week shipwrecked in an isolated bay when his anchor chain broke one night, and gained weight in this time.

Murihiku came abreast of the entrance to Pickersgill Harbour. It is an indentation of the shore partly shielded from the main reach of the sound by a small, high island, Crayfish Island; only partly and not entirely adequately, as we were to learn. We looked at the narrow entrance to the west of the island. From the journals it seems clear the *Resolution* was sailed in, and not towed by the ship's boats. For us there was not a breath of wind so, shamefaced, we chugged through.

Within, we drifted to a halt on the calm water, wanting to moor precisely where the *Resolution* had, but not sure where to go. None of the journals was specific on this point, simply talking of 'a cove', or 'facing Astronomer Point', which is ambiguous. A number of minor promontories with intervening creeks faced us. The nautical chart showed Astronomer Point clearly enough, but not the anchorage, and in any case seemed not very accurate. In the end we turned up the facsimile of a chart drawn by Henry Roberts, a fifteen-year-old draughtsman on the ship, and only here did we find firm evidence of the place, in the cove south of Astronomer Point. We dropped the bower anchor in eight fathoms and then, using the dinghy, warped *Murihiku* in by the stern until she lay a few yards off the rocky bank, in four fathoms, much as the *Resolution* must have. Thus secured, we sat on deck in the sun and looked around at the historic place. After the immediate entry to the sound it was, I think, the supreme moment of the cruise. But not a peaceful moment, not for very long anyway, for sandflies descended from the over-towering bush and attacked — an inevitable thing in this land and one that with the recurrent rains may preserve it for a long time from the *pox tourista*. 'The most mischievous animals here,' wrote Cook, 'are the small black sandflies, which are very numerous and so troublesome that they exceed everything of the kind I ever met with; wherever they bite they cause a swelling, and such an intolerable itching, that it is not possible to refrain from scratching, which at last brings ulcers like the smallpox. The almost continual rains may be reckoned another evil attending this bay . . .'

We coated bare areas with insect repellent and sat on deck drinking tea. A large fishing boat came through the small entrance and edged alongside. It was bigger and more luxurious than anything we had expected to encounter on this coast. The skipper stepped over. He was Maori.

'I'm Cardie Waitari,' he said. 'This is my wife Mary. You're lucky, you've struck the best day we've had for weeks. But you should come over to Luncheon Cove, there's a nor'wester on the way and this place won't be comfortable.'

'We'll be all right here,' I said, surprised, for Cook himself had written: 'Pickersgill Harbour, where we lay, is not inferior to any other bay.' 'At least tonight. We want to look round.'

'I'll come over tomorrow and show you into Luncheon,' said Cardie. 'Food? How are you off?'

All the crayfish boats have their own massive freezers, so the crews can live well. We muttered a few gaps. Mary went below and returned with an abundance. Then *Minerva* moved off, and we were left to the evening and the historic place . . .

In the morning we went ashore and spent some time replenishing our water supplies from the stream the *Resolution* had used; and later followed it to its source, a mournful-looking minor lake, utterly forest-enclosed, without a single strip of beach, about twenty minutes up in the bush. Afterwards we built a fire by the stream and roasted a leg of our venison on a spit of green wood. The weather was catching up with the weather office, for the sky clouded over, and when we went back to *Murihiku* after mid-day the wind was coming in briskly past Crayfish Island and she snubbed so vigorously on her chain that we were compelled to put a spring on — the last thing we had anticipated doing in this famed harbour. But we were to learn that the popular conception of the fiords as vast havens for vessels, full of splendid anchorages, was fallacy. To some extent this may be true for ships, of something more than, say, a hundred tons. But for boats, for small fishing vessels or something like *Murihiku*, this just is not so. In all of Dusky there is only one anchorage beyond criticism, and that is Luncheon Cove, and similarly most of the other fiords seem to have only one acceptable anchorage.

When we'd attended to the warps I went below and out of interest looked up Pickersgill's log during the stay of the *Resolution*. They were fortunate with the weather, for in five weeks they did not have five days of strong winds, and the direction is not specified. Certainly a ship the size of the *Resolution* could have lain there more comfortably than we, and I could not, in turn, see us in serious trouble. The fact remains that Pickersgill is no marvellous place for boats, though to shift to the first cove within the narrow entrance would place one in calmer water with plenty of depth. Indeed only Henry Roberts' small drawing convinces me the *Resolution* was not moored in this more sheltered place.

At mid-afternoon, when we were bouncing well on our several warps and cables and not feeling enthused, the *Chappie* came churning round the corner, with Cardie and Billy Maquarie. Cardie came aboard as pilot and Billy went on ahead. This was the only occasion we had a pilot, and here it was necessary. Cook, while surveying the south-east side of Anchor Island, where a confusion of rocks and small island lie, wrote: 'I found here a very snug cove sheltered from all winds, which we called Luncheon Cove, because here we dined on crayfish, on the side of a pleasant brook shaded by the trees from both wind and sun.' The cove was accurately shown on his chart. When the *Acheron* seventy years later came to resurvey the sound Luncheon Cove was somehow missed. The name appears on the nautical chart, but slightly misplaced, with the approaches utterly wrong.

'We might sail over,' I said.

'You won't sail over,' said Cardie. 'It's blowing out there.' So without any canvas up we motored through the narrow entrance, and straight away things went wrong. Tide and wind against her, *Murihiku* was not happy, and out there it was blowing far harder than I had realised. She kept on course for a moment and then slewed to port. With the wind abeam and the tide pressing on her long keel she defied correction and just ploughed on for the cliff face. There was nothing to be done, there was no room to wear ship, and I simply pushed the engine revs up to the limit and leaned on the helm. Away ahead Billy saw our troubles and came churning back in the *Chappie*, which with its flat bottom and minimal windage, no spars aloft, was untroubled. But he was far away. The rock came up and I remember thinking, rather sadly, that it was at least a noble place to finish. Then, just a few feet short, *Murihiku* felt the rebounding wind off the wall, and this sufficed. She answered, the whole hull churned round, and we ran into the wind alongside the steep-to limits of the entrance, so close we could just put our hands out and touch the rock.

'I'm putting back,' I said, but Cardie said, 'No, Billy'll tow,' and he flung us a line. With our thirty horses and his sixty champing we plugged across the sound. I can't imagine what it was like at sea. Here, in the sheltered waters of the sound, the air was white with spray, willy-waws swept over us, and three or four times *Murihiku* was close to lying on her beam ends. Then we came between the small islands and into Luncheon Cove, and a few minutes later *Murihiku* sat comfortable alongside Cardie's large and luxurious *Minerva*.

Here we dined in the evening while the wind howled beyond us, occasionally dropping into the cove to toss up a bit of spray. It had not been a proud day, towed across Dusky after near-disaster. What would Cook have thought?

'I've never seen it blow in here like this,' said Mary.

'I've never seen it blow in here like this,' said Billy.

Cardie nodded in assent. We felt happier.

Philip Houghton, *Land from the Masthead —*
a circumnavigation of New Zealand in the
wake of Captain Cook, 1968

Leaving England, 1885

WHEN THE *Jessie Readman* left East India Docks in London on 8 August 1885, bound for Auckland, New Zealand, one of her youngest passengers was 11-month-old Ernest Wycherley — my grandfather. His father Charles, judging from the diary he kept of the 106-day voyage, was a well-educated man, curious, observant and God-fearing, head of a family of ten. From a respected family of Shropshire saddlers, he established businesses in Wellington and Palmerston North.

In 1885, emigration to New Zealand had been in full swing from Britain for forty-five years and from Europe for fifteen. The *Jessie Readman* was well known on the New Zealand run, enduring the gales, calms, tropics and once round the Cape of Good Hope, the bleak and furious southern ocean — non-stop. My grandfather's passage was her eighteenth. Built in 1869, she was a 200ft three-master, 962 registered tons, carrying twenty-three sails. Young Ernest had his first birthday aboard, three degrees north of the equator, on 18 September — 'a grand doll's tea party attended by all the dolls and children aboard'.

Unlike today's liners, an emigrant ship didn't just cast off from a London dock and that night put out to sea. She might wait for favourable conditions at Gravesend, opposite Tilbury, for some days, and wait again with others in the English Channel itself, in the area just south of Ramsgate known as the Downs inside the Goodwin Sands. Then, freed at last by a favourable wind, she'd raise sail and set off down the English Channel. Imagine it, *forty* of them . . .

The day of sailing was fixed for Saturday, August 8th, the passengers having received instructions to embark in the East India Dock on Friday evening. Happening to call at the office of Shaw Savill we were told to be on board on Thursday evening, the vessel to sail next morning. It was fortunate for us that we were able to comply with these instructions, as the experience of some of our fellow passengers was not pleasant.

Some of our party left with all our baggage and drove direct to the ship, the rest of us filled one side of a 'bus' and in due course were deposited at the gates of the East India Dock close to which the ship was lying. After the usual formalities had been complied with, viz., the payment of dock dues, amounting to about 2/- a package, we were allowed to put our baggage on board. We found a few passengers already in possession and soon we, like them, began to set our house in order, not an easy task with a lot of baggage and very little room to stow it. We reached the dock at 4 o'clock. The rest of the evening was devoted to unpacking. By 9 o'clock the little ones were put to bed and soon after the dock's police came down to see that all lights were out except the ship's lamps, which went out of their own accord about 12. We passed a quiet night and were awakened only by the ducks and fowls on deck and soon after, the men began to prepare for leaving the dock.

The ship was towed by a tug controlled by ropes from the wharves, and at 9 o'clock we passed into the river, the crew came on board, and at once set to work sending out a ringing cheer as we slowly moved away from the dock gates. We climbed to the poop and took a last look at loved ones waving us a loving God speed, and lingered there till a passing ship hid them from view. Happily for us we had no time to spend in grief, though saddened by parting with those we loved and from whom we had received so many tokens of love. We soon reached Gravesend, where we took farewell of a brother and a sister who had accompanied us thus far, and so the last 'Goodbye' was said and the last link, as it were, broken that had still joined us to house and friends.

The ship was moored now, mid-stream, and we learned that she would remain there until next morning to wait for passengers and tide. About 5 or 6 we descried boats with passengers and baggage. They were much discomposed by having to come by rail and embark in small boats. One poor lady sat quietly waiting to be hauled up in a chair, and we found afterwards she was almost helpless with rheumatism. Suspended in mid-air the order was given to lower, when the chair tilted forward and she, being unable to help herself, slipped off and would have fallen on deck but for a rope which was passed round her body. As it was she came down before the chair, but fortunately reached the deck without more serious harm than shock and fright. We had now all got aboard. They had gone to the dock and found the ship gone, so had to take train to Gravesend and embark as described. We were very thankful to have gone aboard in the docks, especially when we saw the experience of others.

About 8 o'clock I went ashore to get a baking tin and more condensed milk and malt and hops for a fellow passenger. The ship serves out flour and cook bakes the bread, but passengers are not supplied with yeast, so at the last minute there is a scramble to get malt, hops or baking powder and tins to bake in. Returned about 10 and soon turned in, after giving new arrivals benefit of our night's experience. About 4 o'clock next morning we heard the order given to let go the ropes. The splash of the water told us we were being towed down the river, there was no perceptible motion like a steamer.

In two or three hours the water began to take effect upon the ship, and in two or three more, upon the passengers and most of us in the steerage began to look and feel white. We each had a turn, except the baby, so that when the dinner bell rang our party declined roast beef, and we contented ourselves with biscuits and water. The wind increased, the jib and spanker flapped against the ropes, the order was given to lower both and as we passed Ramsgate preparations began to let go the anchor. Deal soon came in sight; several large ships and a number of smaller ones lay in the road. The tug headed for the bay, we got into quieter water, the anchor dropped, and the ship lay in peace, just rising and falling with the waves. The children now began to recover and were racing around the deck. The evening was wild looking, and it appeared uncertain how long we should remain here, and so Saturday night came, and in our novel circumstances we turned into our berths and passed a quiet night.

Sunday was a bright and beautiful day, tho' dull first thing, yet but little like the Lord's Day we had been used to. The morning passed away almost before we could get the children together for a little reading, and the call to an early dinner disturbed us. After dinner we did better, read John X, and had a few words with the children. The sound of singing brought others together like-minded and to whom the name of the Lord was dear, while we could not fail to notice how some gave us a wide berth, as having no part with us. Then we had prayed, the first on board openly, then separated. During our little service the wind was rather cutting, so we had Haswell's hammock brought up and fixed it as a screen from which we derived great comfort. There was no church on board . . . Some of the second class joined us, including Mr and Mrs McKay, known to some of our friends, and one guest from the 'saloon' joined in.

93

In the evening our time was fully occupied with domestic matters and it was late before the little ones were put to bed, also we had intended having a little reading in the forecastle; as it was, the watch off duty was resting so we could not even sing a hymn forward. Miss Read, one of our party, brought out a hand organ and with some others spent an hour singing hymns which we much enjoyed, and then I heard my name called out and coming up was desired to close the day with prayer. This we did seeking the Lord's blessing on Captain, passengers, officers and crew, and asking Him to give us a prosperous voyage.

Monday: We have been lying here 36 hours and though not making much progress the delay has been of much service to us, as we have been able to get used to the ship, arrange baggage, unpack boxes wanted, stow away things not now required, and, generally, to arrange our new home which we expect to occupy for three months. We now find everything comes in handy — a screw or a nail is a treasure, a bit of wood for a shelf more valuable still, an old cardboard box very useful. The hooks for the ceiling especially necessary. My tool case full of nails, screws, hammer, odds and ends of all kinds, is an important adjunct and has done good service for all the cabin. Hitherto we have not been put on rations but have had food and water ad lib. After tea last night, the order came to carry forward watercans, and from this time every drop has to be carefully preserved. The mate came down and divided our party into seven messes. Ours, No. 2, is the largest mess: our allowance is 6 gallons, 1 quart, 1 pint, the latter baby's allowance. Then we have to allow the cook 5 qts. a day for breakfast, tea, and so much for soup, porridge or rice. Today, Monday, we are to have a week's rations served out in the raw state, and have had to make bags for flour, rice and other dry materials. These in turn are handed each day to be dressed as required. Jars are wanted for pickles and treacle, and canisters for tea, coffee. Miss Read brought out a sewing machine and was seen at work making bags for the company.

This is a lovely morning. Deal is about 2 miles away, Walmer Castle surrounded by trees opposite us, Ramsgate distance behind. Last night when all was quiet, we came up on deck and greatly enjoyed a walk round. The stars were shining brightly, the sea smooth, the beacon or light ships showing steady, or flash lights in all directions. Everything was quiet and peaceful. As the wind seemed shifting from the west, the order came 'All hands out.' The cable was shortened, the yards braced, and preparations made to put to sea. When all was ready, the wind again shifted, and when we awoke this morning found ourselves still off Deal. The French coast is plainly visible, the Pilot who brought us from Gravesend left us on Saturday, when we bade farewell to 'Uncle Sam' (the tug). We have another on board waiting to take us to Portland or the Start according to weather. That will be the last chance of sending letters home. This morning, Monday, everyone is happy as we lay in the sunshine, the children are amusing themselves on deck, reading, writing, sewing or watching the men at work. Arthur is a great favourite, and Mercy gets on well. Clement and Harry work with the tools some kind cousin gave, baby is very fond of ship's biscuits and begins to eat nicely. The cook is a West India man, fine looking fellow, and his dark face frightened the little ones at first, but a lump of sugar put them on better terms with him. We have on deck two pens of fowls, and two of ducks, 7 pigs, 7 sheep, which are a source of amusement to the children. Arthur and Mercy are fond of eating out of hands. Yesterday one pig treated himself to a walk around the deck and caused much amusement by a chase from the children. He was finally caught and escorted to his pen tail first.

We have just had our first week's rations served out, and quite a business it was. We have more than sufficient of each kind. I have arranged with the cook for a fresh supply of bread. He is to have 10/- now and 10/- at the end of the voyage. That is for making and baking it.

Monday, 3.30: I think it is now time I gave an account of our fellow passengers. Our cabin is just under the hatch, tolerably light and plenty of air. There are five smaller cabins partitioned off from it. The first contains Mr and Mrs Satman and two children. They are returning to the colony after a visit to their friends at home. He is a smith and not finding work at home among his friends he is leaving them behind. Next comes the single man's cabin in which Charlie and Alf sleep. Mr Winn, a young fellow of 17, a Christian, a Mr Young who is going out for his health and to get work, is a kind fellow, quiet and obliging, then two little boys named Howard, who with their sister, a girl of 15, are going out to their father. These children have been disappointed 5 times, the Company declining to take them along. Their Uncle brought them to the dock, we promised to give an eye to them. Since then Mr and Mrs Satman have taken them under their care. In the boys' cabin are two others named Osborne, whose parents and three children occupy the next. Then comes ours, almost in the centre of the ship. One large berth and two small ones, 8 feet long and 6 wide. We get a space underneath for boxes, and it is quite full. They allow as much as you like in the berth. The store room where the 'wanted luggage' is kept joins ours. Access may be had once in two weeks.

Next comes the single women's cabin, where Jessie, Theresa and Grace sleep. With them Miss Winn, sister of the one already named, their aunt — the invalid lady who nearly fell overboard, Miss Read, the lady of the organ, and Miss Downard, the young lady who goes out to her father. This is our family and very happily we have managed to live so far. The Winns are all Christians, the others are quiet girls and may be. The Osbornes and the Satmans stand aloof from our reading and prayers. In the 2nd class are Mr and Mrs Mckay, and three others in the saloon, the Captain, his wife and two gents and one lady.

Just as we turned in last night, the mate came down to warn us to have our water cans tied up as we were about to proceed to sea, but 24 hours later we are still in the Downs opposite Deal. The Goodwins are a little on our left, that is, when the bow is towards Dover. Sometimes we go to bed with it on the left, the ship having swung round during the night, an operation most perplexing to the uninitiated. We have now been four days afloat, and we are beginning to get a little used to the motion of the ship. We found the lemons refreshing when the worst of the sickness was passed, and acids of any kind are very gratifying. Although the four days have been very agreeable, our time has been so fully taken up that there has been no time for dullness, had we been so disposed.

Tuesday, August 11th, 1885:—When we left London, the ship had been in dock some time and had not had the usual 'wash and brush up'. She now presented quite a different appearance; every morning the decks are scrubbed at 6; they tell us the boards will be white by the time we arrive in N.Z. Then the brass work has all been polished, even the hoops round the buckets, cabin windows, ventilators, lead compass, all bright and clean. It is now blowing hard from the west and probably our friends are thinking of us as being tossed up and down in the Channel or away at sea, but our good ship is safely at anchor off Walmer Coast. With the glass we can see people ashore very plainly, and the coast from North to South Foreland is stretched right in front of us. The Captain had the cable lengthened this morning on account of high wind. The pilot has an easy time of it. He came aboard at Gravesend, takes charge here and leaves at Portland where we hope to post these. This morning we had a general clean-up, floors scrubbed, etc. Satman is an old hand, and has been hard at work with bucket and brush. We have to do all our own work here. No washing put out. Cassie is mother to the young people. Miss Read scrubbed the ladder, the boys carrying water. It is pleasant to see how most adapt themselves to the new circumstances. Though the ship is rolling, no one seems to mind. The children are as merry as possible. We have not been able to undertaken any routine work and they have had a fine time of amusement. The call has now come to dinner, so I must away and assist.

Dinner over, perhaps our friends would like to know how we fare. Today we had beef, potatoes, pickles and bread; then boiled rice with sugar or treacle, then a bit of Grandma's cheese. For breakfast, porridge, coffee, bread and butter — meat if you like. This is William Winn's birthday, so each has contributed material to make a family cake in honour of it.

The wind seems to increase. There are four ships like ourselves waiting for a change to get away down channel. Jessie, though pretty well on deck, is not sufficiently used to the motion of the boat to remain very long at a time, though we like the deck best. We are thankful that the weather has been such that we could be in the air instead of being all ill together down below, which might have been the case. Down below the motion is more apparent, everything is on the move. We are obliged to suspend many things and they all swing to and fro. The covers of Grandma's provisions boxes came in very usefully. They had ledges at the end, so we cut up a cardboard box and nailed strips along the sides. This makes a capital swinging tray to suspend from the ceiling. Then Mrs Haswell's hammock came in very nicely to hang up as a curtain to divide off one side of the cabin as a dressing room for the ladies. Six in one cabin found it difficult to dress together in such small space. For the benefit of intending immigrants, I suggest a good supply of ceiling hooks to screw in, small screws, french or wire nails, 2 or 3 inches long, hammer and chisel, a small shovel and funnel. The last two articles none of us have.

At Gravesend I bought a small spirit stove, but we are almost afraid to use it not wishing to offend against the regulations of the ship. Cassie asked the steward if we might and he gave us permission. This we found a great comfort. The oil stove fails to bring to the boil.

I am pleased to be able to say the discipline of the *Jessie Readman* seems good. The Captain and the first mate and second, as well as the petty officers, viz., carpenter, boatswain, cook and sailmaker all seem steady and sober men, and no bad language of any kind is heard from any of them. This is a comfort with so many children about.

Evening—The wind still keeps up and tho' foul for us is fair for others. Today we have been much interested watching homeward bound vessels sailing beautifully past. One, a four-master, had 17 sails set; another was from N.Z., with a cargo of frozen meat. We exchanged signals with the latter. I timed one to see how long it was from the time her top masts were first seen till she came up with us and found it 3/4 of an hour. I should think 10 or 12 full rigged ships have gone up during the day. There are several tugs cruising about in search of a job, besides a great many small craft. Two or three pleasure parties from Deal have passed close to us, yet not near enough to have a letter passed to them. One boat came off the shore on Sunday with bread and onions, but the steward said he was not to be trusted. This man came aboard this morning and I have sent one letter and four postcards by him which I hope our friends have received; for the benefit of intending emigrants, I should say do not trust to agents to supply you with necessary articles. Some of our companions paid for flock beds and had straw sent, and various things paid for not sent at all, a very serious matter now that others cannot be obtained.

Numbers of souls on board — Captain, his wife, 3 saloon passengers, 5 second class, 30 third class, 2 stewards, 1 cook, 2 helpers (these last are working their passage out), carpenter, boatswain and sailmaker, a crew of 22 — 70 all told.

The wind increases. The twin steamer, *Calais Douvies* with four funnels, lies just hove in sight and has anchored for the night under the South Foreland, too much sea to put into Dover Harbour. A large timber laden ship has just passed sailing on her beam, and it is supposed the cargo has shifted; as she passed one of her top sails blew away. It is fortunate she has a fair wind; she is deck laden.

Thursday: The ship rolled a good deal during the night, but everyone slept well. The children have all slept every night. The *May Queen* which stood alongside over in East India Dock has just passed; she is bound for Wellington. Our time here is very short now. Fifteen fathoms of cable have been drawn in this morning; 45 are still out. The sails are now being set and all is bustle on deck and up aloft. We are glad to be able to send you detailed account of our life afloat, as you will see we have much cause for thankfulness. I think I may say we have gained the confidence of the stewards and of the cook by consideration of them, instead of trying to grasp all we can as one seems disposed to do, and has been the loser, in consequence. When anything is required for below, my name is generally called out. I mention this only to show we are on good terms with the officers. The first mate is a very nice gentlemanly fellow. We have had an extra allowance of candles to burn all night if required. This will comfort dear Mother.

Friday, 8th day out: Yesterday was a busy day; about 11 a.m. the anchor was lifted and we bore away for S. Foreland, followed by a fleet of ships, more than 40 in full sail. Most of them kept very close to shore to avoid strength of tide. Our Pilot stood away more to sea and we passed Dover about three miles away. The first day at sea is always a hard one for the men, so many sails having to be newly set. It was great fun seeing the men and boys, perhaps 20, in a line running the whole length of the ship, tramp, tramp, to a lively tune that seemed improvised for the occasion. All seemed to work with a will, so cheerily, that it was more like play than work. After the delay of nearly a week everyone seemed glad to be off. As the night closed in we were off Dungeness, which has one fixed and one flashlight. We could just discern the glare from the Calais lighthouse, on one side, and the reflection of lights at Hastings on the other, some of you will remember a ship called *Centurion* painted green — we left her in the docks. When we got up this morning we found her at our starboard bow, having been towed as far as Beachy Head which we passed during the night. She is bound for Melbourne. This morning we have a light fair wind and smooth sea. The ship seems almost as steady as a house. Cassie had another turn of seasickness yesterday and I was very queer for a time, but after a little sleep in turn we each got better. Jessie, too, was done up for a time. The little ones do not seem to mind it now.

I have just opened a packet of books. On the cover is written, 'a parting present from the Religious Tract Society'. One was given to each passenger at Gravesend. It contains a leisure hour, children's hymn book, and a number of tracts. With the permission of the boatswain I nailed up a card with text of Scripture over each berth in the petty officers' house. They were part of those sent by Mr Grove of Kingston-on-Thames. I hope to make use of more as we proceed, but up to now everyone has been much engaged. I find my glass a very interesting companion and should recommend sea-going travellers always to take one if possible. This morning we have the illustrations before us so often found in geographies. There are four ships near together, each showing less and less, the most distant only showing top sails. The horizon appears to be so very near and the tops of the ships below appear distinctly visible.

Saturday morning: The cry has come 'Letters for the shore'. We are now in sight of Portland with all its associations brought to mind again, and one would fain linger over there . . .

Extract from 'The Diary of Charles Wycherley,
voyage on the *Jessie Readman*, London to New Zealand,
1885 (Captain Gibson).'

From Alaska to Canada

FOR THEIR FAMILY DREAM CRUISE around the Pacific in the mid-eighties, Coromandel dairy farmer Dennis Webster and his nurse wife Jenny chose an 11.1m Albert Sedlmeyer catamaran, *Catalyst*. With three young children aboard, Joanna, Mathew and Hamish, they valued the greater speed and interior space of a cat. Clocking up more than 20,000 sea miles over a total of three years, *Catalyst* was to remain in the family until 2001.

The voyage northwards to Japan via the Fiji Islands, Vanuatu, Solomon Islands, Truk, Guam Atoll and Guam took sixteen months. Jenny and the children then wintered over on the yacht in Valdez, Alaska, at 61 degrees N, while Dennis worked as a commercial fisherman in the Bering Sea, well paid but away for up to two months at a time. All learnt survival techniques in sub-zero conditions which were to stand them in good stead for the next stage, from Alaska south to Canada.

We wintered over in South Alaska, in Valdez, which is at 61° North. Almost two years had elapsed since we had left New Zealand, and with cruising funds at an all-time low, it seemed as good a reason as any to spend a year in one spot.

The three children and I lived on board *Catalyst*, our 36' Sedlmeyer catamaran, while Dennis joined the crew of a large US dragger. He fished the treacherous and icy winter waters of the Bering Sea, while the family and I practised basic survival techniques in sub-zero conditions on board a boat built with the tropics in mind.

Although the fishing venture was to prove most lucrative, the trials of the severe Alaskan winter were a supreme challenge to us all: a New Zealand family used to warmer climes. We emerged with characters strengthened by a unique experience and incredible memories of a crystal world frozen in time; of 35 inches of snow on deck, solid-ice squabs and long, glistening icicles inside the boat. Valdez was committed to memory forever. In late September, the dragger sank during a perilous storm, fortunately with no lives lost. Obviously the fishing days were over, so we decided to sail south before another winter was upon us. A year in Alaska was enough for this cruising family, thanks.

In fact, summer was gone, the snow geese having flown south a few weeks before in beautiful formations of graceful birds, honking loudly. The crisp smell of snow was already in the air, and the days were beginning to draw in. We decided it was now or never.

The autumn equinox had passed, bringing its usual storm right on cue. We observed the weather patterns for the northern gulf of Alaska at the Valdez coastguard weather station. The situation didn't look promising for October, so we divided the gulf into three stages; the first leg to an anchorage between Kayak and Wingham Islands, only 60 miles away, then to Yakutat, a further 150 miles and the final leg of 300 miles to Cross Sound and the protected waters of the Inside Passage.

I was extremely dubious about the wisdom of this Gulf crossing and felt it would prove to be the biggest challenge of our Pacific circumnavigation.

It was too late in the year to expect anything else. We set sail on 1 October, with the barometer already sitting on 995 millibars. A light wind out of the southeast was forecast to increase to 35 knots, which we weren't too bothered about. The boat goes to windward well in stronger winds.

Two hours later the wind died, so we motored. The proverbial calm before the storm. The barometer dropped a further two points, and it was blowing the predicted 35 knots. Visibility was poor, and we were in the lee of Kayak Island. Without a radar, we couldn't go in and anchor so we took all sails down to wait for dawn.

At 3.30 a.m., the barometer was down to 987 mbs. The air temperature was 10 below zero, with wind-chill plummeting it down further to an appalling 40 degrees below!

The east wind, now 45 knots, and the strong current had effectively blown us eight miles off-shore into the teeth of a rising storm. At dawn, the wind was 60 knots. With four reefs in the fully-battened main and the storm jib up, we began to tack our way back.

Dennis wore his float suit, a wool hat and gloves. I was enveloped in his outsized Edi Bauer snow coat, its fur-trimmed hood designed to warm inspired air. The children all wore thick wool sweaters and stayed in the relative warmth of the wing deck cabin. In extreme cold such as this, we should have been wearing survival suits.

The ocean floor rises in the Gulf and is shallow compared with the Pacific Ocean, so within a short time the seas had become volcanic rather than mountainous; short and terrifyingly steep. By 6.30 a.m., it was blowing 70 knots and we were helming in an open cockpit, completely unprotected from the raging elements. The air was filled with foam and spray and the sea was completely white with driving spray. Some forecast! This was our Cape Horn.

Dennis struggled against the wind to raise the tri-sail, while I clutched the helm, sick for the first time ever. I remember reading that if a sailor has never been sea-sick, then he hasn't been in a big enough sea or a small enough boat. Wind-chill was in excess of 45 below zero. Tears ran down my whipped cheeks, turning into frozen tracks of ice. An icicle formed at the end of my nose as it dripped, and my eyelashes froze behind the iced lenses of my glasses. Dennis's face was protected to some extent by his beard, even though it was ice-encrusted.

I went inside to the relative warmth of the cabin. The two boys were fighting. How could they? I put the kettle on, and hung on to it for grim death, standing braced beside the stove. The 3/8 inch ply hull shuddered as each wave crashed and vibrated with the force of thousands of pounds of pressure against it. Back in the cockpit, I gave Dennis his coffee, but the wind promptly funnelled it out of the cup. He quickly drank the dregs.

The wind showed no signs of abating; screaming and clutching at us like some rabid animal. The boat couldn't go about in such extreme conditions, the trisail and storm jib had insufficient sail area, so we used the 25hp outboard for each tack and that did the trick.

Dennis looked across at me, his brown eyes warming with a lovely smile which began a glow deep inside of me. Love at 40 below? We were both frozen to the marrow, shivering with hypothermia, but that smile made my day. We glanced up as the sun, a weak, insipid, arctic orb, glowed briefly through a grey hole in a black sky. It looked like a malevolent eye surveying its foul brew.

At noon, the barometer began to rise rapidly to 1000mbs. We put the main back up with four reefs in and the wind dropped to 45 knots. Just a stiff breeze by comparison. The boat tacked easily now, but we were still very cold. I heated some soup. The kids were okay — they were firing paper darts around the cabin. The bathroom mirror revealed an apparition, a creature with a blue hat on top of a bunch of strangled, frozen curls; bright pink cheeks, cracked and bleeding lips. I looked like a witch. The original wild woman of Borneo.

Finally, we got right in close to Kayak Island and by 3 p.m. were safely anchored beside a fleet of fishing boats. *Catalyst* rocked gently in the quiet, green waters; brave and enduring. We all ate hugely and fell into bed, exhausted.

We stayed there for four days, as yet another storm passed over. On the evening of the 5th, we listened to a promising forecast, and decided to leave via a channel between Kayak Island and the mainland. The chart showed a shallowest depth of 3½ fathoms, sufficient for our 2½ ft draught. This route would have saved us 15 miles to Cape Saint Elias, compared with the way we had to come in.

With one hour of daylight remaining, we motored to the channel, watching the depth sounder constantly. An uncharted reef shook our confidence momentarily, losing precious time, then just as we began to enter the passage came the cry, 'Breakers ahead!' We cautiously approached the line of white water, checking depths, altering course parallel to the coast in the hope of finding a gap. As total darkness descended, there was no choice but to drop the anchor and review the situation. It was dead low tide with only a 3 ft swell and a very light breeze.

We finally radioed a fishing boat and explained the situation. He replied 'It must be kinda interesting out there, to say the least!' and informed us that it was a very tricky passage at the best of times. The bottom had uplifted 20 ft since the 1964 earthquake and should only be attempted in daylight and on a high tide. The moon began to shine through the clouds, and very cautiously we sounded our way back to the anchorage without mishap. When we did leave for Yakutat the next morning, we went the long way instead.

On this leg, a beautiful full moon illuminated the northern sky each night, and we encountered only light head winds, a huge southeast ocean swell and just the occasional ice-rain squall. With the auto-pilot out of commission, we continued to helm. It was only 20 below zero and quite pleasant by comparison. Everything is relative.

The children were able to continue with their correspondence schooling and update their journals. Someplace I had read a quotation by Goethe: 'All theory is grey beside the tree of actual life.'

Our children, now aged 13, 11 and 8 had climbed an unusual education tree, jumping from branch to branch, learning as a squirrel does that each jump is a challenge. They were certainly receiving an education, albeit an unconventional one.

After a brief stay in the tiny fishing Indian village of Yakutat, 12 October saw us out in the gulf again, for the third and final time, we hoped. Optimism was high as was the barometer at 1023mbs. To windward as usual, helming in a clear, crisp air; a hint of snow on the decks. Six hours later, the southeasterly wind increased to 30 knots, the 12 ft southeast swell rapidly becoming huge breaking waves. The barometer dropped six points ahead of a weather front. By 6 p.m. the wind was 40 knots, gusting 45. Vicious ice rain and hail squalls lashed our frozen bodies and the wind-chill was once again in excess of 50 below zero, with the wind howling off thousands of square miles of Arctic ice and glaciers. To heave to, rather than sail all night was an easy decision to make. Throughout that long bitterly cold night, we kept a lookout for ships, and our anchor light hung dimly in the rigging. We even slept some. In retrospect, we should have set the parachute sea anchor (the stress of extreme cold influenced us some-what), because by dawn the wind and current had dragged us back 15 miles. By 8 a.m. we were tacking off a lee shore and the wind diminished gradually and became west. The morning sun shone pink on the massive glaciers, a truly magnificent sight which we were too cold to appreciate. In fact, I didn't care if I never saw another glacier for the rest of my life. The second night was so cold, it hurt to breathe. The air crackled and we all gazed in fascination at an incredible display of the aurora borealis; curtains and waves of green, pink and yellow swept the night sky. We wished we were viewing it on television. Below zero temperatures made it just a bit too realistic.

The forecast at dawn warned us of an imminent storm, approaching at 40 knots. Intense weather systems were tracking northeast across the Gulf of Alaska every 24 hours, sometimes less. With the wind already rising, we sailed into Dixon Harbour, rather than attempt notorious Cross Sound. We anchored and rode out the 50 knot sou'easter in relative comfort and warmth. It snowed, hail littered the decks and the sheets froze solid, but we didn't care. We were warm and dry for a change.

By now, it was 16 days since we had left Valdez. On 17 October, we sailed out of Dixon Harbour's sheltered arms, and rounded Cape Spencer into Cross Sound with a following breeze. Huge hailstones littered down, pitting the paint work. The children were full of energy now, with the end clearly in sight. We thankfully lowered the sails and motored into Elfin Cover. There we located hot showers and a laundry, a fisherman gave us a king salmon for lunch. No fish ever tasted so good.

Catalyst, sturdy and strong, had endured a severe beating and had carried us steadfastly across this most treacherous piece of water. I'll always be thankful. It wasn't the boat but the human element which gave up on occasion, due to the extreme stress of freezing conditions. My fingernails had turned from a healthy pink to pure white.

We continued on the Juneau and motor-sailed down the Inland Passage for the remainder of the year. Being winter, it snowed, hailed, rained — you name it! By Christmas, however, the days were too short and dark with only about four hours' light, and frequent intense storms were hindering our progress somewhat. So we stayed in Prince Rupert, Canada, for three months.

In March, we set sail for Vancouver, delighting in the warmer temperatures and occasional sunshine. The hatches were opened for the first time in two years! The Canadians often complained of the below average temperatures but to us, 5° above was a heatwave. The Inland Passage, over 1000 miles of narrow channels, provides relatively protected waters and magnificent scenery for the hundreds of North American boats every summer, when the area becomes congested, with anchoring often a hassle. In contrast, we had the whole 1000 miles to ourselves and didn't see one other yacht from Juneau to Vancouver, for obvious reasons.

Sailing into Vancouver heralded the end of winter sailing for us, at least in the North Pacific. I wouldn't do it again, but strangely, I'm glad we did. Experiences like this sure bring out qualities and an inner strength you never knew you had. The boat, now with over 25,000 ocean miles logged, had proved to be a worthy ocean voyager. My trust in her, after this winter gulf crossing, was etched forever in my heart.

Jenny Webster, *When Nature Tests Inner Strength*, 1988

Close Hauled
to Stewart Island
(and Back!)

GRAEME DIXON, a medical researcher in Dunedin, learned to sail — as do many New Zealanders — in Sunbursts and Z- and X-class dinghies, and then as crew in offshore keelers. In 1991 he bought *Faith II*, a 32 ft Woolacott sloop. He and his wife Alison both completed a Coastal Yachtmaster qualification before embarking on their first coastal passage to Stewart Island. The reality, he notes wryly, was somewhat different from the theory, although 'we learnt a lot, and survived as a family, no mean feat.'

The initial Stewart Island cruise remains a memorable one in the collective family history. *Faith II*, still racing and cruising out of Dunedin, 'keeps the family connected, especially when the adult children come to visit'. As much younger children, they could understandably have been rather discouraged from sailing when *Faith II* set out on that first passage to Stewart Island.

*I*t was the second year of our ownership of *Faith II*, a 32 ft Woollacott sloop, and, it was our first attempt at a coastal passage. The trip from Port Chalmers to Stewart Island can be a dream twenty- to thirty-hour cruise in glassy seas with a following wind, or it can be a week-long nightmare with no end in sight and nowhere to hide.

Our preparations had been to get the boat up to Category Three standard and hurriedly complete our Coastal Yachtmasters. We had been unable to afford any of the modern passage-making tools such as GPS's, radars or autohelms.

A stable weather pattern was predicted for three days. It seemed like an ideal opportunity to go. A huge high was centred over the Chatham Islands, an occluded front west of Fiordland. A cold front was predicted for later in the week, which should have given us a good two to three clear days to make the expected thirty-hour trip to the island.

We leave Deborah Bay at 1230 hours, amidst the tearful wails and quiet prayers of grandmothers, clear the entrance motorsailing in a gentle 5–10 knot NE breeze, and set off down the coast. Crew are myself, my wife Alison, and our two trusting and naïve children Naomi (9) and Demian (14).

The journey is agonisingly slow, with the breeze dying as we approach the notorious Cape Saunders. Sights off Green Island confirm that our speed is slightly over five knots over the ground, but the day has started to deteriorate. The sky is lit by streaks of lightning followed increasingly closely by loud peals of thunder. What's the rule? Every five seconds is a mile or is it every second is five miles? Finally the inevitable rainstorm appears and the sea turns into a giant milkshake. We think ourselves lucky to have an accompanying adverse wind. As darkness approaches we have made about 50 miles and are 10 miles out to sea. I have calculated that steering a 210-degree magnetic course through the night will see us about five miles off the Nuggets at first light.

I have taken the night watch — well, because no-one else volunteers — with the understanding that others will keep me company throughout my ordeal. A beautiful moon makes a joke of the expression 'the dead of night', and, as I steer Naomi keeps me awake and company with a lively conversation punctuated by more lively conversation. She's the first to spot the Nuggets light. We have several hours' debate as to whether it is Gp Fl 2 every 12 seconds or is in fact a stern light of a fishing boat that is disappearing in the swell. *Faith II* is booming along at six to seven knots but any attempt to turn off the motor reveals that the breeze is very light and our speed drops to an untenable three to four knots. As we motorsail through the night the phosphorescence bubbles in our wake, and the moon pokes out from behind the clouds.

My navigation appears pretty reliable with dead reckoning based on compass course and the log. Taking running fixes and two bearing fixes is frustratingly unpredictable. Either the current or a tide (there are exceptional spring tides at this date) pushes us further out from the Nuggets and I waste a couple of hours going back into land when morning breaks. I later find a newspaper article on shipwrecks on the southeast coast indicating a westward pull to the tide, toward the coast. Demian joins me as we approach Tautuku lighthouse and then our blissful morning is destroyed as we encounter a stiffening breeze from the southwest, which initially finds us relieved that we can stop motoring. This turns to concern as we are forced to change headsails and tuck in two reefs as the breeze rises to thirty knots and the sea builds.

Steering a course for the Slope Point lighthouse, we are dismayed to find we cannot fetch it as our only gaining tack pushes us further out to sea. The boat below is a shambles and everybody apart from me is seasick, miserable, battered and bruised. The boat resembles a submarine as seas sweep the foredeck, hit the cabin front, rise to crosstree height and crash down into the cockpit.

Naomi has been unwisely reading *The Wreck of the Rose-Noëlle* and thinks that our time has come and has visions of *Faith* upside down. Her visions are prophetic. We have managed to beat about thirty miles toward Slope Point since 0700 hours when we hear the welcome voice of Val, our resident friend in Stewart Island, calling us from the Golden Bay wharf where he is installing a new prop on his floating home. As we attempt to answer his call a fisherman interrupts and carries out a matey conversation. He sounds as though he is in two minds about being out in such a sea and behind his joviality is more than a hint of tension. I radio my rising concerns about the weather to Val.

With the sea and winds increasing to new heights, we decide to turn around and seek shelter at the Nuggets or, failing that, run back to Dunedin. Places to shelter on the southeast coast of the South Island in this sort of weather are few. We are all pretty frustrated in that we have come so far, but there seems no end to this gale. Val informs us that there is shelter at Tautuku Bay and as he describes the anchorage to us — enter the middle of the bay on the northern side and anchor about 300 metres off the telegraph road signs by the cribs on the hill and drop back and lie to a long anchor — we hear a somewhat surprised voice saying what are undoubtedly a sailor's last words: 'Turnover, I've just turned over'.

The radio goes silent. We have other things on our mind as we broad reach down the face of waves and surf at what now feels like twelve to fourteen knots, attempting to cover in three hours a distance that had previously taken us six hours. We later hear that these are the last words heard from local fisherman, Basil Mortimer, whose upturned boat is found several days later still floating in the leftover storm waters of Foveaux Strait.

We eventually find Tautuku Bay and enter. Although the sou'wester is screaming out from the shore, we find an anchorage, though one fraught with danger. If the wind shifts we'll be right on the edge of steeply shoaling shorelines. If our anchor drags we will be dashed to bits on the beach. I would prefer to anchor a little further out although it looks like it may be more uncomfortable.

We try to dry out after a quick hot drink of soup and some toast, then we all collapse into bed. I haven't slept for thirty hours, yet I only doze in snatches, alternatively worrying about the anchorage and the boat rolling madly in the big swell coming into the bay. The south-west wind also rises to new heights. Lying below in such conditions is really frightening, but less so than being out there battling.

By morning, the wind has pretty much died and there is even a light nor'easter blowing, so we rapidly fire up the motor and head out to sea at 0500. There is a big leftover swell running and even with the sails up the motion is awkward, but we are going in the right direction. I manage another hour's sleep as Demian takes the helm, which turns out to be a daylong job for him. We decide to cross the strait from Slope Point rather than go any further and we steer a 230 magnetic course, which we predict will take us past the southern side of Ruapuke Island. We can see what we think is the island (which is in fact a series of islands and rocks) and are steering for it when we work out that it is in fact the Bluff Hills. Ruapuke miraculously appears out of the sea, low lying, and we pass safely to the south in a dying breeze and, unfortunately, with a dying engine. It started smoking, then missing a beat, and finally the steady drone of the engine got steadily weaker. I am at a loss to diagnose the problem but resting it, then running it at low revs, temporarily alleviates the symptoms. However, clouds of black smoke herald the demise of yet another flexible exhaust coupling and I am left cursing the parenthood of the man who assured me that this was the right material and would last years before needing renewing.

I effect a temporary repair with a roll of exhaust manifold tape that I have stored in the bilges for such an event. Another repair sees us with a fully functioning motor again, albeit somewhat fumey as the pipe is nearly severed.

We finally clear Ruapuke after what seems an eternity, and Val calls to inform us that he is back in the water and heading for Little Glory for the night. We seem to be almost there and are becoming excited at the thought of finally making a landfall. Silly us! We should know by now that the god of the seas has us figured for four mugs. This is confirmed when Val finishes his sked with the welcome information that another south-west front is forecast and that it is becoming quite lively in Little Glory. From my previous holiday at Stewart Island this probably means it is blowing fiercely in the inlet, but as it is calm where we are, I hope this is all some cruel joke. As we approach Bench Island, we are indeed hammered by a south-west wind blowing out of the inlet. A change down to No. 1 jib and two reefs is required, but at the end of a gruelling three days and in our tired state, it is a frustrating process. Jib halyards go flying out of control, I get smacked over the head by the boom as Demian Chinese gybes, Alison gets hit in the face as I try and wind up the jib and we are all thrown around.

Faith, of course, is in her element with the lee rail buried in the water and creaming along at five to six knots. We are also a little confused as to where we are. I discover that the course I had decided to steer would have ulti-mately taken us out on the seaward side off the Neck and back down the eastern shores of Stewart Island towards Port Pegasus. However, it is finally sorted out and we eventually sight Glory Cove. As we round the point a fresh gust heels us appropriately and we surge into sight of Val amidst cheers and roars of 'You made it — that's my old boat' (a familiar catchphrase for the rest of our holiday). Delightful offers of hot showers and beer, crayfish tails and laundry are accompanied by more personal declarations such as 'We are all at sea and need to look after each other' — which are ultimately the more valuable of the gifts that Stewart Island has to offer.

Our holiday in Stewart Island is filled with fishing, eating and weather. On my second journey to Oban I stopped on the track and talked to a local about the weather. When I commented on the fact that it rained and blew a gale virtually every day he replied, 'Stewart Island is the cleanest island in the world. It's washed and blow-dried at least once a day.'

I am faced with an awful dilemma. The prop shaft has sheared off the connector unit and shattered the housing that locks the whole affair to-gether, and we have no motor to fall back on. I have talked to an (well, *the*) engineer on Stewart Island and although a repair is possible, the boat will have to be slipped. The only slip on the island is likely to cause further damage to the boat. I have a family to consider and I must let them individu-ally decide if they wish to return with me or make other travel arrangements. To my delight and surprise, they all agree to come back with me.

From Monday the awful routine of closely monitoring the weather fore-casts starts. This is a part of yachting that I could well do without, as no weather forecast is perfect and every person has different views on what constitutes favourable.

We finally decide to chance a battering in the strait in order to ride the breeze to Dunedin and set off from Little Glory in thirty knots. We are immediately flattened as we enter the inlet and the storm jib alone is unable to hold us up to the wind. In order to gain steerage I am forced to put up the double-reefed main, which claws us off the reef on the Neck and out into the inlet. Alison later admits that this part of the trip terrified her, as again *Faith* is mostly underwater until I can clear the Neck and set a more downwind course to pass inside Whero Rock and the Neck (a local deviation on the Carter Passage).

With only storm jib and double-reefed main we are constantly surfing down waves, and for a brief, glorious, orgasmic five minutes we ride two wave systems with the log going crazy.

The next day (or is it four days) leaves me with a bitter hatred of one of the worst aspects of sailing I can think of. Being becalmed. From virtually 2100 on Day 1 to 1200 on Day 2 we are left in the same piece of water off the Nuggets, seemingly going forward then backwards. I can feel and see breeze, but, without a motor, cannot get to it. Alison tries her best to console me but I have fallen into the depths of a great depression until I manage to hook on to the farthermost reaches of a light north-east breeze fetching down from Dunedin. I feel that the Nuggets is where the Chalmers and Foveaux weather systems meet each other, and through the course of the day this two to five knot breeze builds into a fantastic mother of a wind which has us rocketing along at five to six knots with the No. 1 genoa and full main. This ranks as one of the most exhilarating sails of my life. The day is beautiful and I manage to get below for an hour's sleep. How wonderful it is to be below with the water rushing past the hull and the log steadily ticking the miles away as we power up the coast.

This lovely north-east breeze (which really deserves the name of an exotic yet fiery Spanish woman) takes us just south of Taieri Island. I decide that to lay the Cape Saunders light we must tack out to sea approximately fifteen miles and we should come in on a tack which will leave the light just to starboard of us.

As we tack out to sea Alison gets to see her dream of the night before when a container boat gently slides down to Bluff with its mysterious cargo. We are alone on the ocean apart from crayfish pots and one or two fishing boats. We turn to make our approach to the coast as the sun sinks gently into the sea and the moon makes its appearance in the sky.

To our horror, as we approach the coast we find that the warm day has enshrouded the coastline with a layer of fog and low cloud, and we cannot make out any familiar sights. To add to the confusion, night falls rapidly. We then spot some lights but are uncertain as to what they might be. I am sufficiently perplexed to head back out to sea, but the Spanish wind now decides that it will leave us and we are becalmed once again. We suddenly realise that some of the lights belong to squid boats, which must place us twelve miles outside the coast. But night brings even further terrors as the moon is suddenly clouded over and the air holds the promise of a sudden change in the weather. We are also troubled by a total loss of battery power. The motor can no longer charge or run the navigation lights, as they are in such a low state of discharge. Luckily, I have emergency navigation lights on board, which prove to be a godsend.

Then the cloud lifts, and we see that we are directly off the coast of Dunedin and St Kilda beach. It is with welcome relief that Alison sights Cape Saunders light flashing once every ten seconds and the south-west wind enables us to make slow but steady progress towards it under storm jib alone. I lay the light as morning breaks and have another hallucination that we are drifting backwards. The main is raised to give us more motive power away from threatening rocks. I then retire below for sleep as we sail down the coast in a nasty sloppy sea. When I awake we are just approaching the Taiaroa Light and I am greeted with the news that albatross have been flying and the water is alive with kahawai feeding.

I have never felt such a sense of relief when the mooring line is safely on deck. The family hug serves to remind us all of the experience we have shared together, which will change our lives in many ways. We have made it through a large degree of adversity and we have proven that we can work together as a team.

I have been impressed with everybody's ability to produce an effort when required, given that we have all been incapacitated with either seasickness or tiredness or frustration at various times during the journey. I feel that this is a significant change in our attitudes towards ourselves and the boat and the ocean.

As we drive home to bed and rest it is hard to believe that the dream is over for another year and we are back to the reality of our urban existence, away from the relatively protected life we have been living for the last month. We have crammed so much into that month it almost feels as though we need a further month's holiday to recover.

Graeme Dixon

Las Palmas to the Cape

AT EIGHTEEN, a sailing dream prompted Stephen Prinselaar to quit his job with TVNZ and go to sea. He answered an advertisement for a crew position on a vintage 44ft Bermuda cutter bound for the Pacific, and found that yacht hiking became the ideal way to travel and enjoy island paradises and their oceanic people.

Back in New Zealand and with a c.v. that read more like a sailing log, Stephen got work in ad agencies but every few seasons was drawn back to voyaging. At thirty he returned to set up his own creative advertising shop, begin a family and get his own boat, a 10m Turismo catamaran.

Now Stephen's next dream is unfolding. Called *Parallel Life,* the bridge deck catamaran will take his partner Natalie and their two young children, Luca and Saskia, on an extended Pacific cruise, to bestow upon them the beauty of nature at sea.

In the following passage, Stephen recalls a memorable voyage from his earlier yacht-hiking days.

*N*ovember, and I had arrived at Las Palmas, in the Canary Islands, one of the last stepping-stones for most of the cruising yachts heading west in the wake of Columbus. Yachts crammed the marina, overflowing out into the harbour. Makeshift marquees turned on a party every night. This was a cruising regatta's ideal conditions and a yacht hiker's heaven.

It's not often you change your life's direction in the time between sipping and swallowing an ice cold beer in the tropics. Yet this is what happened when an English skipper told me he couldn't find any crew.

'But there's tons of crew looking for boats here,' I said incredulously.

'Not to where I'm going,' he lamented.

'Where are you heading?' I asked ahead of a hearty slurp.

'Capetown.'

I swallowed. My mind was made up. I was on the edge of realising my desire to cross the Atlantic Ocean to the Caribbean and see it in all its moods.

Essentially, by cramming hours of reasoning into one biological timeframe, an oesophagus' spasm enabled a moment of unparalleled lucidity. By going to Capetown I would be spending three months exploring the Atlantic instead of three weeks. And by travelling latitudinally I was guaranteed to see the many faces of this ocean.

Jeanne II was a 31-foot Sadler (I found that out the next day). It had sailed from South Africa to the UK and was now being delivered home. Sailing down from England it had weathered comfortably a couple of Bay of Biscay beauties. I figured the hard part was over.

We picked up one more crew on the day of departure. Simon was an 18-year-old student and countryman of the skipper, John, aged 64. My 30 years provided a handy fulcrum to balance the generation gap.

On leaving the gently swaying palms of the Canaries behind, one soon enters the infamous wind acceleration zone. Using the high peaks like a ski jump, the wind blasts out to sea in a sail-shortening thirty knots. Like a slingshot we were propelled out into magnificent blue swells. We surfed our way to the Cape Verdes in six days (that deserved a bow wave) and were fortunate enough to see it half a day away.

The next morning in the safety of the harbour all the surrounding mountains had disappeared. When the Harmattan is blowing the air becomes laden with dust blown from the African deserts some 645 km to the east. We'd discussed our choice of route and agreed. The options: do what everybody does and dog-leg it via Rio; or tack against the trades and visit a single big rock, called St Helena, somewhere in the windswept South Atlantic.

As a catamaran fiend from way back, I'd always enjoyed a good beat to windward so here was the chance. Besides I seemed to have been following in Napoleon's shackled, shuffling footsteps since Elba. So why not all the way to his final resting place on the last bastion of British rule, St Helena island.

A couple of days out from the barren Cape Verde group we had our first good blow. We reefed down, then battened down and in the end just watched the storm unleash great rolling 'grey beards' that thundered down like a succession of trains.

It's interesting how there seems to be a moment of awareness of when a storm has passed. When relief is replaced by exhilaration despite the on-going assault of the waves. We started sailing again, tentatively unfurling the roller headsail and one by one shaking out the reefs in the main.

That night, at 2 a.m., while sailing hard in the still lumpy sea I was visited. The rush of air was like a knock at the door, and soon I was host to a pod of dolphins careering in our bow wave. Carefully harnessed on, I made my way to the bow where I was met by a sight I shall never forget. Phosphorescent green dolphins, their bodies glowing silhouettes in the black sea. They swam like torpedoes shooting from our bow. Suddenly, two peeled away in mirrored synchronicity, looping back to form a lumi-nous figure eight, then leapt from the water in an explosion of shattered sparkling green jewels. They stayed for an hour and afterwards I made my way back along the high windward rail stunned by the sight I'd seen. It was then I saw how we must have looked to them. The fin keel stirred up a million swirling green lights cutting a swathe of fluorescence under our hull. The rudder and self-steering rudder slashed another luminous chasm in the sea while the hull pounded out an aquatic version of fireworks. It is such unearthly displays, coupled with the lights of the universe above, that makes the solace of the night watch such a valuable time.

The beautiful thing about travelling continents is the varied terrain, ris-ing from desert plains to snowy alpine ranges. They appear like geographical signposts telling you where you are on the globe as effectively as a street sign. The ocean is no exception. It is far from featureless, and as the miles slid by under the stern at about 100 a day and the degrees N on the chart continued their countdown to zero, the signposts around us grew ever more apparent.

The Trades lost their puff. We had an invisible band as tangible as the sound barrier to break through. The swell disappeared and the sea became glassy and mercuric, not even rising to break its serene surface against the impertinent line of our hull. Our sails hung uselessly, abandoning any re-sistance in their slow flip flop swagger. They did not even afford us the luxury of shade from the vertical sun. The absurdly blue sea offered res-pite from the heat and the boredom with its peculiar concoction of refresh-ing swims braced with irrational panic at the incomprehensible depths below us.

Sometimes you could imagine you were being held fast, sandwiched between the deep blue sky and the deep blue sea. A sense of humility overwhelmed me, an emotion all too often suppressed in the 'real' world. Conversations readily became theosophical.

Towering cumulus clouds would often spill their guts to you. It was 'All hands on deck' for a fresh water shower. Our first attempt at collecting drinking water from sail runoff showed us just how pervasive the dust carried on the Harmattan was.

'There was wind in them there clouds too' — fifteen, twenty knots breaking the glassy sea. In the heat of the day you could spot little threads of the clouds' dark, grumpy underbelly twisting away towards the sea. The wind would circle around you like a predator, duck in and ruffle your hair, then go.

At night lightning silently strobed the horizon while above the majesty of the universe was reflected in a myriad of lazily sparkling reflections. That was the night watch's reward. The only sound was an occasional far off rumble, more audible down below, as a ship passed somewhere over the horizon. Sometimes its lights would appear in a shallow arc then sink below the black horizon again. From a cruiser's viewpoint the slow and unsteady progress through this invisible limbo was trying. Heaven help the racer's psyche. The multi-purpose sail was kept in its sausage skin on deck as the easiest and lightest sail to raise and dowse without undue flopping.

All eyes were on the GPS, willing its coordinates towards that magical moment when the N would change in the blink of an eye to S. Of course it's unwise to rely solely on electronics so we implemented our fail-proof backup system. And yes, we are pleased to announce, water does go down the plug hole the other way.

Crossing that imaginary line was a huge morale booster. For a start, I was at last in my home hemisphere. And suddenly it was summer again.

We decided to set the iron spinnaker and lose some weight in diesel (and perhaps even motor in those elusive south-east trades). The next twenty hours was a lesson in abject relativity — that perception of distance covered is relative only to things that move past you. On a flat calm ocean the only relief came from a long-lost plastic bucket. Even the sea life had melted away except for our little troop of camp followers that sought protection between our self-steering and rudder stem.

Then one day there was a signpost. It was even all lit up — with lightning. We motored over to the wall of cloud, through its drenching curtain and into the other side. This was the point on the planet where the winds were literally stonewalled by the Inter-tropical Convergence Zone. The resulting friction created the electric light show and a signpost no one could miss. We were through, but still with a long way to go.

The following days' progress on the chart resembled the famous Lombard Street in San Francisco. A concertina that seemed to resist every degree of southing. Our position was like a flea stuck in the armpit of Africa. Even the weather was dull, with a constant mantle of cloud and insignificant winds.

Ten days passed, then late one afternoon we came to the edge of the cloud. It looked exactly like the western edge of Australia when flying out into the Indian Ocean. The huge flat shelf, that looked about a hundred feet thick, just suddenly stopped. Everything turned blue. With the sun came wind and the prospect of Christmas ashore at St Helena.

Optimism is a wonderful thing. When that deadline fell overboard we had New Year to aim for. We arrived on New Year's Eve after thirty-five days at sea.

Saint Helena island is a rock. Albeit a bloody big one. A veritable prison with no natural harbour, no airfield, no beaches, no islets. No wonder they sent Napoleon there to die. HRH put him up in some nice digs reminiscent of our own Governor's house in Waitangi, Bay of Islands. He had a chaise longue, a full-size white velveted pool table and some pet tortoises which are probably the same ones you can see on the lawns of the present Governor's residence.

The 'harbour' was temporary home to about six cruising yachts on their way to the Caribbean from South Africa. (Plus one confiscated drug ship that was rusting away on its mooring while its skipper did a 'Bonaparte' in the not so lavish common criminal cells for nine years.) Any swell that developed would roll into the bay, crash up against the flat walled harbour edge they were building, then roll back out doubling up with the incoming seas. If the weather turned bad you skidaddled.

After two weeks of St Helenian hospitality we reprovisioned and set a course of 180°. Our plan was to sail to 36°S, turn left and ride the westerlies for the thousand miles to Capetown.

The South Atlantic Ocean is a very lonely place to be. That was until sunset one evening when a concerted effort to check the narrow blind spot in front of the genoa revealed a billowing spinnaker 500 metres ahead. My jaw literally dropped. We were beating, they were running and hadn't seen us. We couldn't pinch up and didn't have the speed to go under them.

At last they spotted us and passed close by with some incredulous shouts (telling us we were going the wrong way) and waves from the stunned crew. On the VHF they told us they were part of the inaugural Cape to Rio race reinstated after the fall of apartheid. There were ninety other yachts in the area. Things suddenly felt very crowded. Over the next twenty-four hours we spotted four more racing yachts.

The further south we got the more signposts we started to see. First we began to see a cross-swell building from the west. Each day it got more pronounced. At 34° S I started to scan the swells for albatross. A book on board said to expect them from 36°C. With the next dawn and two degrees further south they appeared. That was our sign to hang a left.

For the next ten days we watched these beautiful creatures surf the massive swells, riding the cushion of air across their undulating face before subtly twitching a wing tip and barrelling up and over to join the next wave behind. They'd 'S' their way across the marching ranks of swells, tucking in behind our own gull-winged sails as if to offer encouragement. For as long as they were about, I was in the cockpit marvelling at their existence.

Our first view of Capetown was in the early morning. It was still a day's sail away for us and the Cape Doctor was paying a house call. As if to welcome us our hosts had put out their finest 'table cloth'. That is the layer of cloud that forms on the plateau of Table Mountain and overflows, cascading down the sheer sides before evaporating. It is like an ethereal waterfall that never reaches the bottom and ranks as one of the most spectacular natural wonders of the world.

Sea-lions heralded our arrival as we left the open sea behind. The voyage was soon to be complete. It had been a journey so rich and diverse as to equal any adventure on land. As we stepped giddily ashore onto the African continent and the new adventure I was about to embark on, I was pleased to know in my heart that at last I had been to and seen the Atlantic Ocean.

Stephen Prinselaar

Under Squares off Akaroa

ROBIN GRIGG manages a high country station in mid Canterbury, but his holiday passion is running away to sea, especially on sailing ships.

A volunteer since 1989 on coastal voyages for the Spirit of Adventure Trust, which runs the barquentine *Spirit of New Zealand*, Robin has also clocked up many ocean passages in the Dutch *Tradewind*, the English *Søren Larsen* and *Eye of the Wind*, the Norwegian *Anna Kristina*, the Australian *Bounty* and the giant Russian naval training ship *Sedoy.*

Sailing before the mast, he says, provides endless challenges and pleasures, among them night watches contemplating the things of nature, and the sense of achievement in going aloft in Force Eight to furl sails — sometimes just one step at a time up the upper ratlines between rolls of the ship, then out along the yards to the weather yardarm. You hang on with the backs of your upper arms to the yard while wrestling with the lively canvas until it is subdued and safely gasketed.

And the mate says, 'Right, now we'll do the main topsail as well!'

*I*t sometimes happens at sea that strong bonds are formed through adversity shared.

In the early nineties a company specialising in air conditioning (and to avoid embarrassment it won't be named, but they may recognise themselves in this account) chartered the sail training ship *Spirit of New Zealand*. The purpose of the weekend was to get together technicians and repairmen for a product update and to meet a senior representative of the air-conditioner manufacturer from Japan.

The charter was to sail from Lyttelton on the north side of Banks Peninsula to Akaroa harbour on the south side. We would then sail the ship to

Lyttelton for its next youth development ten-day voyage.

About eight or ten of us, regular volunteer crew for the Spirit of Adventure Trust, were rostered on to form the nucleus of the sailing crew as mates, watch officers, etc, with the remaining forty-odd of the charter group contributing the muscle for sail handling.

All mustered on board ship late Friday afternoon, the guests (as we are required to consider them) gathering in small groups of local acquaintance, making tentative connection with others on board. After the official welcome and safety briefings, we set off to sea. The first leg of the voyage was an easy run down Lyttelton harbour, out through the heads, along the north side of the peninsula and into Pigeon Bay to anchor up for the night.

Easy. To the sailors new to ships and the sea it was a gentle introduction. There was the impression of towering areas of sail, and working the ropes made it all happen. At the end of it all, the old hands and the intrepid climbed aloft into the gathering dusk and spread out along the yards to tie up the sails and put them away for the night. All in all, a good start to the weekend.

Apart from those on anchor watch, everyone else headed to bed. Those who made the hustle and bustle happen slept in bunks in the officer accommodation, the esteemed gentleman from Japan had a bunk made up for him in the sick bay, and the rest of us slept for'ard in the trainee accommodation, racked up three and four high on the pipe and canvas bunks.

Saturday morning dawned overcast and cool with a bit of a southerly blowing. After breakfast, all on board gathered at 0800 on the dot for 'colours', the raising of the ensign, and a discussion of the plans for the day.

The charterers had produced wonderful little passports which included a timetable for the weekend, showing that on Saturday the ship would sail from Pigeon Bay to Akaroa arriving mid afternoon, followed by cocktails on board for our guests and their wives.

It is an axiom of the sea that under sail the weather rules the day.

The old man (as the captain is usually called at sea) and the more experienced sailors pursed their lips upon being informed that sailing to Akaroa was the order of the day, and frowned when they contemplated what a southerly off the eastern end of Banks Peninsula means. Since no real harm could happen if the ship was properly handled, it was agreed to set off for Akaroa.

Anchored close in under the land things were relatively calm, but as the ship gathered way down the bay under increasing amounts of sail, the strength of the southerly and its effect on the sea became more and more apparent. The old salts said the wind was about Force Six with a two- to three-metre swell away from the land.

Once clear of the bay and turned eastward across the wind, the ship was moving quite lively so only the volunteer crew and some of the more hardy souls were answering the call to set the inner jib from the foredeck. The bow was rising and falling two or more metres, so working on the foredeck you experienced the rush of the up, and the swoop of the down. Before long your stomach tires of being weightless and then leaden by turn and rebels, and that's when people began parting with their breakfasts.

Soon people were leaving their positions handling the sail and ropes, staggering down the deck to the lee rail to 'talk to Rupert'. The more resolute then made their way back up to their sail station and were welcomed back by the diminishing group left to set the sail.

Things fairly quickly fell into a routine. As each new victim of the 'mal de mer' appeared up on deck they were bundled into yellow wet weather gear, fitted with a safety harness and clipped to the safety lines along the lee rail. By the end of the day only about eight or ten on board had not been sick at some stage, and volunteer crew seemed almost as susceptible as new sailors.

It is a feature of seasickness that the focus of thought rapidly closes in on the process of being sick. Thoughts about the safety of the body or even of survival rapidly lose their importance, so it's up to those with their sea legs to watch over the safety of the afflicted.

Being watch-officer midships and one of those with their sealegs, I found myself after each tack onto a new course, cajoling the seasick to unhook from what was now the windward side and struggle around the deckhouse and down to the lee rail. Those who tried to be sick into the wind soon realised the need for the shift.

With the wind, a certain amount of spray and sickness hypothermia sets in fairly quickly, so once the unfortunates had plumbed the depths of their stomachs it was time to hand them a bucket and herd them below decks where at least it was warm.

Beyond the end of the peninsula the old man turned the ship towards the wind and began the battle to gain miles to windward by tacking, first away from the land for several miles, then smartly turning the bow of the ship up through the wind and onto the new tack back towards the land.

A sailing ship, particularly a square rigger with its big yards across the ship, cannot sail very directly into the wind and instead has to make do with sailing almost as much across the wind as into the wind on each tack.

So began what was to be several hours of tacking, first on the starboard tack out to sea, and then on the port tack back to land. As the end of each port tack neared, we would look anxiously at the approaching land, trying to identify landmarks to see whether we had gained any ground against the wind. The gains began to get less and less with each tack, and the same landmarks seemed to mock our efforts each time we returned to land.

It was during this tacking that the esteemed gentleman from Japan appeared, first from below up into the deckhouse, and finally when necessity overcame dignity, to join those suffering in the lee watch. In this sharing of the common travail the distance of position dissolved and bonds began to develop.

Back to the slow process of tacking into the southerly. At the extreme eastern end of Banks Peninsula there is a rock pillar which stands up out of the sea, known to sailors as Pompey's Pillar. It's a signpost that you're about to turn the corner of the peninsula.

For two or three tacks we were gaining only a few hundred metres on each return, and those still capable of thought were beginning to wonder whether we would get to Akaroa at all, or whether we should turn tail to the weather and run back to Pigeon Bay.

Eventually it was my turn to take the wheel and do my turn at the helm.

With the squaresails — and because of the wind strength we were now down to two — the trick is to keep the ship heading so that the wind is blowing on the back of the sails, pushing the ship forwards. Let the wind come round on to the front of the sail (said to be 'taken aback') and the sail acts like a brake, slowing the ship down and frustrating the efforts of the fore and aft sails to push the ship forwards.

By the time I took the helm we were just past Pompey's Pillar but still not far enough up into wind to safely begin the long tack across the southern side of the peninsula to Akaroa.

The old man wanted the ship held really close up to the wind on each tack, with the windward ends of the yards pointed directly into the wind so that the windward ends of the squares were neither filling nor being taken aback, a very delicate balance. In this situation the half of the square sail on the lee side of the mast is still filled from behind, or drawing, because of the effect of the fore and aft sails on the wind flowing past them.

I can still see him, as I momentarily lost concentration or allowed the ship to fall slightly off the wind. The old man would pop up into view somewhere up for'ard where he had been having sheets tweaked to fine-tune the set of the jibs, and wave to windward indicating that the helm must be put down and the ship brought back even closer to the wind.

Finally, the windward searoom had been gained and the port tack went on, and on. Close in, the wind was being deflected off the land, subtly shifting the local wind direction, giving what sailors call a 'lift off the land'. Taking advantage of this effect we were able to begin our westerly run.

The thing sailors fear almost above all else is being caught on a lee shore, hopelessly trapped between the wind and the shore. For some time it was a case of maximum care with the helm and sail until we were clear on a comfortable reach past the southern bays. With a three metre swell, comfortable is perhaps not the term the seasick would have used.

Akaroa harbour is an unusual place to approach from the sea. When the navigator gives the word, you turn the ship into what appears to be a narrow gap in high cliffs with no room for second thoughts and no sign of the wide open harbour you know is in there somewhere.

With the southerly at your back, you push on into what looks like another short cliff-bound bay and disaster. Then, about half a mile in, the cliffs together turn gradually to starboard and you pop out into the wide crater of an extinct volcano.

Out of the open sea swell and comfortably moving to the gentler waves of the inner harbour, life began to return to those laid low. In literally a matter of minutes, the lassitude of sickness was thrown off, heads came up, deep breaths of welcome air were drawn in, and colour returned to faces. There was positive exuberance as those who had suffered tasted the simple joys of life again. Hands returned willingly to handling lines as the sails were taken in and furled.

A quick but thorough clean-up below followed the setting of the anchors, and promptly at 5 p.m., as stated in the passports, a local launch appeared alongside with wives and non-sailors on board. Soon the newly minted sailors were regaling their guests with tales of mountainous seas and strong winds.

On Sunday morning the ship was taken for a brief sail within the harbour and the new hands were able to show off their newly acquired skills as sailors, working together as a crew to handle the big sails and brace the yards.

Even now, ten years after this voyage, when the volunteer crew gather on the ship or in Christchurch someone may ask the question, 'Were you on that trip to Akaroa?'

Robin Grigg

Night Life with Oars
in the Atlantic

ROB HAMILL, a rowing world silver and Commonwealth gold medallist, was training in Virginia, USA for the 1996 Olympics in Atlanta, when he saw a notice in a locker-room seeking a partner to row across the Atlantic. It was the beginning of a dream.

Plenty of obstacles stood in his way. The $27,000 entrance and kitset fee, for a start. Raising sponsorship money, building and equipping the boat, finding a partner.

Phil Stubbs read in a newspaper about Rob's determination to do the race. Aged 36, and a policeman, Phil had done plenty of blue-water sailing and competed in Iron Man, surfboat, dragon boat and kayak events. When the first Trans-Atlantic rowing race from the Canary Islands to Barbados began on 12 October 1997, Rob and Phil were there in *Kiwi Challenge*. Thirty boats and sixty rowers faced 3000 miles of lonely ocean, storms, capsizes, seasickness and madness. Friendships would be put under extreme pressure, and in the case of Hamill and Stubbs, come 'perilously close to blows'.

Forty-one days and nights of non-stop rowing later, *Kiwi Challenge* crossed the finish line, first by eight days.

'After 101 years, a two-man crew had finally rowed the Atlantic faster than the legendary Norwegians, Habro and Samuelson. And now I didn't want the journey to end,' wrote Hamill, before both flew home to an ecstatic Kiwi welcome. He and Stubbs agreed that though they would mount another challenge, they would not row together again. Tragically, at the end of 1998, Phil Stubbs was killed when his Piper aircraft nose-dived into the sand at Karekare Beach on Auckland's west coast.

*D*usk, the most pleasant time of the day. Then the glare of the sun, now long past its zenith, would reflect off my back. As the temperature dropped I would begin to feel better, the permanent headache would almost disappear and a freshness in the air was invigorating. Then, as the sun's orb touched the horizon, cutting its power by half, one sensed the impending darkness looming like a prowler in the back yard. Reality was that another long night was ahead. For the moment I enjoyed the spectacle, glancing over my right shoulder observing brilliant colour changes from bright reds and yellows through the spectrum to shades of violet and, eventually, darkness.

Sometimes when the cloud cover was dense and low the *Kiwi Challenge* would plunge into a total blackout, leaving only a red glow from the compass light as the night sky's sole luminance. At these times my imagination would take over, making the universe as small or as big as I so desired. Sea monsters lurked, then appeared through the darkness, serpents with multiple heads and darting tongues. It was a game I sometimes played to make myself more alert to the surroundings and, hopefully, more aggressive on the oars. I wondered if such monsters really did exist. John Ridgway saw them on his Atlantic crossing with Chay Blyth.

One thing I definitely did see — on two separate occasions — was some kind of brightly lit craft hurtling across the sky at a speed far in excess of any aircraft. I wondered what these could possibly be; other than a UFO. The best explanation I could come up with was that they were military weapons. I knew from listening to the short-wave radio receiver — our only form of communication with the outside world — that there were new tensions in the Gulf. Could they be rockets streaking in the direction of Saddam?

Steve Boga, *The Oceanrowers*
Jan and Daniel [mother and son team] were prepared for squalls and huge, aggressive seas; what surprised them were all the calm, glassy seas. 'So many of the nights — especially in the second half of the race — were windless and calm,' says Jan. 'We began to call our ocean, Lake Atlantic.'
She recalls one of the many nights: while Daniel slept . . . Jan rowed on a satin sea beneath a full moon. She wore only a bikini and her Walkman earphones. Classical music — Debussy — echoed through her head. With each pass of the oars through the water, she churned up glittering bioluminescent creatures. 'Like scooping up millions of

emeralds,' she thought.

Occasionally a shooting star plummeted towards the horizon. A dozen dolphins suddenly appeared around the boat, cavorting, gliding effortlessly through the water, their backs glistening in the moonlight. It was possibly the most beautiful moment of her life. One she would cherish forever.

Let me take you through a couple of night shifts. On the night of October 28 — the night of the day I had first rowed naked — I came on at 8 p.m. when there was little natural light. Later on there would be a new moon, but it had yet to rise. My eyes were a little sore from the bright day just gone, resulting in me not being able to see the compass easily. I slid right forward on the trolley seat, got my bearings and was away.

A swell came through and lifted the stern so with a little extra effort on the oars we swished, gurgled and slapped along, surfing a smidgen. When we were in the lowest part of the trough I would put in an extra couple of quick strokes, a little more effort to get us moving before the next swell caught us sitting in the water. I was pleased I was working well with the boat, but the early evening shift was rarely a problem. The temperature and brightness were lower and the colours were enhanced, a great time to be on the ocean.

'That's better, Rob,' I thought. 'That will get us home a little quicker.' The shift was uneventful, and I had kept a steady three knots with the assistance of the current, a light easterly astern of us, 6.5 miles for the shift.

The midnight to 2 a.m. shift was a gutbuster for me. We thought at that time, after 16 days, we were a quarter to a third of the way through the race and I was getting worn down at night. It was a struggle to stay alert. I rowed, but I wanted to sleep. When the sea is demanding you are awake and concentrating, but this night was as regular as it got and I had my eyelids closed, rowing by sound and feel. If I slept, I didn't stop rowing.

WHAM! I felt that!

I was wide awake in a flash, looking for the sea monster and the monster seas arriving with it, wondering what the hell was happening. Out of the west a tiny 10 cm flying fish had hit me in the middle of my back. A juvenile with learner's licence overcooked the glide and arrived, blat, in the middle of my back, and flopped in the boat. The fish, still a little stunned by its exuberance, slid towards the gunwales as I slipped my foot out of the rowing shoe to guide it through the scuppers back to mother sea.

I was sure it would have a whale of a tale to tell its mates. It gave me a fright; three times on the journey I was jolted by a hotshot flying fish, twice in the back and once in the neck. Yep, each one brought me to life with a start, just a minor adrenalin rush, although nothing compared to the mother of all frights I got when that storm petrel attempted to land on my shoulder.

Just as I thought everything was back to 'normal', an unexpected cross-wave from the port side lapped ever so accurately into the stern cubby cabin, wetting the bedding and Phil. Even at night the temperature was in the mid-20s; so we often had the stern hatch open. In the half-light of the new moon I couldn't see the following sea and sliding up the stern a crest could flop into the cabin all too easily. Then for good measure another cross-wave did it again, just to remind us who was boss. Thankfully Phil had shut the hatch after the first gentle splash.

Throughout the middle part of the journey we had poor light at night, simply because of the phase of the moon. Under those conditions it was difficult to see the waves coming. Occasionally I could hear waves, but I still wouldn't know where they were and, apart from bracing myself, there was little I could do.

Thus it was always the unexpected and at night, the unseen, which caused chaos. This shift I hauled the boat 5.5 miles.

If the midnight shift was a gutbuster, the 4–6 a.m. shift was a gutbuster plus a headshrinker when my eyelids felt like sandpaper. The Sleep Monster homeopathic remedy helped but not nearly enough for my liking. Waking the other person up became increasingly problematic. To begin with I had to call three or four times before an answering murmur would signal Phil had heard the wake-up call. Then as the days passed I would have to call louder. Loud, four to five times calling Phil's name whilst I was rowing, occasionally (the occasional became regular at the end of the odyssey) shouting when I got no response.

Likewise when I had been sleeping and then heard Phil's voice, I could tell from the tone and volume that this was not the first time he had called. I would wake up thinking, 'Shit, Phil must have called me.'

I would lie doggo for a little, waiting to hear Phil's, 'Come on, mate, rattle your bones. The time is five minutes to four, your shift!' If this didn't happen I was asleep again.

At least half a dozen times, maybe more, I awoke and thought something along the lines of, 'Damn, I've gone back to sleep,' so I called out, 'Yeah, yeah. I'm coming.'

I would struggle into my shorts, put on my smelly, cold and damp rowing T-shirt then stagger out of the hatch to confront a startled Phil.

'What are you up to, Rob?'

'What do you mean what am I doing? You woke me up. Didn't you yell at me to go on the next shift?'

'No. No, it's only 3.25, mate. You've got a good half hour to go yet.'

I turned and flopped back into the pit, totally brassed off with myself.

Another difficulty was the effect a sleeping person had on the trim of the boat. I guess I had a similar effect but when Phil slept at night frequently he would sleep chest down, head tucked into the stern corner on the starboard side. This unbalanced the boat, making rowing more difficult. Generally I waited for 10 minutes or so when this happened. Sometimes he would automatically centre himself, sometimes he wouldn't. If he didn't, I would have to stop rowing, clamber down the deck, open the hatch and tap him on his feet.

'Phil, could you centre yourself, mate?'

He would shuffle back to the middle, 'Thanks, mate.'

Quite often he would not recall being woken.

While my body was taking the rhythm of the rowing, my mind was attempting to estimate time. I had a goal of going for 75 minutes without looking at my watch. Counting strokes was too mind-numbing and stupefying.

Instead I would look at the compass bearing, a star on the horizon, the wind on the water, the wake, the wash, anything but the watch! I would try to fathom the ocean's mood, but my mind would lose the plot, so I'd begin an intellectual medical, going over my body minutely, checking responses from my neck, shoulders, arms, back, butt, thighs, privates, knees, ankles. Later, as the race progressed, I would notice that my pulse was getting stronger and stronger.

I'd listen to the rhythm of the row, watch a cloud form, move, dissipate and reform. Then I'd go through the same process again through the water, the sky, the body, the boat, the second haul on the water bottle. When I felt reasonably sure that the 75 minutes was long gone I would row for another '10 minutes' and then check my watch. Damn, only 40 minutes. Try as I might to increase my 75 minute accuracy I hardly ever made it.

Chocolate bars were one of the staples to help keep our energy levels up at night. In the middle stages Phil had a philosophy that worked well. One bar of chocolate had seven pieces or knobs in it. Phil would watch the log like a seagull and the moment he completed a mile he would have a knob of chocolate, row another mile and have another knob of chocolate. This would spread a bar over the entire shift. Not a bad idea, eh? Invariably he would have a chunk or two left over to celebrate the completion of his shift.

The phosphorescence in this part of the world was unique. In New Zealand waters the phosphorescence seems to be evenly spread, but here it was patchy. When you hit a patch there would be almost an explosion of light. On an ill-lit night, irregular pools of phosphorescence would well up at the tip of the blade, quickly bloom in intensity and then equally quickly dissipate. I would think, 'What is that?' Another exhausted bird about to land on an equally exhausted human, or another 'L'-plate flying fish playing shark with the boat? No, nothing dramatic like that; it was just the plankton playing.

The night settled in long and hot. The head wind faded. It was funny watching each other go through our get-up routine at night. It was a huge struggle. I had to will my eyes open; they refused, my brain short-circuited. I thought harder, the eyes opened, but they didn't seem to be part of the rest of me. My brain re-attached, I then got the rest of me to shuffle to the hatch, hitting my head on the ceiling joist in the process, hit the light switch and rummaged around for the smelly, sweaty shirt that I had been wearing only two hours before.

The shirt dried in the day, but never at night. I pulled it on, usually bumping my head on the hatch while exiting to get my drink bottles and occasionally bumping it going back inside. Now that I had my drink bottles I had to put the powder in. I stepped outside, bumping my head again, clinging to the bulkhead with one arm to stabilise my body, twisting to the right and pumping the water, then filling the plastic water bottles with water. Shaking the bottles was not a difficulty and neither was the inelegant collapse into the cabin, while bumping my head again. During the trip huge scabs would fall off my scalp like bark from a tree.

Nearly awake now I would climb outside again, bumping my head, and stand up, wobbling from side to side, struggling to catch up with the roll. Standing in the outside well I stretched for two minutes, then had a scratch and a grizzle about the calm, the head wind or the tail wind. The ritual proceeded as I wobbled and rolled up to my rowing position. I then applied silicone barrier cream to my bum, sat on the woollen seat, positioned the drink bottles in their individual holders and placed my feet in my shoes. I would now be ready to row although still half asleep. I took a couple of strokes with Phil and forced myself to wake up. I began to stiff-arm the Atlantic again.

One clear night I decided to make a huge effort and try to find a few constellations in the night sky. My father went to sea on a merchant ship during the war; transporting arms across the Tasman Sea and up the coast of Australia. He ended up as second mate and navigation officer. He had lent me a battered old star chart that had all the Northern Hemisphere's constellations laid out, with lines drawn connecting the stars and names for each one.

I used this map to identify the constellations one by one. There was the Great Bear (or Ursa Major), with two of its stars acting as pointers to the Pole (or Northern) Star. Then there was the Little Bear (Ursa Minor), Pegasus and the brightest star, Sirius. The most distinctive constellation — for it is also found in the southern hemisphere skies — was the Greek god Orion, with his sword ready for action.

And then I spied a huge shooting star. It was as if the string holding Sirius in the sky had been severed and the star left to drop into the atmosphere to multiply a hundredfold in brightness, streaking across the black night looking for anonymity on the other side of the world. Then it was gone, leaving only its blinding flash etched into the back of my retina for a few moments.

Until we rowed naked, the Walkman was often clipped onto my shorts at night and so was Frank Sinatra. I have always enjoyed him, most of all 'New York, New York'. Great song, great song. I learnt to row in sync with it. That is one tremendous advantage crooners have; they go well with scullers. To be successful at either you need unrivalled timing. In an endurance race we synchronised really well.

There was 'New York, New York' of course, and 'I did it my way', which incidentally is the first song on the tape, most appropriate. '*Regrets I've had a few. . . .*' Sinatra was fun and fitted well with the 4 a.m. shift, and I genuinely enjoyed 'New York, New York'. '*I want to be a part of it. . . .*' Anyone can see the appropriateness of 'For once in my life', 'The best is yet to come' and 'They can't take it away from me'. Here was my own concert, in my own theatre. It was warm, I kept to Frank's rhythm, we were working well together.

The music was my consolation and my inspiration. Phil never understood this.

Later in the journey, when we were further westward, the sun rose on the 8–10 a.m. shift. The faint purple hue over the stern registered the imminent arrival of another day. The water began to change from jet to ethereal black, a little later to dark grey, followed by a yukky grey-blue. Likewise the sky lightened to reveal few clouds and signal a thirsty day ahead.

Quickly, very quickly, the sky would lighten right through the colour spectrum, and day would come racing. Then came the golden blind. Horizontally, unswervingly targeted into my eyes. The shafts of the first rays sought you out, as though to register back to the sun, that you were still here on the sun's planet, still sitting on the water, still paddling away, still present. My lids were screwed up under the sunnies to shield my eyes from the sun's laser probe.

The intensity of the rays precluded much else other than being forced to acknowledge the dominance of the new light over the old dark, watching the sea with peripheral vision, acceding to the assertive power of the full-on, high-beam light still coming right into my eyes. 'Ah yes,' my mind would say, 'but we are further around your planet, we are making miles away from you.'

Rowing within myself, waiting as the sun rose a little and the light beam dipped a little, but then quickly the reflection off the sea twinkled to torment me for a while. The warmth of the sun began to register on my shoulders, then chest and waist, while my eyes did battle with the light of this new day.

We did not alter our watches during the Atlantic crossing, which meant the shifts altered in real time for the longitude we were at. For example, the first of the night shifts at 8 p.m. watch time became 6 p.m. real time halfway across. Although our shifts stayed the same sequence on our watches, the light intensity appeared to increase as we progressed westward. Unconsciously it gave us the perception that we were rowing out of the night and into the dawn.

'Yeah. We really are making progress around the girth of Earth. We are doing it.'

The night was calm, the next day a doldrum-like Karapiro calm. A small pod of dolphins hung around curiously then disappeared on their journey;

131

we were just too slow for their interest. It is amazing how much noise rowing the boat actually makes. The seat wheels roll, the axle rubs on the plastic, the oars clack in the gates. The oar tips rip the water, water drips as your oars exit the water, the boat shifts water in front of it, the sea closes in behind and around you, each making a differing swish, gurgle and fizz.

Morning ablutions, and in the dark hours before dawn it was incredibly humbling sitting on a plastic bucket in a plywood dinghy on an endless ocean. Just before dawn, sitting on the throne, an audible still pervaded, the sounds silent, I could hear the blood rushing through my eardrums, a deafening quiet. I felt out of place, like a fish in a desert, a pollutant in an ocean stadium intruding on Mother Nature's turf. Would she tolerate this irritant? I hoped so but at the same time I wondered about the bigger picture.

Would she tolerate the prolific problems we humans thrust upon her daily? The self-cleansing environment that is our planet has long since been overloaded by a variety of pollutants causing change. It reminded me of the boiled frog syndrome: a frog placed in a pot of hot water will immediately jump out. But place that same frog in a pot of cold water and begin to heat the water slowly over an element and the frog will happily remain, unable to detect the gradual change in temperature that reaches the point where the frog will be cooked alive.

As individuals, we cannot detect the subtle changes that are occurring as nature tries to balance out the polluting intruders we create and thrust into the air, soil and water. It is only our instruments that tell us that the average global temperature is rising or that our ozone hole grows bigger with every passing year, yet we still fail to act with a sense of urgency. Like the frog, our senses are unable to pick up these subtle changes on a daily basis to constantly remind us that, should we fail to act soon, it would be to do so at our peril. Ultimately our apathy could lead to our extinction.

Adding to the problem, I chucked the bucket contents, swirled seawater in the bucket, chucked again, cleaned the inside, stowed it, picked up the oars and rowed.

We are a species of Kermits.

Phil checked the hull late that morning. I thought it was quite courageous, really. During the previous night, as he was washing his hands in the sea after a crap, there was a flash of phosphorescence below his hands and he had then seen the outline of a really big fish 2–3 m long. Now, the next day, he was about to enter the water with a reinforced nylon scrubbing pad 20 cm by 20 cm in hand, scouring the hull.

I grabbed the video camera and began to record the event, then felt suddenly guilty. 'What am I doing here with the camera when you are going in with the sharks, Phil?' 'You kind of volunteered for the camera, Rob,' he replied good-naturedly.

He held onto the grab line (the nylon safety line strung along the outside hull just above the water line) with one hand and scrubbed with the other, slowly working his way around the boat.

Brave Rob stood guard, looking out for intruders. After Phil had completed the job and was back on board, he said there were even baby barnacles attaching themselves to the hull. I got the *Kiwi Challenge*, now clean and shiny on the underside, under way again and this time Phil was happy to take a photo of me, naked but equipped with a strategically placed Sunsmart drink bottle. It seemed as if we were trying to have some fun at last . . .

Colin Quincey, *Tasman Trespasser*
I think there is a very thin, very precarious line which separates the uttermost striving to achieve something and obsession with the achievement to the exclusion of common sense. To survive it is essential to maintain sufficient mental faculty to know where to draw this line.

The last day of October, the 31st, had been another long, hot day, the third in succession. During the day we had our second big food dumping session. I dumped the contents of 14 day packs. That took us down to 56 days' supplies. The packs were torn apart, we kept the plastic bags and wrappers and dumped freeze-dry meals, energy bars, fruit bars, milkshake mix and cereals. I was particularly tough on the honey soy chicken. I guess we lightened the boat by 10–14 kg, maybe more.

I was taken aback by the energy required to stay out in the boiling sun, opening the bags and deciding which to dump. It took only 20, 30 minutes maximum, but it sure was a tremendous drain on energy, or a huge cutback in recovery time. Whatever, it amounted to the same outcome; I was stuffed. The last time we dumped food the weather immediately changed and we had that three-day storm. This time I hoped it was not going to be a harbinger of adverse weather.

Neil Hitt, *Hospicare*, July 1999
We were rowing along after about three weeks when the ocean was

totally flat. Both of us were rowing and it was about two hours before sunset. We were both aware of a rumbling noise gradually getting louder. Pete was rowing in the bow seat and looked over his shoulder to see a large cargo ship coming straight towards us.

They had cut their engines some time before and had been coasting towards us, trying to work out what was causing the small blip on their radar screen. They passed so close to us that we were able to shout across at the crew and say that we were fine and rowing to Barbados. As they were still moving we were soon out of earshot and the VHF radio didn't seem to be working.

We sat down and started to row again, putting about 1/4 mile between the two boats. It looked as if they were altering course, but they continued to turn their ship. They were coming back!

'Ships don't stop,' said Pete. 'The certainly don't turn around for a chat!'

The ship came back and stopped alongside us. We were tiny compared with the mass of this cargo ship. We got the VHF working and chatted with the captain. He invited us aboard for a meal and a drink but we said that we were in a race and couldn't accept outside assistance. Two seconds after I had said that I regretted it but after a couple of hours when the ship had gone we were glad that we hadn't got on board. We may not have wanted to get back off.

The ship was from New Zealand, bound for Europe. The captain's parting words were, 'Only MAD dogs and Englishmen. . . .'

Little did he know there were two Kiwis out there as well!

Sometimes, once the shift was under way, all I could think about was when it would end. And the worst thing I could do was to keep checking the time. This had the effect of slowing time down, making two hours drag on for what seemed an eternity. And when the wonderful moment arrived when I could call out to Phil for his shift, I would then hawkeye the watch, making sure he did not fluff around too much.

When I noticed Phil was between one and three minutes late on some shifts I made a point of being one to three minutes early on all my shifts, or at least I thought that was the case. However, in the middle of the day I was four minutes late as I was adjusting the solar panel to maximise incoming solar radiation and greasing the seat axle. Phil just stopped rowing, in a slight huff.

The next morning I accidentally woke Phil one minute earlier than usual for the 2–4 a.m. shift so he woke me two minutes early for the 4–6 a.m. shift. That gave me an extra two minutes' stretching time and I used them. Then the irritation Phil felt came out. 'Jeez, mate, I think you need to start your shifts on time, not a bloody minute late each and every shift.' Not a major, but it was interesting to note how we were watching each other like hawks. The nights were so tough it was easy to get annoyed like that.

Rob Hamill, *The Naked Rower*, 2000

Travelling by Sea

YOU HAVE TO BE a certain age to remember the last days of sea travel, when the only way to cross oceans was on the scheduled runs of the great passenger liners run by companies like P & O, Shaw Savill, Cunard, Union Castle, the New Zealand Shipping Company. By the mid 1970s the trans-oceanic passenger trade was all but over; sea travel had given way to the delights of being entertained on cruise ships.

Tessa Duder made her first sea voyage at the age of five, from New Zealand to England via Panama, beginning a lifelong fascination with the sea and watery pursuits. Swimming, sailing and sea travel have featured strongly in her own life and in most of her ten novels for young people and her choice of non-fiction subjects.

In recent years she has enjoyed her work as a trustee and occasional sailor on the three-masted *Spirit of New Zealand* (the Auckland-based youth training ship) sailing a Micron dinghy and long weekends afloat with friends. In 2001, in the early Norwegian winter, she relished the unique pleasures of the famous Hurtigruten ferries which take local passengers, freight and tourists from Bergen up the spectacular coast of Norway and into the Arctic circle to Kirkeness, close to the Russian border, and back.

It wasn't her first encounter with snow and ice at sea. In the spring of 1964, just out of New York in the north Atlantic, there'd been an iceberg or two off the *Seven Seas'* port bow .

*A*fterwards, we were told that the woman was English, returning home with two young daughters following the failure of her American marriage. And that it was a miracle that first, she survived an hour and twenty minutes in the icy grip of the north Atlantic and second, that we ever found her.

The alarm had sounded late in the afternoon, when the May light was beginning to fade, and thoughts on any passenger ship are turning towards happy hour and the evening meal. We were two days out from New York, ploughing uncomfortably through a grey, sizeable swell and past smallish icebergs on our port side. To appreciate just how cold salt water of 42°F feels, you only had to stick a toe in the swimming pool, which the day before had been refilled as we passed through the Labrador current, which flows south direct from the Arctic. There'd been few around the pool that afternoon and only one swimmer. Most people had left the decks and retired into the warmth of the public rooms below when six short blasts reverberated throughout the ship.

A moment's indecision: do we go down and get lifebelts as per the drills? But this wasn't the long unbroken ring of a general alarm — meaning fire? collision? a stray iceberg? a mini *Titanic*? — but something more specific.

'Someone's overboard!' My new husband had been that solo swimmer in the pool the day before, resulting in a knotted intestine. He'd been discharged with the threat of surgery if it didn't clear itself, but while in the hospital, had been aware of another patient, a woman, in distress.

On deck, with the ship now rolling heavily, it was clear that already we had slowed, or even stopped. There was activity around one of the big lifeboats on an upper deck. We could hear urgent shouts in German. And some way off on our starboard quarter a tiny single light could be glimpsed occasionally, riding the grey swells and becoming more distant by the minute.

It soon got around: a distraught woman in a night-gown had escaped from the hospital and the pursuing doctor, and leapt to an icy and certain death. The doctor had the presence of mind to throw over a lifebelt with a light on it. Now they would go after her in the lifeboat. Very likely they would find a frozen body, if they were lucky; no one could survive that cold for more than a few minutes. Some sighed or shrugged their shoulders, or said a prayer, and went down below to warmth and the first sitting of dinner.

Passengers on a sea journey of any length get used to seeing crews' drills involving lifeboats, but not usually for real in such conditions. The swell made the lowering, and later, raising of the lifeboat an extremely hazardous operation for the crew. Added to the absolute necessity of keeping the descending lifeboat on an even keel was the pendulum effect created by the ship's movement. Not only was the lifeboat swinging crazily back and forth along the ship's side, like some mad fairground installation, but the bigger swells sent it swinging outwards as well, away from the ship — and crashing back against the steel side. This was a smallish liner, of German registration, that didn't have stabilisers. Nor, with the life of a passenger at stake, did its crew have any choice.

Maybe it took ten minutes to lower the lifeboat into the water; maybe it was twenty. The drama, and likely tragedy unfolding before us, blotted out all else, even thought of dinner. With the four or five crew aboard hanging on for grim death, the lifeboat finally hit the water and quickly got clear of the ship. Suddenly smaller, seemingly unequal to the task, it headed purposefully off into the dusk towards a light that was no longer visible, a woman certainly dead of cold or drowned. We heard that the doctor was among the lifeboat's crew. The ship was hove to, and my husband speculated that the navigators on the bridge would be plotting likely areas for the lifeboats to search by dead reckoning. There was no other way, with sea and sky that bleak monochromatic grey for which the north Atlantic is famous, no hint of a sunset indicating west and east, barely a horizon and visibility maybe half a mile. Though frozen to the marrow, with nothing to see, we could not yet go below. A young mother temporarily out of her mind had died out there. What a desolate, ghastly, lonely way to go. The ship was moving again.

In 1964, there were no GPS, electronic aids or cellphones. But there was good seamanship. Sometime over an hour later, in the final stages of dusk, those few of us still keeping a silent vigil on the deck were rewarded by seeing the lifeboat's lights reappear. It was too dark to be completely certain that there was an extra body in the boat, well swathed.

Now they faced the final challenge. Getting the falls attached and the lifeboat raised and swung inboard was, if anything, worse for the crew than before. We winced with every clang against the ship's side, willed the fore-and-aft arcs to get no wider, please. After what seemed an age, the lifeboat was eventually aboard without a further tragedy.

And the woman, we heard later, although not over dinner (we'd missed our sitting and were firmly turned away from the second one) had — incredibly — been found alive. She was back in the hospital. One could only assume that when she came up spluttering and gasping to see the ship bearing her daughters steaming inexorably away, she had cast a vote for life. She knew she'd been seen jumping, and in her flimsy night-gown had perhaps lain on her back, waiting. Maybe she'd clung onto the doctor's lifering with its tiny beacon of hope, instinctively hugging her knees (ordinary folks had never heard of hypothermia in those days) to conserve what little heat she had.

A week later, on arrival in Southampton, a canny passenger sold a picture of the lifeboat hanging half-way up the ship's side to a major London newspaper. It was given a full half-page, headed *Rescue in the Atlantic*, or something like. Today someone on board, crew or passenger, would have captured the drama on a video or digital camera, and sent images within minutes all round the world. The shipping company's PR department would have gone on to red alert, arranging for interviews of the captain and hopefully, the rescued woman. They might even have tried to get the daughters to speak to breathless journalists on the ship's phone. Mother and daughters would be mobbed by the media on arrival, with chequebooks poised.

But then, forty years ago, journalists still respected privacy and passenger ships were still the preferred form of global travel, and passengers falling off ships were a rarity. When I did my obligatory Overseas Experience three years earlier in 1961, air travel was still an expensive alternative to travel by sea. For ordinary passengers wanting to get half way round the planet, the transition to air would take another few years yet. Within a decade, the passenger sailing ship and later the noble liner would have come to the end of that proud chapter of maritime history so intrinsically linked with the growth of empire and the nineteenth-century migrations of millions of dispossessed Europeans and Asians to the new world. By 1980 large ships appeared doomed to carry only oil and freight, but in the 1980s the pleasures of sea travel reasserted themselves in the form of seagoing temples, majestic cruise ships plying the oceans. As high above sea level as ten-storeyed apartment blocks, better equipped than most small cities, these ships dominate a harbour and terminal area.

There is a fundamental difference, though, which only those of us old enough to have done a passage by sea *when there was no alternative* can really understand. The modern cruise ship is one long party, hedonism expensively indulged and unrestrained. Are we actually in the Carribbean, the Med, the Pacific, the Indian Ocean or South China Sea — who cares as long as it's warm on deck, the beer's cold and the music's great? We might, if we can get out of our bunk before midday, pop ashore at the next port, do a spot of sight-seeing. The 'guests' — for so they are now artlessly called — are self-selected as moneyed party-goers and holiday-makers in an environment where the pursuit of pleasure is paramount.

Passengers, on the other hand, endured a sea voyage to get from A to B in the most congenial way possible given the chosen ship's comforts, the sea conditions, the climate and the company. Departures to the northern hemisphere were festive occasions, with huge crowds, bands, streamers; these passengers would be back. From northern ports, they tended to be gloomy affairs, with tearful families being wrenched apart, bereft grand-parents left standing on the wharf clutching their limp streamers. Like today's flight attendants, ships' crews had to serve the diverse variety of human beings who walked on board, united only by their desire to go to wherever the ship was going and ability to afford the fare, whether in wood-panelled first class or stinking 6-berth steerage.

The day I set off on my first sea voyage, aged five, I got mumps. It wasn't a passenger ship as such, but the 7527-ton *Port Dunedin*, built in 1925, noted as the first refrigerated motorship carrying New Zealand's farm produce to Britain. My father, aged 32 and not long returned from five years' war-time field hospitals in North Africa and Europe, was the ship's doctor to the crew and twelve passengers. The afternoon of depar-ture, one of the twelve passengers delivered an ultimatum: 'Either that child and her family get off or I do.' Captain Hazeldine, who valued his doctor more than an obstreperous Scotsman, invited Mr Mahon to have his bags put ashore by 1600 hours.

We sailed on schedule, with my father and I quarantined to a separate cabin, straight out into the teeth of a North Cape gale. It was to be an early introduction to seasickness, to a headache so blinding I can remember it to this day. Through the tightly closed porthole, green seas streaked with spume surged past. The ship, built for the roughest oceans, took a bit of a battering. Water broke through that porthole and flooded the cabin. Com-panionways on deck were ripped off. In my cabin, my mother read me stories. I must have slept a lot.

The best part of a week later, I was allowed on deck and saw those raging Pacific seas calmed to long, majestic indigo swells. I spent hours staring down into that gorgeous radiant navy blue which you only see mid-ocean, spotting flying fish skimming across the surface and rarely, a school of dolphins. I don't remember even a box of crayons being provided for a child's amusement, let alone whole restaurants and 'kiddie worlds' de-voted to keeping third millennium children from ever uttering the dread word 'boring'. The air grew balmy, the skies bluer than ever, the tropical sunsets golden and sublime.

My mother got mumps. The Scotsman walked through games of deck golf, kicking the pucks out of his way. He played bagpipes in his cabin late at night, wearing, it was rumoured, tartan pyjamas. My mother hoped he or his wife, preferably both, would catch her mumps. He got instead an ingrown toenail, which my father (apologetically, of course) treated without anaesthetic. The crew stooped to a rarely used revenge: they apple-pied the Scotsman's bunk.

The days passed quietly, soberly, gracefully. The day's run was posted on a notice board. In between meals and lifeboat drills we chatted with the other passengers, listened to crews' yarns, played deck quoits and golf. There were no films, no swimming pool, no entertainment officer, no chardonnay, no cocktails, no *bar*. Mr Preston took to beginning his day at 6 a.m. with a whisky in his cabin. On the ill-tuned piano in the saloon young Miss Whittington practised assiduously, day in, day out, for an ATCL piano exam she was to take on arrival in London. The scales got on everyone's nerves, but they respected her zeal and capacity for work. No one complained. Mrs Nike's suspect appendix stopped rumbling, to my father's great relief. The Scotsman and his haughty wife were left pretty much to themselves.

We passed through Panana's docks and refuelled at Curacao. Across the Atlantic it got colder and the days seemed longer, but we were clocking off the miles, 250-odd each 24 hours. Expectations of seeing other ships and land rose. We must have sighted the coast of England as we sailed up the English Channel, though I remember only Dover's stark white cliffs in the distance. One morning we threw our lines alongside a berth in the Royal Docks, and as we walked down the gangway the ship's crew and cranes were already hard at it, unloading New Zealand's wool and dairy produce for a still hungry and exhausted Britain. We had arrived.

Less than two years later, we did the return trip on the *Waiwera*, a liberty ship. Male and female passengers were separated into 4- and 6-berth cabins. Again it was a month, the days broken by meals and drills, the southbound journey broken by engine trouble resulting in three days in a Jamaican hotel — where I was so entranced by the sight of a sailing ship with three masts at anchor in Kingston Bay that I stepped backwards fully clothed into the hotel swimming pool, giving my parents a hell of a fright. Then Panama's donkeys again and the long Pacific haul to Auckland. Again those wondrous indigo seas, the flying fish, the quiet companionship enjoyed between passengers, and between passengers and officers. This time we were spared a North Cape gale.

I am grateful to have had those sea-passages as a child, which led to my OE voyages in my early twenties. I left on the *Oronsay* via the enticing west-about route of three Australian ports, then Ceylon, Bombay, Aden,

Suez, Cairo, Marseilles and Gibraltar (I remember the steamy night the Southern Cross, visible in the heavens all the way across the Indian Ocean, finally sank into the Red Sea — *now* I had left home) and returned on the radically new *Northern Star* via two long hauls: Southampton to Cape Town, and thence to Perth, Melbourne, Sydney and home. Unlike the *Port Dunedin* or *Waiwera*, these were purpose-built liners, where the passengers' comfort and entertainment were as important as merely getting there.

But the writing was on the wall. In 1964 we went to England via Panama and New York, and fished that poor woman out of the Labrador current. By the time we were ready to make a return trip to New Zealand, five years later, there was no doubt that we would travel by jet aircraft, a DC-10, I think. Waste a month on an enforced holiday at sea when at a competitive price you could do it in three or four days? Jumbos, cutting the time between New Zealand and UK to two days, were just around the corner. Today's affluent, restless young on cheapies, the hoards of air travellers at the world's airports facing the discomfort and tedium of a long cattle-class air flight, know nothing else. With the blinds pulled shut and movies to pass the hours, they cross the greatest oceans with only a toy aircraft on a computer screen to indicate that below are the vast seas which their own grandparents could traverse only by ship. Probably most have never set foot in a ship of any size, nor ever will — a pity. As food for the soul and spirit, there's not much to beat a well-run ship's steady, stately progress towards her destination across an ocean's glistening swells, through sunrise and sunset, storms and calms, under blinding sun and crescent moons, a world unto itself.

My daughters are luckier than most. In March 1981 we deliberately booked on the mighty P & O flagship *Canberra* for the first leg of a journey to Malaysia, to give them a brief taste of passenger travel before it faded into history. The experience also gave them a taste for starting the day with freshly baked croissants from the galleys, for continuous entertainment and for the large upper-deck swimming pool. We hardly saw them, though I recall we signed plenty of drink chits. They were certainly not spending their hours quietly marvelling at the blueness of the Tasman Sea.

Ironically, there was an airline strike on at the time, and hundreds of desperate travellers had besieged travel agents' offices for every last available berth on the *Canberra*. That week it was the fastest, indeed the only way to get across the Tasman.

Tessa Duder

PART TWO
RUNNING FREE

So Many Days

So many days on the water.
The light lay on it like silk,
the wind ruffled it, darkening
its surface, till the water was
a small familiar voice rustling
against the hull. Rain fell, warm
and steady, blackening the teak.
Afternoons the wind came in,
full of spirit, and evenings
it died away, leaving the water glassy
at the head of the bay, the trees dark
on the headland, the sky pale behind.

So many ways to be happy,
until at last the best one:
on our last morning in the Bay
you came walking towards me
out of the crowds on the quay.

Sailing home that night, with the moon
a sliver in the black sky, a thin rind
above the shoulder of Cape Brett;
the whole coast was ahead of us,
with all its dark islands, and the rushing
water under us, and the stars glittering.

The summer now shrunk to these:
your face in sunlight, and the sickle
moon.

Anne French

The Adventures
of the Good Ship
Whimaway

SARAH ELL, although brought up in the seaside suburb of Takapuna, never showed much interested in sailing as a child. She got into dinghy racing in her late teens, sailing Sunbursts from Wakatere Boating Club in Devonport.

From there, she moved into keelboat sailing, including the *Whimaway* years, serious stints racing on women's crews on the MRX and Ross 930 classes, and in 1997, sportsboat sailing, when the Magic 25 class was introduced to New Zealand. Her current thrills come from being on the trapeze and going as fast as possible.

Trained as a journalist on the *Auckland Star*, Sarah covered yachting for many years before she moved to *Boating New Zealand* for five years as sub-editor and eventually editor. Her published books include an acclaimed full-colour guide called *Dinghy Sailing*, an historical anthology and *Fired Up*, a popular sailing novel for young adults.

*B*rent's dad said he called her *Whimaway* because he bought her on a whim, to go away.

She was a Farr 38, an 11.6m, one-design, racer-cruiser keelboat. Brent's dad — better known as Captain Gribble — bought her on the aforementioned whim to enjoy a bit of cruising, and kindly allowed Brent and his pack of mates — myself included — to race her on a regular basis. Sometimes he attended, offering useful advice and winding up Brent in that way that only fathers can wind up their sons, and sometimes we just had the boat to ourselves, a bunch of 20-somethings with the common aim of sailing hard and having as much fun as possible. Over a period of about five years we regularly campaigned in the Royal New Zealand Yacht Squadron's various series, including some very memorable Squadron weekends at Kawau, plus numerous other local races and four Coastal Classics, the 120-mile Auckland to Russell race at Labour weekend.

Due to the size of the boat, she was best sailed with eight people, but quite often we sailed with only six or seven. When we really couldn't find any friends, we could sail her with as few as four (we took line honours in the Te Kouma race one year only four-up). The make-up of the crew varied over the years, but there was a hard core of usual suspects, a group of friends who also played indoor netball and touch rugby together. Some of the crew were sailors of international standard — Andy S went to the 1996 Olympics in the 470 class, with Mat as his training partner — and sometimes we had to make do with a bunch of ring-ins, who were quickly inducted into the ways of the *Whimaway*.

By virtue of his parentage, rather than his organisational skills, Brent was the skipper. Brent had been a champion dinghy sailor, and went on to be a professional yachtsman, but he constantly ran on 'Gribble time', which varied from between ten minutes and half an hour behind New Zealand standard time. Whenever he told us what time to meet at the boat, we always asked, 'Is that regular time or Gribble time? Should we show up a quarter of an hour later?'

While we always put our all into the racing, having fun was definitely a big part of the equation. Boating and alcohol are not a good combination out on the water, but back at the marina, yachties and drinking go together like rum and Coke. Music was also a very important part of the experience. To a generation raised on FM radio and music videos, having an appropriate soundtrack to your life is vital. Fortunately, *Whimaway* had an excellent stereo system, including that must-have for the modern racing yacht — cockpit speakers. Because the speakers were mounted in the backs of the cockpit seats, it meant that the skipper and tactician got the best sound quality, but also meant they had to put up with excessive volume at times so the crew on the rail could enjoy the music. Music came in handy for psyching up the crew between races — something hard, fast and loud usually did the trick — and for whiling away the time when there wasn't enough wind to start. When we were doing serious short-course racing the stereo usually got turned off at the ten-minute gun, but on the longer races we quite liked to have some music on when rocking along. I remember one day creaming along on a tight kite reach along the north side of Motutapu, the crew lounging on the rail in bright sunshine, with The Feelers' *Venus* blasting out of the speakers — heaven on earth, *Whimaway*-style.

Occasionally when the portable CD player was not an option — usually because Brent had been on Gribble time and had forgotten it in his rush to make it to the boat — we had to resort to Captain Gribble's collection of tapes. The only remotely bearable ones were Neil Diamond, and many's the time we rocked back to Westhaven on the rum and Coke, singing along to *Cracklin' Rosie* and *Sweet Caroline*.

Another advantage of the cockpit speakers was not only to psych ourselves up, but also to psych out the competition. If we could beat people with the stereo on, it implied we didn't even have to try that hard. One Wednesday night race finished with an intense tacking duel up the Westhaven wall against one of the top 38s. Tack for tack we slowly gained on them, and passed them, all the while blasting out a hard dance song with the repetitive motif: 'get *down* to the funky *shit*'. It must have been incredibly annoying!

Another 'soundtrack' incident — fulfilling our desire to have our heroic moments backed with suitably climactic music — came at the end of the Round the Islands race at Squadron weekend. We had led most of the way in ideal conditions, with most of the race downwind. However, it was a long beat home from Motuora, our two chicks and four puny boys on the rail versus the massive combined weight of a crew we nicknamed Captain Najork and his Hired Sportsmen, after the Russell Hoban book. As the wind freshened, we got as much weight out to windward as we could, cranked up the stereo and prayed for the finish line to come as Captain Najork closed on our stern. We managed to hold them out, and crossed the line to the strains of Radiohead's *Karma Police*: 'This is what you get/this is what you get/this is what you get/when you mess with us!'

We all leapt to our feet cheering and hugged each other, including Brent, who eventually realised he'd let go of the helm and that we were in grave danger of running into somebody if he didn't take urgent evasive action.

As we motored up Bon Accord Harbour to anchor and thence to drink, Radiohead still blasting, our competitors caught up. To our surprise and delight, the Hired Sportsmen were lined up on the rail, chanting our (unofficial) theme tune 'A-wimoweh, a-wimoweh' in tribute. It was a proud moment.

Later in the evening, as we partied frantically ashore (there's no point in winning on the water if you can't cut it at the bar later), one of Captain Najork's crew approached, with a message from the great man himself: 'Captain Najork says well done.' Brent was too taken aback to do anything else but smile and nod, but later on we howled with laughter and plotted that the next time Captain Najork beat us, we would send over one of our crew to say to him sincerely, 'Brent Gribble says well done.'

We were always grateful for the competition provided by the Hired Sportsmen, of course, and the entertainment we got out of using cunning and skill to beat someone who could afford to buy speed. We also admired Captain Najork's fantastic, black, traditional-style launch, which had a cannon mounted on the foredeck, like Captain Flint's boat in *Swallows and Amazons*. One of the Hired Sportsmen would blast turnips out of this first thing in the morning in response to the Squadron's 8 a.m. morning wake-up shot (whereupon you are supposed to leap out of bed, hangover and all, and hoist the burgee).

Which brings to mind another story. One day we were so hung-over we had no idea we had hoisted the burgee upside down until we had sailed all the way home and circled around the Squadron committee boat a few times, as they started some match-racing off the Westhaven breakwater. Eventually the gesticulations of one of the white-clad race officers alerted us to our breach of etiquette. As we hurriedly lowered it to the deck, Brent was heard to mutter, 'And while we're at it, we may as well piss on it and set it on fire.'

Speaking of hung-over, such a state of dehydration and low blood sugar was never unpleasant for too long, thanks to Brent's tried and true, proven morning-after revitalisation foods. There is nothing like waking up to the sound of water slapping on the hull (usually as some poor fool from a nearby boat dives in for a morning swim, without thinking that quite a few people have already been up and performed their morning ablutions), not sure if you should sit up and activate the latent headache lurking behind your eyes, and have someone bring you cold orange juice and cream crackers slathered with butter and Vegemite, then lie there feeling warm and comfy while they fry up a huge feed of bacon and eggs.

We always ate really well on *Whimaway*. Captain Gribble was a fantastic cook, and even though Brent would have difficulty organising a social function in a brewery on land, he was very good at provisioning. He always managed to procure just the things we felt like eating after a long race or a hard night (see above). All food tastes better when eaten in the open air, especially when you've earned it by racing good and hard. Brent's mum always made us a wonderful casserole to keep us going in the Coastal Classic, to be consumed just before it got dark (which varied between somewhere off Leigh and somewhere north of Tutukaka, depending on the breeze). To the poor suckers on the rail, these little bowls of steaming stew, dotted with peas, accompanied by a slab of white bread coated in butter, tasted better than any gourmet restaurant meal and were just the thing to make the long, dark night ahead seem bearable

The exception was on our last Coastal, in '98. When it came time to heat up the casserole we discovered that we were out of gas for the stove. Even though we were having a cake walk — already north of Tutukaka on a spanking reach and no sign of the wind dying — the idea of there being no hot food until the Duke of Marlborough nearly caused a mutiny. Initially we cursed Brent for not checking there was enough gas before we set off. Then, the next morning after arrival in Russell, we cursed him again when we discovered that in fact we had a nearly full tank of gas, it was just that the solenoid connection had come loose.

The other time we missed out on our Coastal casserole supper was during the hell race of '96. We made our quickest time ever — just over 14 hours for 120 miles, not bad going — but it was also the most unpleasant piece of yachting I have ever done.

We had a blustery easterly the whole way, providing us with a beam reach and a huge, rolling, side-on swell. Frequently, the only part we could see of the boats next to us was the tops of their masts, and I was constantly poised to let the vang go in case we broached. It was way too windy for any of us to come off the rail for the whole 14 hours, and too rough for us to heat up the casserole anyway.

The only time I went below was to go to the toilet, whereupon the motion of the yacht caused me to fall on to — and break — the kauri louvres on the cupboards opposite the head. When I came back on deck, Captain Gribble warned me not to lean against them. I told him, thickly, that it was a bit too late for that.

Once we reached Cape Brett we had to gybe, which was hairy to say the least. I had naively thought that the final twenty miles into Russell would be the easy part of the trip, with the wind well aft and a nice broad reach into the Bay of Islands. Wrong again! The wind had swung round more to the north, so we found ourselves on a tight two-sail reach in pitch darkness. *Whimaway* was a bitch to steer at the best of times, and in these conditions keeping her from wiping out was a major struggle. She constantly wanted to round up, so helmsman Andy S had to bear away almost constantly. Because the steering was so heavy, it was my job to sit down to leeward and, when Andy yelled that we were about to wipe out, shove the tiller hard to windward to help him bear away. I then had to let go suddenly when the boat responded, or else he'd scream at me again. It was testing, to say the least.

The other thing that made the trip unpleasant was my allergy to cold water. Seriously. I suffer from a rare condition called cold water urticaria, which means I get an itchy red rash and hives when my skin comes into contact with water colder than blood temperature. The easy way to avoid this occurring is to take antihistamine before going sailing — a simple enough precaution, but one which I neglected on this occasion. My reaction probably started out as hives, but by the time we got to Russell, my hands and feet were so swollen up with fluid that my knuckles were invisible and it felt like I was walking on cushions. By the morning most of the swelling had gone down, however, and the magic bacon and egg breakfast made the world seem all right again.

I was just about to write 'I have never wanted to get off a boat more in my life', when I realised that isn't actually true. On the way back from our first *Whimaway* Coastal, I wanted to get off so badly that I rang my parents from Tutukaka and asked if they would consider picking me and some of the crew up from there.

'Are you sick?' asked my father. 'Are you injured? Are you in danger?'

'No,' I replied. 'There's no wind and a huge swell and we're going to have to motor the whole way and I'm bored.'

'Well, get back on the bloody boat then,' he said kindly.

I'm actually glad I did get back on board, because otherwise I would have missed probably the most magic moment we ever experienced on *Whimaway*. Towards the end of the trip home, which had taken much longer than we expected, we were sailing down the Rodney coast in the dark. It was raining, and our visibility was further hampered by the fact that I wasn't wearing my contact lenses, Andy S was wearing glasses but couldn't see because it was raining on them, and Brent and Andy K just can't see that well. Everyone else was either seasick or down below, asleep. We were trying to find Flat Rock off the seaward side of Kawau, quite a large lump of land which we did not particularly want to hit, upon which there is a light which flashes every seven seconds. As you can imagine, we were having some difficulty finding it, and feeling rather nervous.

Just as we were starting to get really worried, we realised we were not alone. Shooting past the boat in arrows of light, illuminated by the phosphorescence which seems to be particularly strong around the Kawau area, were two or three dolphins. They were just playing with us — cruising in the bow wake, dropping back to the stern, then shooting off out to the side and back up to join the ride at the front again. Under the water, their bodies were completely outlined in light, with a fiery train flowing out behind, like waterborne comets. When they jumped clear of the water or broke the surface to breathe they disappeared, black on the black water, then lit up again as they submerged. We watched in awe, our own bodies covered in glowing particles as the waves broke over us too and flowed down the deck like showers of sparks.

Knowing that dolphins are traditionally good luck for mariners, we felt confident that they wouldn't let us hit Flat Rock. In fact, the dolphins grew tired of us and cruised off into the dark when we were still a few miles from it, but we appreciated their support.

Although we saw dolphins quite frequently while out racing or cruising, our only close-up encounter with a full-size whale was with a dead one. We were out training (or drinking and chatting more like) in the Rangitoto Channel when we saw a large white object floating in the channel. Initially we thought it was a capsized boat, until we sailed closer and found it was the white underside of a very dead minke whale. Floating upside down, its striated throat distended with gas as it decomposed, the whale was almost as long as the boat. A single seagull stood bewildered on top of it, as if it had found so big a meal it didn't know where to start. It was most definitely a hazard to navigation.

We radioed the Coastguard: '10-4 Rubber Ducky, we got ourselves a dead whale here.' No, seriously, we did the whole 'Coastguard, coastguard, this is *Whimaway*.'

'Go ahead *Whimaway*.'

'Um . . . we've come across a dead whale in the channel and we thought someone should know about it.'

'Thanks very much, *Whimaway*, we've had quite a few calls about the whale. Where are you now?' Quick check.

'By a buoy.'

'Right, well it seems to be coming in on the tide. Thanks for keeping us updated.'

It wasn't as good as a live whale sighting, but we were pretty excited anyway. And it was on the front page of the *Herald* on Monday.

All good things have to come to an end eventually. The *Whimaway* era drew to a close when Brent's dad decided he would get more use out of a launch, and Brent wanted to take his sailing and organisational skills overseas. Reluctantly, she was sold to a Dutch father and son out at Bucklands Beach.

Our last outing was the Red Sock Salute at the start of the finals of the 2000 America's Cup. Along with hundreds of other boats, we motored around an inner harbour circuit to show our support for Team New Zealand. The new owners were on board, and I chatted to the son about his plans for giving our beloved girl a bit of TLC.

'Well, if you're going to paint her, you can get rid of that horrible orange stripe,' I said cheerfully. 'Dreadful colour — we've always thought it made the boat look terrible.' He stared at me for a few moments, before replying gravely, 'Orange is the national colour of Holland.'

I have never seen her since.

Sarah Ell

Learning to Capsize

IT MIGHT SEEM unlikely that a high-profile rock musician should also be an expert and experienced sailor. In Andrew Fagan's case, the sailing came first — as a kid growing up in Wellington, in arguably the toughest combination of boat and conditions imaginable.

The harbours around wind-swept Wellington are demanding enough in any sort of sailing craft, but especially in a P-class, those racy seven-footers which since the 1920s have been the first boats of nearly all New Zealand's top sailors. Sail a P-class and you can sail anything, it's often said. And one of the essential skills learned early by their young skippers is the not-so-gentle art of capsizing.

*T*he wind was on the water. No doubt about it. I saw it and thought at times that it could see me. Dark patches pushing fast across the Port Nicholson Harbour surface. 'Here it comes' — talking to my uncertain self.

I'd seen it before, safe on my push-bike on the way to school, or on extremely 'windy' days, from the window of the bus going around the Cook Strait bays, the wind urging the sea into huge breaking waves. Terribly windy Wellington. Most people didn't pay that much attention to it. Wind seemed always to be just there, around the rugged edges of Cook Strait, in the day, or late at night, pushing light rubbish down empty streets, keeping the trees on the move, an annoying background player. It meant a lot, from what I could see. White sails on the Wellington white-capped sea, heeled over hard, going somewhere, it had to be me. Gender unspecific, user of the wind, sailor of the sea, I volunteered to see what it would involve.

Before you learn to sail you must learn to capsize. First time I fell over (capsized) the bottom of my seven-foot P-class looked a lot larger than I'd noticed before. Instead of being above the water, I the sailor, appeared to be actually in it. All 'coldy' body shock on spontaneous immersion, and a hull floating higher than I'd ever noticed before. The instruction label on my *Titanic*-style, overly bulky lifejacket should have read ' Do Not Attempt to climb onto Centreboard to Right your Vessel'. It was what I urgently needed to do but couldn't, so I clung on getting chilled and despondent, my well-varnished centreboard the focus of many seemingly desperate moments. Someone came to save me, a soaked post-race victorious R-class crewman chest-high in salt water and miraculously walking on the close inshore seabed. My P-class came ashore upright, pushed from behind, all wet and suddenly dangerous, mainsail flapping its machine-gun malevolence.

Safely ashore, sodden mainsail banished to its nasty sail-bag, I realised that 'sailing' in Wellington was the last thing I ever wanted to do again. I'd made a big mistake. It wasn't for me. No way. The paper round to pay for the boat, the whole enormous pre-adolescent enterprise teetered on the brink of a collapse dictated by authentic, primal, wind-driven fear. I'd lost it. There was no way forward. I would have to learn to capsize or never again return to that 'theatre of gusting danger', Port Nicholson Harbour. My sailing future felt bleak.

Over we went again, capsized by the wind, this time the chance of a 'dry roll' as the sail hit the water, clambering over onto the centreboard, high side up, no wetness to be felt anywhere. Standing up on the leverage platform called centreboard, wishing the thing up, then there it is, the salvation of mast and sail rising from the spooky depths of salt water, into view, swiftly rising up, then above you, the way they should look: wet sails and a mast blocking out the sky. Rejoining your 'command' afloat once more, water dripping everywhere. The desperate rebirth of a sailing entity.

It wasn't all bad, and seemed to get better. Summer light airs, coffee aromas drifting north from the factory south of Evans Bay. Peer group pressure to capsize for 'fun' and the inevitable familiarity bred from practice. I thought I'd earned the confidence of a hardened capsizer. I'd continued to practise the 'art' involuntarily for a few years until the P-class trials arrived at the top of Evans Bay. It was my last season in P-class and if I was to defend the honour of the Evans Bay Yacht and Motor Boat Club I would have to pull my finger out. Was I a 'wuss' when it started blowing? I had my suspicions. I'd had a bad start . . . all that capsizing. Horrible P-class. Huge sail area, mast too far forward, too much weather helm.

Surfing off the top of a short north-westerly wave, pleased with my competitiveness having rounded the top mark up with the front bunch, the bow of my *Born Free* seven-footer refused to respond to the usual oxygen requirements. Down, down deeper into the saline solution of Evans Bay. Then goodbye helmsperson, the expected catapult forward, skipper touching the mainsail, upside down goes boatland and wetly shocked be the sailor at the interruption to a fiercely important race. This was not the right time to stop and we needed to go again. The recovery started well, up came the wet sail, then over she went again. Of its own volition a P-class cannot be expected to point up into the wind mercifully when you need it to. Multiple capsizes became the order of my wet morning. My competitors raced on, down to the bottom mark, then . . . I lost sight. Sodden and slowly chilling, I let the wind get the better of me. Hanging grimly on to my diligently polished upturned hull in Balena Bay, mast in the mud, patrol boat rescue, sole defiant survivor angry with the early signs of exposure. A 'Did Not Finish' ruined my overall chances and reinforced at a subconscious level a resounding sense of having once again been defeated by that relentless Wellington wind.

Having consolidated my fear of capsizing on numerous P-class occasions, I finally graduated to Des Townson's Starling Class and a realisation that not all sailing boats are such unforgiving dogs. I got more confident at capsizing. OK dinghies brought the realisation that some New Zealanders are more 'strapping' and better to windward than the lighter 'weakling' ones, and that us weaklings had to strap on two stones' worth of salt water-filled, hot water-bottled 'weight-jackets' in order to be competitive on windy Wellington days. That was okay except when the wind inevitably triumphed, to leave me in the water clinging to the recently capsized and righted boat. Worn out but still wearing a 'weight-jacket', too tired to climb up and aboard, just clinging, hanging on to the hull, the sonic assault of wet flapping mainsail, desperately removing and flinging the heavy jacket aboard, hopefully followed by my non-drowned self.

Lifting the surface from the sea, sometimes the Wellington wind can legitimately be seen as 'demonic'. Riding downwind aboard my fourteen-foot Ron Given Paper Tiger catamaran on a club day, Saturday raceland competitive moments. I had no reason to expect anything malevolent in wind world. Capsizing was no longer surprising; over the years I thought I'd been practising. I didn't see it coming , but it probably saw me. Down went the catamaran, twin bows elevating the sterns and off fell I, forward and flying into the fully battened mainsail, stoically clutching the long tiller extension arm. It was a tiller extension arm once attached to a pair of rudders and boat, now adrift and alone with me. The boat got away, wind grabbing at the half-exposed windward hull and webbing, flipping it up and over, far out of reach, multiple capsizing on its own, way down the bay, not a thought for me . . .

My buoyancy aid kept my head above water. Other madly keen racers ploughed past nearby. 'You all right? Can't stop, crucial handicap race.' It was quite relaxing, floating on the surface, all buoyant and stranded, waiting to be rescued, rudders dangling nearby under the surface, hung onto by me. Sort of peaceful, resigned, floating defeated, knowing that the wind was the winner. Took my boat away. Left floating, and thinking, I'll never learn to capsize.

Andrew Fagan

Caul of the Sea

CHRISTCHURCH WRITER Barbara Newburgh's story will ring bells with those apprehensive novice sailors, especially adult novices, who've experienced their first capsize and found that the sea, in this case the Christchurch Estuary, is not necessarily a deep and dangerous place.

She has enjoyed sailing *Happy Cat* with her husband many times since, in the Christchurch Estuary, Akaroa and Lyttelton Harbours and the Marlborough Sounds.

*M*y enjoyment of the water began and ended at the age of eight during a class trip to the local swimming baths. Descending into the pool, the water had only reached my midriff when I started gasping for breath. My lungs were imitating a deflated balloon when the impatient teacher yelled, 'Get out of the water, you silly little girl!' I left and never returned.

My mother was full of sympathy, not being a swimmer herself. In those days mothers didn't storm the principal's office, ring talkback or contact 'Fair Go'. She did, however, assure me that I would never drown, because I had been born with a caul over my head. This was exciting news. What on earth was a caul? Apparently it is a thin sheet of membrane which is usually removed and discarded straight after birth. In olden days cauls were greatly treasured by seamen, who wore them in tiny bags around their necks. Possessing one or being born with one, my mother said, meant that you would never drown. It was nice to be unique in this way, but I wasn't keen on testing the principle.

By teenage it was great to own an up-to-date bathing suit and frolic in the sea, but I never ventured further than hip-height, the spectre of that standard 3 teacher always hovering nearby.

Twenty years ago came one of those moments in time when nature supersedes one's misgivings and doubts. I had met a charming man who owned a small catamaran, and one Sunday it was arranged that Bruce and I join some friends for a sail on the Christchurch Estuary. This could be the beginning of a Fine Romance.

Then I saw the *Happy Cat*. I had sailed around the world in my late teens, but that was on a 20,000-ton ocean liner, not a little trampoline on floats, without even proper seating arrangements! Love may be blind, but I couldn't bring myself to undertake the caul test just yet. So it was decided that Bruce, Patty and George could get their pants wet on the *Happy Cat*, while I would sail in style with Peter and Karen (Patty and George's daughter) on Peter's Sunburst.

Initial nerves gradually gave way to pleasure as Peter nimbly tacked across the water, telling us to move when we went about and duck our heads whenever the boom came near. I began to enjoy the flap of the sail and the salty air. The Sunburst was sturdy, I was in good hands, all was right with my world.

From time to time I would glance across at the *Happy Cat* with its purring crew, quite content to sit on their mobile puddle while we seemed to be only slightly damp from the spray. Yes, this was the best boat, that was for sure. Heave ho, my hearties!

We had begun some sort of turning manoeuvre, and supposedly Peter had everything completely under control, when suddenly there was a mighty gust of wind which caught him (and us) unawares. Within seconds we had tipped over into the briny.

Of course, as soon as the water reached my midriff away I went, gasping and spluttering, my chest heaving for air, complete and absolute panic setting in. Karen and I had landed near the upturned bottom of the boat, with me nearest the bow. I heaved a sigh of relief as I grabbed the bit sticking out the front and held on for grim death. Grim death! Now the caul theory would certainly be tested.

Meanwhile Karen, being a good swimmer, thought the whole thing one great joke and was placidly treading water. I bravely tried to join her laughter but as the cold water gradually froze my lower extremities, all I could produce was a breathless sort of wheeze. So that I wouldn't be looked on as a complete coward I gave a toot on the plastic whistle attached to my life-jacket, bringing hoots of delight from the crew of the *Happy Cat* who were circling our wreck in high spirits.

'How's the water, Barbs?' George always had a good sense of humour. 'Didn't think it would be warm enough for a swim!' Patty and Bruce were grinning. You could go off people, I thought.

My breathing wasn't quite so laboured by now — annoyance (or was it despair?) starting to take over quite nicely — when I was aware of someone calling my name. 'Barbara? Barbara?' It was the well-mannered Peter.

'Y-y-yes, P-P-Peter?' I gasped, my castanet teeth making speech very difficult.

'I wonder if you'd be so good as to let go so I can right the boat, m'dear?' He was so polite.

'Oh, O-K-K,' the coward answered. *How was I going to stay afloat if I let go?*

'Yes, won't be a tick,' he assured me, but by this time I had closed my eyes, cursing that useless caul and thinking, well, you were wrong there, mother! *And* there goes this great romance! Oh well, maybe it wasn't meant to be. He'd find someone much braver than me, a female crew member on a Whitbread perhaps . . . or a Naomi James . . .

Gradually my fingers loosened their manic grip, and taking what was surely my last breath I slowly sank down to my watery fate. My mind was certainly playing tricks by now, as I imagined my feet being caressed by some soft creature of the deep . . . but wait a minute! What was this? Oh no! Don't tell me I was standing on the bottom?

We were obviously over one of the Estuary's banks, and by straightening my legs I could stand on the bottom and still have head and shoulders above the waterline.

Suddenly I was laughing with everyone else — aren't we mad? Isn't this hilarious? I gave my whistle a toot of triumph.

Sheer relief took me up and on to the now-righted boat. Peter was pulling on the rope that controlled the sails while Karen grabbed a plastic bailer and I used my bloodless hands to scoop out as much water as I could. Peter then thankfully headed for shore.

I was still 'as blue as your jersey', as Bruce commented when he helped to pull me out later. 'I'm very proud of you, you did well for a novice sailor!' Followed by a rather enjoyable kiss, I might add. And what a relief to get into dry clothes and enjoy a mighty swig of rum. That must have been how the sailors felt in the old days, after a night's watch on the mighty main, steering their ship through turbulent waters, then going below for a meal and a tot or two. Oh yes, this sailing lark was great, I could thoroughly recommend it. I couldn't wait to get to work on Monday morning.

'Have a good weekend, Barb?' I would be asked.

'Oh, great thanks, we went sailing you know — and we capsized.'

'Oh really? Gosh, you were brave, I'd be too scared.'

'Nah, there's nothing to it. And anyway, I was born with a caul over my head, so there's no fear of my drowning,' I would assure them.

That day proved to be a watershed in more ways than one. Bruce and I have been together ever since. He has shared his love of sailing with me, introduced me to the *Happy Cat* and all its delights, from sunbathing while becalmed in Kenepuru Sound to pounding the waves in a 30-knot southerly on Akaroa Harbour.

Today I am grateful that the water no longer holds the fears it once did, either due to my mother's superstition, or maybe by just having the right teacher.

Barbara Newburgh, *Boating New Zealand*, 1997

It All Happened
at the Beach

TED DAWE was born in Mangakino in 1950 and, as a child of a teaching family, grew up in Ruatoria, Otaki and New Plymouth.

Childhood summers were spent first at Waipiro Bay and then at Otaki Beach where his grandmother lived. Later, as for many young Kiwis, languid beach days gave way to the intense cult of the teenage surfer, chasing the perfect wave at the multitude of Taranaki beaches between Oakura and Urenui.

Twenty years an English teacher in Auckland, Ted has just bought his first boat, a 12ft dinghy, powered by a two hp Johnson outboard, to use off Reotahi, on the Whangarei Heads.

*T*he day must end. We all know this. Fine white sand squeaks under our feet as we all labour back to the bus. The line stretches more than a hundred metres, the children tiring and we adults bringing up the rear. From the gloom of the sand dune I watch each emerging tramper become incandescent as they step clear into the low sun. Oblivious of their own enchantment they struggle on. From here they look like extras in a biblical epic reaching the promised land. I turn to Maurice; he sees it too and nods, as though answering a question. The sea bewilders and renews.

As a small boy my vision of happiness was constructed from salt water and grains of sand which were baked in sunshine. This was before anyone had invented Playstations or worried about skin cancer.

At the end of the year, when my parents went on holiday, we would load up the old De Soto and make the tortuous journey from Ruatoria to Otaki. Once there we would take over my grandmother's house for four or five weeks and our lives would move to a different rhythm. I can't remember what the adults got up to. You don't tend to notice that sort of trivia when you are a kid, but I clearly remember what we got up to, and it all happened at the beach.

We would arrive at the beach early, the black sand smooth and unwritten on, the lifeguards at home in bed and the only figures distant fishermen. The sea was always gentle and well behaved first thing in the morning but it made no difference; we weren't allowed in until those lazy lifeguards had planted their red and yellow flags. By this time the beach was no longer ours. People were starting to appear.

Old people with bags collecting seaweed and driftwood. Friends and enemies we had made from the previous day. And of course, worst of all, the families. Colonising the beach with umbrella, rug and picnic basket. Cricket and badminton sets. Marking out a space that was their private property. A piece of sand that became their turf for the day. Something was taken, something was lost.

Then the teenagers would arrive. The bodgies and widgies. Listening to Elvis Presley and Tommy Steele. Hanging about in the dunes where they could smoke and do other forbidden things. Learning the rituals of adulthood from their safe vantage-point.

Sometimes there was drama at the beach. A school of pilot whales lost their sense of direction and tried to head inland. Some of them were saved but most of them were dragged away tail-first behind a tractor. Another day I could see a group of people gathering in the shallow water. I ran down to see what they were looking at. A man had been carried and he lay face up on that wet margin of hard sand while a lifeguard punched his chest and blew in his mouth. A heart attack. Dead in the surf. Someone's dad I suppose. A big, heavy man without a hair on his head. It was horrible but I couldn't look away. Finally, the guard gave up and an impromptu cluster of pallbearers carried him slowly up the beach. I was nine years old. I went straight back in for another swim.

Some days the sea was angry and wouldn't let us in. Huge waves charged in all directions, like a giant splashing his feet in the bath. The grown-ups warned us about a mysterious thing called the undertow. I could see this giant wiggling his toe under the waves. On other days the water was thick with bluebottles and we would come out with red lines drawn across our chests and legs, as if we'd been scribbled on with a thick red pen. A woman from the surf club would rub vinegar on the marks and then we'd run back in and get a few more.

In the afternoon as the tide retreated we would dig for pipis and toheroas.

Sometimes we would stay till dark and my grandmother would arrive with a billy and milk and bread. We would build a fire and roast the pipis on a piece of old tin. There was always a piece of old tin on the beach. Later we would drink coffee essence and milk and listen to stories. When my grandmother was young she rode a Harley Davidson, so you see she had a lot of stories. We would bury our legs in the warm sand and lie back and stare at the stars. They seemed to hover just beyond our reach. Every now and then you chance upon paradise . . . but you never realise until later.

Later . . . years later . . . as a sixteen-year-old, I would wriggle out of bed at first light and consult my fickle god, the Tasman Sea. From the top of the cliffs in New Plymouth the sea billowed below me like a swathe of grey silk. Would I favour school with my presence today, or spend the day in meditation and worship, kneeling on the altar of my surfboard? After a moment of indecision I would ring Wayne and suggest he pick me up in his smelly old FJ Holden. We would argue about whether it should be Fitzroy or Oakura, or maybe chance our luck with the tricky breaks that rolled in between the two islands at Back Beach.

On arrival we would check out our fellow worshippers. There were the high priests who were out there. I mean *out there*! in the full meaning of these words. There were the rank and file like us, and then there were the pseudo-surfers who hung around in the carpark. The boards were big; mine was a nine-foot four Del with triple stringers. It was heavy, but you had to carry it as though it weighed nothing. We weren't tied to the fin, or skeg as we used to call it. If you came off, it was a long swim back to shore and you always assumed that any broken wave had a rampaging runaway surfboard buried in its angry heart, so you dived deep. No wetsuits of course. You'd have been laughed off the beach.

Once you were out there, it was a matter of waiting and watching. Although the sea throws the same waves at everyone, there the equality ends. Some surfers always seem to be at just the right point. They would carve their way across the face of an unbroken wave, showing their dominance and artistry. We watched with silent respect, recognising in their moves the intangible beauty of the human heart. We mortals would be pounded, time and time again, our boards were like unbroken horses desiring only to shed their clumsy riders and be free.

Imperceptibly, as the day got warmer, the legendary masters would withdraw. The waves no longer measured up to their high standards. The rank and file would fill the gap, fighting it out for position and dominance. Eventually even we would leave and attempt to fit back into land-locked society. It was a struggle, and we didn't try very hard.

Years later, travelling around Europe in a dying Volkswagen, hunting down the cultural masterpieces of the old world, I take a detour to revisit the sea. I wind down the cliffs into Nice and there it is, an emerald arc stretching forever. The river of cars makes it hard to stop. At the point where I am about to give up, a space presents itself and I clamber stiffly on to the pavement. Below the promenade the beach is a writhing blanket of people. No sand visible. To get to the water takes great care, each tense step perilously close to a face, every route violating some personal space. Finally the Med stands before me, glistening like a rainbow. Not a broken oil tanker but the slick from thousands of oiled bodies. The sea seems limp and warm like the body of a freshly dead animal. It lies around my ankles beaten and defeated. I can't bear it and head back up.

We're all on the old bus now, chugging along Ninety Mile Beach, the seats on the right side ablaze with the afternoon sun. Back for a kai at Whangape. The kids strangely silent, some sleeping but most lost in their remembering.

'Weren't we lucky with the weather, Maurice? It could have rained, like yesterday.'

He nods and then adds, 'It still would have been a good day at the beach . . . just a different sort of good day, that's all.'

Endless sand, green waves, not a person in sight.

On we go.

Ted Dawe

Making Music
in the Adriatic

GWEN SKINNER was a violinist with the New Zealand National Orchestra at 19, and her colourful life has included many years playing with the National Orchestra, the New Zealand Symphony Orchestra and the Auckland Philharmonia. She also worked in London, Sydney and New Zealand as a model, and published books on cruising, food and her mother's final years, as well as a satirical novel on orchestral life. Now 'retired' to a lifestyle property in south Waikato, Gwen runs horses, gardens and writes.

At 40, Gwen married champion yachtsman Bernie Skinner. Gwen had previously never stepped aboard a yacht, but when he suggested they build a boat and cruise the world, she took a course in navigation and was the navigator on *Swanhilde* during six and a half years' cruising between 1968 and 1974.

*B*y the time we Skinners reached Yugoslavia in our home-built forty-foot ferro-cement yacht *Swanhilde*, we had been living aboard for five years. We'd left Auckland with a complement of four: myself, husband Bernie, daughter Megan aged seventeen, and son Paul aged seven. But Megan had fallen in love before we set off, and after fifteen months afloat, had flown home from Acapulco to live in Devonport with her boyfriend and his family.

'At least,' we'd said, watching her disappear through the airport gate, 'our lives will no longer be governed by the next mail pickup!' But we felt terribly sad and bereft. For the rest of the trip there would be only three of us on board.

Megan and her fiancé John joined us eighteen months later, and we put on an amazing wedding in Jamaica. Recalling the sheer theatricality of the ceremony and colourful reception that followed, flamboyant might seem a more appropriate word to describe it. There was a massive and statuesque black priest in flowing gold and white robes, his face lit by an equally dazzling white smile; a wildly enthusiastic flamenco band in straw hats, gaudy streamers and shocking pink shirts twice as loud as their music. The reception was ablaze with rainbow-coloured flowers in yellows, bright blues, oranges and hot reds, and tables overflowed with colourful tropical fruit and exotic spicy food.

The ceremony itself took place in an old white stucco church, newly painted for the occasion, at Port Antonio on the north-east coast of Jamaica. The reception was held on Navy Island just off Port Antonio, where *Swanhilde* was tied up. It had been Captain Blye's naval retreat in the good old days, but was owned more recently by the late actor, Errol Flynn, who raised peacocks there. His actress wife, Patricia, was currently operating a dress boutique further down the coast.

An American couple normally resident in Jamaica but vacationing back in the USA, loaned the newly-weds a luxurious house complete with staff and swimming pool in which to honeymoon. Bernie and I were, of course, happy for them, but nevertheless it was with mixed feelings that we left them to their Jamaican idyll and continued cruising.

We visited Haiti, Bermuda and the Azores, then transgressing from our plan to stay within thirty degrees of latitude either side of the equator, decided to spend spring and summer in England. We were determined the trip should not become an endurance test, and sailing fifty degrees north might well become exactly that, but we had friends and relations in England.

We arrived at Falmouth on 15 June, early summer and a perfect time of the year. I remember the date because it was my mother's birthday, and we spent the day trying to locate a Post Office in order to send her a telegram. We then continued round the south coast to Sussex, and for most of our stay *Swanhilde* lay in Birdham Pool, close to Chichester, where expatriate friends ran a shop. We had every intention of leaving England before the cold weather arrived, but the ship's motor had developed a problem crossing the Atlantic, and we had to wait for new parts to arrive.

Snow had begun to fall on us before we were able to cross the English Channel, step the mast, and motor down the inland waterways of France heading to the Mediterranean. The weather was crisp and lovely most of the way, but we had definitely stayed in England too long. I took numerous pictures of Paul making snowmen on the quay at Lyon, and skipping to keep warm. Although he was now twelve years old, we had to teach him how to skip.

We exited the French canal system at Sete, and after a leisurely cruise along the French and Italian Riviera, eventually reached the Adriatic and made our way to Dubrovnik. Then we sailed up the Yugoslavian coast and dropped anchor off Otok Hvar (Hvar Island) south west of Split.

In order to understand the incident I'm about to recount, I must explain the circumstances leading up to it, otherwise I might be considered a weirdo or a crank — or at the very least someone suffering serious delusions. I might still stand accused! But I assure you I have the musical accreditation to back up the story.

I was in the original intake of musicians when the New Zealand National Orchestra came into being in 1946, later to become the New Zealand Symphony Orchestra. I graced (I hope) both New Zealand and overseas concert platforms for more years than I care to be exact about. I think I can say quite truthfully that I played in every Auckland orchestra that came and went — or came and stayed, in the case of the Philharmonia, of which I was a member for twenty years.

So when Bernie and I decided to build *Swanhilde* in our backyard at Birkenhead, then set out on what was intended to be a three-year world cruise (though it turned into seven), I made one non-negotiable condition. We would build into the boat a compartment to accommodate my two violins. Bernie, well aware he had an eccentric wife, was not even surprised.

Therefore we set off around the world with a German and a French violin stored in a watertight compartment below the waterline. In that location, the fish glue that holds fine wooden instruments together would be less likely to melt in the tropical temperatures wherein we had every intention of remaining. And now we were in conditions that would truly test the theory, cruising around the Adriatic in steaming hot summer, not a woollen sweater in sight. In fact, exactly the opposite.

Yugoslavians are nature lovers and overwhelming supporters of nude bathing. If you're cheeky enough — or your desire for a titillating shot or two for the family album is so strong that ethics don't come into it — all you have to do is cruise with your zoom lens at the ready. You don't even have to search for subjects. Entire families lie in unembarrassed serenity on the shingle foreshores on wooden boards, totally unfazed at being viewed in their birthday suits.

Otok Hvar was, and probably still is, one of the most popular nudist colonies on the coast, so if nudism is your thing, you've reached Utopia! But with a forty-foot boat at our disposal and memories of New Zealand's white sand beaches still vivid, we on *Swanhilde* felt no need to row ashore with scrub boards tucked under our arms to lie on the equivalent of Winstone's Quarry.

My own preference, in tropical heat, was for a bikini, and I happened to have purchased a particularly gorgeous leopard-skin one in Paris. Tanned from years of sunbathing and exposure to the elements, threats of melanoma not yet loud enough to worry itinerant seafarers, standing tall, blonde and in good shape, I was wearing the bikini the day we anchored off Otok Hvar.

Swanhilde was catching a gentle breeze, just strong enough to evoke that pleasant leisurely feeling of contentment that allows one to go with the flow, so to speak. We'd tucked in around a few rocky outcrops, sufficiently far from shore and the tourists of Hvar to luxuriate in that sublime feeling of independence and self-sufficiency that rewards those who cruise on well-found, well-provisioned small boats — as opposed to ocean liners.

Bernie and Paul had gone off for a sail in our little dinghy, so I had *Swanhilde* to myself. I lazed around, read a book, poured myself a drink. Then I decided that a little music would make my day. I would entertain myself, disturbing no one in the process. I would practise my violin for a while — get my fingers working — see how well or how badly I was playing after so long at sea.

I went to the compartment and took out my latest acquisition. While we were in England I had visited the world-famous music establishment Hills of London, and by exchanging the two violins I'd set out with and adding more money, had bought a beautiful old English violin built by Daniel Parker in 1714. The most senior member of the Hill family, over eighty years of age at the time, had been thoroughly intrigued at the thought of my bringing two violins on such a hazardous sea voyage. Some time after my purchase, he'd arrived unexpectedly at *Swanhilde*'s side as we lay in Birdham Pool and gifted me his own prized Hill bow. 'You can't do justice to one without the other,' he'd said quietly. Surely, I thought, on such a calm day and under the shade of a sturdy blue-striped canvas canopy, I would harm neither.

Picture the scene. A calm sea, a bright yellow day with sunshine reflecting off the distant parched yellow land, a blue sky with not a suspicion of a cloud, a white yacht at anchor flying a New Zealand flag and a tall tanned blonde standing in the cockpit in a leopard-skin bikini playing unaccompanied Bach on a violin.

Suffice it to say, the curious rose up in a body from the shingle. First one, then a few more, in canoes, on paddleboards, even swimming bravely, converged on *Swanhilde*. They shouted, clapped, called out for more and spluttered their requests, fascinated by the uniqueness — by the sheer mind-blowing incredulity of the sight.

'Tchaikovsky! Tchaikovsky!' they chorused. So I complied — and gave them Vivaldi, Brahms and Dvorak for good measure. They yelled and applauded, nearly drowning themselves in the process. There's nothing to equal a free concert with not even a collection bucket in sight.

Eventually those treading water began to head for the shore, followed by the paddlers and the rowers and the stragglers, until finally my audience had dwindled and disappeared. Enough was enough, I thought, I'd earned a long John Collins.

Then I saw a shiny red runabout approaching at speed, massive white jets of spray spurting from its sides as it cut through the water. It looked like a dame out of vaudeville arriving on stage in red satin and white feathers. Was someone about to arrest me for disturbing the peace? Was I to be accused of obscene exposure? Hardly likely, considering the naked bodies on shore.

The driver executed a flamboyant U-turn then cut the motor, and with an engaging smile and a great show of courtesy, handed a note up to me. I accepted it with a mixture of speculation and trepidation. Would I be able to read it? And assuming I could, would I feel flattered or flattened?

'We are enjoying your recital' it read. 'Please do not stop'. It was signed 'Amadeus Quartet', only the most famous string quartet in the world!

I wondered whether to accede to the request? Not to do so would be like ignoring a royal command. And why should I be shy? We were all on holiday.

I decided to play one of my favourites, 'Meditation' from Massenet's opera, *Thaïs*, the tear-jerker of all time, and followed this with 'God Defend New Zealand' — the part we all know before the words fizzle out — as a cryptic way of letting them know the show was over.

Then I poured the aforementioned John Collins. The day had been rewarding. My fingers were still working and my bikini had stayed in place — not that anyone would have turned a pubic hair if it hadn't!

Gwen Skinner

Two Records before Breakfast

ANTHONY SWAINSON'S passion for fishing has taken him off every coast in New Zealand and a few of the more remote islands. He has chased fish across the world, from the North Atlantic to the Coral Sea via the Baltic.

In the Celtic Sea he tried, but failed, to catch Atlantic pollack over the wreck of the *Lusitania,* but went on to write about the sinking of the torpedoed liner as well as the disaster that overtook the German High Seas Fleet in Scapa Flow.

Now 'exiled from the sea', living with his wife in semi-retirement at Wairakei Village near Taupo, he has settled for the gentle art of fly-fishing for trout in a different ocean — Taupo Moana.

*A*ndy Warhol said, in one of the most quoted epigrams of the twentieth century, summing up the zeitgeist of the Swinging Sixties: 'In the future everyone will be famous for fifteen minutes.' My fame lasted slightly longer, in fact as long as it takes for the *Pursuit* to run from White Island to the weighing dock at Whakatane.

It was late January and we had a three-day charter on the *Pursuit*. I have fished on the *Pursuit* for years. Each time has been a delight — a superb boat with an excellent and knowledgeable crew — but this was different. It was one of the best fishing trips. We trolled for tuna as far down the coast as Cape Runaway, then across to White Island and beyond, out to the Rangitira Reef where the wind increased and we couldn't jig for the legendary kingfish, but made do with big albacore and a rare short-billed spearfish.

In the evening an electrical storm came up as we approached our anchorage at Factory Bay on the northern coast of White Island. I went ashore to a landscape incandescent with lightning, and sheltered in the ruins of the sulphur factory. The pale nimbus that hung perpetually over the island glowed in the evening sun.

The skipper expertly anchored the *Pursuit* so we were out of the snow-storm of volcanic dust, and yet comfortably sheltered from wind and swell that quartered the bay from the northeast.

At first light I was spinning off the bow of the *Pursuit*, casting into the shaded water that the early morning sun had not yet reached. I hooked a large fish that circled around the boat. The skipper appeared and netted it for me at the stern.

'Trevally!' he said, 'and a big one — a very big one! What line are you using?'

'Five kg,' I replied, removing the small silver spinner from its lower jaw.

The skipper disappeared into his cabin and came out minutes later clutch-ing the IGFA Record Book. We live in measuring times; the International Game Fishing Association measures an angler's ability by the breaking strain of his line. It has a needlessly complicated system of declaring records; the different weights of each species have a line category in as-cending order of breaking strain.

'Let's weigh him, it might be a record.'

We did and it was; at 5.44 kgs it was bigger than the current record fish for the breaking strain.

'You must put in a claim,' and I said yes, but not immediately, for there was still good water at the bow of the boat that was slowly coming into the sunlight.

It would be wrong of me to suggest that on the next cast I hooked an-other fish; but a little later, again at the front of the boat, I hooked and landed a lovely 3.62 kgs kahawai (these are quite rare off the Island). It had *déjà vu* written all over it. The Book was brought forth and consulted, heads were scratched, and indeed this too was a record. The category was vacant, and the skipper wanted to be the first in the book.

Again that evening we anchored in the same bay, but the wind increased during the night and changed direction. The boat was covered with fine white ash. We washed it down and by late morning we were heading out into the swell and starting on the long haul back to Whakatane. The skip-per called up the weighmaster on the radio and asked him to be ready to weigh two record fish.

'Didn't tell him what they were — keeps 'em on their toes,' he added.

As we quartered around Whale Island the local Radio Bay of Plenty came within range and we heard a newsflash announcing that the *Pursuit* was due in at four o'clock with two potential record fish.

'Tell me, skipper,' I asked, sharpening my pencil, 'will I have to sign any autographs? Does Whakatane have any Record Fish Groupies — you know, like the Rolling Stones?'

'Not really,' he replied, 'but you will get a big kiss from the mayor's daughter.'

'Oh goody,' I said, clapping my hands.

'Have you ever seen the mayor's daughter?' he asked archly.

We came slowly across the bar and could see people milling around the weighing dock. Crowds were everywhere. Mothers clutched babies and held them up to see the boat coming up the river against an ebbing tide. Big men with the sea etched in their faces toted camcorders and speculated among themselves in low whispers. Perhaps on board the *Pursuit* was Whakatane's first 225 kgs yellowfin tuna, a record marlin, a rare broadbill swordfish, or even a dirty great hapuka seduced from the abyssal chill and as big as a small milking cow, its carcass swelling black in the sun. It was the year of the warm sea, when anything was possible.

The weighmaster started to swing the davit out over the icebox. The skipper, puzzled, indicated we didn't need it. It squeaked back into place. We opened the box and lifted the two relatively small fish out on to the deck. Only the people from IGFA would have been impressed. There was a collective sigh of disappointment, like a breeze that makes the sand run along a dry beach, and my fifteen minutes of fame were over. Everyone vanished as if on some secret errand, and we were left alone with my embarrassment and a pair of scales to weigh and verify the catch.

The rest can be quickly told: the fish were weighed and forms filled in. In the only photograph I have, it seems that even the weighmaster has turned his back and is closely examining the paintwork on the door of his office. He was good enough to shake my hand, congratulate me and charge $40, that is $20 per fish. There was still no sign of the mayor's daughter.

Footnote: Neither fish was accepted, both being disqualified on technical grounds. A lot of people have delusions of grandeur; all my delusions are trivial. Instead of a kiss from the mayor's daughter, a week later I received a letter containing my $40. I'll never know which was the better part of the bargain.

Anthony Swainson

On Being the Skipper

POET AND EDITOR Anne French read *Swallows and Amazons* at the age of 10 and longed to go sailing, but didn't start learning until her early twenties, when her ex-Sea Scout brother bought a trailer-sailer. Together they had many adventures in Wellington Harbour, sailing out of Greta Point (the outboard, she says, never started).

She began crewing on a Townson 32 after moving to Auckland, and discovered the joys of Hauraki Gulf cruising in 'the most beautifully swift and sea-kindly boat you could hope for'. When she won the New Zealand Book Award for Poetry in 1988, she bought her first boat, a wooden Sunburst, followed by her beloved Townson 32, *Sir Christopher*, which she keeps in Auckland, and a part-share in a famous Spencer yacht, *Saracen*. She currently races on an Elm 36 with the Royal Port Nicholson Yacht Club.

Her summer holidays usually include a trip in *Sir Christopher* to the Bay of Islands, and she's thinking about entering the next Two-handed Round North Island race in 2004.

The first thing that goes is a good night's sleep. At first I found it hard to imagine why that should be the case. After all, I reasoned, I've been crewing on this boat for years. It's the same vessel, anchored in the same places. Now I own it, and I'm in charge. What else has changed?

But in the middle of the night the conscious mind isn't in control of thought. Something darker takes over. It wakes me every time the wind changes force or direction, whenever the zephyrs and puffs from the SSE that wrinkle the black water in the bay turn into baby breaths from the SE, or peter out altogether. The boat stops rocking with the wind's gentle kisses, and instead turns slowly, so slowly that the turning is imperceptible, pulled by the slow unseen force of the moon that slowly, inexorably drags the slick wet sac of the oceans towards itself, and then, ever so gently, like a slim girl pulling off her wet lycra bathers, with a soft ping, releases them again.

The moon's long fingers drag, the water under us slides up silkily over the rich dark mud of the shoreline, and the boat turns on its chain above the quick clouds of little silvery fish like a pale moon hanging in their firmament, like an anchored blimp in an empty sky advertising human pleasure. And in the skipper's bunk I am awake yet again, looking out through the companionway to match the silhouette of land and sky offered to my retina against the memory of what was last time I looked, and what it should be if we had not moved; listening for the water's rustle against the hull, or not, to decide whether we *have* moved, from what cause, and whether the anchor, which at dusk dug into the black mud on the sea's floor, is still holding.

Cruising yachtsmen, drinking in some salty bar, or getting noisily plastered in each other's cockpits at sunset, always tell each other stories of anchors dragging. No one who's capable of managing a vessel around the waters of the New Zealand coast hasn't dragged a few times. By day, and on land, when the rational self takes over, the skippers discuss the various kinds of anchor they swear by, or swore by until such-and-such an incident involving high winds or embarrassing loss of face convinced them to switch their allegiance from Danforth to CQR, or CQR to stockless, with chain all the way, or an anchor buddy, or a float, or two anchors out forward in a big blow in preference to a stern anchor as well . . . And all of it reasoned, with worked examples, diagrams drawn on bar napkins or old envelopes containing boat-builders' accounts, and frequent invocations to the implacable God of Physics.

But at night, lying alone and awake in the skipper's bunk, each of us is deserted by reason. We lie still, breathing steadily, trusting instead to religion. Religion, the blind faith that has holy Hindus spear their tender body parts and walk barefoot over hot coals; that makes good Christian ladies feel unworthy, whose smudgy sins amount to no more than occasional mild irritation with the grocer and a certain lustful dependence on crème-filled chocolates in front of the telly of a Saturday evening, yet has them lowering themselves and their creaking corsetry down to balance on swollen knees each Sunday morning, knowing that they will walk out the door in another seventeen minutes as pure as their own crisp, starchy bed-linen, the better to thank the vicar for a lovely sermon and pour tea for the other grateful parishioners, formerly sinners. Theirs is an entirely religious confidence that when the vicar says 'Go and sin no more', each mild soul is now as clean as a load of Monday's washing flapping in a good brisk breeze. It is a deaf and blind but devout faith that keeps the holy man's bare soles cool and airy as he strides across the black and red mosaic of fire, with no sensation of warmth or sizzle; and it is the same passionate faith that the cruising skipper pins her hope to in the middle of the night, riding at anchor. Religion may not be rational, but it can be a powerful comfort.

This — what happens in the skipporial brain in the middle of the night — is not the realm of science. Science is over. Forgotten. Irrelevant. Science helped you decide where to anchor, as you motored gently into the bay in the late afternoon, assessing the possibilities. Science gave you the words of instruction to the crew. 'We'll head up gently into the wind. When we come to a halt and start blowing back, I'll give you the word.'

Science assisted your foredeck hand to flake the anchor chain on the deck, to pay it out evenly, as the boat slid backwards towards the gap in the sea you had identified as the perfect spot, giving everyone sufficient swinging room not only now but for the forecast to come. Science, cool and precise, ensured that you fetched up more or less where you had always intended, with the anchor's tine well dug in to the mud, and the chain laid out, if you could only see it, along the sea-floor in a sinusoidal curve, impersonally recording that, in spite of your best efforts, once again you didn't quite manage to steer backwards in a perfectly straight line. Science told your crew how much warp to let out, and science ensured that they had made it up properly on the bollard, locked and safe, yet easily removed when the time comes to weigh anchor and go.

Science has played its part, it is true. But it is now the middle of the night, and reason departed hours hence. The skipporial brain is anxious. Night mares are galloping around it, eyes rolled back in their heads, baring their teeth. By day or on land, Stephen's story about the time the Piedy dragged in Waikalabubu, at the top end of Motutapu, is an interesting anecdote, ripe for analysis. Which way was the wind blowing? How strong was it? Would they have blown straight across into Woody Bay on Rakino, missing all reefs, isolated rocks and the Three Sisters (no chart handy to work out whether this is possible, so speculation can run riot), or would they have fetched up in the extensive area of foul ground at the northern end of the island? Either way, a Pied Piper would not have survived much past the first rending crash. But at night, reviewed from the skipper's bunk, the story takes on the force of prophecy.

'The wind had been blowing over the hill, into the bay, so there was a bit of noise. At about three in the morning we both woke up. Everything had gone quiet. We thought the wind must have dropped. Someone else might just have rolled over and gone back to sleep' (not me, you think), 'but my brother and I are a bit anal that way so we both got up to have a look. Sure enough, we had dragged, and were heading towards the top end of Rakino at a fair clip. Lucky we noticed.'

A Pied Piper is a Twilight's little brother. Only 22ft 6in long, but with the same sexy sea-kindliness of the 32, fast and as much fun as two young guys can manage with a spinnaker in a place like the Hauraki Gulf. Its anchor (I didn't ask what kind of anchor it was, since an anchor that is in the process of dragging is just a piece of failed technology and needs to be dealt to first, analysed later) couldn't have been that big. A 22ft boat, even a Piedy, doesn't need a 30kg lump of galvanised iron holding it in place. And Waikalabubu has reasonable holding, but I don't recall spending the night there. Nor wanting to, though in a light southerly it's probably OK.

All of which thoughts rattle around my brain at 3 a.m., causing me to heave myself up from the skipper's bunk and out into the cockpit (mind the creaky floorboard), just to check that all the seamarks I identified at dusk over my post-anchoring glass of gin are in the right orientation to each other, and the Stewart 34 next door is still the right distance away, and the shore is no closer and no further away than it was at sunset. Having satisfied myself, I resume my bunk and its slightly cooler sleeping bag for some more prayerful contemplation of the Infinite.

On a windy night, or one with a change of wind forecast, I'm up more often, every time there's the least change in the factor conditions. Amazing how, even after a hard slog out to the Barrier, ten delicious hours of proper sailing followed by dinner with wine, I can still wake with the least ruffle of new breeze to peer out. On a still night, though, I'll also be up to check how things look, even though the water is like glass, and the only movement is coming from the tide as it enters the bay, turning the hull to face its slight attentions.

It is, I have learned, the price of being the skipper. In the good old days, when the original skipper slept in the skipper's bunk, and I curled up round the sails in the forward cabin as befitted the Gulf's keenest forward hand, I'd wake only for major events, like big gusts, major wind shifts, or — once in a cyclonic moon — being roused to prop myself up against the mast, still tucked in my sleeping-bag, to watch the willywaws thumping down the hillside and hitting the anchored vessels in the bay till they twirled like bath-toys on the end of their strings. On a night like that, with the remains of a tropical storm battering the island, a term like 'swinging-room' takes on a whole new significance. But even then, I thought dragging was something that other vessels did. You watch, you call warnings at the dragees or fend them off, you long for dawn, but I confess I never expected that evil would befall our own trusty anchor. After all, I put it there. I knew we were well in.

Oh innocence! For it is not until you have dragged a few times that you understand the essential Zen truth of anchors. Any anchor can drag, except the anchor that has already begun dragging. All anchors, once in the seabed, are in a state of potential dragging. The only useful observation you can make about an anchor's tendency to drag is that it doesn't drag until it drags. The current state of the anchor has no predictive force. The half-life of an anchor cannot be determined, unlike that of uranium. And in the murky green waters of the Hauraki Gulf its position cannot be ascertained, nor its orientation, though the scientific mind knows that it has both position and orientation for as long as it chooses.

Heisenberg would have had a field-day with anchors. Indeed, it may have been Erwin Schroedinger's previous anchoring experience that helped him with hard problems in quantum mechanics. Schroedinger's Cat could so easily have been Schroedinger's Anchor, thus saving him from a thousand undergraduate misunderstandings. The anchor's potential to drag cannot be calculated nor predicted, except that it tends not to happen when it is under active surveillance, such as when skipper and crew are standing on the foredeck pretending to admire the view but actually wondering whether they are in and holding, or beginning an embarrassing drag into that gin palace 20 metres downwind. No, the anchor prefers to wait until its existence has been forgotten, when the dinner is nearly on the table and the cork is out of the bottle and the wine is being poured . . . or until everyone is asleep, and only the tired skipper's ear is half-cocked to unexpected noises. No self-respecting anchor bothers to drag under surveillance, unless it truly cannot help itself. Usually they wait, even then, for the instant of distraction. Even Schroedinger's Cat was the victim of the poison gas. The anchor is an active agent.

But once a cruising sailor has lost his or her anchorish virginity and understands the essential First Law of Dragging, banish all sleep! Welcome care! For now the novice skipper must lay down her head knowing that science and the old fella's sea-lore are insufficient to hold the boat in one place. The anchor may drag notwithstanding, and she, dear God, is designated responsible for noticing it and setting all to rights. She must rouse the crew from their frowsty bunks and send them forward to retrieve it (fending off any other vessels) while she gets the engine going and they motor out of danger in order to do it all again.

On *Sir Christopher* we use a fisherman's pick as our main anchor. Also known as an Admiralty anchor, it is the most anchor-like looking of anchors, a piece of nautical equipment even a landlubber would recognise and unhesitatingly be able to name. It was bought to replace, I was told, a Danforth that failed regularly in Squadron Bay, down in Te Kouma, on the western coast of the Coromandel. This was thought to be due (so the story went) to the large number of cans and bottles that lie on the sea-bed, emptied now of their pale amber contents and covered over with mud. The fisherman's pick was tried, and the fisherman's pick was found to hold in Squadron Bay. (Not always, I have learned, but that's another story.) The Danforth was consigned to the forepeak, and the fisherman's pick became the main anchor. It was somewhat after that when I made my first acquaintance with the skipper, then with *Sir Christopher*, and ultimately with the anchor. After nearly a decade of crewing, making the foredeck my own domain and mastering everything (anchor included), I bought the boat. The anchor is now my problem.

The pick is awkward to winkle through the pulpit, but it's light (too light to be safe, say the doubters), and it could do with more chain. Nonetheless, it holds in most places most of the time, and it's easy enough for me to manage on my own. For *Sir Christopher* does not have a motor-driven windlass; nor yet the convenience of a chain locker. (Spoil the teak decks?) Indeed, *Sir Christopher* lacks self-tailing winches. There are no self-furling sails on *Sir C*, no lazy-jacks, and nothing sheets back to the cockpit. There is also no depth sounder, no GPS, and no log fitted, although I can see that all of them would be useful. *Sir C* is not that kind of boat. We have a second and third anchor. We have a full wardrobe of headsails, a good set of charts and a *Nautical Almanac*, cruising guides, a VHF radio, a hand-bearing compass and a lead line, a decent respect for weather and tide, and we sail within our limits.

But the fisherman's pick has taught me, in a benign kind of way so far (*so far!*), that anchors can sometimes drag, and not always when you expect them to. It has also taught me that it's entirely my responsibility when it does. And that is why, now that I am the skipper, I get such a wretched night's sleep.

Anne French

Stoney's Story

GRETCHEN BRASSINGTON, re-named Brassi by the pre-school children she taught, grew up as one of six children on a Taranaki farm, with visits to the beach as rare treats.

Later she moved to New Plymouth, enjoying its nearby wild beaches, and eventually to the Mercury Bay area, where she and her husband owned launches and fished recreationally. She has three children and has published four successful books for young readers, three of them with nautical themes, under the pen-name of G. Brassi.

Her brother-in-law Stoney began his fishing career at Whitianga as a young 16-year-old just out of school. At present he lives in Te Anau with his wife, Gretchen's sister Meg. When not skippering the ferry to Manapouri he is building a boat of his own, a fine catamaran along traditional historical lines which he plans to use for charter work around the New Zealand coast.

*M*y brother-in-law raised his face to the stars and stretched his jaw in a yawn.

'Crikey, I'm tired.'

'You've got good reason to be,' I said.

Stoney and my sister Meg had been married here earlier, a simple ceremony beside the lake. Now, hours later, we were still on the beach, sitting around a dying bonfire under a thin crescent moon.

It was a great night for a walk, someone decided, and off they all went through the moon shadows, leaving Stoney and me in charge of the fire. A little later I heard my sister's distinctive shout of laughter ring out from further around the bay. She seemed very happy. I remembered her bridal kiss, and smiled.

The voices grew distant. Nearer at hand the black water at the edge of the lake breathed in and out, but all else was silent. Stoney yawned again. It's a strange sensation to gain a brother in middle life and know nothing about him.

'I hear you've been a commercial fisherman,' I said.

'Sure have.' He grinned, his teeth gleaming in the moonlight. 'My grandfather started me off fishing when I was five. Y'know, once he caught a salmon as big as himself.'

The slant of his head challenged me to disagree with his statement. So I did.

'Sounds like a fishy story to me.'

'It's God's truth. The old man was famous down Fairlie way for a retriever he had. Granddad used to stand on the bridge there, aim his shotgun over the side, and shoot the salmon in the river. Then his dog would swim out and retrieve them. Well, one year Granddad shot a fish that was as tall as he stood.'

'You don't say.'

I pushed a half-burned log further into the fire with the heel of my boot and watched it flare into flame. 'Did you live with your granddad?' I asked.

'Not for long . . .'

Stoney was silent a moment. I threw more wood on the fire and used my boot heel again to stir it into a blaze. 'And your parents?' I prompted.

'Mum and Dad were divorced when I was about knee high,' he said. 'We kids were scattered and lived all over.' He smiled. 'But the summer I turned eight — now that was a big one. Mum collected all of us kids from the various relatives and took us to the Pelorus Sounds. That's when we met our new father. After that we lived on Dad's farm on the coast, along with the dogs, pigs, sheep and goats. The boats and the beach too. No roads, no power. For me it was paradise.

'All the creatures in the rock pools on the beach — we kids found them straight away. The crabs, the sea anemones, the limpets and the sea squirts that spat like water pistols; that whole place was fascinating for us. We learnt how to catch snapper off the beach with those green cord lines kids use. We'd toss some broken up blue mussels into the sea to entice them in, one would take the bait, and *wham,* we'd have a major tussle on our hands. Eventually we'd drag in a big golden snapper and slide it carefully ashore. We'd smack it on the head with a rock and loop a piece of flax through its gills to carry it home.'

'Sounds like a good life,' I said.

'The best. Most warm days we'd be swimming in the bay. I remember one afternoon I saw a blue shark just after we'd all come out of the water. It was in the surf, idling along with only its dorsal and tail fins out of the water. It was the slow, side to side movement of the tail fin that caught my attention.

'I was pretty indignant it had chosen our particular bay to swim in. On an impulse I slid quietly into the water, and when I got out far enough I stood very still, trying to imitate a rock. Well, that shark passed within an arm's length of me. Its tail wagged by so invitingly I lunged out and got a grip on it. What a mad dance! Us kids, the dogs and the shark, all frantic with excitement. I backed up, out of the water, and landed what was probably the smallest blue shark in all the Pelorus Sounds, but I felt like a hero that day. I was the lifeguard who'd caught a killer fish barehanded!

'Weeks later, while my father and I were offloading a dinghy full of firewood on our beach, we spotted another blue shark. This one was much larger. Dad grabbed our harpoon from the boat and walked back into the sea up to his waist. I stayed at the head of the beach where the angle of the sun on the water was better for me to see under the surface. As the shark swam past Dad, with its dorsal and tailfins above the water, he gave it a mighty prod with the harpoon. The trouble was, I'd blunted the harpoon earlier when I'd speared a rock that I'd thought was a stingray, so the spear just bounced off the shark's side and I saw it race away flat out.

'But apparently it was annoyed, because suddenly the crazy thing spun around, flexed its body like a cat hunting prey, and it took off, accelerating straight for my father. The speed of it was awesome. I could see the power bulge of water at its head getting rapidly closer to Dad while he stood in the water wondering why there wasn't a shark on the end of his harpoon.

'"It's after you," I shouted. "Get out of there, Dad!"

'The shark got bigger and faster as it got closer. Dad was still waist deep in the water. From his lower view he wasn't able to see what I could, but perhaps he was lining up with that power bulge of water because he was holding the harpoon below the surface in roughly the right direction. He took a step back towards the beach and braced himself.

'The hurtling shark charged right onto the shaft of the harpoon so that the point entered through the mouth and came out through its gill slits. The creature was hardly wounded at all. Up the harpoon shaft it came, thrashing and chewing and trying to get Dad. He was backing away as fast as he could. I grabbed the firewood axe from the dinghy. Dad and the shark got as far as the beach, with the shark becoming even more violent and heavy as Dad hauled it half out of the water, and then the harpoon pulled out. The shark thrashed around, trying to get back into the sea. I aimed a couple of swipes at it with the axe, but missed and only raised sparks as I hit rocks. By now Dad had got the monster by the tail. He dragged it up the beach while I chopped more rocks with the axe.

'"Give me that, will you!" Dad yelled. I threw him the axe and he let go the shark's tail and waited for the right moment. Then *whack*, he hit it hard on the skull with the back of the axe. The shark lay still. I gazed at it, admiring its long, slender shape and iridescent blue and silvery-white colours. Such a thing of beauty . . .'

A knuckle of wood in the fire sighed and shifted in its bed of ashes. I felt behind me in the chilly bin for a couple of cold beers and threw one across to Stoney.

'I was sixteen years old before I met my first mako shark,' he said. 'Now those fish fairly bristle with teeth. They're similar in colour to the blue shark, but they're much tenser. They compare like a schoolboy would to a samurai.

'When I came out of school I scored myself the job of deckhand on a line fishing boat working the north-east coast of the North Island. We mainly set bottom longlines for snapper, but when the weather and tides were right we'd put the land over the stern and steam out into deep water to fish for hapuka with handlines.

'Small mako and blues were common then. We saw them most days. They took fish off our longlines, leaving only the heads, and sometimes one would hang under our boat and become a real pest, dashing out to eat our catch right before our eyes. We'd toss a strong line over the side, baiting it with half a fish on a big hook, and *bam,* it'd be mako madness. Those fish could leap way out of the water, end over end through the air. We'd pull one alongside, thrashing and fighting, and use a pick handle to hit it on the head.

'We didn't target mako, but small ones were a regular part of our catch. They were saleable, but as a rule they were too much hassle and danger to land. Even hours after they were caught those jaws could slam shut in a nasty bite. Once, when I was pulling up our longline, I found we'd caught a small mako by its dorsal fin. There are no hooks in a hauling line but this little guy had got snagged somehow. It was about the size of a baseball bat, and as stiff as one. I thought it was dead, but as I gripped it by the tail its eye moved. That fish was watching me, still alive and very angry. I worked the rope clear of its body pretty gingerly, I tell you! I gripped it in one hand and called to the skipper.

'"Hey," I said. "Look at this!" Suddenly there were splinters of wood and paint falling on the deck and darned if that fish hadn't chomped into the side of the boat before I realised what was happening. And there was the skipper yelling, "Go easy on my boat, will you!" '

Stoney laughed. He picked up his can and drank the last of it down.

'Hapuka fishing was great fun,' he said, 'but it was hard work. We used large weights and heaps of heavy line, with five baited hooks on each one. Those hooks could go through your hands if you messed up. We'd pull the lines up using a kind of power hauler we called a surge drum.

'Late one summer afternoon we were fishing for snapper, and when we'd pulled the last line in the skipper headed our boat out to sea while I stowed the fish into the ice box. The skipper got us positioned over a high peak of rock that the echo sounder showed had a large school of fish over it. There was a light breeze, so the skipper motored up the breeze and stopped the boat. We lowered two handlines each over the side, and as the boat drifted back towards the reef we felt the thump, thump of fish biting hard.

'For the next two hours we fished by drifting over those rocks, hauling in lines with three or four hapuka per line, then we'd motor back up the wind and drift back again with the motor idling all the time so we could use the surge drum. We were hand-hauling lines in as well, so busy catching fish we had to leave them lying around our feet. Just before dark the skipper motored up the breeze again, but this time he dropped the anchor so that we could hang back over the rock for the night. We were going to clean up the fish, have tea, and then work right through to daylight with one of us fishing and one sleeping in turn.

'When the engine was cut the silence was magic. Just the lapping of small waves against the wooden hull. The skipper cooked tea and I dealt with the four handlines. I secured them to the boat and cleaned and gutted the hapuka, throwing the entrails overboard and holding each fish over the stern by its head while I scrubbed it clean with a scrubbing brush. Usually caught fish were scrubbed on deck under the seawater hose, but that needed the engine running to work the pump. Rather than shatter the peace I used the ocean itself this time.

'I was very tired. We'd had a long day and it wasn't over yet, but I loved fishing and I wasn't about to stop. After cleaning half our catch I had room to move on deck again, so I hand-pulled one of the lines up. Darkness was closing in but my eyes adjusted to it as I followed the routine of hauling a couple of kicking hapuka to the surface. I took a firm hold of the line just above the first fish; and then I must have turned my head a moment because suddenly there was this violent jerk on the line and the sea beside the boat exploded, soaking me in a huge cascade of water. And instead of landing a large hapuka I brought in only its head.

'"Hey Skipper!" I yelled, "there's something out here stealing my fish!" '

'My senses were straight away heightened by fear. Have you ever experienced that? I could hear the tiniest ripples on the water, my skin was itchy with the hair standing up on my arms, and that dark water all around me was full of menace.

'The skipper came out and switched on the deck light. He stared out to the lit area beyond the stern and pointed.

' "That'll be it," he said.

'I looked, and saw a large yellow eye reflecting our deck light, zigzagging backwards and forwards behind the boat.

'"Grab a decent snapper from the ice," the skipper ordered, and he disappeared inside the cabin, to return a moment later with a heavy wire trace and the biggest hook I've ever seen. He tied a spare length of anchor rope to it and attached the other end to a bollard on the deck. Then he threw the gigantic baited hook out into the water. We stood there in an eerie stillness and watched that yellow eye approach the place where the bait was slowly sinking into the inky blackness.

'The rope line bumped and began to move through the water. The skipper braced himself with one foot on the side of the boat.

'"Pull like hell!" he yelled.

'It felt like we'd hooked an express train. The rope whipped off the deck and flew over the side faster and faster. Friction heated our hands even though we'd grabbed a sack each to protect them. As the length of rope came nearer to the end the skipper yelled, "Jump clear!"

'Together we jumped back and the rope snapped tight. The boat lurched sideways and we heard a huge splash out in the darkness.

'"It's a big mako," the skipper shouted, "and I'll bet that sudden stop gave him a headache!"

'The rope fishing line was bar tight and the boat continued its sideways progress.

' "Grab the biggest berthing rope and make a running noose in the end," the skipper yelled as he raced inside to start the engine. He shot out again and pulled enough slack in the rope to get two turns around the surge drum. The weight on the rope made it crack and pop as we hauled on it, and I was impressed by how efficiently everything worked. The boat was a giant fishing line and slowly but surely that mako was drawn in.

'" Here he comes," the skipper said quietly. Seeing the bulk of it made me almost wish it had broken the line and taken off. It was a mean looking critter.

'And then it seemed to lose the will to fight suddenly, as if it was sulking. Carefully we drew it up to the side of the boat. I leaned over to drop the noose over its tail thinking Dear God, don't let there be another one out there. I pulled the rope tight.

'Well, it was a good thing that shark was too big to bring on deck. With the tail rope tied off at one side of our stern and the rope with the hook still in the shark's mouth tied to the other side, the beast woke up. It began to roll and chew at the side of the boat. The skipper leaned over the side and whacked it on the head with the pick handle — no difference! The shark just got angrier.

'"We'll have to tow it by the tail," the skipper grunted. "That'll kill it."

'So we pulled up the anchor and began the long steam home through the oily black ocean. We couldn't fish any more anyway with the biggest shark I'd ever seen dragging from our stern by its tail.

'The next morning, safe in port, we used the wharf crane to haul that massive mako out of the water. It was longer than two men. I couldn't touch hands when I put my arms around it.'

There was laughter from further up the beach. Women's voices drifted on the breeze.

'Ston-eeee . . .' That was my sister. Her husband lifted his head and I knew I'd kept him to myself for long enough. Stoney said softly, 'I'm glad I stopped scrubbing those hapuka when I did. If I'd cleaned one more fish I wouldn't have been here to marry your sister today.'

'Yesterday,' I corrected, pointing to where the moon sat spiked on a treetop over the other side of the lake.

'Yeah,' Stoney said. 'Whatever.'

Gretchen Brassington

PART THREE

WORKING ON WATER

Sea Call

Let the radio pip and shudder
at each dawn's news

Let the weatherman hint
a gaunt meaning to the chill
and ache of bone:
But when the new moon's bowl
is storing rain, the pull of time
and sea will cry to me
again.

And I shall stuff my longing
in an empty pack
and hasten to the secret shore
where the land's curve lies
clad in vermilion — and the green
wind tugging gravely

There let the waves lave
pleasuring the body's senses:
and the sun's feet
shall twinkle and flex
to the sea-egg's needling
and the paua's stout kiss
shall drain a rock's heart
to the sandbar's booming.

Hone Tuwhare

Ship-Handling

JACK WELCH joined the Royal New Zealand Navy in 1959 as a seaman officer cadet and retired nearly forty years later as a Rear Admiral and Chief of Naval Staff.

Following his initial training at the Britannia Royal Naval College at Dartmouth, he specialised as a gunnery officer. During his time at sea he commanded four RNZN ships and served in the Antarctic, Indian and Pacific Oceans.

His second command was in the former minesweeper *Inverell*. Fifty-seven metres long, home to six officers and sixty-three crew, she had a reputation as a difficult ship to handle. A visit to the port of Gisborne in 1976 was to teach the 35-year-old Lieutenant-Commander a lesson he never forgot.

On a clear, calm, March evening in 1976, I stood on the bridge of HMNZS *Inverell* as the ship approached the port of Gisborne. We were to stop there overnight before proceeding to the Chatham Islands the following day. *Inverell*, one of the two surviving minesweepers in the Royal New Zealand Navy, was employed in sea-training of junior officers and ratings as well as fishery protection patrolling around the coast of New Zealand and its outlying islands.

The ship had assumed a high state of damage control and the sailors were at their special stations for entering navigational waters. Having sailed from Auckland two days earlier, we were to pick up some stores and personnel for transport to the Chathams. I was the commanding officer and naturally somewhat nervous as we were to berth in a port unfamiliar to me. Gisborne port has a small basin at the head of a dredged channel. In the channel, large ships lie alongside to work their cargos while smaller ships, such as fishing boats, make their way up to the basin to berth.

Inverell, at about 900 tonnes and 57 metres in length, was at the large end of vessels able to secure safely in Gisborne basin. However, there were no other berths available and we had little choice but to accept the wharf offered. It was theoretically a simple evolution as there was room to turn the ship, there was no tidal stream, the wind was negligible and the local small tug *Takitimu* was available to assist us in safe berthing. Certainly there were other considerations to add to my concerns, such as two feet of water under the keel and fishing boats already in the basin, but a well-organised and briefed team, together with our collective experience in ship-handling would see us safely through. Or would it?

For the commanding officer, or captain, the safe handling of a warship under his command is a major reflection on his professionalism as a seaman. There is an expectation that he will display élan and flair in manoeuvring the ship at sea and while berthing and sailing from a berth. He will have been well versed in the theory of ship-handling and, over many years as a junior officer, will have observed his former commanding officers as they carried out close manoeuvres in the company of other warships or berthed their ships in testing conditions. But it is not until he is placed in the exacting position of commanding officer that he will have the opportunity to demonstrate his acquired skill or lack thereof.

Those who can handle a warship well are sometimes described as having mastered an art that eludes many. Others are attributed with a combination of luck and divine intervention. The reality, as ever, probably lies somewhere in the middle. Rather like a car, there are good and bad ship 'drivers' — those who can do it naturally and those who struggle despite their best efforts. Some commanding officers, fortunately few, who are in all respects qualified and experienced to achieve command, never manage to display the necessary ship-handling ability expected of them. In some cases this has led to the limitation of otherwise successful careers, and almost certainly being restricted to one command.

Successful ship-handling is not easy, for many reasons. There is the expectation of the ship's company, or crew, that the boss will handle the ship in a manner of which they can be proud. Fairly or otherwise, many other human failings of the captain are forgiven if he can demonstrate that 'their' ship is well handled. Thus pressure is not only from on high, but also from within. A bad berthing can see the captain's reputation suffer and his prestige take a hiding.

Warships of the Royal Navies, unlike most vessels of the merchant service, are expected to go into waters and situations that are potentially dangerous. Close manoeuvring in a fleet situation with other ships is a necessary activity. Ships will need to refuel and restore from tankers and other support ships while at sea. This entails bringing the ship close along-side the supplying vessels for the transfer of fuel, food and stores while underway. Although well practised, this is a particularly hazardous activity, especially in rough conditions and at night. The chances for collision are greatly heightened and the captain is required to bring all his experi-ence to bear to carry out restoring safely.

Similarly, warships often need to manoeuvre at high speed in the close company of other warships, for tactical reasons. Manoeuvres will see war-ships at speeds of 25 knots or more, passing within fifty meters of each other. One slip can be catastrophic, as history demonstrates.

A more routine activity for warships is berthing, or mooring, at a wharf. Again, unlike most merchant ships, this is almost invariably carried out without the use of a pilot to assist and the captain uses his judgement to make the berth safely, without damaging the wharf or the ship. Every berthing is different, not only between wharves but also on each occasion at a familiar wharf. The weather and tidal flow will vary from day to day and present a different challenge to the captain.

Warships also do not normally have bow thrusters, or propellers situ-ated near the bow, which can assist the captain in keeping control of the bow when manoeuvring at slow speed. Tugs are sometimes used in more extreme conditions such as when there is very tight room in which to man-oeuvre or if tide or wind make their use mandatory. In most cases, how-ever, berthing is carried out without tugs assisting. The underlying policy for not using outside assistance is to ensure captains are able to practise ship-handling and develop confidence for the occasions when it is not available.

To add to an already complex array of challenges common for all ships, there are also huge variations of characteristics between ship types. These are very obvious when manoeuvring, especially at slow speed, as a ship's windage (that part of her exposed to the weather) makes her 'sail' in dif-ferent ways. The amount of power available and how this is applied intro-duces exciting moments until the propellers bite and the expected effect is realised.

Obviously size does matter, and a ship's inertia is directly related to her displacement. A large ship will 'carry her way' much longer than a small vessel. This also relates to the power a ship has and how quickly the way, or speed through the water, can be taken off when approaching a berth by putting the engines astern. Clearly arriving at the allocated berth with speed still on the ship will lead to collision and general disaster. The desired outcome when berthing is to arrive at or very close to the wharf with the ship stopped and parallel to the wharf, when the berthing lines can be passed and secured.

Each ship has its own characteristics that are a direct function of design. Most warships have large propellers, ample power and big rudders that are sited in the wash from the propellers, making steering much more sensitive. Others, for a variety of reasons, are designed less favourably for the ship-handler.

As *Inverell* and her trusty crew of seventy made her way along the approaches to Gisborne basin, my mind cast back to a word of wisdom which had been given me by the Commodore in Auckland, my senior officer and a former commanding officer of a ship of *Inverell*'s type, soon after I had taken command. It went something like this: 'Hmm, commanding *Inverell*, eh? No doubt you will get plenty of free advice on how to handle her and I won't offer too much. My suggestion is that you should make your approach in the usual way, allowing for wind and tide. When you judge you are at the right place, put the engines astern, turn round and face aft, close your eyes and count slowly to ten. Then turn forward and see what you can do to save the situation.'

The reason for this and other gratuitous suggestions was that *Inverell* had been a minesweeper. She was powered by two steam reciprocating engines of considerable power necessary for towing the sweeps she had earlier been fitted with. Unfortunately she had only one small rudder placed between the propellers and so needed to be making speed for it to be effective. To add to her unique characteristics, the propellers rotated the 'wrong' way and as astern power was applied to the engines, the stern was unpredictable as to which way it would swing, unlike frigates that are entirely predictable in similar conditions.

I had taken note of the good Commodore's advice during earlier berthings in Auckland, and until Gisborne had achieved considerable success in placing the ship safely alongside the wharf. Clearly I had enjoyed much luck and possibly my building confidence was misplaced.

Inverell entered the basin at slow speed and secured *Takitimu* to the bow on a short line. The master of *Takitimu* had been told of my intention to place the ship with her starboard side to the wharf. My plan was to go straight alongside and turn the ship for departure as we sailed the next day.

As the way steadily reduced, I asked the tug to pull *Inverell*'s bow to starboard, towards our allocated wharf. Meanwhile, I ordered the engines astern to stop her in the water while we passed lines to the wharf. To my great surprise, the gentle turn to starboard suddenly accelerated and I found the ship spinning at a rate which was getting uncontrollable. Ever alert to making the best of a rapidly deteriorating situation, I instructed the first lieutenant (in charge of securing the ship) to prepare to berth the ship with her port side to the wharf. With alacrity he took charge of the sailors and rearranged the lines and fenders for this revised plan. To my complete surprise and pleasure, Inverell's crazy swing stopped after 180 degrees and we were neatly placed alongside the wharf, pointing towards the channel along which we had just steamed.

With engines stopped and lines firmly secured to the wharf, I accepted the local, barely audible muttering about 'making up his bloody mind', and ignored the sharp looks from the seamen who had been put to unexpected trouble in changing sides at the last moment. Indeed, I made a rather lofty remark about flexibility and the need, as seamen, to be able to respond to fast-changing situations. Not wanting to kick over the traces for too long, I retreated to my cabin for a large whisky and to toast the god of ship-handling who had intervened on my side. Perhaps I was lucky in not colliding heavily with other vessels in the basin or with the wharf, but luck of course follows those who make it. Of course.

The night passed pleasantly enough. We loaded stores for the Chatham Islands and embarked some passengers. I remained on board and turned in early to prepare for an early departure. I gave considerable thought to what might have caused the sudden turn rate we had experienced in the basin and concluded that it was a combination of very shallow water (there had been about two feet below the keel) which can have a very severe and unpredictable effect when the bottom interacts with the ship's hull, and possibly an over-active tug which had pulled too vigorously. No matter — there was no need for me to disturb my superiors as we had broken nothing. As my airmen colleagues would say, 'Any landing you walk away from is a good one.'

The next day broke fine and clear. The sailors had been preparing the ship for sea since 5 a.m. and the engines were warmed through. Routinely, the engineer and first lieutenant reported at 5.45 that we were ready to proceed. I talked with the master of Takitimu and explained what we wanted her to do in assisting us from the basin. This included taking a tow from the bow and hauling Inverell's bow towards the basin exit. This requirement was acknowledged and at 6 a.m. all berthing lines were let go.

As the tug commenced to pull the bow I ordered the engines, one ahead and one stern, with the intention of moving *Inverell*'s stern to keep the ship lined up with the channel. Great in theory.

Having apparently learned nothing from the previous night's experience, I discovered to my increasing concern that the stern was quite happy to remain where it was. Nothing was happening, except that the tug continued to take our bow towards the other side of the basin. The tug was directed to cease pulling to starboard and to commence hauling us towards the exit. This she did, after a long delay.

The result of the increasingly heightened number of anxious orders I was issuing was that *Inverell* was making a rather rapid approach to the other side of the basin and I needed to take urgent action to lessen the impact of what was clearly an impending collision with the wharf. With both engines going astern in *Inverell* and the tug hauling hard to port, we arrived on the other side of the basin quite neatly except we had about three knots of way on the ship.

Inverell continued her way alongside the wharf with engines by now at full power astern, but having little effect in the shallow water. To my horror, I noticed a small shed that looked very much like a privy ahead of us on the wharf. The sheer of our bow was overhanging the wharf, and I watched in paralysed helplessness as it made contact with the shed (a crude corrugated iron structure). With much crunching noise, the sheer passed neatly along the side of the shed which initially resisted but finally succumbed to our superior weight and collapsed neatly onto the foredeck.

My immediate concern was that there might be an early user of the 'privy' who would have had his peaceful moment utterly upset, but investigation showed that it was empty of any human life and was in fact a store shed. The sailors showed much initiative in returning it, damaged beyond all repair, to the wharf. By now some control was returning to the ship-handling situation and we managed to make our way along the channel to the open sea without further untoward incident.

Seamen from other ships who had been disturbed by the noise of our antics had assembled to give us a loud cheer as we made our way past them. Much unsolicited comment was received, most of it uncomplimentary, and I was delighted to arrive finally in open waters, out of earshot.

It took my ship's company a long time to forgive me for exposing them to the derision of other mariners. If body language could talk, I would have been left in no doubt as to my parentage and lack of skills as a 'ship driver'. But time does heal, and after some months without further major disasters, I was once more accepted as a part of the family. My superiors too were benevolent in their judgement as I was later to command two frigates, handling them in an acceptable manner and damaging neither wharves nor ships.

The lessons I learned from this particular incident remained with me for the remainder of my career and never again was I to take for granted the hazards of handling a ship.

Jack Welch

A 'Boatscrew'
Wartime Wren

IN DECEMBER 1966 Jane Taylor answered an emergency call to skipper the Russell-Paihia ferry *Kewpie* and thus became, for three enjoyable years until pregnant with her fifth child, A. E. Fuller and Sons' first female captain.

There were some dark mutterings around the Bay of Islands waterfront. A skipper in those days was also ticket collector, engineer and cargo handler, and responsible for keeping the vessel clean and refuelled. Eventually on three occasions she was to skipper the famous Fullers' Cream Trip on *Kewpie Two*. It was pioneering stuff in the 1960s.

A decade earlier, Jane had sailed with her husband Pete to New Zealand in *Beyond*, a 45ft aluminium alloy cutter designed by Laurent Giles and owned by another adventurous young couple, Tom and Ann Worth.

Earlier again, in her mid teens and determined one day to serve in the Royal Navy, Jane had signed on as a bargee on canal cargo boats. Wartime England opened up many such jobs to fit young women. But a badly twisted knee saw her reluctantly signing off the canal barge and returning home at the age of 17, more determined than ever to realise her dream.

*A*s I unpacked my bag, my mother was horrified at the sight of my callused hands and the smell of my filthy clothes. She told me to burn the lot immediately in the incinerator as they weren't worth the expense of being sent to the laundry. At that time, no washing was done at home.

I hobbled around for several weeks, regularly massaging my knee with linament. I can't remember anything special about my 17th birthday but as soon as my knee had fully recovered, frustrated and bored, I suddenly decided one day to have a try at joining the W.R.N.S. before I was actually old enough.

I've no idea how I achieved this. Possibly birth certificates weren't required, which seems strange to me now, but I know I filled in a lot of forms, presumably lying about my age, because at the end of 1942 I duly reported to the W.R.N.S. training establishment at Plymouth. However, I had only been there a short while when a sore throat saw me in sick quarters with a high temperature which refused to come down. My age was then questioned and I was unceremoniously told to get back home and enrol again in 1943. They did allow me to remain until at last my temperature dropped to normal.

This brief period in Plymouth was important though, as it resulted in my meeting again, quite by chance, the two New Zealand girls, Virginia and Gillian Carlyon, with whom I'd been at school at Priorsfield. Older than me, they were both already serving in the W.R.N.S. in the 'Boatscrew' section, something I hadn't known until then existed and which employed only a limited number of women.

When I met up with Virginia and Gillian, they were both wearing the usual Navy-blue uniform jackets, but with bell-bottom trousers, the same as the sailors wore and with white lanyards stretched across their jackets from lapel to lapel, the special distinction of the 'Wrens' who worked afloat, handling harbour craft.

Immediately, taking into account the knowledge of boats that I now possessed, I set my sights again not only on joining the Navy but on becoming a seagoing member of the W.R.N.S.

Of course I still had several months to fill in before this could be achieved and I certainly couldn't sit around at home doing nothing. There was an obvious answer right there in my home village. I could join the Volunteer Women's Land Army on a temporary basis for as many weeks as I wished to pick dwarf beans on a farm growing them by the acre only a few miles from my home. This could have been a boring occupation, though a very healthy one, except for the fact that the 'Tip-and-Run' raids by German planes on the south coast were now almost a daily occurrence, especially in our area on the railway line which ran close to the coast between Exeter and Teignmouth. These only took place during the day and were very speedily carried out, bombing the railway lines and machine-gunning the trains.

After carrying out these attacks, the German pilots would amuse themselves by machine-gunning other completely innocent targets, such as us females picking beans. We'd hear the planes, usually two or three together, roaring in over the sea, and immediately we'd rush to the side of the field and hurl ourselves under the surrounding hedge, hoping we'd not been seen. It was very terrifying but soon over. The planes were so low we could see the grins on the faces of the pilots and the swastikas on the wings, but none of us were ever hit and I think maybe the pilots never intended to do more than scare us and give themselves a few laughs. Still, they were responsible for my only war wound. Throwing myself under a hedge one day, I landed on a bumble-bee which retaliated by stinging me viciously, resulting in my having a swollen and painful arm for several days.

Finally, having spent several months bent over, picking thousands of beans, the much longed for day arrived. I duly reported this time to the W.R.N.S. training establishment at Mill Hill, in the London area.

Quite honestly, however hard I try, I cannot remember much of my two (or was it three?) weeks' training. I know, on arriving in London I gazed in awe at the hundreds of huge silver grey 'barrage-balloons' floating in the sky above the city, the cables attaching them to the ground providing an almost impenetrable network and thus making it difficult for the German bombers to reach many of their targets.

For the first time I was to feel the ground vibrate as the bombs fell during the nights, after the wail of the air-raid sirens sent us hurrying to the basement clutching our bedclothes. We slept, or tried to, until the 'all-clear' sounded.

Most of our training was spent on learning the correct way to march, stand to attention, stand at ease and to salute. I'll never forget the day when our training finished, and we were asked which branch of the W.R.N.S. we wanted to serve in and if we had any preference as to where we'd like to be stationed.

I stated most emphatically that I wanted to be a Boatscrew Wren and I was then asked to give details of what boat handling experience I'd had and this was all noted. I also asked to be posted, if possible, to a submarine base, as by now my brother Tony was serving as an R.N. lieutenant in the submarine *Ursula*. I said I'd also like to be somewhere on the south coast, as my home was in Devonshire.

It was a great day when we were issued with our smart uniforms. I had never worn a hat in my life, never feeling at home in one, and this was the case, even with the delightful little round hats that were part of our uniform. The front of these was supposed to be worn just above the eye-brows but I felt happier with mine perched on the back of my head and I regret to say I was reprimanded for this many times in the years that followed. During wartime the silk ribbons around our hats and those of the sailors too, only bore in gold the letters H.M.S. The names of ships or bases were left blank.

I could hardly believe my ears when I was informed that I'd been accepted for Boatscrew and that I was to report to the submarine base H.M.S. Dolphin at Gosport; I guess that was one of the most exciting days of my life. I'd actually made it. I'd joined the Navy.

I had to go to Portsmouth first to get to H.M.S. Dolphin and here I had my first look at a town which had somehow survived hundreds of air-raids by enemy aircraft. Devastation and ruined buildings were everywhere and yet there were people everywhere too, still smiling and laughing and going about their daily tasks. I realised more than ever how close the war had brought people together and the sense of comradeship that existed, especially in places that had suffered terribly.

In the harbour itself, there were grey-painted ships of every size and description and the sight of them sent shivers of excitement through my body. This was the Navy of which I was a part, at last.

H.M.S. Dolphin or Fort Blockhouse as it is also called, lies at the mouth of Portsmouth Harbour and was at that time approachable both by sea, by naval launches and liberty boats for the personnel based there, or by road from Gosport, to which a ferry ran, from Portsmouth. This road ran past Haslar Creek where there was a large naval hospital and also the Coastal Forces base of H.M.S. Hornet. From there the road narrowed, continuing down the isthmus to Fort Blockhouse itself. On this road I was later to ride a bike hundreds of times, past the anti-aircraft emplacements situated there, going off or on duty from Dolphin to the W.R.N.S. quarters, some two to three miles inland.

Reporting to Dolphin for the first time, I crossed over on one of the liberty boats and on landing, had my first close look at the submarines based there, their long, grey, sleek hulls berthed alongside the concrete jetty as I walked along it above them. I was greeted cheerfully, in true naval fashion, by members of the submarines' crews, wearing their off-white submarine jerseys and bell-bottomed trousers. My excitement grew. There were naval officers, matelots (as I soon learnt sailors were called) Wrens and Wren officers, all around me.

I found that there were quite a lot of Wrens at Dolphin, but only five that were Boatscrew. I was introduced to them soon after I arrived.

Bridget Child, fair haired and fair skinned and rather a serious person, who lived in Gosport was the only Wren coxswain there at the time. She was entrusted with actually handling the high-speed 'barge' used by Captain, Submarines at Fort Blockhouse. The crew members were 'Billy' Eddy, small and dark, older than the others and the only married one. Then there was Pauline Sheffle, blonde haired and very glamorous, Lesley Pilkington, rather reserved and quiet, and Eileen Parnell, an attractive girl whose parents owned the Red Lion Hotel at Cosham. Eileen and I became very good friends but we all got on well together.

The Captain's other coxswain was a man and a chief petty officer. Tim Haley was a Cornishman from Fowey who was not enjoying very good health. Apart from being a coxswain of the barge, Tim was also the Captain's manservant so to speak, in charge of all his requirements ashore as well.

Tim was a darling and completely at home with his female crew members. He was to teach me all there was to know in handling a craft so completely different to a 'narrow boat'. It was Tim who introduced me to 'my' Captain, Admiral 'Reggie' Darke (known also as 'Pusser' Darke) who had been retired but who had returned as wartime Captain of Submarines at H.M.S. Dolphin.

To have girls as his crew must have been a horrendous shock to him, but he, like Tim Haley, seemed to be very proud of us and apparently often referred to us as his 'painted Jezebels'. Tim made it clear to me immediately that it was an honour to be a member of the Captain's boatscrew, that I must look smart at all times, the barge must be kept spotless at all times and that the handling of it must be done to perfection, whatever the weather conditions.

The high-speed craft had a black hull which I think was approximately 35ft long, with white topsides. The decks had a covering on them similar to lino, which we scrubbed every morning and was easy to keep clean. For'ard was an open cockpit containing all the controls. Passenger cabin amidships and in the aft cabin were the twin 60 HP Meadows petrol engines controlled by Bendix gear. The engines were maintained by an E.R.A. (Engine Room Artificer). He didn't go to sea with us unless a problem was suspected.

I had been issued with my bell-bottomed trousers and white gym shoes, both of which we wore when on duty, and the white lanyards which we wore across our jackets from lapel to lapel at all times when in uniform. Hair had to be worn up, off the collar, and I copied Pauline Sheffle's style of winding a narrow scarf around my head and tucking my hair up all around it. It was a style that many women in the services adopted during the war.

As the newest member of the crew I began as 'sternsheets-man' responsible for letting go or making fast the stern line or holding the stern alongside using a boat-hook.

We had been taught smart boat-hook drill, i.e. twirling the boat-hook then holding it aloft over one's head with both hands, and this drill was always performed prior to using it for holding the boat alongside while passengers came aboard or disembarked. When performed correctly, this boat-hook drill looked very impressive. My seagoing duties began straight away. I gained practical knowledge through experience. We were on duty for twelve hours by day or night alternatively. We were 'piped away' over the base's loud speakers when we were needed to take the Captain either alone or with other senior officers across to the Portsmouth side to one or other of the various landing places at the dockyard or collecting them and bringing them to Dolphin.

We sped across the harbour and took a pride in 'coming alongside' without even touching. I admit, though, envying on occasions the Boatscrew Wrens from H.M.S. Hornet who rushed around the harbour in their tiny 'skimming dishes', as they were called, just one Wren usually with a single passenger. Handling these skimming dishes looked great fun and far less formal than we had to be.

By now the worst of the air raids were over but they still did occur. If we were out on the harbour when this happened there was nothing we could do except watch as the bombs fell and the fires started turning the sky red above Portsmouth. If we were ashore in our duty cabin at base it was compulsory that we hurried to an air raid shelter as soon as the sirens sounded. Our shelter was in the small garden that separated the Captain's living quarters from the building in which we lived. From his building the Captain looked out over the jetty alongside which the submarines lay berthed, and he could also see his barge alongside the floating pontoon on the inside of the main jetty . . .

As the weeks went by, because of my previous boat-handling experience, I was fairly quickly promoted from sternsheetsman to bowman, and from then on into taking the controls when there were no passengers on board.

I was hooked immediately by the amazing manoeuvrability of a twin-screwed boat with Bendix gear controls. I had always enjoyed skippering boats and handling this one seemed incredibly easy. One could literally make her do anything.

My keenness and perhaps my ability must have been noticed, because before long I found myself also having instruction on the other launches used at Dolphin. For instance, how to use the incredible 'wheel-whirling' Kitchener gear perched on the stern of the long slender-hulled pinnaces and also taking the wheel on the large heavy diesel 'Liberty boats' which carried Dolphin personnel to and from base.

Meanwhile Tim Haley's health was deteriorating until the day came when he was medically discharged and I was promoted to take his place as the second coxswain, doing alternate duties to Bridget, but only where seagoing duties were concerned, not ashore. Before long I was rostered onto duties on the 'liberty boats' too, a job I thoroughly enjoyed.

Here I must mention the first horrendous error that I made not long after Tim Haley left.

For the first time, I and my crew had to take our boat over to fuel at the jetty at H.M.S. Hornet. I had never done this as coxswain before and to this day I feel ashamed of the mistake I made. Our barge, always being berthed alongside a floating pontoon with no tide to worry about, was made fast with short, fairly light lines, with an eye-splice in both ends placed over bollards both on the boat and on the pontoon.

On this occasion the tide was high and we were lying level with the top of the jetty. Without giving a thought to using different lines or to the fact that the tide might be ebbing, we used our short 'made up' lines. Having fuelled, one of the H.M.S. Hornet E.R.A.s who had been giving us a hand, suggested we went and had a cuppa with him. Knowing we had no duty trips due, off we happily went. I've sometimes wondered if this might have been intentional on the part of our engineer 'friend', because when we returned half an hour or so later, both lines fore and aft were absolutely bar tight due to the fast ebbing tide. Luckily, hacksaws were readily available and our 'friend' soon returned with one and saved the situation for us by sawing through the ropes, but not before the Captain's barge was hanging unceremoniously in the air. The story soon got around but I never found out if it reached the ears of Admiral Darke. From that day on I was known at Dolphin as Calamity Jane. Jane I've remained to this day.

Winter night call-outs were often chilly and wet. We wore thick jerseys, oilskins, our bell-bottoms, seaboot stockings and gumboots. I remember one quite amusing occasion when 'piped away' and still half asleep we rushed off down the jetty to the perpendicular iron ladder down which we descended usually onto the pontoon below. On this occasion however, the barge for some reason was at a different pontoon to its normal one which, unknown to us, had floated itself a couple of feet away from the foot of the ladder, something our usual pontoon was not able to do. I was first down the ladder and thinking my feet would as usual automatically land on the pontoon, I continued descending until I suddenly realised that both my boots were filling rapidly with water as I'd gone clean down into the sea. No time to change, I had to carry on with icy cold wet legs and feet until the trip was over.

Actually, at the finish of many of our cold, winter night call-outs, we were frequently welcomed on our return by some kind submariner offering us a swig or two, or many more, from a flask of 'pussers rum'. How welcome it was and how warming. Ever since my navy days, rum has been my favourite drink.

I earlier mentioned 'Bendix' gear with which by moving the two control levers in the cockpit one could literally make a boat do anything, but there was one problem which I encountered myself one day. If you moved the controls too fast through neutral to 'full astern' for instance, from being in 'ahead', once in a while you could find that you were still in 'ahead' and thus go 'full ahead' instead of 'full astern'. It was quite a recognised fault and could, of course, have disastrous consequences. We actually had an engineer working on our engines one day. We were on the inside of the main jetty and bows on to the concrete access 'bridge' which connected the main jetty to the shore establishment. We were having a trial run and moving forwards when the E.R.A. called out to me to go 'full astern both' which I promptly did, but going too fast through neutral, the result being that we went 'full ahead both'. The tide was fairly high, leaving just enough clearance for the boat under the 'bridge' as we rushed forwards but not enough for me. My top half was therefore swept backwards over the cabin top, as I pictured myself noseless and minus my breasts (things of which I was very proud incidentally) as in this position I was unable to reach the controls until clear again. Whew, I was only grazed but it was a near thing and a mistake I never made again. 'Calamity Jane' once more.

One other misfortune that befell me was on an important occasion when we had to collect two high-ranking naval officers from the Portsmouth side. With the boat performing beautifully I came alongside faultlessly at the landing, going astern to slow down. Unfortunately and without knowing it, as I went astern I picked up around one of the propellers a length of frayed rope that had been floating just below the surface. Instead of speeding proudly back to Dolphin with my important passengers aboard, I discovered to my horror that I could only crawl, and crabwise at that. Most upsetting to a cocky young female coxswain.

Sadly, although the reason I'd asked to be stationed at a submarine base was because my brother Tony was in 'subs', he was in the Mediterranean in the submarine *Ursula* at that time and never came into Dolphin in her, though he did come in briefly later on, in command of *Venturer*.

I find it rather difficult to recall the names of the subs that were at Dolphin while I was there. Two midget subs or X-craft were tied up near our boat and I remember *Telemachus*, *Tally-ho*, *Torbay*, *Rorqual* and *Porpoise* but there were many more. We all felt that submariners were very special men with a special relationship having to live together in such confined quarters. We admired them greatly.

At Dolphin, suddenly, several months before D-Day occurred (that famous day in June 1944 when a magnificent Allied invasion fleet of hundreds of ships and thousands of servicemen crossed the English Channel and landed on the Normandy beaches) a rather shattering event took place. All 'our' submarines slipped quietly away and with the roaring of powerful engines, their place was taken by a flotilla of Coastal Forces M.T.B.s (motor torpedo boats). Everything at that time being kept very secret, of course, we had no idea that this was about to happen, and were taken completely by surprise. From then on their almost unceasing movements coming alongside or leaving were, to say the least, extremely noisy, compared to 'our' subs. It always seemed to be the inside boat that had to leave, necessitating its neighbours having to start up their engines and move out of its way into Haslar Creek. It was almost too much for poor Admiral Darke, so used to the stealth of submarines. He was obviously quite upset over the transformation of 'his' base.

This flotilla carried out regular patrols into or across the English Channel, laying mines and in other ways generally preparing the way for the invasion fleet. For the first time, we witnessed the harrowing sight of craft badly damaged by enemy action, limping back into our base. I actually had a date one evening which never eventuated, my date's dead body, along with several injured sailors, being carried ashore that day, right in front of my horrified eyes. I guess we young folk matured fast during those times. But life went on . . .

At last, on 15 May 1945 came that most memorable day of all, V.E. Day —

Victory in Europe — when the end of hostilities was announced. Germany had surrendered. What fantastic news it was. I honestly think we all temporarily went mad.

Everyone was hugging and kissing. The sound of sirens, hooters and church bells filled the air and the material for a huge celebration bonfire miraculously began to appear in the centre of the parade ground right in the middle of H.M.S. Dolphin. When darkness fell lights shone forth everywhere — gone were 'black out' restrictions. Flames from the bonfire lit up the happy faces as many of us rode our bikes round and round and round it. We were all totally inebriated, either with or without the aid of alcohol, and some of the bikes finally ended up on top of the bonfire. I don't recall anyone trying to stop all this crazy behaviour. Authority seemed to have temporarily ceased to exist. Such exhilaration had to be accepted on such a momentous occasion.

Within a few days, of course, things had quieted down again and we carried on with our usual routine.

In July I turned twenty and then on 15 August we heard the literally earth-shattering news that an atomic bomb had been dropped on Hiroshima, soon followed by an even bigger one on Nagasaki and that Japan had also surrendered. V.J. Day had followed three months after V.E. Day. The war was finally over. Strangely, I don't think there were the same crazy celebrations on this occasion. I think perhaps we just accepted it calmly and thankfully, though perhaps with rather mixed feelings realising what a change was about to happen to our lives and being overawed by the fact that a lot of us would soon be out of uniform and back into 'civvy-street' again, leaving so many friends behind. As it happened, I and my crew didn't leave Dolphin until November. A few nights before our departure we celebrated with a last game of cards down aboard one of the submarines. The story later went around that it was 'Strip-poker' that we were playing, but I'm not going to enlarge on that. Regulations decreed that we had to be in our cabins by 2200 hrs (10 p.m.) but because of our imminent departure, having rather a 'to hell with it all' feeling about life, we threw caution to the wind and remained on board till midnight. We were seen leaving and reported. I suppose it couldn't be overlooked and we had to appear before the Captain and were duly reprimanded. This was my very last 'calamitous' effort at Fort Blockhouse. I was rather apprehensive about what would be on my Discharge Report, but I needn't have worried. It read: Kathleen Jean Marshall employed on Coxswain Duties in W.R.N.S. Boatscrew Jan. 1943 — Nov. 1945. 'An energetic W.R.N.S. rating with a pleasant personality and capable of very good work.' Signed C.R.M. Wood, 1st Officer W.R.N.S. (for Captain).

Luggage in hand, I climbed aboard the 'liberty boat' I'd handled so often and was taken across to Portsmouth dockyard, swallowing a big lump in my throat as for the last time I walked past Nelson's old ship, H.M.S. *Victory*. I'd achieved my ambition. I had actually served in the Navy, but those days were now sadly over.

What did the future hold for me, I wondered, as I sat in the train travelling south to Devon. Surely it was going to be dull after the life I'd been leading? It so happened that I needn't have worried at all.

Jane Taylor, *Rudders to Udders*
— and back again, 1996

'A Near-Derelict'
in Wartime

AS A BOY, Hank Cavendish got used to the constant upheaval and long sea passages demanded by his father's work in China, USA and Europe as importer, exporter, agent and broker. Home was Shanghai, then one of the world's centres of trade, commerce and corruption, its river crammed with junks, naval ships and traders endlessly fascinating to a small boy.

After the Wall Street crash of 1929 the family left China for good and settled in San Francisco. Young Hank, restless and bored, became a high school dropout and vagabond. In 1936 he joined his first ship, a 9000-ton Pacific tramp, beginning a career as a merchant seaman that would eventually encompass a hundred different ships under the flags of five countries.

In mid 1938 he'd been accepted for the crew of the *Research*, a brigantine being built for the Hydrographic Department to explore the South Atlantic and Indian Oceans. On 3 September 1939 Britain declared war. Hank's dream of wandering the oceans under square rig vanished. After two weeks' training, he began five years of war as a qualified merchant seaman gunner.

Not until the war ended did I realise it, but for five years I'd held a winning hand. Lady Luck hadn't merely smiled in my direction, she'd had her arm around me. The *Brockley Hill* was an example.

She was a London Greek; a 5000-ton, coal burning, clapped-out tramp built in 1919. And for twenty years, under five names and for five different owners had been worked hard, and thoroughly neglected. We knew nothing of this when we signed articles in Dock Street.

Ernie May and I shared a cab, and the remains of a half bottle of Scotch, on the way to the Surrey docks. Crossing Tower Bridge, the cabbie's comment was reassuring. 'You'll never see the swastika over the Tower, mate.' He turned out to be right. The Union Jack was still over the White Tower when we next saw London, but the rest of the area had been devastated.

Had it not been for the drink, I doubt we'd have gone up the gangway. We stared at the hulk in disbelief. 'Jesus Christ,' said Ernie, 'a floating antique, a collector's item.' She was truly a sad sight; rusted, battered sides, bluff bows, high poop and counter stern. A wrecker's yard would have rejected her. And as well as the dirt and rust, a month's stoke hold ashes lay piled around the galley and bunker hatch. We later heard that she had been due for the breaker's yard that year; that the outbreak of war had saved her bacon. Refusing to join the vessel though, would have been desertion, and meant trouble. We dragged our bags aboard.

Choosing a ship was never a problem for me. Having waited until I was penniless I would have to accept the first job offered, then do my bitching later. Yet surprisingly, this near-derelict turned out to be one of the happiest ships I ever joined.

Mick Kinsella, the Irish bos'n, accepted a tot and laughed at our petulance. He was short and greasy, a happy soul and I liked his style. He pointed out spare bunks, agreed the ship was a wreck but listed the compensations. Apart from essential work, he said, nothing was done about the decks; the mate just wasn't interested. Discipline was unknown, and although the food was rough, the cook was doing his best. She sounded better than she looked. Ernie May went ashore for another bottle and I made up my bunk.

There was no rush, we had a week in which to get her ready. The derricks had to be housed, hatches battened down and gear stowed. Once squared-up, she was seaworthy, but with hold sweepings ankle deep about the decks she looked more like a garbage scow than a merchantman. Yet, once at sea, with the ashes dumped and washed down fore and aft she'd be in better shape.

We had joined the ship in mid August, the week the Battle of Britain started. The German triumph in Europe had given them possession of the French airfields lining the Channel coast. From these, Goering intended destroying the RAF, the first step in the proposed invasion of Britain. During July, constant raids were made on our coastal convoys and Channel ports, and in early August south-east coast radar installations were badly damaged. At the time, 100,000 German assault troops prepared to cross the Channel. Britain had lost a thousand aircraft before the evacuation at Dunkirk, yet despite the shortage of planes and pilots, the RAF held on. It was touch and go — history was made during those few weeks. And high above our heads, over the Surrey docks and the middle reaches of the Thames, we saw some of that history being written.

Ten days after joining, the tugs eased us out through the locks and, as they did on every sailing day, my thoughts raced. A touch of exhilaration, that 'glad to get away' feeling; apprehension too. And a tinge of regret — for once I had met a woman who had seen something in me — and she'd had tears when we parted.

We steamed slowly down Limehouse Reach, the Isle of Dogs on our port hand. On the Greenwich side, in a setting of lawns and trees stood Wren's naval college and hospital, impressive and elegant. Between us and the foreshore, the Thames was slack at high water; the river of Pepys and Conrad; of two thousand years of history. The river I'd dreamed of as a boy, and would learn to know well in later years . . .

At Southend we joined the north-bound convoy. Before the war, sunken ships were noted on the chart and marked by buoys. Now, in the Thames estuary there was no need for these warnings. In the shallow waters outside the swept channel there were more sunken hulls than fairway buoys, the graveyard stretched for miles — masts and funnels the tombstones. And having kept to the unwritten wartime code, these sinking craft had struggled to get out of the fairway before going down. Over a hundred ships, a third of a million tons, had been sunk by mines alone that year in this area — the Nore Command. A sobering sight on the first day out.

Eight hours steaming saw us off Yarmouth and into 'E-Boat Alley'. These were small raiders powered with aircraft engines and capable of forty knots. They would lie off the buoys, inshore of the swept channel, and with hardly having to alter course, launch their torpedoes and race back across the North Sea. Fast, deadly, and always in the dark, they were seldom seen, but left in their wake burning and sinking ships.

The sky was black, the rain squalls heavy and frequent, and finding our way about in the dark that first night was difficult. The war was still new, and the knowledge that we were losing was depressing. Suddenly action broke out at the head of the convoy and speed was reduced to dead slow. A number of ships opened up, the gunfire was heavy, flares blazed overhead, and from the escorts and leading ships, streams of tracer squirted away to the east. Not slowing quickly enough, we nearly rammed the ship ahead, and I stood amidships with a mug of tea, my feelings a mixture of helpless defiance and loneliness.

Yet it could have been worse. At least we were taking part, could see the action and hear the racket. It wasn't the drawn-out anxiety we were to know in later years in those same shallow waters. When, in addition to the magnetic mine, the Germans were laying the acoustic and photo-electric mines. By mid 1942, serious air and E-boat attacks on convoys had eased off, giving us far too much time to wonder just what was waiting below the surface.

The last of the coasters turned off at Blyth, leaving six ocean-going ships, and ourselves leading the starboard column. I remember nothing before the incident, only that we were south of the Moray Firth, somewhere off Aberdeen. The weather was fresh and cold, a half-gale blew from the north-east, and just before dusk I was lookout on the bridge. With a snarling roar a plane passed overhead and was gone. There was the dull thump of an explosion on our port side. 'Gun's crew,' I yelled to the mate, and raced aft. And there, with the rest of the lads, watched helplessly as the raider swept wide to the north, turned, and came back down the port column. And knocked out two ships.

The first went up in a sheet of flame, a frightening, awesome sight. The second was one of Houlder's 'Grange' boats. Both lost way and dropped astern. The Grange boat, gutted, was still under repair on the Tyne seven months later. A near miss and two direct hits on a convoy of only six ships. By one plane. And he'd only missed us because of the reduced target area, his coming in from abeam. He raced away low over the water, heading for the fatherland.

The first ship burned fiercely, brightening the nearly dark sky. We steamed on, leaving the sickening picture astern. I was angry, frustrated — wondered how many had been killed. Any survivors would be crippled, burned, scalded from burst steam pipes. Our own defence against aircraft was an elderly Hotchkiss machinegun, a relic that usually jammed after getting a few rounds away. As planes didn't attack in the dark there was no need to stay on the gun platform.

We started to climb down, but our ex-passenger-ship steward-type gun layer protested. He insisted that the four-inch gun be loaded. I took my spite out on him. 'That's for surface raiders and subs, you dumb bastard,' I shouted, 'not for fucking planes.' We left him up there in the dark, alone with his dreams of glory.

We crept cautiously through the Pentland Firth, the degaussing gear destroyed by the near miss. The Navy patched it up in Oban and we joined the next convoy for Halifax.

The surface of the Western Ocean was unusually calm when we rounded the Butt of Lewis. An hour later, the signal flags went up. At first, speed was reduced to dead slow, followed by the order to stop. Our escort of two destroyers and a corvette swept through the convoy dropping depth charges. Deafening explosions rang through our empty hull, dislodging rust, sending the compass card spinning madly in the binnacle, and prematurely ageing the engineers and firemen down below.

With no way on them, ships drifted out of position and came close to colliding. Unable to manoeuvre, masters and mates verged on heart attacks. There had been no sign of a hit, no oil or wreckage came to the surface. The silence between explosions was uncanny. An hour later, the last explosive upwelling settled back on the surface. The Navy called it a day. We resumed formation and crawled on.

Some days later I scribbled a few notes. From the crow's nest that morning I had watched the convoy, fifty-odd ships spread over three square miles of ocean. The slow-moving, rusted and salt-encrusted cargo liners, tankers and tramps, together with the escort, made an impressive sight. The clouds were low, the sky a monotonous grey and the sea colourless. But there was an occasional touch of colour. These came in hoists of bunting, coded signals from the commodore, often for us alone and passed down the column, ship to ship.

Our old vessel, well past her prime, was powered by a wheezing, triple expansion, steam reciprocating engine. In good weather she could maintain a comfortable eight knots, but head winds would hold her back. She would also lose speed when the boiler fires were being cleaned. This resulted in a loss of steam pressure — and the slowing of the screw. As last ship in the column we endangered no one astern, but the eagle eye of the commodore missed nothing. The flags would flutter. 'G-7,' or whatever our position number was, headed the signal — followed by a terse 'Keep station.' This happened in nearly every watch — with a slight variation, an occasional 'Don't lag.'

Burning coal as we did, smoke resulted — a considerable amount at times. Before sailing, all masters and chief engineers had been cautioned about this — smoke was a dead giveaway to submarines. Our convoy number, followed by 'Make less smoke' became so familiar we no longer referred to the code book. And after one particularly black display the comment was long and sardonic, 'G-7, please, we are trying to avoid the enemy.' Our captain, outwardly calm, fumed inwardly. Our answering flags were always at the ready — 'Message received, doing our best.' A Nelson-like reply from a clapped-out Greek tramp.

The convoy dispersed on 28 August, and we arrived in Sydney, Cape Breton on 5 September. We made the run to St John, and two days later watched the first slings of cargo come aboard — in dismay. It was pig iron. 'Christ,' said Ernie May, 'If we cop one now we'll go down like a greased anvil.' A subdued breakfast hour was half-over when a shout, 'Hey, come and look at this' brought us out on deck. It was worth seeing. The few tons of iron already loaded were being discharged. The foreman didn't know why, but the orders had been changed and we were to load pit props — a full cargo. Five thousand tons of buoyant, worry-free Canadian timber. Just how fortunate we were we found out later.

For ten days the prevailing westerlies helped push us along. The autumn weather wasn't bad; half-gales much of the time and overcast skies; an everlasting greyness that suited my mood.

We had joined the eastbound HX75 on 21 September 1940. A week before sailing, conscription had started in the US. It looked now as though they might join in, despite the isolationists. That was the good news.

On the other hand, Japan had signed the Tripartite Pact, and was now allied to Berlin and Rome. That same week, the Germans started their mass bombing of London. U-boat attacks on convoys hadn't stopped.

And neither had my alcoholic remorse, I suffered for days. A classic bout. A long session in St John had been followed by withdrawal symptoms — and the depression wouldn't lift. For a while I almost considered abstinence.

Later that month we heard that our convoy had been attacked — that ships had been lost. We weren't there. Our own skirmish had taken place two days before — but not with the enemy.

It happened before dawn on 4 October, ten days out of Halifax. Our watch had just been relieved.

I was thrown out of my bunk, sprawling, fighting to come awake, cursing and dragging on boots as the vessel came upright. I made my way amidships over an obstacle course of chain lashings and slippery timber. The crew was assembling by the bunker hatch in total darkness. No explosion had been heard, but the ship had gone well over. There was now no way on her, and the engineer and firemen had come up from down below. I got through to the fore deck but could see nothing except a mass of jumbled timber.

On the bridge, the helmsman gave me brief details. The ship had lost steerage way, and he had shouted to the mate from the wheelhouse. Unable to signal or show lights, the mate could only ring down 'Stop engines.' By that time we had swung well out of position. A ship in the next column, the *New Westminster City*, one of Smith's of Cardiff, rammed us.

A corvette appeared alongside. Through the crackle of his loud-hailer we heard, 'You're on your own. Good luck.'

The system of rod-and-chain steering gear had not changed since the early days of steam. Though crude, it was efficient — if well maintained. At sea it was under continual strain and in port subject to damage by cargo work. It was also clumsy and at times it carried away.

With shielded lights we found the trouble. A link had parted on the main deck, by the engine room. Fortunately the weather was kind, with no wind and a long, low swell. Dawn wasn't due for another hour but we dragged tackles and gear midships and got started. And by breakfast time had the links joined up, and were under way once more. We went aft covered in grease and black-lead, a job well done, and rather pleased with ourselves.

For the next three days we steamed on, alone. The water in the hold was the same level as the sea outside, and the logs that washed free left an untidy trail astern. But, thanks to the Almighty, and to thousands of little Canadian tree-trunks we floated. With the degaussing gear sliced through we were again a target for magnetic mines in shallower waters. But even with the bottom blown out of her we would still float. She was like a great iron-bound raft.

We made it to the Firth of Clyde and anchored. The deck cargo, pushed halfway up the foremast, amused the pilot. 'You looked more like a drunken haystack than anything else,' he said. The old man didn't see the funny side.

A good little port, Greenock, downstream from Glasgow, and across the Clyde from Loch Long. A town famous for Robert Steele's yards where the tea clippers *Taeping* and *Young Lochinvar* were built. Late in the last century, Steele's were considered the foremost designers and builders of clipper ships in the world. Apart from this reputation, the town also boasted three delightful hostelries. We were made most welcome.

The gash in the ship's side was immense. She was opened up from the bilges to the fore deck, and nearly into the hatch coamings. The yard foreman was optimistic. 'We'll have you out of here in a couple of weeks,' he said. He hadn't allowed for the ship's decrepit state, nor for wartime delays. The same man told a good yarn. His own grandfather had been an apprentice shipwright in Steele's and had helped to build clippers — ships still admired worldwide.

My thoughts only of London, I applied for leave, and was promptly refused. I sulked. To hell with the ship, I thought, I'd get out of the bitch, and considered ways and means. A small injury would do the trick, or a minor illness. I tried to talk Ernie May and Mac into leaving, and finding a ship out of London on a tropical run. I listed the benefits, the sunshine and albatrosses, girls and wine. Neither showed any enthusiasm. 'Hell, man, take it easy,' said Mac, 'we're safe up here for a while.'

Apart from the collision damage, general repairs were being carried out. The surveyor had condemned the funnel and a new one had been made up in the workshops. Tug Wilson and I were on the boat deck the morning of the changeover. The new funnel was on the wharf. A rigger had placed a wire strop around the old one, the crane driver had positioned his jib, hooked on and gently taken the strain. A boilermaker with a gas torch then cut the old funnel free. As expected, the top swung down, the base rose, and the load levelled out, ready to go ashore.

The idea was sound, but not the funnel. Twenty years of acid smoke had left a well-painted, brittle cylinder of rust. No longer rigid, the two ends gradually sagged. We watched, entranced, as this former smokestack slowly described a great inverted V. And showered the boatdeck, ourselves, the surveyor and mate with soot and rust, the accumulation of years. But this was not all. The prevailing wind also carried much of this black cloud across the dock site, liberally fouling another target — an immaculate, until then, naval vessel. The disapproval from her lower-deck ratings was loud and coarse.

Shortly after our arrival in November, the *Admiral Scheer* had sneaked into the North Atlantic, the first German battleship on the prowl since the sinking of the *Graf Spee* off Montevideo. She attacked an eastbound convoy, sank the *Jervis Bay* and five merchantmen, and left the tanker *San*

Demetrio shelled and on fire. With 8000 tons of petrol aboard, and well aware of the possible outcome, the crew abandoned ship. The following day, with her cargo still blazing, some of the crew re-boarded her. For two days they fought the fire, and finally doused it. And then, having managed to start the main engines, they steamed for the UK. A week later she came up the Clyde, charred and blistered, the steelwork ripped apart and holed by shellfire. The crew had painted six-foot high S.O.S.s across the bridge bulkhead. We gave her a cheer as she passed.

We finally got away in mid January, in OB 272, and steamed for the Minches, the passage through the Western Isles. Once around the Butt of Lewis, we met a westerly gale. The escort was hardly reassuring, one destroyer, two corvettes and a rescue tug — and this was when the Germans were sinking a quarter-million tons of British shipping monthly. To farewell us, a German reconnaissance Condor circled, well clear of the escort's gunfire, and no doubt reported our position and course before flying off.

That night a ship was hit. She went up in a great orange flash that lit the sky and silhouetted the ships. The only casualty, she dropped astern, blazing, and we crawled on. No wolf-pack had made this attack. It had probably come from a lone U-boat, heading back to her base, and getting rid of her last torpedo. The rain didn't stop, and I left the bridge, soaking, and stood in the stokehold fiddley to dry out.

By dawn we were into a full gale and heavy sea, weather that lasted for a week. In ballast, and well out of the water, station keeping was difficult, but we somehow managed. We bounced and twisted and dived, and when we punched into the heavy stuff, the entire ship shuddered. We also shook like a wet terrier when the bows dropped and the stern lifted clear. It was then that the exposed screw would race, and endanger the shaft. This acceleration and the sudden strain has at times resulted in the shearing of propeller shafts — and the foundering of vessels. These shocks ran up the masts, and from the crow's nest it felt as though the sticks were coming out of her. Yet, bad as it was, we all hoped the weather would stay foul — would worsen, even, and keep the bastard U-boats well below the surface. Davy Jones was quite busy enough as it was.

The Atlantic gales were bad that year, and south of Iceland there was also the cold to contend with. The world was grey, and with the sprays and rain squalls, the decks never dry. Without birds, or sun, or colour, the ocean was drab and monotonous. The convoy was still an impressive sight — a fleet of fifty ships had to be, but I'd seen enough of it. The wind eased north-east of Newfoundland. Two days earlier, Canadian corvettes had relieved our escort. By then we were well across, out of the range of German spotter planes, and U-boats would have to search for us unaided. Occasional bursts of sunshine brightened up the national flags painted on the hulls of the neutrals. To prevent damage in the freezing temperature, our cargo winches had been turning over slowly for a week. It was the standby man's job to go around once a day with an oil can. A wet assignment. But now, with the Canadian coast just over the horizon it wasn't rain that fell, but snow. Long-johns went to the head of my mental shopping list.

We tied up again in St John on 24 January, the ship's side rust-free, scoured by our final passage through broken ice. That trip I eased off, and did my drinking aboard. As did most of the others; night temperatures had put a damper on any shore-side pleasure seeking. There had been much speculation on the next cargo. Pig iron had been ridiculed, we couldn't be that unfortunate — or could we? Ammunition didn't sound all that healthy — we'd go up instead of down. That left rolling stock, planes and wheat. Naturally, we all favoured pit props, the previous load still a cherished memory. But the chances of a second cargo quite that user-friendly seemed remote.

When the rail trucks did arrive there was a general fluttering of hearts — it was timber. And not untidy little tree trunks, but dressed Oregon pine, long and straight, sweet-smelling and light. We'd hit the jackpot again — and promptly celebrated. Fully loaded, we joined convoy HX 110 in mid February.

The commodore set the pace, and we were again the last ship in the column. The danger was no greater here, ships went down from any position. We felt, and not unreasonably, that with this cargo, not even two torpedoes could sink us. Timber had saved us the previous trip, and our chances were again excellent.

The coal-burning fireman had the worst job in the world. Any man who spent eight hours a day below the water-line, in semi-darkness, and shovelled and sweated in fierce heat, more than earned his crust. When he did this in wartime, he was a hero. In ships hit by torpedoes in the engine room, the death toll was appalling. The men not blown to pieces were scalded to death, and those who didn't die violently drowned.

Most of our original firemen had left the ship in Greenock, and been replaced by Glaswegians. What with the retirement of older men, of others going into oil burners and the casualties at sea, there was a shortage of experienced men. Concerned by this, a worried Minister of Shipping appealed to the courts.

Throughout history, men have been reluctant to join certain ships. In Phoenician times, oarsmen had to be chained to their benches, and less than two hundred years ago the Navy still employed press gangs. As late as the last century, crimping and Shanghai-ing were common in the merchant service. But by 1940, the old strong-arm tactics were over. In criminal courts, magistrates now gave some offenders a choice: 'Either go to jail or go to sea.' The unwary joined the merchant service as volunteer firemen. Four of those novices sailed with us.

German surface-raiders had been active for weeks in the north Atlantic, and to find one of our own battleships with us one morning was no great surprise. She stayed with us for three days, slipping away by night and rejoining at dawn. A strange guest, welcome but disturbing. 'I t'ink we're de cheese in de trap,' was Mick's wry analysis.

On the third day she was away at full speed, leaving us to decode an unfamiliar signal. 'Turn about and scatter,' read the flags. The faster ships were soon hull-down on the horizon; the old and slow tottered along behind.

There was no attack, we saw no action and heard nothing. For a full day we steamed in the wrong direction, then received orders to re-group. More time was lost while the escort rounded up stragglers. Some ships never rejoined; had been lost or made a run for it. When finally tidied up, the formation continued eastward. But again, not for long.

There was the morning I stood by the galley door waiting for eight bells — the first wheel in the forenoon watch was mine. The four-to-eight trimmer had emptied a sack of coal into the galley bunker, and then stepped out on deck. 'There's enough bloody coal to keep the galley fire going today, and that's it — the fucking bunker's empty.'

Our fuel was gone, squandered on extra days steaming, on delays, on miles lost through endless zigzagging. And now, with the Scottish mountains just over the horizon we were out of coal. Ten minutes later, the way was off her, she wasn't steering, and I left the wheel. A corvette came alongside, offered sympathy, and left with a cheerful 'Goodbye and good luck.'

From the bridge I watched the conference below — master, mates and engineers. About the bunker hatch the rest of the crew, the stewards, the radio watch keepers and cook stood and waited. The discussion was short.

A minute later, chain lashings were thrown clear of the deck cargo aft, and timber was dragged amidships. Saws and axes appeared.

The carpenter made up chopping blocks and sawhorses. And we chopped, and sawed, and broke up timber, and dropped it down the stokehold ventilators. The black gang then tossed it into the furnaces.

The activity relieved the strain. The convoy had vanished but we laughed and sang, and joked about our floating sawmill. The old man hovered about and made encouraging noises. He even hinted at additional leave — and the Lloyd's medal for conspicuous gallantry. But he didn't bring out a bottle. Nor was he amused when I suggested that a photograph of the proceedings would be of national interest.

Marine boilers are designed to burn coal, and the better the quality, the greater the steam pressure. But the worst coal available would have outshone wood. The stuff blazed and crackled but raised little steam, and our top speed was under three knots. Dead slow — in the Western Approaches.

We crept into Stornoway sixty hours later, relieved and shamefaced. A little boy who'd wet his pants would have been more dignified. Tied up to the coal hulk, we relaxed, and shore officials came aboard to arrange our run to the mainland. A lucky ship, they said. There were handshakes and congratulations.

Since the first day of hostilities, the merchant service had suffered heavily. From September 1939 on, crews had known violence and death and despair. Acts of bravery had been frequent, and for hundreds of men and women in open boats, the slow torture had been terrible. During the first three months alone that we spent in that vessel, 351 Allied ships went down.

And all we could brag about was a collision — and a shortage of coal. The bell just wasn't ready to toll for us.

But I'd had enough, and left her.

Three months later, on 24 June 1941, the Brockley Hill *was torpedoed and sunk by the German submarine* U651 *while on a voyage from Montreal to London. Loaded with grain, she was in Convoy HX 133. The crew of 42 were rescued.*

Hank Cavendish,
Albatross Years — a life at sea, 1994

Storm in Mid-Atlantic

PETER TAYLOR'S first ship, as a 16-year-old runaway from small-town New Zealand, was a British tramp called the *Algonquin Park*, a Liberty-type utility ship run to minimum Board of Trade standards and bound for London.

Taylor could box a compass and tie a clove hitch and bowline — and that was about all. The Chief Officer didn't believe either his stated age or the glowing reference from a 'Mr Bill Smith', fishing boat owner.

But the *Algonquin Park* was the beginning of a long and colourful career as a merchant seaman, later writer, photographer, public servant and lighthouse keeper (an earlier book, *As Darker Grows the Night*, published in 1975, documents the final days of manned lighthouses round the New Zealand coast).

Taylor's second ship was the *Leicester*, one of the adapted pre-war British Ocean class tramp steamers that were built by the thousand during the Second World War and became the backbone of Allied convoys. Burning oil, not coal, and her crew provided with fresh bread each day, she was a step up from the *Algonquin Park*.

On the *Leicester*, Taylor was to experience the sailor's 'deep, almost primeval fright' in his first real storm at sea: the heaving grey Atlantic in November . . .

November's English Channel is bad enough, grey, coldly miserable, unpredictable and dangerous. November's Atlantic can be profoundly worse.

The barometer began dropping rapidly and radio messages began apparently telling of something afoot — 'apparently' because generally the only way of knowing what was happening was by the helmsman relaying remarks between captain and officers, or by what was told officially to the bosun who may or may not then tell his men.

Confirmation that the worsening weather was the outrider of something considerably greater came when the captain ordered rope lifelines rigged both sides of the main deck from bow to stern. The watches below were turned out to place steel storm battens across the hatch tarpaulins and check and tighten the wooden wedges that held the tarpaulins against the holds' coamings. Hold ventilators were turned off the wind and thick canvas covers tied tightly across their cavernous circular mouths to prevent the entry of any water. Thick steel cabin porthole deadlights were lowered and screwed home.

All the while the ripped black clouds thickened and lowered. The rain fell heavier. The wind blew fiercer. The seas rose higher until their collapsing tops were blown away like misty smoke so that the division between ocean and atmosphere became indistinguishable.

We were finally enveloped in the primeval uproar of a North Atlantic winter storm.

The ship laboured up each curling-crested wave. At the top it paused briefly amidst the spume of the breaking water. As the wave passed beneath, her forward length was left suspended above the following trough. Then, no longer supported and sometimes with a speed that momentarily made a human body feel almost weightless, her 8000 tons fell down the other side and crashed to a standstill with such breakneck power the hull trembled and the steel masts jerked and pulsated like trees in an earthquake.

With each tumble the stern angled high out of the sea. The propeller thrashed the air and shook every plate and rivet. The engineers struggled to reduce revolutions until the stern was again thrust deep until, throwing her bow clear, *Leicester* climbed the next moving hill. Water streamed from her decks like a surfacing submarine as she reared sometimes high enough to almost bury her stern.

Despite the helmsman's efforts to keep her shoulder to the seas, *Leicester* was regularly and derisively thrust aside to slide sideways down their lengths. Then she was engulfed from bow to stern, the 'midships superstructure in which we lived little more than a steel tidal rock. She strained at every seam as she struggled to emerge, water cataracting over her sides in furious torrents.

High on the wave tops, their tumbling crests disintegrating in flying spume and driving spray, the spectacle was awesome; immense valleys and endless rows of almost vertical hills, rank upon rank of liquid hordes charging from the horizon like a teeming cavalry in an undisciplined onslaught.

The cooks were ordered to abandon regular meals. Despite steel bars across the stove tops to keep a semblance of order among wildly jumping, sliding, clattering pots and pans, nothing needing liquid could be cooked. It was enough for the galley hands to avoid being thrown against the hot stoves without the added danger of burns or scalds from spilled hot liquids.

Bacon, steak, tea, toast and tabnabs were the order of the day for some time. We could not eat at the tables, despite tablecloths soaked with water to stop things sliding across the table surfaces that were themselves divided by wooden 'fiddles'. Instead, we stood wide-legged and pressed against the messroom bulkheads, plates flattened into our chests as we fought to keep upright. Sometimes we were knocked completely off our feet.

Off watch we lay wedged in our bunks amid the wet-dog smell of damp clothing, continually shocked awake as the ship rolled far to one side and slid down the wall of a wave, or a huge sea rampaged across the deck and smashed against our accommodation, rolling us so far over that oilskins on their coathooks streamed out almost horizontally and any loose objects hurled like projectiles. The more violent occasions were the stuff nightmares are made of. Green water crashing many feet deep against our portholes made their protective steel deadlights seem thin indeed.

At the height of the storm the seas reared so high, sometimes nearly 100 feet, that the wind could not reach us in their sometimes quarter-mile or longer troughs. But it scourged us with a ripping shriek as we topped their cliff-like tumbling summits. It was beyond belief the air we breathed could move with such speed.

The bosun and carpenter and several of the most experienced ABs later struggled on the boatdeck taking off the lifeboats' canvas covers. Then they refilled freshwater tanks, added blankets and extra stores and ensured the davits were greased and rope-falls in readiness. And, although the lifeboats' survival, never mind our own, in such conditions would have been unlikely, the captain had the mast cargo lights kept burning at night.

'Just in case,' he told the bosun matter-of-factly. 'You never know what might happen.'

The lights turned the night-time scene into something out of hell. Each breaking sea came spuming out of the darkness and into the pale illumination as a singular, clamorous messenger from the demons. In daylight no wave assumed an entity of its own unless of extraordinary size. It was just one of countless monsters. But such extraordinarily sized individuals could be seen in the distance. There was time to prepare for their towering inevitability as best we could. In the darkness, however, each was an individual with no hint of the stature of its follower until it fell with indifferent savagery, as if intent on forcing the ship to the ocean bottom.

On lookout, crouching alone and clinging to the binnacle behind the dodgers on the monkey island above the wheelhouse, events seemed even more climacteric. We seemed to be the only sentient living things in a consummation of chaos.

The screaming wind; rain driving like ice splinters; seas thundering unseen until they came in their spuming fury into the lights' weak periphery; the violent rolling, climbing and precipitate falls; the creaking, groaning, straining, stretching hull, all combined to elevate a sense of impending calamity.

It gave meaning to the words I had sung with such feeling in church not many years before. I felt truly in peril on the sea and utterly unhappy. But I could not fail to be impressed by the sheer natural brutality around me. There was a monumental honesty about the savageness of something with neither brain nor soul and so insensible in the exercise of its power.

Along with the hymn another childhood event had buried itself deep in my cognition. It resurfaced over the years whenever I felt a momentary and foolish intimacy with the sea. It may have been what kept me from fantasising about it. I knew it was a barbarian.

In the morning I had been playing in the wavelets and building castles in the sand. In the late afternoon I sat silent and shivering in a storm wind near a drowned man whose boat had been overwhelmed in the breakers. My father and several others tried to resuscitate the cold blue body. They gave up as the sun set. They pulled the dead man beyond the waves' grasp, wiped his face and closed his eyes and covered him with someone's overcoat, then sat with him until a policeman took him away on the back of a lorry.

My relief at the end of a lookout missed his footing climbing to the monkey island. At the same moment a vicious roll swung him wide from the ladder. He lost his grip and crashed to the bridge deck. He rolled around momentarily stunned and in danger of sliding through the rail into the sea.

I looked in disbelief then clambered down to rescue him. He was a heavy man and another massive roll slid us against the rail with our legs protruding through it. It was only with a great effort that I was able to drag him back and prop him up out of harm's way.

When he regained his sensibility he shook his head, shivered, coughed and opened his eyes.

'Fuck,' he said. 'What happened?'

I cleared my eyes and mouth of spray and told him.

'Fuck,' he said, as he stood up and resumed his way to the monkey island.

I reported the event and the captain ordered the man below, and me to continue on lookout on the lee bridge wing. Its weather side was too dangerous because of the seas sometimes reaching it. Maintaining a lookout was impossible, anyway. Eyes slitted against the miscegenation of wind, rain and spray could see nothing through elements bent on slicing heads from shoulders.

The captain spent much of his time on the bridge. A tall, ascetic man, despite his studied calm, Captain Andrews was plainly not happy. Sometimes he uttered a slow and well-enunciated 'Oh, shit!' when the ship fell unusually heavily off a wave and the next came rolling down the deck or over the side in a solid wall burying the hatches and deck housings before bursting against the bridge.

In intimate contest with a wholly hostile force it is difficult not to dwell on the chances of survival. I felt for my life. It was a deep, almost primeval fright. It permeated every part of me, body and consciousness, and severely dented the customary youthful belief that unlike everyone else I would live forever. I had begun to believe the future could be predicted only in increments of about ten minutes. It shortened to five minutes each time the captain said, 'Oh, shit!'

Everyone was also mindful that in similar circumstances, only a couple of voyages before, the captain's predecessor had been hurled from this same bridge into the sea. Only by a promiscuous stroke of chance had he been carried back by the following wave. A similar event now was unlikely to have the same result. As seamen rarely lose their deep-rooted suspicion of the sea, when Captain Andrews swore it was with a considered and measured passion which seemed to come from deep within him.

Survival lay in his capabilities and the merits of the shipbuilders and enginemakers. And since each had their fallibilities, one also had to trust to luck. Or as some might have it, God. On the other hand, since presumably He was responsible for the tempest in the first place, trust in such a tyrant could have been entirely misplaced.

The unconcealed unease of the most hardened and experienced men, normally taciturn Hebrideans who had been at sea all their lives, sharpened the misgivings of the less experienced. An occasional remark showed their full awareness that in similar weather *Leicester* had lost six men and had narrowly escaped being totally lost herself. And there was *Samkey*, too, her sister who had disappeared without trace along with all her crew, some of our crew's relatives among them.

The ship's increasing reluctance to resume an even keel indicated something amiss among the cargo. The chief officer and bosun fought their way along the deck to the holds. Fortunately, Liberty ships' hold-access was by ladder through deckhouses at the base of the masts. On many other ships it was necessary to lift exposed hatch-covers.

The two men found hundreds of bags of basic slag in the No 2 hold broken free of their dunnage restraints and sliding across the sheet steel cargo, on top of which they had been loaded in Antwerp. They were fetching up on one side of the ship and causing her to list. It was a dangerous state of affairs.

All hands were turned-to. Wearing life jackets we were sent in relays to drag as many back into place as we could. We worked in the gloom of cargo light clusters lowered into the holds. We were continually thrown off our feet and into each other as the seas echoed around us, smashing against our thin steel sides and sweeping across the hatches above us.

We worked twenty minutes at a time before being relieved. Then, signalled by Aldis lamp from the bridge when it was judged safe to do so, we raced in pairs down the deck, clinging for our lives to the lifelines and sometimes reaching safety by seconds.

Eventually the elements ran out of energy. They left a rolling, confused surface as though great submarine creatures had just finished fighting. The sun began showing occasionally from behind the slowly dispersing clouds. Still with a considerable list from the shifted cargo, we resumed course for Willemstad in the Dutch Antilles island of Curaçao in the Caribbean. The weather finally calmed and we made good time through a sparkling tropical sea to Sombrero Islet and the Anegada Passage between the Virgin and Leeward Islands.

Willemstad's tiled roofs, gables and baroque facades of its eighteenth-century Dutch architecture were a welcome sight as we passed behind an assisting tug up the narrow St Anna Bay Channel, to come to rest well inside the Schottegat. Europeans first visited Curaçao in 1499 and by 1527 it had been settled by the Spaniards, after deporting the entire Indian population to Hispaniola in 1515. The Dutch took over in 1634. They needed Caribbean salt for herring preservation. The English took the island off them for a while during the Napoleonic Wars but returned it under the Treaty of Paris in 1815. The Dutch found oil in Lake Maracaibo in Venezuela in 1914. Because the lake was too small for ocean-going ships, Royal Dutch Shell built refineries on the island and brought the oil from Maracaibo by small 'mosquito' tankers for refining and transhipment.

Our cargo was restowed and some deck damage repaired and we were moved to nearby Caracas Bay where, overlooked by a stone fort established by Captain Morgan, one of the Caribbean's more notorious pirates, our oil bunkers were refilled. We may have stayed had the captain known the real state of his ship following the Atlantic storm. But he didn't. And so we set off for the Panama Canal.

In the sixteenth century the Spaniards had ideas of building a canal through the Panama Isthmus. A local Spanish official suggested a route close to that of the present canal. Later several other plans were suggested, but no action was taken. And then in 1880 along came Suez's Ferdinand de Lesseps.

'I maintain that Panama will be easier to make, easier to complete, and easier to keep up than Suez,' a confident de Lesseps said.

He planned a sea-level canal similar to the Suez Canal and began the job with a symbolic blow from a pick-axe wielded by his small daughter Ferdinande. But for the next nine years malaria and yellow fever decimated the diggers. Some 20,000 died. De Lesseps, by then a publicly maligned man, died in 1894 at the age of 89.

In 1904 the Americans, although haunted by de Lesseps' failure and French graft, extravagance and swindling, began anew. Their efforts were also unsuccessful until 1907 when President Teddy Roosevelt handed the job to the US army under the charge of an engineer, Major George Washington Goethals. The redesigned canal and its locks were opened in August 1914. It had been the most costly single effort ever undertaken anywhere in the world.

Today some 15,000 ships pass through the canal each year. They are lifted 85 feet by locks at one end and dropped at the other, on the way sailing through the mountainous spine of the Isthmus of Panama. Each time the locks are used around 50 million gallons of water are pumped in and then flushed out to sea. Most of the water comes from the artificially created Lake Gatun and nearby Lake Madden, formed in 1935 for extra water.

When *Leicester* passed through, much of the route was through rainforest covering 1300 square miles of the watershed. Most of the time it rained in steamy tropical downpours. By then, 20 per cent of the original forest had been cut.

About 70 per cent of the forest has now gone. This is bringing less rain to fill the lakes. As well, half a million tons of soil are washing from the denuded hills into Lake Madden each year and reducing the amount of water it will hold. Lake Gatun is suffering the same environmental damage.

In the early 1960s the canal was already too small for some of the larger ships then being built. Nuclear bomb builders exhibited an alarming enthusiasm for another bigger canal using their 'devices' to burst apart the mountains of Darien.

And their predecessors had reckoned de Lesseps was mad!

Except for a couple of strategically posted engineers to pass orders from the pilot to the engineroom should the bridge telegraphs fail, the canal transit was an idle time for most of us. Canal authorities provided helmsmen and men to handle the lines attached to the 'mules', small locomotives that pulled us in and out of the locks.

There was also an armed guard in the wheelhouse. Some said he was there to prevent anyone attempting to take over the ship and block the canal. Others said it was proof of Americans' preoccupation with guns. Sceptics said it was to provide ex-soldiers with jobs. Most professed no interest. It was enough to lean over the rails with mugs of tea and be idle spectators of proceedings for a change.

The voyage from Panama to New Zealand was generally pleasant. The ship rubbed her cheeks fondly against the Pacific's long, lazy swells as if having forgotten their Atlantic brothers' earlier conduct.

We were traversing the world's largest and deepest ocean. It is immense, more than twice the size of the Atlantic, 64 million square miles covering more than a third of the earth's surface and holding more than half its free water.

We passed few other ships and no land except one or two tropical islands in the hazy distance. Life ran its normal tempo in which the sounds of a ship at sea become so regular as to be accepted as silence, her movements so continuous as to be stillness.

Outward bound ships on the Britain–New Zealand–Australia run were generally cleaned and cargo working gear overhauled. In the coastal ports the hull was painted. Homeward bound the masts, derricks and superstructures were painted. Apart from the usual watchkeeping jobs of steering and night lookouts, our work during the three weeks across the Pacific to Wellington was mostly soogeying paintwork, chipping rust, repairing or replacing cargo-handling wires and ropework and odd painting jobs.

Rounding Cape Kidnappers on the way north from Wellington to Auckland we crossed *Leicester*'s track from the previous voyage from Napier. At that point I had been around the world.

In Auckland, while being readied to load wool for New York and Philadelphia, the bottoms of the holds were found to be buckled. Marine surveyors discovered even greater structural damage. The Atlantic storm had badly deformed our hull. Divers found heavy steel hull plates indented several inches between the frames. In some cases the frames themselves were badly distorted.

We were towed to the Devonport naval drydock where *Leicester* underwent New Zealand's biggest-ever and most intricate ship-repair job. Damaged steel was replaced. Frames were straightened. Some 700 intercostal plates were fitted to the double bottom to provide extra stiffening fore-and-aft. Extra girders were installed beneath the main deck to strengthen the hull full length.

As a wartime utility-built ship, the ship was welded instead of riveted, using a shipbuilding technology not then anywhere near its prime. It was later believed not all Liberty ships disappeared during the war because of enemy action but in many cases because their hulls broke apart when welded seams failed in heavy weather or extreme cold. Fortunately, *Leicester*'s owners had structurally strengthened and riveted her more vulnerable points. She would not otherwise have survived her Atlantic battering.

After all, as Joseph Conrad wrote about the *Titanic* enquiry, 'there is not much mystery about a ship. She is a tank . . . ribbed, joisted, stayed . . . and for the hazards I should think about as strong as a Huntley and Palmer biscuit tin . . . well, perhaps not quite as strong. Just look at the side of such a tin and think of . . . a ship and try to imagine what the thickness of her plates should be to approach anywhere near the relative solidity of that biscuit tin.'

If kicked by a mule, Conrad went on, the tin 'would come back to earth smiling, with only a sort of dimple on one of its cheeks. A proportionately severe blow would have burst the side of . . . any triumph of modern naval architecture like brown paper — I am willing to bet.'

The homeward voyage was uneventful. Anyway, 'events' were something we could do without. The company thought so, too. Before we reached London the ship had been sold to the Nassau Maritime Company in the Bahamas. She was renamed *Inagua*. She was sold again and renamed *Serafin Topic* and later again *Jela Topic*.

Several years later, as *Viking Liberty*, she ran aground off Trinidad on her way to New York. She was refloated and towed to New Orleans. But she was beyond repair and in 1966 was broken up in Santander on Spain's Bay of Biscay coast.

Peter Taylor, *Wet Behind the Ears*, 2001

Heirs of Tane

DAVID LEWIS'S long-awaited autobiography *Shapes on the Wind* was published in 2000. Through a lifetime of adventure and risk, as doctor, mountaineer, sailor, navigator, scientist and freedom fighter, he had written eleven acclaimed books, including one of the finest survival stories ever written, the classic *Ice Bird* (1974) about his extraordinary single-handed voyage to Antarctica in 1972–74.

An earlier book had confirmed his reputation as one of the great navigators of the twentieth century, also one of the most controversial. *We, the Navigators: The Ancient Art of Landfinding in the Pacific*, the story of his 1600-mile voyage between Tahiti and New Zealand using only traditional Polynesian navigational techniques, was a major contribution to the 1960s debate about the settlement of the Pacific. In his autobiography he looks back at the voyages he and his family undertook in a variety of craft around the Pacific and Indian oceans between 1964 and 1980, furthering his lifelong quest to chronicle humankind's maritime past.

In Tahiti my insatiable curiosity brought my long-cherished project on Pacific settlement to the point of a practical sea trial. From the outliers of Asia across the ocean to Easter Island in the very shadow of the Andes, from Hawaii in the north to New Zealand in the south, the great canoes had reached every speck of land. What part had been played by conscious navigation? To me this seemed to be the key question.

The subject of just *how* the islanders accomplished their unique maritime achievement had recently become a matter of hot debate, spearheaded by New Zealand academic Andrew Sharp. He effectively debunked the earlier uncritical acceptance of traditions, often edited, that had ancient Polynesians quartering the Pacific like jet aircraft. Unfortunately, in their place he substituted the assertion that the Polynesians had hardly navigated with deliberate intent at all, but had made their longer landfalls by accident. This theory made good sense to many anthropologists and historians, who were all too ready to doubt the nautical expertise of pre-literate Stone Age, native people. But Sharp's glaring misuse of book-derived nautical data made no sense at all to Pacific small-boat sailors or, indeed, to anyone personally acquainted with the islands of the South Seas.

One important issue, that of accuracy without instruments, I had already addressed in theory well before I left England. With invaluable help from Professor Harry Maude of the Australian National University, who was visiting England, I had written papers in the *Journal of the Polynesian Society* and the *Journal of the Royal Institute of Navigation*, demonstrating how relatively easy it was to target any of the huge Pacific archipelagos or 'blocks' of islands, and then to use pointers like clouds, deflected waves and homing birds to locate individual islands, which would generally not be very far apart. It was only several years later, in 1968 and 1969, that this speculation was dramatically confirmed by the navigators of the Pacific themselves. 'You steer,' explained Hipour, my Polowat mentor in the Carolines, 'towards the *screen* of homing birds, clouds, deep reefs, disturbed waves and islands that stretch across your pathway.' He then proceeded to demonstrate the process both ways across 450 miles of unbroken ocean. Similarly, the Hon. Ve'ehala, a senior member of the Tuita Navigator Clan of Tonga, revealed this telling saying from their secret lore: 'You do not aim towards an individual *puko* tree but towards a *grove* of *puko* trees — only then do you look for your particular tree.'

Here I must tread a delicate line: I have written a good deal about Polynesian navigation, and the newly revised edition of my book, *We, the Navigators*, is in print and doing well.[1] But, as far as Polynesian navigation is concerned, this book is not the place for a detailed treatise.

What was clearly timely back in Tahiti in 1964 was to subject my theories to a sea trial. We therefore resolved to navigate Tahiti–Huahine–Rarotonga–New Zealand in the manner of the navigator-priests of old. We would follow the directions of Kupe, legendary discoverer of New Zealand, to steer a little to the left of the setting sun in early November. No instruments, neither compass, nor clock, nor sextant, would be used to navigate the vessel. However, for safety and for the record, Priscilla would log our true positions but would not reveal them, except in an emergency, until journey's end. The stars and the sun would be our compass; stars arching overhead in the zenith and the Southern Cross sweeping the horizon our sextant; wave forms, birds and clouds our warnings of land.

The first leg to Huahine in the Society Islands of French Polynesia went well, and there I met Curt Ashford, who was to become a lifelong friend. Curt and his wife Jenny's little schooner *Sea Wyfe* had lost her rudder and had been swept over the reef. The couple had built a *kikau* shack on the beach and spent a year making repairs. Their three-year-old son Eric spoke only Tahitian and their daughter Ngaire was about to be born. We were to renew the family's acquaintance a decade later in Hawaii in dramatic and tragic circumstances.

Our course for the next 500 miles through the Lower Cooks was indeed arrow-straight, but we overshot the islands through my ignorance of patent bird clues, and Priscilla had to break her silence. The last 1600 miles from Rarotonga to New Zealand culminated in a landfall only twenty-five miles south of my estimate.

There was one particularly embarrassing occasion in Auckland that did nothing to enhance my reputation as a navigator. I was to take the chair at a public meeting at Auckland University for Thor Heyerdahl of *Kon-Tiki* fame. I thought I knew the way to the university from years before, but toiling up streets that had become somehow unfamiliar, sweating with anxiety as the time got later and later, I knew I had let down the distinguished audience and the eminent speaker. When I eventually arrived very late in the piece, Heyerdahl, far from showing irritation, went out of his way most graciously to put me at my ease.

Regardless of Heyerdahl's theories of Polynesian origins from South America (disproved by excavation, carbon-dating, linguistics, even by the discovery of the bones of *kiori*, Polynesian canoe rats, on Easter Island), the Norwegian explorer did demonstrate dramatically how the oceans were potential pathways, rather than necessarily barriers, to the simple craft of yesterday — a truly revolutionary change in perspective. I encountered Heyerdahl again in Hobart, Tasmania, where we were both speaking at a diving conference. Subsequently, he provided invaluable introductions to people in Russia, particularly to Yuri Senkevich, the doctor on his *Ra* and *Tigris* voyages . . .

Once the 1965 cyclone season in the tropical South Pacific was over we continued on our way round the world. The first stop was Tongatapu, the main island of the ancient Kingdom of Tonga, after which we planned to visit Nomuka, Captain Bligh's last landfall before the mutiny.

'You steer two hands' breadths to the left of that star rising in the north-east,' explained *eikevaka* (cutter captain) Koloni Kienga, pointing to the star. He was giving me directions for our passage through the archipelago. I could hardly believe my ears. The 'extinct' art was alive!

'When that star rises too high for convenience, follow the next in line, directly or at an angle. This is called the *Kaveinga* or Star Path. You follow the succession of stars till dawn,' Koloni continued. 'Yes, I do have a compass. It is in the bilge somewhere. I never use it.' He explained how the long ocean swell lines were distorted by land, being bent on each side of an island and ultimately joining beyond it in a complex interlocking pattern. On the windward side a back swell was reflected. 'If you know what to look for these swells can be interpreted twenty miles from the smallest atoll, and you yourself know well enough that an atoll's palms can only be seen ten miles away from a boat.'

If you know what to look for. That was the rub. There must be other Kolonis. How could I find them?

Fiji, Vanuatu, Papua New Guinea! Everywhere we came upon fragments of the old knowledge, and tantalising rumours of active, living star-path navigators in the Carolines, Kiribati and elsewhere. It was in Port Moresby that it all came to a head. I had been holding forth to Ron Crocombe, then head of the New Guinea Research Unit of the Australian National University and married to a Rarotongan 'sister' of mine, about the need for someone to make a systematic Pacific-wide search for these navigators, go to sea with them and record their methods before it was too late. But how?

'Apply for a research fellowship from the ANU, why don't you?' Ron suggested.

'I'm not an anthropologist, nor a historian,' I objected. 'They would never appoint me.'

'Give it a go,' said my fellow New Zealanders, characteristically. So, fuelled by rum toddies, we drew up an application that very night and Ron put it into acceptable academic form. It was in the post before we sailed, but neither Ron nor I gave it much chance of success, and I thought no more about it . . .

Rehu Moana traversed the Indian Ocean via the Cocos Islands to Durban.

It was January 1967 before we rounded the Cape of Good Hope, only having to lay-to twice in southwest gales, and prepared to sail from Cape Town. I was glad to be leaving South Africa, where *apartheid* was in full swing and distasteful racist myths were very much in vogue, even among people who should have known better. Rather than take the usual (and more sensible) route up the South Atlantic, we decided it would be more interesting to follow the coast northward, calling at South-West Africa (Namibia), Angola and Zaire (Democratic Republic of the Congo), before rounding the great bulge of West Africa.

So it came about that we were in Walvis Bay in South-West Africa when the news arrived: I had been appointed to a four-year Research Fellowship at the Australian National University, with the terms of reference Ron and I had proposed. Australia! Our lives were about to take an abrupt about-turn.

There was only one problem, or two, to be exact.

In the first place our ship was, literally, beached. We were in the thick of reconstruction work, knee-deep in plywood, fibreglass and glue, when the message came through. I quote from a transcript of a recorded film interview, without apology for the rather intemperate language: 'Near Walvis Bay we got rammed by a tug, skippered by an Afrikaner moron who had been demoted from every job in the bloody harbour. Skippering a tug was the lowest job a white person could do. They should have shot him. That was *apartheid* in practice. A sudden nor-wester came up and just about all the boats had to shift, and this tug crushed us against the sea wall. We had to run up on the beach or sink. We did a deal with the harbour board that we wouldn't make a fuss if they helped us with repairs.'

A kindly harbour pilot and his wife took in the little girls, for their bridge deck cabin had been destroyed. They attended the local kindergarten, apparently not disconcerted at finding the teachers spoke only Afrikaans and German. '*Eins, zwei, drei, eisenbahn, alle kinder waschen sie,*' they learned to chant, while marching in line to wash their hands. For years thereafter Susie and Vicky insisted they had been to school in Germany.

The second problem was that the faithful *Rehu Moana* would not be the most suitable craft for the proposed journey. What would be needed was a 'motorsailer' with a range under power substantial enough to seek out navigators in obscure islands without having to worry too much about fair winds. *Rehu Moana*'s narrow hulls would never take a heavy motor or the necessary fuel. This all meant that we had to complete our circumnavigation, and sail from England to Australia in another boat.

The repairs at Walvis Bay were eventually completed and we continued up the vast West African coastline to Lobito and San Antonio do Zaire in civil-war-torn Angola. Crossing the Congo River to Banana in what is now the Democratic Republic of the Congo presented something of a problem since the two countries were theoretically at war. They were, however, happily trading Congolese chickens for Portuguese wine and agreed to let us cross the closed river frontier unmolested. Both sides treated us with the utmost kindness.

Back in England David purchased the gaff ketch *Isbjorn*, a Scottish trawler-type double-ender, 39ft long and crossing a square yard on the foremast. In this vessel they voyaged across the Atlantic, through the Panama Canal and across the Pacific.

Leaving Fiji in late 1968, Barry and I set out on a year's systematic investigation of traditional navigation, setting the seal on what, for me, has become a lifelong quest to chronicle humankind's maritime past. The aim was to sail with the traditional Pacific navigators either in their own vessels, or, by default, aboard an *Isbjorn* stripped of compass, sextant, timepieces, radios and charts, to learn, in the words of Chief Beiong of Pulusuk, 'the secrets of all the reefs and islands under the stars'. The disciplines of medical research were relevant to my way of thinking, perhaps more so than academic ones. For academic speculations may remain forever unproven in default of objective confirmation, whereas in a medical study, the drug either works or does not; the patient either does or does not get better. It seemed to me that here we had a similar situation. The stern test of landfall would be the criterion of accuracy (in fact, this never failed; the island always appeared where the navigator predicted).

I cannot speak highly enough of the great tradition-bearers Tevake, Hipour and Mau Piailug. Tevake has long returned to the ocean that was his heritage; Hipour, at eighty, is teaching traditional navigation to children in Chuuk; and Mau Piailug (of *Hokule'a* fame) is currently sailing the double canoe *Makali'i*. All three are immortal — cornerstones of the renaissance of ancient star-path navigation that is now sweeping the Pacific.

Tevake's home was Nifiloli, one of the Polynesian-speaking Reef Islands of the isolated Santa Cruz archipelago, whose geographical complexity is only matched by the inaccuracy of the single chart (the Reef Islands are laid down seven miles too far to the west, for instance). While politically it is regarded as the Temotu Province of the Solomon Islands, the Santa Cruz Islands lie north of Vanuatu, with which it has ancient trading links. Indeed, in 1606, when the explorer Pedro Fernandez de Quiros visited Taumako, sixty miles beyond the Reef Islands proper, Chief Tumai told him of seventy islands that he knew. The 60-foot claw-sailed *te puke* outriggers that Quiros saw ranged from Malekula in Vanuatu north to Sikiana, and from Tikopia in the east to Santa Ana and Rennell in the main Solomons chain, more than 500 miles each way. Nor was this voyaging anything new. As long ago as 1100 BC, Lapita pottery makers (ancestral Polynesians) were shipping obsidian for stone adzes 900 miles to Santa Cruz from Talasia in New Britain.

Tevake himself had made two 200-mile *te puke* voyages to Tikopia and another to Vanuatu, as well as everywhere in his own extensive Santa Cruz archipelago. His *te puke* having been wrecked these five years past, our own voyages together were in an *Isbjorn* stripped of instruments.

The best way to appreciate something of the ancient arts to which Tevake was heir, and which date far back over as yet uncounted millennia to when the first seafarer ventured with intent out of sight of land, is to recount an actual passage. One that stands out in my mind was sailing with Tevake on the sixty miles from Nifiloli to Taumako.

We sailed at dusk that December 1968, and the star path was our guide: first, the rising Betelgeuse, then, in turn, Pleides, Castor and Pollux, Procyon; rising either ahead or at a known angle to the course. Just before dawn the navigator picked out the rugged outline of Taumako. The return was in daylight, in blinding rain squalls that blotted out everything. For eight solid hours the lean old man stood on the foredeck, sopping wet lavalava (a wraparound cloth) flapping round his legs, an umbrella palm leaf over his head, gesturing from time to time to one of the young crew members, Kaveia[2], guided only by the ill-defined 'sea swell' that had travelled a thousand miles from the north-east trades beyond the equator. He only relaxed when the dim outline of our destination emerged from the murk half a mile ahead. On a later journey to Vanikoro 100 miles to the south-east, Tevake demonstrated more star-steering, told of wave and current lore, and revealed the strange underwater luminescence called *te lapa* . . .

Barry and I bade a reluctant farewell to Tevake on Ndeni in the shadow of the perfect cone of the sacred volcano Tinikula with a white tropic bird, tevake, his namesake, wheeling overhead. He wrote me back in Australia: 'I am getting very old now and very sick. Have you written down all I taught you?' I replied in the affirmative. Months later, the increasingly infirm and dying navigator had bade a formal farewell to his kin on Nifiloli and paddled out to sea on a one-way voyage of no return. The world of seafarers is diminished by his passing.

From the Santa Cruz archipelago Barry and I headed north across the equator to the Caroline Islands in Micronesia, the one part of the Pacific where traditional voyaging was most intact. Even so, sailing-canoe crossings of the unbroken 450-mile stretch between the Carolines and Marianas had been discontinued around the turn of the twentieth century.

The two-way voyage was repeated by Hipour in an *Isbjorn* denuded of navigational aids. All he had to guide him were oral traditions three or four generations old, which laid down star courses for different wind strengths and weather conditions, the expected complex swell patterns, and what homing birds would be encountered. Yet, using this long-dormant word-of-mouth data, he navigated us successfully both ways, with birds each time providing the final clues to land. I received my first tattoo, a Caroline Islands navigator's design, in his honour. We exchanged names and became 'brothers' . . .

A shorter voyage with Hipour back in 1969, this time to the island of Pulusuk in his own 29-foot sailing outrigger, was only permitted by the powerful Polowat chief and leading navigator, Manipy, on the condition that Barry would take a turtle-hunting party in *Isbjorn* to Pikelot, a hundred miles away. I was to encounter this same Manipy at the South Pacific Arts Festival in Samoa in 1996, where he allowed his 'son', Sosthenes Emwalu, himself a worth successor to Hipour, to reveal secret navigational lore. Manipy appeared virtually unchanged after a full quarter century.

Barry and I had other mentors — from Ninigo, Tikopia, Kiribati and Tonga — during that eventful year on *Isbjorn*, a year of research and discovery that continued what the *Rehu Moana* test voyage had begun, and which laid the basis of further navigation and route-finding studies in the Pacific and Indonesia, and from the Central Australian deserts to the shores of the Arctic Ocean.

What has been the point of it all? This is the era of electronic navigation, of Global Positioning Systems that have rendered even the sextant a museum piece. Why bother? We should bother, because without those innumerable nameless captains of yesterday who paved the way for us today there would be no GPS; we owe a debt to their memory that we can never repay. Nor were the followers of the 'voyaging stars' limited to the Pacific. There are close parallels with the age-old techniques of the Arabs, Persians, Indians and Chinese, and early European maritime heritage bears similarities with the Polynesian. Here are 1000 AD pre-compass Viking sailing directions from Norway to Greenland:

From Helte Fjord north of Bergen leave the Shetlands just in sight to the south. Go north of the Faroes keeping the sea horizon half way up the mountain slopes. Then sail due west. South of Iceland there will be a multitude of birds but you will not sight the land . . .

However, only in the Pacific are such ancient arts still extant to provide a unique window through which we can peer back into the distant maritime past, to which all seagoers are heirs . . .

In 1975 an invitation arrived to participate in a canoe voyage that could not possibly be refused. The girls and I accordingly flew to Hawaii for me to take up a research fellowship at the East-West Center, Honolulu. I was to go to sea the next year aboard *Hokule'a*, a 65-foot replica of an ancient Hawaiian voyaging double-hulled canoe. *Hokule'a* was built of modern materials, but her underwater proportions (on which performance depends) were based on measurements obtained by Captain James Cook in Tonga and Tahiti. The project had been initiated in the main by Professor Ben Finney, Hawaiian artist Herb Kane and canoeman Tommy Holmes. The idea was to sail the 2500 miles from Hawaii to Tahiti, all of it navigated without instruments by initiated Caroline navigator Mau Piailug of Satawal in the Caroline Islands, neighbour and rival island to Hipour's Polowat. He would be assisted by me for zenith star latitudes south of the equator, and by veteran Tahitian seaman Rodo Williams for local landfall signs.

From the start there were cultural strains. This is hardly surprising, since at that time the native Hawaiians were at their lowest ebb. They were a minority in their own land, not even included on the census; once proud soldiers of Queen Liliuokalani a mere ninety years earlier were now Waikiki beach boys tinkling ukuleles for tourists. The art of deep-sea navigation had long since been forgotten and there was profound resentment of outsiders having to be brought in to fill the gap (this understandable prejudice was still apparent in 1996 at the Pacific Arts Festival in Samoa, where I was co-opted into the Cook Islands and New Zealand Maori delegations, but never the Hawaiian). Different Hawaiian factions were at each other's throats back in 1975–76. Crew selection for *Hokule'a* was marred by prejudice — at least two Hawaiian sailors with more deep-sea experience than any of the men were excluded because of their sex . . .

Of course, we were sailing in the opposite direction from the original discoverers of Hawaii, but this was hardly relevant to the navigation involved, nor to the twenty-two plants we carried, all species introduced by the Polynesian seafarers. The plants — including coconut, gourd, sugarcane, sweet potato and yam — were wrapped in moss, matting and tapa cloth, which is made from the inner bark of the paper mulberry tree. All survived and flourished when planted in Tahiti after our arrival.

I will describe only one incident, since it illustrates so well one aspect of Mau Piailug's navigation skills. This was our planned landfall in the Tuamotus after a month at sea. The Tuamotus were deliberately chosen as being upwind and upcurrent of Tahiti itself. Mau Piailug's confident estimates of distance run and observation of the southern stars which now arched overhead showed we were in about the right latitude for the archipelago. One set of ocean swells was rolling in from the north-east and another was coming from the south-east. Towards nightfall the latter swell was abruptly cut off, suggesting the proximity of the extensive Tuamotu atolls in that direction. A pair of large terns, that had been circling the masthead, flew off to the south-east.

'Those *ititahe* never fly more than thirty miles from land and always sleep ashore,' Rodo Williams told us. We altered course to the direction the birds had taken and, shortly before dawn, the silhouette of Mataiva's palms broke the horizon ahead.

In many ways the voyage had been an imperfect enterprise, but the consequences exceeded all expectation. We had hoped that the practical reenactment of a proud tradition would enhance Polynesian self-respect, but I for one was not prepared for the magnitude of the renaissance of far-voyaging that has resulted. The great part of the credit belongs to a young Hawaiian, Nainoa Thompson, who was trained by Mau Piailug and who has in turn trained a school of young navigators from Hawaii, the Cooks, Tahiti and New Zealand.

---

1   *We, the Navigators: The Ancient Art of Landfinding in the Pacific*, 2nd ed., University of Hawaii Press, 1994.

2   Chief Kaveia of Taumako, one of the ship's company, is now the senior traditional navigator of Santa Cruz.

David Lewis, *Shapes on the Wind*, 2000

The Jonah Divemaster

THESE DAYS Sid Marsh's focus is on birds, notably threatened forest bird species such as kokako, kiwi and kaka. He works as a Department of Conservation ranger based at Franz Josef.

During the 1970s and '80s he built up an impressive record as a diver. He first put on a mask for paua and mussel dives around the Whitianga area in 1973, and has since dived extensively around the New Zealand coast and throughout the South Pacific, also in the Sea of Cortez.

His 1991 book *Diver's Tales* brought together salty stories of diving on wrecks, exploring the fiords, crayfishing, or simply enjoying favourite dive spots such as the Kermadecs and Three Kings islands, which he describes as wonderful but always 'unpredictable'. And then there were the waters around White Island, where dive parties went down with an active volcano playing nearby . . .

I could feel its presence. Out there in the void something — some creature — was watching us.

Malcolm and I were 36 metres down and intent on following the lubber line of my compass. On a due east heading and still sorting out our neutral buoyancy with the b.c.d.s, we had only just begun the U-patterned search of the seabed. Another two atmospheres below, naked slabs of rock were swallowed up by the sands of a great plateau that stretched on for about 60 metres before dropping vertically over the edge of the continental shelf. We paused, gazing down from our 36-metre vantage point at a meadow of featherstars, a bushy black coral tree, and lots of *Diadema* urchins. After turning left 90 degrees and moving forward past a school of blue maomao, the search was continued on a northerly bearing.

A trail of tiny rising bubbles drew our eyes to a silica-rimmed fumarole

— a house-sized area on the bottom, pocked with vents that puffed hot mineralised water. As this mineralised water chemically reacted with the surrounding cold seawater, silica was precipitated in a murky cloud of white dust-like particles.

Three minutes later we again altered course, this time to the west, but still there was no sign of what we were looking for. Instead, several kick-cycles into this run, a number of splendid perch, drift-feeding on invisible plankton, appeared below. The colourful males were gaudily splashed with purple-blue heads, orange hind bodies, and yellow tail fins edged with purple. One straggler drew my eyes away from the main school, and it was only then that I saw it — down on the grey sand, resembling a toy miniature of the real thing.

I signalled to Malcolm to stay where he was while I descended for the pick-up. He too could see it, and responded with an 'okay' signal before I dropped out of formation like a diving Skyhawk — down 40, 45, 50 metres. Hitting the bottom, I snatched the camera unit, a Nikonis II with strobe and light meter, then quickly pushed off to begin the long ascent back to the surface. A few metres away lay the other piece of jettisoned equipment — her weightbelt. It could stay there; no way was I going to try lugging that back to the surface! Back at 36 metres we linked up again and together continued the long upwards slog. After a couple of staged safety stops in the shallows, the two of us finally popped back to the surface half an hour later.

Our anchored charter boat, M.V. *Nautilus*, was about 40 metres away, her name painted boldly in black on her square white stern. She was an old-fashioned boat, comfortable and seaworthy, with a deep cockpit and a superstructure topped off by high-flying outriggers and aerials.

We swam on towards her. Malcolm was mad keen to inspect the salvaged camera, so I passed it over and watched him as he caressed and tinkered and even clicked-off a photograph.

'Holy mackerel, that was a bit of a fluke, coming across it like that on only the third run,' he remarked, snapping off one more. 'What do you plan doing with it, Colin? Surely not return it to her?'

'No way. Finders keepers, mate — marine salvage rights and all that,' I replied. '[An American] lost her camera. She was lucky she didn't lose her life.'

'You're telling me.'

Behind the *Nautilus*, White Island rose, high and mighty, into a clear blue sky. White Island — a boulder-tossing geyserland that belched thick clouds of steam and sulphurous fumes.

Dubbed the 'weather vane of the Bay of Plenty', White Island is a steep-sided cone around an enormous crater. Along with two remnant volcanoes — the precipitous lava plugs of the Volkner Rocks to the northwest and the Club Rocks just south — it lies 50 kilometres offshore, right in the middle of the bay.

With a thunderous rumble, the volcano shook as Malcolm and I reached the boat's stern. Using one hand to steady myself against the dive platform, I lifted the camera rig up out of the water so it could be retrieved by the skipper. Malcolm and I helped each other off-load the scuba units, and they too disappeared into the boat. Next were the weights and then the fins, before we ourselves followed by climbing up the ladder.

The 'old man' was inspecting our find, and judging by the look of incredulity on his face he was more than a little surprised to find himself holding the 'lost' object in his hands. After it had been abandoned the previous weekend, he probably figured it was gone for good. But that didn't stop him from having a playful jab.

'Gee, what took you guys? You were down over 40 minutes.'

I responded testily. 'Up your nose, Jack. We recovered it at 50 metres, so most of that time downunder was spent decoking in the shallows.'

Malcolm backed me up. 'Jack's just trying to needle you, Colin. I mean, let's face it, in exchange for a single risky dive you've scored yourself a camera rig worth 1500 bucks.'

Jack told him where to go, and Malcolm retaliated by pulling a face and poking out his tongue. That really cracked us up.

From where I stood, I could see the buddy-board with its list of divers still down. Malcolm and I were the first back. Two buddy pairs, plus an instructor with six students, had yet to return. While I had been away searching, Jack had temporarily stood in as divemaster, assisting and checking off divers as they entered the water.

'When did Peter finally get his class underwater?' I asked him. Another rumble from White's scooped-out cavity made us all glance over in its direction.

'About 15 minutes after you two went down,' he replied, before adding. 'Boy, sometimes this place really gives me the creeps.'

'So they should be up any minute, then. Good.' . . .

His eyes were drawn to White's steamy plume, then down to the tip of the cone, where a sinister-looking haze swirled before being dispersed out to sea. Anchored downwind, the *Nautilus* copped the dregs of this foul-smelling gas. The three of us coughed and spluttered.

'Smells like a mixture of methane, ammonia and rotten eggs,' gagged Malcolm, quick to cover his mouth and nose with his handkerchief.

'Whatever it is, it's probably highly poisonous. Cripes, look at my brasswork! It's gone black,' sighed Jack. 'Not again! It took me hours, not to mention the three tins of Brasso, getting it right after last weekend's trip.'

He continued to grumble as Malcolm wiped a finger along the rail and studied the smudge. 'It'll be a reaction between the copper base in the metal and something in that gas — a form of oxidisation, greatly accelerated.'

The unpleasant fumes wafted on.

'There'll be more of that to come if we stay anchored here much longer,' I said.

'As soon as all the divers are aboard, we'll motor on down to Wilson Bay for lunch,' said Jack, coughing and spitting over the stern.

I packed the last of my gear away while Malcolm headed for the galley to put a brew on. Jack fiddled with the compressor, getting things ready for the up-and-coming filling session. Just then, White's volcanic rumbling ceased. For a minute or two, an eerie silence prevailed. As it turned out, it was the lull before the storm.

Nearby there was a splash, and then the first plaintive cry carried across the water.

'I'm dying. I'm dying.'

Malcolm caught it too and in a flash was on the dive platform beside me. Not 15 metres from where we both stood transfixed, a diver floundered, with blood oozing from her nose and mouth. Her eyes were closed. 'I'm dying. I'm dying.' The words gushed out of her bloodied mouth as her head lolled back. At that instant another diver, probably her buddy, hit the surface.

'Hey. Hey you!' I yelled to get his attention.

He looked over.

'Tow her to the boat. Get that mask off her face — quick.'

He snapped into action.

Blood was running down the girl's face and dripping off her chin into the water. As she was brought in, she gabbled non-stop. It looked bad. Jack joined Malcolm and me at the stern, volunteering his services.

'Do you want the oxygen?' he asked me.

I nodded, and he bolted away below decks, emerging just as the victim was pulled up to the boat.

'Ditch her belt. Help me take her scuba unit off,' I ordered. Between the diver, Malcolm and myself we managed to jettison the bulky equipment. We dragged her up onto the platform and then manhandled her limp form onto the *Nautilus* — thankfully clear of divers and gear. She was in shock but still conscious. Blood discoloured the front of her wetsuit.

We laid her out on the deck, and I did my best to reassure her.

'You're going to be all right. Just relax here. Breathe slowly and deeply.'

She groaned again. Jack finished assembling the regulator/mask attachment to the oxygen cylinder.

'Oxygen's ready to go.'

'Okay. Turn it full on,' I instructed.

Both of us were crouched on either side of the girl. I took the mask from him and placed it over her nose and mouth. By now the bleeding had stopped and she breathed steadily, inhaling and exhaling the oxygen. It gradually flushed the tenseness from her body.

Her partner had by now boarded the boat and was intently watching Jack and me administering the oxygen. Malcolm approached him, hoping to find out what exactly had gone wrong, but he was spaced out and still catching his breath. I turned to the girl.

'You're going to be all right — Lisa, isn't it?'

She looked up to me and gestured 'yes'.

Back at the dive platform, two more divers had arrived, but Malcolm held them at bay. In dribs and drabs others returned to the boat while Jack and I continued to administer first aid.

Meanwhile, with every oxygenated breath, Lisa slowly recovered, and her buddy gradually regained his composure.

'What happened, mate?' I asked.

Before he had a chance to reply, Lisa spluttered through the mask.

'The instructor left us behind on the way down. We weren't ready to follow . . .' As she paused to gasp in more oxygen, I cut her off.

'Don't talk. Just breathe in the oxygen. That's right, slowly and deeply.'

Gazing at his girlfriend, the guy bent down beside her. She lifted an outstretched hand and he took hold of it. After some deliberation, he started to talk.

'It was how Lisa said. The others went down too fast. They just continued on without us. I was having problems with a leaky mask; after fixing it we descended in a hurry to catch up, but they had disappeared. Figuring we'd find them on the bottom, we kept going right on down.'

'How deep did you go?' I asked.

'I don't know for sure. A little over 30 metres — maybe more.'

'What was your approximate bottomtime?'

He was vague. 'About five or ten minutes.' Too vague. We needed hard facts. I tried to think while Jack checked Lisa's pulse. A few metres away, Malcolm contained the returning divers at the rear of the boat. The guy scratched his scalp and hesitantly offered a little more.

'Come to think of it, Lisa's instrument console might have a bottomtimer and a depth-recorder on it . . .'

He didn't need to tell me twice. Seconds later I was holding the console in my hand, and Malcolm joined me in studying the instruments. Together we gagged at what they divulged. 'Fifty-eight metres!' I choked.

'Fifty-eight metres for eight minutes,' added Malcolm.

Both of us were incredulous.

Talking from beneath the mask, Lisa gave us her version. This time I didn't bother stopping her.

'We knew it was deep. We were stressed out at losing the instructor, but it wasn't until I spun around and saw this great big fish swimming directly at me that I really freaked and bolted for the surface. I panicked, I'm sorry.'

'Look, don't apologise — you're alive, and that's what matters.'

She'd been on the oxygen for 10 minutes now, and despite the appalling depth and long bottomtime I was convinced she wasn't seriously injured. Jack thought as much and told her so.

'You're going to be okay. I'd say all that blood would have been caused by ruptured blood vessels in your sinuses and nasal passages. Not nearly as bad as it first looked.'

'Yes. I'm feeling a lot better now,' she said, continuing to breathe from the apparatus.

'Are you experiencing any bends symptoms? Pins and needles in the limbs, nausea, fuzziness, etc?' I asked. We had to be sure.

'No. I'm feeling okay — honest.' She flashed me a smile.

'All right, that's good enough for me.' I eased the mask off her face and disconnected the oxygen cylinder. 'Just watch yourself over the next few hours, and if at any time you aren't feeling 100 percent, tell me.'

She got up, a little wobbly, moved to a squab nearby, then asked if she could have something to drink. I suggested some juice or a cup of tea, and Jack rose to get it for her. I turned and called out to the waiting divers. 'Right you lot, you can come through now.'

Balanced on the platform and perched on the stern, the eight divers collected their stuff and started moving through, awkwardly penguin-shuffling one by one into the cockpit. Soon they were disassembling their gear and changing into dry clothes. Meanwhile, Lisa downed a couple of orange juices while Jack started ferrying the empties over to where they would be filled by his compressor.

A few metres astern Peter the instructor, the only diver still in, swam back in his leisurely fashion. He wouldn't be a happy man when I told him about Lisa. Out beyond him, White Island shook and disgorged a sizeable cloud of brown smoke that rose into the plume of thick white steam.

Malcolm and I yawned while Peter glanced at his watch and got a shock — it was five o'clock already. If he and his class were to keep to their tight weekend schedule, they would have to get a move on. Yet another dive, a search-and-salvage exercise, had to be done before the day was out. I told him about the anchor and gave its approximate location, and he was enthusiastic enough to incorporate it into his planned dive.

After his small band had been briefed, they all squeezed into the cockpit and started gearing up. The other four divers not involved with the class decided to go for a dive as well, and the end result was a divemaster's worst nightmare — a limited deck area crammed with people putting on suits, assembling aqualungs and donning equipment.

I was trying hard to keep a low profile on the poop deck, when Malcolm's head popped up from below — he was standing on the railing.

'Fancy a spot of fishing?' he asked.

'Yeah, I wouldn't mind.'

'I have to throw a bit of tackle together; be a couple of minutes. How 'bout grabbing the inflatable, and I'll meet you up forward?'

'Done.'

I climbed down, through the divers donning and checking their gear, and worked my way back to the stern, where the inflatable's bowline was hitched. I undid the rope, pulled the tender up to the *Nautilus*, and was about to clamber in when I had an afterthought. I hailed my old mate. 'Jack. How about passing my mask, snorkel and fins from that red gear-bag there.' I pointed in the general direction.

'Sure — this one, is it?' He reached over, retrieved the gear, and passed it on to me via the nearest divers.

'Good one. Thanks fellas — have a good dive,' I said, as I chucked the stuff into the rubber-duck, climbed in and pushed off. I rowed up to where

Malcolm waited at the bow. As I came alongside, he threw in some bait and a couple of handlines then, with a tackle box under his arm, lowered himself down. I moved forward while he positioned himself at the helm. After the eighth or ninth pull, the outboard roared into life.

'All set?' he yelled over the burbling two-stroke. I grunted, bracing myself against the sides and the hard plywood bottom.

'My middle name's Goff,' he bellowed, 'and in a shower of spray we're bloody well off!' The throttle was floored, and we tore away with a drenching lurch. It was a short, exhilarating ride. Several hundred metres out from Shark Bay, he cut the motor and we drifted to a stop.

'This spot looks as good as any — throw the pick over, Colin.'

'What's the magic word?' I teased.

'Now!' he ordered. I chucked it in. It was deep; we only just had enough warp.

Two baited lines soon followed the anchor, and not long afterwards we felt the first tentative nips. I pulled off my soaked tee shirt, spread it over an oar and, drinking in the sunrays, lay back against a pontoon.

Suddenly, with an almighty yank, Malcolm's line was nearly ripped from his grasp.

'Cripes, I've got a bite — something big too,' he said, rising to his knees and bracing himself to do battle. Another colossal tug, then nothing. He waited, then hauled the limp line in.

'I think the rat's taken my hook and sinker.'

As he recovered what was left, the nibbles on my line intensified until, lo and behold, I too had something hooked. I reeled the line in, pulling hard. Soon the fish was at the surface, then thrashing wildly in the bottom of the boat. It was one of those worm-infested things — a barracouta.

'Don't throw it back; it'll do for bait — the bass love it,' he said, plonking his hurriedly repaired line over the side again. I screwed the fish off the hook and cut up some more bait. Straight out from where we lay anchored, something was brewing. Drawn in from all directions, concentrations of gulls and other seabirds circled above a patch of water percolating with fish. A petrel swooped down, followed by a succession of gannets peeling off to dive vertically into the ocean. All of these birds emerged with fish wriggling in their beaks.

Malcolm was watching too. 'That's where the action is — over there, mate. Probably a big school of trevally or kahawai feeding on krill,' he said.

'It's a pity we didn't bring a rod and some lures along. It would have been pretty neat trolling through that lot, eh?' I said.

'An unweighted line with a bit of meat on it might work — depends really on what sort of fish they are, and how hungry they are. First things first though; I'm out to nail this bugger down below.' He only just got the last word out, when once more he was pulled forcefully down onto the pontoon. 'Yours truly is at it again,' he grunted through clenched teeth.

I moved in closer to give him a hand, but he stopped me with a gasp. 'No, mate. She's right — I've got it.'

He struggled and cussed as I rebaited my line, lowered it down, and almost immediately hooked another fish, this time a blue maomao. Once again Malcolm lost his groper.

As quickly as it had started, the feeding frenzy in the distance petered out. The birds took to the air and dispersed in different directions; some maintained their vigil over the surface waters, while others shuttled back to White Island. I landed yet another good-sized specimen — a bright-red pigfish.

The groper down below stole yet another hook and sinker from Malcolm, while I scored my fourth fish, which I gutted and cleaned for the pot. Perhaps attracted by the blood, several gulls alighted nearby, and soon other birds were amassing overhead. A gannet tucked its wings away and plummeted into the sea, before surfacing to fly off with a single, squirming anchovy. More and more birds arrived — gulls feeding at the surface, and gannets and petrels pursuing their quarry further down. Next to our hull, an urgent flurry developed into a rushing splash of white froth and foam — a sizeable school of fish caught feeding in the shallows. On the outskirts of this activity, a long scythe-like dorsal cut through the water — yellowfin tuna. The mass of anchovies was stampeded even closer to our anchored craft. Malcolm was spellbound; so was I.

'Try some bait on a floating line!' he hollered over the noise of the birds. In a futile bid he tried, with his bare hands, to rip the sinker from the thick nylon fishing line. I proffered my knife, and he snatched it away.

Caught up in the spectacle developing before us, I abandoned the fishing and leaned over to have a look below. At that instant, about eight metres down, a big dark form tore through the mob of small fish.

I squawked in delight. 'There's a whopper down there!'

Herded closer and closer by birds above and tuna below, the harassed school broke the surface forward of the bow — thousands of pulsating silvery bodies displacing an area several metres across. It was an awesome, stunning sight.

'Holy hell!' swore Malcolm. From where he was positioned, he stood up for an unobstructed view. 'It's a bloody meatball!'

'Meatball' is a term used for a school of baitfish herded by predatory fish into a terrified, tightly bunched ball.

Approaching the shadow cast by our hull, the school compressed itself still tighter, tucking in close to the protective bulk of the inflatable. Setting his sights on a tuna, Malcolm threaded a hunk of barracouta flesh onto his hook and then cast his line over to where the water boiled. Soon he was fighting a creature at the other end — not a fish, unfortunately, but a big gluttonous gull. The bird launched itself into the air and in a state of confusion gyrated above.

From all quarters, the meatball was crashed again and again. The birds squabbled and screeched, while the golden sickles of tuna flashed in the sun. Malcolm freed his line and joined me in watching the packed baitfish being busted up by the rampaging tuna — big, black, silver and gold. In a matter of minutes the meatball was smashed and dispersed.

'I've never seen anything like it,' I babbled. 'I mean, we were right there, slam-bang in the middle of it all.'

Malcolm shifted his gaze to look beyond where I was seated. 'Yeah,' he grunted hoarsely. Still looking in the distance, he paused, and then added, 'It was something, all right, but the way things are shaping up you ain't seen the half of it — have a gander behind.'

I twisted around. Over a huge school of what looked to be a mixture of baitfish, trevally and kahawai, the birds had again regrouped, this time in their hundreds — another massive meatball was in the making. Half a hectare of water erupted with a rippled splash, a signal for the birds to begin their assault.

In record time the anchor was back in the boat. Malcolm started the outboard and then gunned it, steering straight for the column of working birds. As we came up onto the plane, I thought about what we had just experienced. It had been a staggering spectacle — one could only imagine how it would have appeared underwater. Underwater? The notion suddenly hit me. I stretched across to retrieve the snorkelling gear, and Malcolm immediately twigged.

'I'll drop you right in the middle of it — don't go until I give you the word,' he shouted above the din of the two-stroke, adding with that characteristic smirk on his face, 'and watch those bities.'

We rapidly closed in. I managed to don the fins, with difficulty, then placed the mask on my forehead. Just in front now, petrels and gannets fell headlong into the melee. Malcolm closed the throttle, threw the motor into neutral, and then pressed the kill-switch so we coasted the last few metres to where the fish swirled at the surface.

Such was the fear of the baitfish that those on the outside were jumping on the top into the middle of the meatball, until it was built 15 centimetres above the waterline. Several yellowfins harassed the anchovies, circling around and charging in and out. The bird noise was deafening.

Malcolm gave the order, 'Right, Colin — go!'

I held the mask against my face, did a backwards roll, and thudded into the numbing cold. I blinked both eyes open — no fish? Against a blue backdrop, trails of tiny bubbles rose from my body as it righted itself and bobbed to the surface. The snorkel needed clearing — a quick blast, before twisting around to find, not three metres away, a wall of anchovies — thousands of them, whirling about an imaginary hub. Big predators circled this rotating ball of fish. One big 'fin swam up and smashed into a cluster of individuals on the edge. The resulting blood and guts drew in another 'fin, and then another — again and again.

Like a single huge organism, the meatball was driven on. Individual kingfish were appearing on the scene, while at eye level pairs of orange webbed feet dangled into the briny — ravenous red-billed gulls scavenging anything and everything. Shearwaters probed further into the depths, propelling themselves along with an underwater form of flying — beating their wings as a means of propulsion to prey beyond the range of the gulls.

I raised my head from the water to check the inflatable's position. It was adrift 30 metres away, almost blocked from sight by the avian clamouring. Malcolm appeared to be trying his luck with the fishing again, but the gulls, it seemed, had other ideas.

He yelled out to me. 'What's going on down there?'

'It's total chaos — fish everywhere. The 'fins are really getting stuck into it,' I shouted back.

Right then a gull surfaced with his bait, swallowed it and took to the air. At the other end of the line, a livid Malcolm swore and struggled to hold on. I left him to it, lowering my head into the storm of fish below.

I now found myself unwittingly on the inside of the baitfish whirlwind — encapsulated by their dizzying, ceaseless revolutions. A giant 'fin streaked by, uncomfortably close, shaving off a mouthful of fish. I wasn't the only one caught up in the squeeze — circulating in the opposite direction to the anchovies were kahawai, koheru and a number of purple skipjacks.

Suddenly my heart missed a beat. I sensed it before I saw it — a juggernaut flashing past on the outside. En masse the terrified anchovies shifted, and once more I found myself floating vulnerably just beyond their rotating ranks. The tuna had strangely disappeared. From side to side I scanned under and behind — then finally dead ahead.

Like an armoured tank crashing through a barrier, the fearsome spear and then the head emerged as the creature shook itself out of the meatball. Its mouth was crammed and overflowing with a bloodied mass of baitfish. The surviving anchovies scattered to reform while, with an explosive burst, the marlin accelerated out of sight. I urgently hailed Malcolm.

'There's a bloody marlin down here!' I shrieked.

He was busy with the bailer, sloshing an evil-looking concoction out of the boat and into the water. 'Yeah, I know — I've been chumming the water, trying to lure him in closer.'

I was aghast. 'You idiot — there could be sharks around.'

'What do you mean, could be?' he pointed towards White, before shouting in annoyance, 'It's not called Shark Bay for nothing, you know!' He was about to digress further when, right alongside, all hell broke loose.

A body of water and fish ballooned upwards, swelling bigger and bigger until it burst with a mighty splash — the marlin, through a ton of anchovies, launched its body vertically into the air. The nearby birds took to the skies in fright, fish bolted, and Malcolm himself dived to the far side of the tender. A scooping bucket pushed ever higher by powerful sweeps of its tail fin, the creature's mouth spilled over with mutilated silver bodies before sinking back beneath the waves.

Underwater, I watched the marlin gulp down the haul, before casually turning to swim slowly and powerfully in my direction. I froze, oblivious to all else — noise, movement, birds, fish, water. From spear-tip to tail-end, it would have been three and a half metres long. Fully illuminated in the shallows, with muscles flexed and rippling, its sleek body shimmered with colour.

The pectorals flared outwards, bringing the fish to a sudden standstill directly in front of me. At first I felt exposed, terrified, fascinated — but when it gradually dawned on me that I wasn't going to be next on the menu, the old bowel and bladder muscles tightened a tad. Its sword-like bill was as long as my arm and about as thick at the base. Although no longer chewing, its mouth continued to open and close, pumping a flow of oxygen-rich water over the gill region, while its huge bulk was momentarily stilled. The front dorsal fanned out and, as it drifted side on, the black, hawkish eye focused intently.

My eyes likewise had been tracking every movement. I unexpectedly found myself thinking back to the black-and-white photographs in Zane Grey's book — the obscene pictures of dead marlin suspended stiffly from a tripod with block and tackle. I half-wished Mr Grey could be with me now, observing first-hand this regal specimen and its fresco of living colour.

Above a silver belly, a distinctive lateral line emphasised the metallic blue-green sheen on its back. Most striking of all were the 15 to 20 lavender stripes running down each flank, the vivid colour intensified by an aura of vitality and raw power.

Without warning, the marlin unceremoniously departed — vanishing in a blur of speed — and in its place a paddle clumsily materialised, followed by an inflatable pontoon. It was Malcolm. The sea and sky were empty. After the marlin's initial slashing attacks, the fish had broken ranks and fled; the birds had also dispersed. I swam over to the rubber-duck, clenched the rope holdfasts and hauled myself back on board.

'How'd it go?' I asked him.

'No good. Bloody gulls. Without lures it was hopeless. If only I'd brought along my skin-diving gear.' He sighed wistfully — on both counts, groper and marlin, he had dipped out.

'Them's the breaks, mate,' I replied.

Malcolm got the motor going, and we moved forward, gathering speed — heading south around Troup Head rather than back to Wilson Bay. He shouted something about cobwebs as we tore on past Crater Bay toward Otaketake Point. It felt good to be on the move again.

We heard the distinctive 'dook-dook-dook' before we saw it. Cruising just above the wave tops, a helicopter rounded the headland to our front — it was an RNZAF Iroquois. Wide-eyed, both of us watched as it flashed close by and banked out of sight behind Troup Head.

I cupped a hand around my mouth and shouted, 'Low-level exercise.' Malcolm nodded.

We tore on straight ahead. The salt spray stung, and after only a few minutes my tee shirt and shorts were once again soaking wet.

Our joy-ride soon had us abreast of the point, where we smacked head on into a vicious chop, and as we neared Ohauora Point the sea conditions worsened until we were forced to turn around and motor back.

From afar, White's headland crests were iced with snow-white patches — densely packed colonies of the Australasian gannet. Beneath the eroded scoria heights, these breeding grounds stood out in sharp relief, sandwiched between lush green belts of vegetation and strips of scraggy dead pohutukawa trees. In the lee above Otaketake, a bluish smoky haze covered the gannetry, partly obscuring the birds there from view. I knew this smoke was due to the hydrochloric acid in the volcanic fumes reacting with the ammonia in the birds' excrement — how they tolerated such a concoction was anybody's guess. We kidney-pounded our way back around Troup Head in time to catch the air force chopper disappearing around North-East Point.

Back at the *Nautilus* there was a reception committee waiting for us — long-faced and unsmiling. As Peter grabbed the bowline and steadied the boat, he broke the news.

'She had a relapse — we radioed for help. The air force sent a helicopter; they're taking her to the chamber at Tauranga.'

'What are you on about, mate?' I asked, suddenly filled with dread.

'It's Lisa. She's got a bad bend.'

It took several seconds to sink in. Malcolm and I climbed aboard the *Nautilus*. For a minute or two, no-one knew what to do. In the meantime White Island smoked, then ominously rumbled and shook, as everyone except Jack fearfully ogled the volcano. The skipper looked me up and down, then yelled loudly, sprinting forward to weigh anchor.

'Let's get the hell out of here!'

Sid Marsh, *Diver's Tales,* 1991

A Shower of Spray . . .

CAPTAIN FRED LADD and his wife Mabel set up Tourist Air Travel in 1955 with one second-hand Grumman Widgeon. When they bowed out of TAT twelve years later, there were several Widgeons operating. Fred had won an MBE and a devoted following among tourists, crayfish hunters and the remoter residents of the Hauraki Gulf. He took the Duke of Edinburgh on his first Widgeon flight in 1962.

Freddie Ladd stories still get told today, especially his Waitemata swan song of risking loss of licence, hefty fine or jail by flying his beloved Widgeon under the Auckland Harbour Bridge in March 1967. He was discharged without conviction after a rap over the knuckles from the magistrate, and $13.50 costs.

But TAT had been no overnight success. To the Widgeon had to be added a licence, an office, advertising, fuel sheets — and training. Ladd, though an experienced wartime and NAC pilot, had no experience of water flying. He was to learn the hard way about wave sets, good and bad landing spots and the hair-raising tendency of his Widgeon to 'water-loop', or suddenly sheer off to port, on landing . . .

I returned to Auckland to start getting ready. Our secondhand Grumman Widgeon from Tahiti, ZK-BGQ, was giving TEAL's engineering staff a few headaches. It was really just a corroded heap. A combination of tropical humidity, sea water, salt air, and a very hard life with numerous mishaps had left it a really sick duck indeed. The engineers were almost in despair over it, and my heart sank when they showed me parts of the wreck. The scheduled 'quick refit' turned into an overhaul marathon that went on — and on — and on . . .

As week succeeded week, and the Widgeon was still not ready, I found myself more jobs. I dreamed up letterheads, made friends and contacts of anybody I thought might be useful to a budding tourist airline. I went on a tour of the north by car to survey various potential beach landing sites with Jim Weir, of the Department of Civil Aviation.

I was a bit over-keen, and in my inexperience of water flying I wanted to land on all sorts of waterways which were quite impractical. If it was wet, I wanted to land on it. I wanted to land on Hamilton Lake, the Waikato River, all the Rotorua lakes, and most of the beaches from Pahi to Dargaville, as well as Hokianga Harbour and Hauraki Gulf. Jim wasn't really very genned up on amphibians either, but he proved to be a fairly good judge of potential landing areas, and the ones he ruled out were the ones I never sought once I did get amphibian experience.

When I thought I'd done just about all there was to do to start an airline, the Widgeon still wasn't ready. The engineers kept on finding more things wrong with it, spare parts were awaited from overseas, and weeks and months crept by. The Widgeon had cost only £6,000 to buy, but repair work sent the cost soaring to £11,000 before she was airworthy.

It was a very depressing and crippling period for us, because we were spending all our capital, and more, without turning a propeller. I started with the company just before Christmas, but it was May 1955 before ZK-BGQ, my very first Widgeon, was test flown by Captain Johnny McGraine, a well-known TEAL flying-boat captain. I went up with him on my first dual flight and my first flight off water in a Widgeon. It was also Johnny's first Widgeon flight, so far as I know, but he was a pukka flying-boat captain, and TEAL had assigned him to teach me to fly from water. If he couldn't do it, who else could?

And so Johnny climbed into the pilot's seat and I into the co-pilot's, and we were ready for take-off. We'd really been around the aircraft and checked our tanks and fuel and oil, and there was a small but representative crowd of the 700 people from TEAL to cheer us off on our historic first flight.

When all our hatches were closed, Johnny gingerly taxied on to the ramp and down into the Mechanics Bay sea water. It was quite a nice day for flying, with clear skies and a light northerly. Johnny was very thorough. He tried out the undercarriage, and it went into place OK, and after warming her up he turned her round in circles either way, and tested the magnetos as he would have done with a full-sized flying boat. Finally he was satisfied.

'Well, are you ready, Freddie?'

'Yes, I'm ready.'

WORKING ON WATER

He gave her the power, and the Widgeon surged forward and the waves seemed to dash up over the hull and around the windows — there was water and spray everywhere. Just as the Widgeon started to come up 'on the step' in aviation parlance (in layman's words, its hull began to plane like a speedboat's), Johnny suddenly closed off the throttle and eased her back into the ocean again. I looked across to see what was wrong, and saw his trousers all soaking wet and the cockpit floor just about awash — he'd forgotten to close his window and the sea had practically flooded us.

'Well, Fred,' he said, 'I guess that's first blood to the Widgeon.'

I little knew then how many more transfusions I was going to get learning how to fly it.

He closed his window and we started again. This time we got airborne without mishap, and we flew a little way and then landed. We took off again, and did 1 hour 20 minutes flying from Mechanics Bay to Mangere and round about. The next day we did circuits and landings, and I did my first dual flying, learning how to handle the magnificent, multi-engined Grumman Widgeon. On 5 May Johnny rang to say that he was sorry he wouldn't be able to give me any more dual that week because TEAL was sending him to Australia.

I was so angry that I tore strips off Mr Johnny Veale of TEAL in protest. Here we were, putting all our money into flying training with TEAL's pilot, and in the middle of it they'd sent him off to Australia, leaving me high and dry like a duck in the Sahara. I said how we'd been waiting six months to get airborne, and that this wasn't a fair go.

Mr Veale was apologetic, but he wanted me to wait patiently until Johnny came back to finish my training off. I had other ideas. I rang up an old mate of mine in the RNZAF, Squadron Leader J. 'Knuckles' Wilson, a former flying-boat skipper from Lauthala Bay (now a group captain). I asked him if he thought he could give me a dual check-out. I explained that Johnny McGraine had been teaching me but had had to go away, and that we wanted our aircraft flying commercially as soon as possible.

Squadron Leader Wilson said this would be no trouble at all, though he'd never flown a Widgeon either. The Widgeon had been left at Mangere, where I'd done my flight checks from land, but I could not yet fly from water. It fell to me to check Squadron Leader Wilson out from land first, and I took the Widgeon up several times to show him the drill at Mangere. When I thought he was proficient I hopped out and left him to do his solo flying. He picked it up pretty quickly — after all, what's another waterplane to a flying-boat veteran?

When he'd done his land solos, I said: 'That's bang-on.'

'Right-o,' said Knuckles, 'let's get back into my own environment.'

I jumped into the co-pilot's seat and prepared to be checked out from water. Knuckles was to take off, do his first water landing with a Widgeon, and then proceed to teach me how. This may seem to be somewhat unorthodox in the light of modern aviation rules, but it was all right in those days.

We took off and did a circuit of the harbour. There was quite a chop on the water from a strong easterly. Knuckles began his circuit and started his let-down. He was very confident, having had many hours in flying boats, and for him this was just another flying boat, although it was only a fifth of the size of the Sunderlands he normally flew. Even as he came down to do his first-ever water landing in a Widgeon, he was speaking calmly: 'You keep the air speed at approximately 80 miles an hour, and as we get down closer to the water you throttle back a bit — like this — and you check your undercarriage up . . . and you can put a bit of flap on now . . . we're coming down to the water now and we begin our round out . . .'

We landed in a flurry of foam, and there seemed to be waves everywhere. When we came to rest, and all the froth had cleared off my cockpit window, Knuckles said: 'I'm sorry, Fred, but I've broken your aircraft.'

I couldn't believe him. '*What*!' I yelped, 'It looks all right to me.'

'Look at the starboard float,' he said. And I looked, and there it was, swinging merrily on a few bits of wire, and all the struts were broken and the wingtip was in the water, and dropping. We were liable to turn turtle any moment.

'Right-o,' said Knuckles, 'get out and do your wing drill.' I sat there, unable to believe that my own beautiful Widgeon, which I still hadn't really flown, was already broken.

'Come on,' yelled Knuckles, 'you'll lose the aircraft if you don't hurry. Get out quickly, I mean it.'

I could tell he meant it then, and I unstrapped and ran down the corridor to open the rear door. When I looked out there was all that angry sea flowing past, only about six inches away, and I thought I'd better get a lifebelt. I went back down the corridor and was bending down to pick up a lifebelt when Knuckles really roared: 'If you want to save your blasted aircraft *get out on that ruddy wing.*'

I realised then that there was to be no lifebelt. I rushed back, clambered out on to the fuselage above the cruel sea, and clawed my way up on to the wing, which by this time was pointing merrily up to the sky with one tip, and had the other half-buried in the waves. If it stayed there much longer we'd turn right over and sink. I did my best to ignore the whitecapped waves beneath, and crawled right out on the wing. Under my weight we slowly righted.

'OK,' Knuckles yelled, 'you all clear up there?'

'Y-Y-Yes,' I stuttered.

It was May, which isn't the warmest month of the year in New Zealand. I hadn't fully acclimatised from Fiji, I had on just ordinary clothes, and there was a strong easterly making my teeth chatter.

Knuckles started taxying us in to Mechanics Bay. We were at Kauri Point, which is between Hobsonville and the present harbour bridge, and we had about a mile and a half to go. I was really dejected and cold as a frog. I could see the float dangling as Knuckles made a wonderful job of taxying in, and I did a wonderful job of freezing out on the leading edge of the wing, about the saddest thirteen stone of counterweight you could find anywhere. We finally got to the ramp at Mechanics Bay and Knuckles selected his undercarriage down and gave the engines the works and we climbed up on the ramp in fine style, no longer a lame duck on dry land. We went up so smartly that we very nearly overshot at the top, and I thought we were going to have another prang, but didn't.

Coming down past the Auckland wharves I was thinking dejectedly of all the anti-publicity we were going to get by having a prang before we even got officially opened, but this was one time when the press slipped up. None of the newspapers or the radio got on to our mishap, to our very great relief.

It was 11 June before we flew again. The Widgeon had been in a bit of a mess with a crumpled nose and float, struts and wires bent as well as a mainplane, four trailing-edge ribs and one aileron. TEAL's engineers worked hard to get her in shape again and when she was ready I had to rely on TEAL again to provide me with an instructor. The RNZAF, sad to say, had laid down instructions that none of its personnel were to train me because of fear of legal complications in the event of their breaking our aircraft — a thing we never even contemplated.

This time TEAL selected Captain Eddie Tredrea as my check-out captain. We did 1 hour 30 minutes on 11 June getting him acquainted with a Widgeon, as he'd never flown one in his life before. We got airborne without any trouble, and then flew around the harbour circuit discussing how to land. Eddie knew I'd been down to Invercargill watching the experts, and he asked how they did it.

'You land with the nose well forward,' I said expertly.

'You're sure?' he said, a bit dubious, and I told him that was how they did it down south.

He was still doubtful in spite of my confidence, because I think we came in to land about halfway between nose well down and nose well up. As we landed, the plane suddenly shot off to port in what I thought was going to be another water loop, and we came to rest literally in a shower of spray, at right angles to our landing path.

We sat there for a bit, both a little shaken up as far as our nerves went, and neither of us saying a thing.

Captain Tredrea was the first to speak: 'You're sure they said to keep the nose down?'

'I'm absolutely positive.'

'All right,' he said, 'we'll go up and try it again.'

Once again we roared off over the Waitemata, turned round over North Head, came back over Stanley Point, and in for the landing.

'You're *sure* about the nose being down?' Eddie said as we were coming in.

'Absolutely. That's the way they do it in the South Island.'

We touched down, and just after landing the aircraft went *whooshing* off in a circle to the left, giving us another big fright. We sat there in dead silence. I wasn't game to say a word.

'Well, I'm sorry, but it looks as though you'll have to go to Invercargill to be checked out in a Widgeon,' Captain Tredrea said finally. Then he looked at me with a sudden ray of hope in his face. 'Do you mind if I have one go at trying to land it my way?'

I was sweating profusely by now. After all, I'd never been a flying-boat captain, and it seemed that every time we'd ever left either the ground or the sea in this thing there'd been an adventure, first with Captain McGraine, then with Captain Wilson, and now with Captain Tredrea. Each time it had seemed like we'd been dicing with death, and I could see that Captain Tredrea was quite willing to leave the aircraft in my care, without ever checking me out.

'Do it your way — sure,' I said, and once more we roared off into space.

Not a word was said as we came in for the third landing, because Captain Tredrea, the great flying-boat captain, was doing it his way, and I wasn't going to interfere. In any case I was clutching my seat and saying a silent and very private prayer, because I didn't know what was going to happen when it was done his way, and by now I had just about lost all the faith I'd ever had in Widgeons.

He brought her in with the nose well up, and he kept a lot of motor on and had the tail well down, and he came in and put her on the water that way, and she landed so beautifully that we both yelled exultantly: 'Terrific!' It was as perfect a landing as you could pray for.

He took her up and down again a few more times to prove it wasn't a fluke, and that the Tredrea way was THE way, and after that we started to fly our Grumman Widgeon ZK-BGQ very successfully.

I sat with him for an hour and a half while he practised, and then he started to give me my training. We went out for a stint next day, doing dual conversion and dual circuits and landings, and on 15 June it was my turn to do my first solos, flying nose up and tail down the Tredrea way. I made it OK, and after that he never climbed into the cockpit again — I was checked out as a capable Widgeon flyer after 6 1/2 hours training. Tourist Air Travel was at last airborne, a real aviation company that actually flew . . .

I had the audacity to do my first commercial flight into Kawau Island on 19 June 1955 — for the grand official opening of New Zealand Tourist Air Travel. I spent a busy few days acting as TAT's public relations officer, as well as its manager/pilot, and organised a fitting opening, complete with blue ribbon, a mayor to cut it, some newspapermen to watch, and a radio commentator, the inimitable Phil Shone, complete with tape-recorder.

A small crowd gathered to watch us at the old seaplane terminal at Mechanics Bay. His Worship the Mayor of Auckland, Mr J. H. Luxford, did the ribbon-cutting, and Johnny Veale and quite a large turnout of his 700 staff knocked off their various duties to make the crowd look larger and more enthusiastic. I'd cooked up quite a nifty little stunt to publicise our Widgeon's capabilities, by collaborating with the management at Kawau Island to put on a midday feast for the mayor. I'd promised Mayor Luxford that TAT could whisk him away from his mayoral duties at noon, fly him to Kawau for a grand inaugural flight dinner, and have him back in his office at 2 p.m. It seemed an impossible feat at that time. The general manager of TEAL, Mr Geoff Roberts, was invited but was not available, and Johnny Veale represented him. We also invited two newspaper men as passengers, 'Pop' Shaw of the *Auckland Star*, and Jim Duncan of the *New Zealand Herald*. In that pre-hydrofoil era of launches and ferries, such a trip seemed almost impossible, and was shrewdly calculated to wake Auckland people up to the great value of a Widgeon service.

I was a bit despondent when I arrived at the wharf that morning and found a north-easterly wind getting up. A choppy sea was the last thing I wanted, because at that stage all my flying had been done in flat calm weather. I'd never landed or taken off with passengers in waves. Every half hour that morning I was out to check on the harbour, and to my horror the waves were getting bigger and bigger. Mabel said at least a couple of times that I ought to cancel the trip, but I didn't really see how we could without losing a lot of face. We'd put out so much publicity about what the amazing Widgeon could do that to call it off because of a bit of wind would have been a very poor show.

By 11.30 a.m. there was a fifteen-knot wind blowing, and to my unaccustomed eyes it looked as though we were in the midst of a full-scale storm, coming straight out of the north-east, diagonally into Mechanics Bay. The official party duly arrived about the same time as various experts from TEAL were coming out to look at the harbour and saying: 'Are you going to fly in this?'

The speeches started, the tape-recorders were taping, and the blue ribbon fluttered in the gale, imploring to be cut. Mayor Luxford finally put it out of its misery, and we all boarded the Widgeon.

The mayor sat beside me in the co-pilot's seat. I started the motors and it was 'down the ramp into the damp' in capable Widgeon fashion, to the cheers of the crowd. Once in the sea I found I didn't like things very much at all. The waves were breaking right over us. I didn't know it, but my misgivings were shared by my wife, and by some of the TEAL people up on the wharf. I taxied out into the main stream to see how big the waves were, didn't like them any better, but felt I'd passed the point of no return. So I turned the Widgeon around and back to the shelter of the Jellicoe Wharf, turned into wind, finished off my cockpit drill, and fed in the power.

In those days I had not yet coined any magic words to counter the passengers' fright at the great showers of spray churned up by a skybound Widgeon on take off. My poor passengers just had to sit there and wonder as the waves came up right around the cockpit and all around the windows. Everybody, including me, was full of excited apprehension as she came up on the step, beginning to plane. Instead of taking off nicely . . . we bounced all the way across the harbour, leaping like a sea-horse from wave to wave. Back on the wharf all the official people and the 700 folk from TEAL were lining the wharves and . . . every time I bounced, the TEAL boys cheered. They were just about hoarse with cheering by the time we laboriously clawed our way into the sky against a very strong wind. We made Kawau in twenty-five minutes, to find that the landing spot I'd planned to use was now impossible, with waves tearing over it like wild horses.

I found a place off a point at the tip of the Bon Accord, next to Mansion House in the main harbour. The only person feeling any apprehension as we came in was me, landing for the first time with my first load of VIPs on a virgin patch of ocean. But I made quite a creditable landing and felt very pleased as we taxied round the point and rolled up the beach at Mansion House. We were met by all the Mansion House staff and the owner, Alan Horsfall, and he and his merry men and women ushered us all into the diningroom and a very sumptuous luncheon. It was such a very good luncheon that when we got to the sweets the Mayor was beginning to relax completely, and regret all the chores and papers and things he had waiting for him back in his mayoral chambers.

He said what a good idea it would be if they could stay the whole afternoon, and the rest of the party dutifully agreed, as they are supposed to do when mayors suggest things at official luncheons. I was the only one who didn't say 'Hear Hear'. All through the soup and the entree and the fish I'd been listening to the wind getting up until, by the time the main course arrived, it was fairly howling around Mansion House. I kept wondering how on earth I was going to get airborne as I chomped my way through the roast chicken and sipped somewhat abstractedly at my coffee. When the sweets came on I piped up, addressing the mayor: 'I think, sir, that we'd better hurry the sweets and get away.'

His Worship was in no mood to hurry. 'Come on now, I'm enjoying this,' he said.

'Well, after all,' I said, 'the idea of this trip was to leave at noon and get back by two, and if we don't, the whole point of the thing is lost.'

'That might be so,' said His Worship, 'but I'm enjoying this, and I'm not in any great hurry to get back.'

I stuck to my guns. 'If you listen, there's quite a wind getting up. I think we'd better go,' I said.

The mayor agreed, rather reluctantly, I excused myself, and hurried down to warm the aircraft up. I was really apprehensive by this time. Mansion House Bay is a very small bay, and the Bon Accord Harbour is very long and big, and out there I could see the waves marching past in great style, bowled along by a twenty-five-knot wind. The party came out shortly after, and we waved our hosts goodbye and taxied out into the waves. I knew we couldn't get airborne in Mansion House Bay, so we had to taxi into the big stuff in Bon Accord Bay. When we got there the old plane went up and down with the floats submerging on each side, wallowing around like a half-drowned duck.

It was terrible — impossible to get airborne in that stuff — and yet I knew that if I didn't get my guest back it was going to be goodnight to any favourable publicity for TAT's Kawau Island service.

I turned round and taxied back into the bay.

'Why are we going back?' piped up the mayor, and it was fairly obvious that he didn't know much about seaplanes.

'Oh, I always come out here to have a look at the wave situation,' I said. 'Now we're going back into the bay, and when we get in by the beach we'll take off from there.'

'Great,' he said, still full of enthusiasm after the dinner, which was apparently sitting lighter on his stomach than my apprehension was on mine. One thing that came to me . . . was a conversation I'd had recently with George Bolt, the famous New Zealand aviation pioneer and seaplane expert, who'd given me a lot of tips on amphibian operation. He told me that if ever I was in a situation where I wanted to get airborne quickly, it helped to take the aircraft as close in as possible to shallow water, and then take off and allow the ground effect to take the aircraft up on the step much quicker than is usual in deeper water. I decided to try the George Bolt technique, and went right back in towards the beach before turning round. There were no magic words. I just said 'Ready?' and gave her the power.

We came up on the step very quickly and started to roar across Mansion House Bay, going fairly well because we were diagonally into wind. We were only just on the step when we reached the first big wave in Bon Accord Harbour, and the thumping that started then was terrific. The book says that for a cross wind you hold the starboard wing down towards the wind and slowly let your nose come round, down wind. I tried to do that, though in my inexperience I exaggerated the manoeuvre, but I kept the power on and we kept dancing in until finally we got into the troughs and tore along parallel with the troughs in that awful gale. We began to bounce higher and higher, until what I thought were bounces were in fact 'porpoising', but I grimly kept the power on and somehow we came out of the last porpoise leap into the air — just in time to see the cliffs looming up on the other side of Bon Accord Harbour.

We were flying straight at those cliffs, and we just managed to scrape up enough height to clear them before we turned over the top and headed for Auckland.

The mayor was happily patting me on the back. 'Marvellous, Captain, marvellous,' he said. 'I didn't think you were ever going to get airborne, you're a great flyer.'

He apparently didn't realise how pale and sweating and trembling I was. We had the wind in our tail now, and we shot back to Auckland in twelve minutes, fairly racing in the storm — and it really was a storm by now. We landed at Mechanics Bay according to Hoyle, but as I went to taxi up the ramp I noticed something different about it. The concrete shoulders were sticking out at the bottom. The tide was out, and as I gave her the power to climb the ramp she merely went over on her nose. I pulled the power off, and the tail slapped back on the water with a thump, and there we were sitting at the bottom of the ramp, bogged in the Waitemata mud — an inglorious end to a very adventurous first official trip. It was my first low water spring tide, too.

I stopped my motors. Johnny Veale of TEAL looked around at everybody and said to the mayor in a loud voice: 'Well, Your Worship, exactly the same thing happens to us with our big flying boats. It's absolutely impossible at low tide, we've had a lot of trouble like this.'

I was very thankful to Johnny. I knew darned well that he never brought his big Sunderlands or his Solents up on low tide, he was just being kind to me. I signalled the TEAL mechanics and they brought a dinghy down the ramp, launched it, and ferried the mayor and Johnny Veale and the press boys ashore. As they reached dry land on the ramp I opened the cockpit window, and shouted: 'Whatever you do, gentlemen, when you get out of the dinghy you must walk up the *side* of the ramp. Don't step up over the wall on to the ramp proper, or you'll slip and fall and possibly hurt yourselves. It's very, very, slippery.'

The mayor got out first and did what I'd told him. Duncan and Johnny Veale followed, likewise obedient. But Pop Shaw, the *Star*'s man, decided to take a final picture of the Widgeon sitting ignominiously in the mud. He stepped off the correct path on to the ramp proper, which was covered in a very slippery marine moss. I was gazing horrified out of my window, knowing what was going to happen, but before I could get out a yell of warning Pop slipped, and I saw a pair of heels and soles flying straight at me. He was on his back, hurtling down the ramp, and his slide only stopped when he hit the bottom . . . knocked out. The TEAL chaps came artfully down and picked him up and they got him to the top and stood him up. He was groggy enough to be taken off to hospital for observation. I waved them all goodbye from the mud — a most depressing finale to New Zealand Tourist Air Travel's inaugural opening flight.

The only really good thing about it all was that nothing was ever said, either in the press or over the radio, about the bad things that happened. Pop Shaw was in hospital, and couldn't write his story, and the *New Zealand Herald* doesn't seem ever to write anything about a *Star* bloke, so they didn't publicise our disastrous finale.

We got only good publicity and, thanks to the gale, had the mayor back on the wharf at 2.05 p.m.

Fred Ladd, with Ross Annabell,
A Shower of Spray and We're Away, 1971

Across the Tasman
in the Pamir

FOR HIS CLASSIC account of the years of the *Pamir* under the New Zealand flag, Wellington author and master mariner Jack Churchouse was able to draw on substantial and well-written accounts of shipboard life, taken from diaries and letters of former officers and crew.

One was third mate Francis (Bob) Renner, whose classic account of *Pamir* only just surviving a Pacific hurricane on her fifth voyage in 1945 is among several extracts memorably portraying shipboard life on one of the world's last great ships trading under sail. After her return to the northern hemisphere and Finnish owners, *Pamir* was tragically lost in 1957 in a north Atlantic hurricane, taking down eighty of her eighty-six crew.

Another sailor/writer of note was Andrew Keyworth, who had signed on as bosun's mate for *Pamir*'s first voyage under the New Zealand flag in 1942. By his ninth voyage, he'd been promoted to second mate, and (briefly) temporary acting mate. Voyage nine took the ship from Wellington via Lyttelton to Sydney. Three months later, delayed by labour troubles, *Pamir* sailed for Wellington, loaded with 2700 tons of cement and 400 tons of nail wire. Her master was the legendary Captain Horace Stanley 'Two-Gun Pete' Collier.

Keyworth's account of *Pamir*'s last Tasman crossing, largely reproduced below, was written in a letter, happily never posted. Docking in Wellington, *Pamir* smashed into the Jervois Quay wharf, her bowsprit stoving in the skylight of the cargo shed (the result of inattention on the part of the pilot, writes Churchouse). She had taken 12 days, 18 hours and 20 minutes, average speed 4.54 knots. The best day's run was 203 miles and the worst, 25.

*B*arque *Pamir*. At sea. 14 April. Night is closing in: the first night at sea. The lights of Sydney are still twinkling brightly low down under our stern. I wonder how long the wind will stay in the south. The ship has a gentle easy movement. She is pleased, as I am pleased, to be at sea again. I felt her come to life passing through the Heads, embracing the first surges of the Pacific swell. How dead she was at Circular Quay. Stately enough but more like a monument than a living thing. She has a soul this ship. Talk to her and watch her respond and a heart that is as big as herself.

We left the wharf a little later than 1.15 but could not set anything till Pinchgut as the wind was rather close. From then on down the harbour we managed to get most of the sail on her. The courses were left until we dropped the Pilot and then every stitch was put on.

It was rather doubtful if we could sail unaided through the Heads so a big tug was kept ahead in case.

I am a little tired. The tiredness that comes after excitement. Very satisfying. I feel like having a good bath and turning in. There is the 8 to 12 watch to keep and I will not see my bed for another four hours at least. I go now for a cup of coffee.

15th. Dog watch. Twenty-four hours have passed and we are not much further ahead. The land is only 90-odd miles astern. Throughout the night and the day winds were very light gradually diminishing in strength until now it is completely calm. There is a tremendous swell rolling in from the east and the *Pamir* without steerage way is helpless, utterly helpless. She has broached broadside on and rolling both gunwales under. The sails bash madly against the masts and rigging with each roll and we can do nothing to ease her save clewing up a few of the lower sails.

During tea time I heard the sound of crockery smashing from for'ard. Sometimes I wonder if they make any effort to save it at all. I have stowed everything well in my room and not a thing has moved. You must not curse her when in these tantrums, rather humour her. She is never so uncomfortable to be unbearable anyway. Tonight I have the 8–12 below so will have a good sleep. I sleep heaviest when she is rolling hardest.

The day was beautiful, clear sunshine, but unfortunately little wind. It seemed strange getting back into the old familiar sea routine again. Working up sights, trimming yards etc. Always watching the ever-changing sky for warning of approaching weather. Keeping careful check of barometric variation. Becoming part of the sea again. This is the life I chose. I have no regrets. I will read a while then sleep blessed sleep.

16th. 6–8 dog watch. Another day has passed and we are not much further ahead. Maybe 20 or 30 miles to the southward. It has rained heavily and continuously for twenty-four hours and no observations were possible. This morning about 7 a.m. the wind came away from the east (dead ahead) for a few hours and we stood south. It blew about force 5 to 6 and we had the first good sail out of her since leaving Sydney. There was a big swell running and she smashed through it pushing with all her 7-odd thousand tons of ship and cargo and throwing water aside in all directions. She looked very grand, close hauled and loaded deep driving through thick heavy rain. It did not seem to matter we were eight points off our course. I was so glad to see her moving again.

It did not last long for about noon she was rolling about in the swell again. The glass has started falling slowly so something may come of the night. It will be my 8–12 on deck too. For my part I care little how long we take on the voyage so long as she is sailing. Even the calms I do not mind for it is not often the Tasman Sea is without wind.

6 a.m. on the 17th. At 11 p.m. last night the wind came out of the SE with considerable violence accompanied with heavy rain. I immediately reduced sail, taking in the gaff tops'l, topgallant stays'l, flying jib and three royals. The glass fell with astonishing rapidity so took in the mizzen upper gallant. Called the watch below out at 11.15 and clewed up mains'l and cro'jack. The sheet of the cro'jack slashed across my face and cut in above the eye and the cheek. Moral — keep out of the way of flying sheets. The night was very dark, incredibly dark. Sent the port watch to take in fore and main upper gallants and my watch aloft to make fast cro'jack. Got the sail off her in time as the wind increased in force to about 8. 12.36. Sent my watch below and turned in.

4 a.m. On deck again. Third mate had taken in fore and mizzen lower gallants, but had not made the mains'l fast. 'Two-Gun' was on deck but went below shortly after I got there. Took in outer jib and lower spanker. Lower spanker had split along a seam and I believe fore lower gallant ripped. Sent watch aloft to make fast the mains'l. While there and as dawn was breaking could see a seam of mizzen upper tops'l split. Brought down watch and clewed it up but unfortunately most of it was ripped and will have to send down same.

6 p.m. Dog watch. It has blown a gale all day. High seas have swept the decks for'ard and aft and washed most of the grime of Sydney away. The watch on deck this morning sent down the mizzen upper tops'l and bent a new one. Quite a job in the wind that was blowing. As soon as it was bent it was set and the ship kept going close hauled into the teeth of the gale

under main lower gallant, upper and lower tops'ls, foresail and the lower stays'ls.

Heard over the radio of the gale that swept Sydney today. Glad we hauled 'Southwind' out of the way. It is part of the same gale we were in. At noon managed to get a fair sort of position. We are only 100 miles due east of Sydney.

In the afternoon the watch bent a new lower gallant and lower spanker and by 4 p.m. the wind moderated sufficiently to set them and the mizzen lower gallant. We are heading only ENE four points off the course but it could be worse.

There is no moon at nights and it is very dark. Practically pitch black and one relies more on feel than sight. However wet it is outside, my room is perfectly dry and my bunk warm. It can blow a lot harder yet before it becomes uncomfortable. The ship is standing up magnificently to the gale, loaded deep as she is. I wish you could see her now. The long low powerful black hull smashing through successive seas that threaten one would think to engulf her completely. Standing up proudly to each fierce squall that comes down on her every half hour or so and trying her with all the force that is in the wind. She staggers a little under each onslaught then collecting herself and freeing the water from the lee scupper rises steadily to meet the next squall. I go now to get my four hours below.

6 p.m. 18th. The gale increased in violence to about force 8 and we took in the three lower gallants at 1 p.m. By observation this morning we were 137 miles further from yesterday's position. Not too bad considering the heavy weather she is encountering and about 250 miles NE of Sydney. There has been no change in the direction of the wind or in the barometer indicating we are travelling in the same direction and at the same speed as the gale system.

It is blowing hard outside and she is shipping heavy water continuously. The sea has risen to immense proportions and the *Pamir* is almost lost among them. She maintains her course very well and there is nothing to fear, she is certainly a fine sea boat. Many another ship would be hove to now or running with the wind on the starboard quarter to get out of it. She was built just for such weather and is loving it.

At 4.30 this afternoon I sent a couple of men out on the jibboom to make fast the outer jib as it was blowing out of the gaskets. She dipped the boom right under the water in a roaring cauldron of foaming white. When it lifted clear one of the men was hanging below, caught in the slack of the wire jib sheets. He had been washed clean off the boom and by some miracle . . . tangled himself up in the sheets. I would not care to lose a man here. I don't think it possible to launch a boat. He had been longer on the boom than necessary so I gave him hell and threatened to fire him in Wellington.

The sails and gear are standing up well to the wind. It seems as though the first gale tested everything and discovered any weaknesses.

I have the 8–12 watch. I rather enjoy it at night in a full gale smashing through seas that come out of the night. God knows where from. There is a great feeling of exhilaration. Man, puny man, defeating the elements. Wrestling with them and defeating them so that I feel like shouting at the wind. Blow — blow — blow your hardest. The ship is more than a match for you. And the wind as if to answer roars back through the rigging — I'll beat you yet. So Man's endless struggle against the elements. The crests of the seas are spaced almost the length of the ship apart so she has tons of scope to rise to them but sometimes one catches her a tricky blow, so that the bow suddenly seems to fall away and plunges maddeningly into the trough. The oncoming sea rises up to meet her and suddenly stops the mad plunge with such force that it threatens to drive her foremast clean through the bottom. All on board are cheerful. Even 'Two-Gun' I think is enjoying it. The lads have stood up to a lot these last few days. I laugh at your forty-hour week.

19th. 6 p.m. By noon observation we were about 100 miles due south of Lord Howe Island. She made just 104 miles for the day's run. The gale still rages outside. Will it ever abate. We drove her all through the night and the day under tops'ls and fores'l. There is an enormous sea running, smashing into her every few seconds so that it is an awful struggle, a battle every inch of the way. Last evening the wind veered a couple of points and now the ship is just able to lay her course for the Cook Strait. The day passed without incident. It is just a ceaseless battle and now everyone is more or less resigned to it. With all the weather we have not missed a meal which counts a lot for keeping up the general morale, nor for that matter have we missed even our morning or afternoon tea.

The gale has had a good psychological effect on the crew preparing them for harder things perhaps in Cook Strait. Discipline is better understood under these conditions and they take it well. They move smartly round the deck. All the lassitude associated with a long stay in port has disappeared and by the time the gale has finished they will be fit for anything. At the beginning one or two of the newer boys were a little sick but now all have recovered. The only cure for seasickness is a good long voyage with plenty of bad weather . . .

20th. 6 p.m. Today is Sunday, the first Sunday since leaving Sydney. There was little to do with the sails so the crew had an easy day of it. Last night the wind moderated sufficiently to set lower and upper gallants, mains'l and cro'jack and that is everything on her except the royals, gaff tops'l and flying jib. It blew about force 6 all day so she had on all she could stand in comfort. There was an enormous sea running although it has moderated somewhat at present. The sea was coming at us about two points on the starboard bow, breaking clean over the forecastle head and smashing away aft until brought up by the break of the midship section. It was so high and steep that several times I saw the end of the bowsprit which is normally about 30 feet above the water bury itself under green seas. The after deck was very wet, seas breaking over the weather side and crashing right across and over the lee side. At times she put her lee rail under and literally scooped up tons of water. We pushed her fairly hard all day. She was logging between 9 and 10 knots which is not bad with the yards braced hard up on the backstays and punching into a heavy sea.

At 4.30 the wind shifted aft a little so I squared in the yards half a point. This eased her considerably and now with the sea moderating everything is fairly comfortable.

I had a go at sheeting home a little on the jibs at 5 p.m. to make her steer better, but no sooner was the watch on the focs'le head than she shipped a good green one scattering us in all directions so I gave it up as a bad job and sent them below for tea. Too many men have been lost off focs'le heads to warrant risking these lads.

We have [been] driven many miles north off our course, in fact we are north of the North Cape of New Zealand but are now laying the course for between the Islands. The only redeeming feature for being so far up here is that it is not yet at all cold. This is as well as everyone has been wet at times including the 'old man'. At night the galley is like a Chinese laundry with gear drying. There is no chance even yet to dry anything outside. To be wet is pretty bad but to be wet and cold is awful. There is a funny sensation when suddenly finding yourself waist deep in water. The sea rises up underneath your oilskins and sort of takes your breath. Then it flows down inside your sea boots and fills them up. When the water has subsided (it is always as well to catch hold of something and hang there when caught by a sea until it subsides) you find there is difficulty in walking. Your feet are far too heavy and there is a dreadful squelching inside your boots. Of course the boots must be taken off and the water tipped out. The trouble is though once sea boots are wet inside it takes a long time to dry them out. In fact they never really dry at all. So when down in the cold southern latitudes you can imagine what it is like pulling cold clammy boots on in the early morning watch before sun up. I have the 8–12 on deck again tonight. It is very dark outside. No moon or stars. Only a peculiar kind of phosphorescent glow from the sea which provides sufficient light to be able to distinguish the silhouette of the sails. When you go on deck at first of course nothing can be seen for half an hour or so. It is just an inky void. Gradually things take shape and all seems well again. During the 'black out' one just goes by touch and feel. These are the times actually best suited for learning to 'feel' the ship. Like the man who is blind, certain dormant senses attain the facility to relieve the loss of other senses.

21st. 6 p.m. Today is Monday, just one week since we left Sydney. We had hoped to be in Wellington by now but adverse weather such as we have experienced was not reckoned with. At noon we were 440 miles due west of Cape Maria Van Diemen, near the northernmost point of New Zealand and actually are not yet halfway to Wellington. Last night in the 8–12 the wind eased sufficiently to set the royals and later on in the morning watch gaff tops'l and flying jib. There has not been much wind today, about force 3 and from the SW. She has idled along at about 5 knots but the day was bright with plenty of sunshine. There were blankets and bedding airing on the foredeck this morning. Oilskins turned inside out to dry and all manner of wet clothing etc. This is the peace that comes after the storm. The mate had the watch on deck chipping rust, of which there is plenty to do. Fine days such as these are not often found in the Tasman Sea so full advantage must be taken. The sound of the hammers was a little disquietening to the watch below trying to catch up on sleep, but I rather liked the din. It was noise of industry, something going on and poor girl she needs chipping so badly.

How different each day is from the other. There is a kind of relaxation today not like the tenseness in the air when we were driving the ship for all she had. Work goes on just the same but in a different atmosphere. I sometimes wonder if steam ships are like this. It is so long since I was in one I almost forget. This is a very old-fashioned way of moving about the world but I prefer it that way.

There is only a moderate swell running though it is confused and has a restless look and feel. Was this ocean ever completely still? The prospects are for a quiet night though I wouldn't be surprised to see the wind back into the NE before the morning. The ship is out of the cyclonic system and the wind should revert to Southern Hemisphere practice of revolving counter clockwise. I wonder. There are many things to wonder about at sea in a sailing ship. The sea and the stars and the wind. The immensity of it all. The circle of horizon in the centre of which we are. The great star-studded dome overhead. We are all alone in the middle of it all.

22nd. 6 p.m. There was little wind all day. The *Pamir* logged only 62 miles. Throughout the day there was barely sufficient to fill the sails and at 4 p.m. the mains'l cro'jack and spankers were clewed up to prevent chafe. Rolling around in the swell does more damage to the sails than a good fresh breeze. She idled round all day rising and falling to a languid Pacific swell. The sun shone again and most of the crew worked chipping rust stripped to the waist. Her decks, a day or so ago dangerous with breaking seas, are now dry except for a very occasional lapping up through the scuppers as she rolls a little heavier on an extra large swell. There is a general feeling of contentment on board. We are not able now to make a fast passage so it may just as well be a pleasant one. Wellington is a little over 500 miles away.

Early in the morning about 3 a.m. the lookout reported a light astern. It could only be seen occasionally at first going on and off as it dipped over and under the swell. It became more distinct and other lights appeared with it. I called up on the morse lamp and it proved to be the *Port Huon* outward bound on her maiden voyage, her destination Wellington. She would probably be there tomorrow and we . . . She came up alongside quite close. A great pulsating vessel. A blaze of lights. I heard her telegraph ring and saw her slow down and stop. She asked us if all was well and offered to report us in Wellington. She spared us a few minutes of her valuable time while her officers looked down and wondered. Maybe her skipper on the bridge served his time in sail. I could almost see him leaning over the rail of the bridge recalling forgotten times when in a ship such as ours. He would look and I know understand.

There would be young men on the bridge too, men who had never seen a ship like this under sail. Some might laugh a little (behind the 'old man's' back) when he compared his modern up-to-date liner with us. Others may feel a little envious and I know many would give up the comfort of a modern ship like her to sail with us as indeed I did. What their thoughts were I cannot really tell, just surmise, for we spoke but little with the lamp, there seeming little that words can say.

I heard her telegraph ring. She came to life again, mechanical wonder, in the way that steam ships do. Her stern light had disappeared over the horizon ahead before my watch on deck had ended.

Another kind of voyager fell in with us at 11 this morning. A traveller in the sky. The trans-Tasman flying boat. He spoke to us on the radio-telephone and wished us luck but could not stay with us at all. His schedule did not allow even a few minutes as with the liner. Speed more speed, where is everyone going in so great a hurry? What a contrast. This 'boat' overhead like fish a million years ago which spurned the sea and then the land, grew feathers and flew. This plane will traverse this ocean forty-five times to our once. I still prefer the *Pamir* and our way of life.

Stars shine brightly outside. Great clusters of them. Occasionally their reflection is caught on the top of a passing swell. They seemed to claim an affinity with the sea. There is hardly a breath of air. A stillness covers the ocean broken only by the slatting of sails and sometimes a squeak in the rigging high aloft, as the spars sway in and out among the stars. A squadron of albatross are becalmed under our stern, great sea wanderers at rest. Nights like these are the only time I think they sleep. Sometimes when sleeping they drift together the way that ships becalmed occasionally do and awaken each other with deep throated squawking. I marvel at the way these birds carry their sail in a gale of wind, luffing up to lift through a squall. Never heaving to. I think they should have reef points in their wings. Sailors say they are the souls of clipper ship captains.

23rd. 6 p.m. Last night a breath of air floated in across the ocean from the NE rippling the surface of the sea, bringing it back to life, catching the *Pamir* gently alee. The after yards were squared and she wore round on to the port tack. Her sails filled and she came to life like a bird about to take flight, poised a little, then gathered way heading into the south and east. The ripple about her bow had a clear-cut note, played in melody — the music of the sea. The wind freshened gradually and she increased her speed fairly leaping at the sea. A school of porpoises under her lee mimicked her antics and kept company for an hour or three. But the sky clouded over and great cloud banks rolled in over the horizon. At dawn, a grey murky dawn, she was logging a steady 10 knots under a full press of canvas. It began to rain soon after and continued throughout the day. We kept driving her all the time. In the early afternoon the wind hauled aft a point or two so we squared her in a little and eased the strain of her sailing.

The crew were under the focs'le head making baggy wrinkle and any other wet weather job that could be found.

We did not see the sun all day so at noon a dead reckoning position was placed on the chart. It puts us 460 miles from Stephens Island in the middle of Cook Strait. From there it is 73 miles to Wellington. We shall be another two or three days at least. Our latitude is 36° S. Not much further south than Sydney but already the weather grows colder. Standing in the rain all day somehow puts a feeling of tiredness on you. I think I shall turn in now. I'll be out again at midnight.

24th. 6 p.m. I came on deck at midnight. The sky was heavily overcast. It had been raining hard and the night was black as pitch. Earlier in the evening the wind had freshened so they took in the royals. We set them again to keep her driving in to Wellington. The barometer continued falling all night but nothing came of it. It began to rain again heavily at 4 a.m. and the wind decreased. At 8 a.m. she was only logging 5 knots. At 10 a.m. a black ugly cloud appeared on the western horizon on our starboard quarter. I brailed in the spanker and gaff tops'l to prepare for a shift of wind. It came a few minutes after but the course was altered to catch it dead astern and not take us by the lee. It blew hard for a few minutes and the surface of the sea was white. The squall passed over and the sun came out from behind it to warm and dry the air. The squall took the rain away but it took the wind as well and left us with a light north-wester. The yards were squared and we made what way we could. At noon she had covered 203 miles for the day's run. It would have been a great deal more if the wind had remained fresh. The crew were busy all day scrubbing the decks preparing for our arrival in Wellington. The heavy rain pelting at the sails all day washed them as clean as any laundry and when the sun came out they dried very white. The sun went down at half past five and I thought it was the only thing in the sky for there wasn't a cloud anywhere. But a slip of a moon appeared just by the jigger mast. It was the new moon, looking something like a gold ring in the sky with one edge a little brighter, so new it was. Stars came out to keep it company. The larger, bolder ones came first and then smaller more timid companions until the sky was studded. How could I be alone with such agreeable company?

25th. Anzac Day. 6 p.m. Sailors have a saying that if the sun goes down out of a clear sky it will also rise into a clear sky. Today at least that was true for it came up out of the sea a flaming molten ball, saturated, dripping. The stars saw it coming and scurried out of sight not to have their brightness dimmed by a greater star.

The wind held fair throughout the night, just a gentle breeze sufficient for her to make 3 knots . . .

Today at noon we were 148 miles from Stephens Island. All being well we should enter the Cook Strait tonight at about 10 p.m. That rough sea-lane that divides the North from the South Island of New Zealand. The Strait is about 100 miles long. At the western entrance it is quite wide, almost 80 miles, but converges to less than 10 in the narrowest part. The northernmost point is at Cape Egmont marked by that remarkably conical, extinct volcano, Mount Egmont rising 8 1/2 thousand feet out of the sea and likened to Fujiyama in its perfect symmetry. Its perpetually snow-clad top is visible 100 miles in clear weather . . .

20th. 6 p.m. The wind held fair until midnight then fell away to a flat calm and we rolled about on a greasy swell. The loom of Stephens Island light was picked up at 1 a.m. but we saw no more of it until 4 a.m. A light breeze came away and at daybreak the coastline was visible on the starboard bow. The wind just came in fits and starts all day and little progress was made, but somehow or other she seemed to ghost into the straits and at present Stephens Island is almost abeam about 5 miles distant. The day was beautifully clear. Not a cloud marred the sky and away to the north Mount Egmont showed its snow-clad peak above the horizon, the only break in a wide horizon. The crew worked all day touching up the paintwork, endeavouring to make her presentable for her return to her home port, but the passage was too short to do her the justice she is due. Anchors were broken out and cables shackled on and all the various other jobs associated with arrival. Except for Mount Egmont no part of the northern shore of the straits are visible but Wellington is only 73 miles from here.

There is a certain satisfaction when making the land, on finding it where you calculate it to be. The light was picked up just where and when it was expected. All going well we should arrive tomorrow, Sunday. I hope it will be as fine a day as it was today, only a little more wind.

Andrew Keyworth,
The Pamir *Under the New Zealand Flag,* 1978

Visiting South Georgia

IN 1983, master mariner and amateur ornithologist Gerry Clark set off to achieve what had eluded Dr David Lewis ten years earlier: a complete circumnavigation of Antarctica.

Clark (presumably lost at sea in 1999; his beloved *Totorore* later found wrecked on the Auckland Islands) was then 56 — an age when running a Kerikeri apple orchard might have seemed a more attractive option than the treacherous southern oceans. He'd been a merchant seaman and, later, occasional blue-water adventurer. Like Lewis, he would experience and write unforgettably about his several capsizes and dismastings and be tested to the absolute limit of endurance, especially sailing solo during the final third of his three-year voyage.

He had taken seven years to build *Totorore* for his Antarctic quest. She was twin keeled so that she could sit unsupported on a beach or rocky shelf, 10m long, of sturdy kauri. Twenty-six sailors and ornithologists came and went as crew.

The first stage took Clark to Juan Fernandez and then to Cape Horn and the Falklands, where they spent many months exploring, and observing bird life. Then, after narrowly escaping being caught in pack ice on a trip to the Antarctic Peninsula south-east of Cape Horn, *Totorore* headed for the mountainous island that will always be associated with one of the greatest Antarctic survivors, Sir Ernest Shackleton.

*O*f all the places I visited during the *Totorore* expedition, South Georgia stands out as the one I loved most. Lying about 1000 miles south-east of Falkland Islands, it is over 100 miles long and up to 30 miles in breadth, with thirteen mostly unclimbed peaks of over 2000 metres, one of which is almost 3000 metres. More than half of the surface is covered with permanent ice, and there are over 150 glaciers. At the western end there are many rocks and smaller islands, and the coast has numerous inlets and bays. All along the northern and eastern coasts are bays and fjords, in many of which a vessel can find shelter, but the south-western coast where the mighty swells batter unceasingly is very inhospitable. It is a land of breathtaking beauty and teeming wildlife, of sudden violent storms and sometimes calm clear days with sunshine. Although it is in 54½ °S latitude, South Georgia is south of the Antarctic Convergence and is considered an Antarctic island. By late winter the pack ice usually lies close south of the island, and in exceptional years it extends all around it and reaches far to the north. This then was the island to which we were sailing with growing excitement and anticipation.

For two days after leaving Stanley the weather was bad and the sea rough, but the wind direction was favourable. The next four days were gale from the south-east, the worst direction of all, and then the south, which is not much better. My two crew were confined to their bunks with seasickness, but Andreas started to recover as soon as the birds became more interesting. I had many an on-deck battle with sails by myself, soaked in water which was not far above freezing. When the weather was slightly better, Malcolm gamely stitched up the foot of the starboard jib from which the hem was parting.

Wednesday 8 August 1984

Driving snow and a southerly gale continued without a break. A lot of water in the bilges, spilling above the sole, so I hove to on the port tack to make it easier to bail it out. I stayed in the cockpit emptying the buckets, which Malcolm handed out through the hatch, over the top of the heavy washboard. Poor fellow is still very sick and had to make a terrific effort. Andreas is not really sick but still cannot eat. He did the actual bailing inside, getting rid of the water which the pumps cannot reach when she is lying over at a great angle of heel, as she is even when hove to.

If it were not for the trouble of my hands, which hurt a lot at night in bed — probably with arthritis — and always when working outside, I could really be enjoying this. Not the constant discomfort, which is very tiring, but just the fact of being here on our way to South Georgia. It is winter and we had to expect cold and rough seas. But seeing Kerguelen petrels, and especially the Antarctic petrel, have made it all worthwhile . . .

In the late afternoon I had a bad time of it when the wind increased suddenly to Force 10 and I had to reduce sail and heave to. First I found it hard to get the deeply reefed main right off as the wind in it made it hard to wind down. The tail of the halyard went over the side, as it so often does when uncleated, but this time it managed to half-hitch itself around the jib sheet lead-block, which was mostly under water. I lay down to clear it and got soaked. The next problem was to furl the jib; because on the same winch and cleat as the furling line I had the staysail sheet, as neither could be held by their jam-cleats in the strong wind. That took some sorting out on the storm-washed lee side and heavy water broke right over me — I'm very worried about our damaged life-line system . . . The air temperature was −1°C and the sea temperature 3°C and I was very cold and thinking that I should get back down below to change. Suddenly there was a loud clatter and I saw the wind generator lift right out of its socket, still shaking the whole boat with the imbalance caused by having lost another blade. 'Did I just write this morning that I was enjoying this?' I thought grimly as I struggled to secure it with my numbed fingers in clumsy gloves . . .

Back inside I enjoyed a scalding cup of Milo, emptied my gumboots into the sink, stuffed them with clean woollen socks to dry them out, and changed as many of my clothes as I had dry replacements. A solid jet of water came down the Dorade ventilator above the galley stove. 'Now I really do believe what they say about the Southern Ocean,' said Malcolm.

I cooked a big stew with the pot tied firmly on the stove, and my two crew each ate a little out of an enamel mug. My heart goes out to Malcolm. He is feeling it badly that he cannot be of more help, but the poor fellow just cannot get over his seasickness, which has left him very weak. I think both he and Andreas are losing a lot of weight . . .

Saturday 11 August

Ever conscious of the proximity of ice I sleep fitfully for short spells . . . at about 0245 hours I had a feeling that there was something amiss and as soon as I stuck my head out I imagined that I could smell ice. At first I saw nothing, because of the snow, but then the nearly full moon shone on the brilliant whiteness of an iceberg away to starboard. What an exciting moment, my first deep-sea iceberg! I woke my two sleepy crew to have a look but the snow came down again and they could barely see it, so were not over-enthusiastic. I had said that we could eat our last tin of self-saucing pudding when we saw our first iceberg, but tonight suggested that we wait until Malcolm was better so that he might enjoy it too. Malcolm said it did not worry him, at which Andreas demanded 'Shall we have it now?' He has got his appetite back, even though I put an onion in the dinner . . .

Sunday 12 August

Just before Andreas took over the watch at midnight I saw a bright glow right ahead, so stayed up with him to have a look at this monster iceberg . . . a shower passed away and we saw it in all its wondrous beauty, with huge cliffs and rolling ski-slopes on the top, brilliant in the bright moonlight. The whole scene was marvellous beyond description, and we all felt extremely privileged to see it. There were many large pieces of ice floating about within a mile of the iceberg, and as we passed less than half a mile away from it we had to steer between them. Watching the distance from the berg on the radar and taking sextant angles, I calculated it to be a third of a mile long and 56 metres high . . . this, of course, is just a first taste of things to come . . .

The sea temperature has fallen slightly below zero, which is actually four degrees lower than normal, so I am rather expecting that ice at South Georgia will be abnormally heavy and probably very restricting as far as our work is concerned.

Before going anywhere else in South Georgia we were obliged to report to the authorities at King Edward Point in Cumberland Bay, about half way along the north-eastern coast. Since the conflict with Argentina, whose forces had occupied South Georgia, the administration of the island was by the British army major in command of a contingent of soldiers numbering about forty. They were the only human inhabitants of South Georgia, and they occupied the base which was formerly used by the British Antarctic Survey, or BAS as it is known. Meanwhile BAS were operating from a hut on Bird Island off the north-west coast, where three of their scientists were wintering over, and where we were to make ourselves known.

We passed by Bird Island in heavy snow, but by midday on 13 August the snow had gone and the sun shone, treating us to a visual feast as we sailed past the endless array of icy peaks, snowfields and glaciers. We noticed how deceptive distances were in the all-whiteness, with far-off capes looking close, and inlets and bays almost invisible. The day was 'out of the box', as we say in New Zealand.

Monday 13 August

It was dark when we arrived and there was a great deal of brash ice and floating bergy bits in King Edward Cove, which we had to push slowly through with crackling and grinding noises. On the hill above we could see Shackleton House, a huge rectangular building of wood with three stories, which used to be the base for the BAS team but now houses the detachment of the Coldstream Guards . . . Using our spotlight we made our way alongside the wharf on the other side of the point and were greeted by two army officers and several of the troops. They scrabbled under the snow, lying 60cm thick on the wharf, to find ringbolts to secure our lines, and then Major Peter Hicks and Captain Chris Cox came aboard to give us a clearance. They told us we had passed very close to the sunken Argentinian submarine *Sante Fé*, marked by a buoy which I had seen on the radar but I had thought was just another lump of ice.

As O.C. South Georgia, Peter Hicks is the Magistrate, the Postmaster, the Customs officer and the Harbour Master. Having formally attended to the paperwork and then stamped our passports, the two very friendly officers invited us up to Shackleton House for hot baths and a delicious and welcome supper, inviting us to have all our meals with them while we are here and asking if they could help us in any other way. I asked Peter if he could send a telegram home, to say that we had arrived.

Across the cove from King Edward Point is the derelict whaling station of Grytviken; established in 1904 it was the first of six shore-based stations, and it was one of the last to be finally abandoned, in 1965. At one time there were also eight floating factories at South Georgia, and various depots and items of shore equipment can still be seen in some of the coves.

When whaling at South Georgia first started, the whales were so plentiful that the catchers took all they could handle from Cumberland Bay itself. By 1917 the total number of whales caught at South Georgia amounted to 175,250. As whaling continued long after that, it is understandable that the number of whales which still roam the oceans is but a small percentage of the original populations, and some species — the Blue whales, Right whales and Humpback whales — are in danger of extinction.

Tuesday 14 August

We cast off and motored over to Grytviken to have a look at the old whaling station, mooring alongside the wharf close to a steam whale catcher, still afloat, which is apparently going to be restored by the Norwegians and taken back to Norway. Two others in not such good condition lay near another wharf. The buildings were all standing and we were impressed by the size and extent of the whole establishment. Deep snow covered everything; being new it was particularly difficult to walk across without skis or snowshoes, and drifts against the buildings often piled up to the roofs, so our progress through the ghost town was slow. It was fascinating to see the vast machine shops, foundries, storehouses, boiler sheds and the service houses for the community, which must have been quite large during the summer, when they were operational. There was a cinema, dated 1930, but that was one of the few buildings which had collapsed. A pretty little church was apparently also being restored. Abandoned by the Norwegians, the station was leased by the Japanese in 1963 and 1964 and left in very good working order. Since then sailors, mostly from Russian and Polish trawlers, have looted and smashed everything they possibly could. While we were there a military patrol skied through the village from out of the mountains.

When we left Grytviken we motored about seven miles across Cumberland Bay to have a close look at the huge Nordenskjold Glacier, the largest in South Georgia, with a two-mile face . . . we were able to pass only a quarter of a mile from the sculptured crags and columns — blue, green and white — in perfect safety, as it was too cold for much ice to be breaking off. We did see one massive tower come crashing down with a great roar, and we had constantly to steer around floating ice and small bergs. There were not very many birds in the bay, except large numbers of Cape pigeons and the usual Giant petrels, Black-backed gulls and cormorants, but we are seeing the pretty Antarctic terns and a few of the lovely white Snow petrels.

With temperatures down to −10°C and the sea usually sub-zero, we began to know what it is like to work in cold conditions. Even small jobs like taking on fresh water became major tasks. Fortunately the water never froze in the tanks on board, although occasionally our cabin thermometer registered 0°C when the hatch was open, but we did have difficulty with frozen filler pipes to the tanks. We filled our cans from a large hydrant on the wharf which was always left running full bore, and had to be very quick in carrying and pouring in the water before it could turn to ice. To create warmth in the boat to keep the pipes clear meant running the engine, and keeping the kettle on the boil to pour down the filler to prevent blockages.

On our way back along the coast towards Bird Island the wind freshened against us to gale force and it was heavy going. We were forced to take shelter in Prince Olav Harbour, our ship and helmsman, Malcolm, thickly coated with ice from the spray. Ashore we could see another old whaling station, which had been abandoned in 1946, and the stranded hulk of a ship on the point. When I dived down into my bunk for a dry balaclava I found icicles on my sleeping bag, broken off from a stainless steel plate above where the bolts from the sheet winch come through.

Anxious to reach Bird Island before dark we pressed on without stopping, but always looking out for colonies of King penguins and signs of Wandering albatross. Sightings of both made us eager to get started with the work we had come to do. After passing through Bird Sound, a rough and rocky waterway about 0.3 miles wide separating Bird Island from South Georgia, we searched for the entrance to Freshwater Cove where BAS have their hut.

Thursday 16 August

. . . We found it hard to see where to venture in among the surf-swept rocks, and there were moments when my confidence was faltering as I headed *Totorore* into what looked like a dangerous cul-de-sac . . . from the looks on their faces, my companions were even more apprehensive than I was, but when at the last minute the hut came into view, we all cheered. The small, shallow, almost circular cove was full of thick brash and pancake ice through which we forced a way and dropped anchor in the centre.

Thursday 16 August

The three young men from BAS came out to the end of a small jetty to greet us . . . Malcolm had a job to row ashore with the lines. The ice was not firm enough to walk on or slide the dinghy over, and yet was heavy to push the dinghy through. Once the lines were set up it was a lot easier.

The cove is most attractive with a rocky beach, now covered by ice, snow and fur seals, and surrounded by steep snowy tussock slopes. The hut is on the beach; inside was warm and comfortable with a good kitchen and a small bathroom. There was also a bunkroom with eight wooden bunks, a tiny dining room, and a laboratory/office/workroom with benches, desks, radio equipment and beautiful picture windows.

We met Robert Lidstone-Scott, the leader, Simon Pickering who is studying the Wandering albatrosses, and Mark O'Connell who works with both birds and seals. They gave us a nice meal with plenty of liquid refreshment and we talked until late about their very interesting work . . .

Friday 17 August

After breakfast we pulled our dinghy through the ice again and joined our new BAS friends for a walk over the hills. We found walking in the deep snowdrifts between the tussock very difficult, sometimes sinking up to our hips. In other places it was icy and slippery. They were wearing boots with crampons on, and I was wishing that I had brought some.

Everywhere there were Giant petrels of both species — *Macronectes giganteus* and *Macronectes halli* — and it helped us to distinguish between them, now realising that we must have made many mistakes at sea. On a knoll close above the hut, we came across the first Wandering albatross chick on its nest, looking very large and fluffy in its grey down. It clappered its beak at us, but it did allow us to handle it, to see the growth extent of the feathers under the down. There were nests all over the hills, widely scattered. Mark and Simon caught two adult birds which had come in to feed their chicks, and from these we took some lice. Somebody held the bill and somebody else ruffled the feathers of the head and picked out the lice with a pair of tweezers, to put into test tubes. Catching the birds was not too difficult, as they are awkward on land and the two experienced BAS men used sticks with crook wires on the ends to catch the birds by the necks, and then grab them with their hands.

We walked across frozen ponds then down to Johnson Cove, the western end of the island, also already crowded with seals and a colony of Gentoo penguins. Malcolm enjoyed scratching the back of an elephant seal pup, but we had to be rather wary of the fur seals, which are becoming aggressive as the breeding season approaches. Mark told us that in the summer they're a real hazard, as all the beaches and lower slopes are packed and several visitors from naval ships have been badly bitten.

Simon and Mark showed us where the Fairy prions and Blue petrels have their burrows, and as we walked back along the tops of the spectacular north coast cliffs, the places where Diving petrels nest, and a few burrows of the White-chinned petrels. Down below was a peninsula which will soon be populated by about 40,000 Macaroni penguins. Altogether a most enjoyable day, finished off with a nice hot shower and a good steak dinner . . .

Saturday 18 August

During the day a pair of large leopard seals came into the cove and while one disported himself on the ice on the beach the other came over to make our acquaintance. In spite of their reputation I think they have kind faces and this one certainly seemed to be smiling at us. In the afternoon we invited the BAS team on board for coffee, and later went ashore for their special Saturday night dinner. And what a spread! We three from

Totorore had second helpings of all five courses, followed by liqueurs. It was delicious and we felt really full, hoping that the cooks would be pleased by our appreciation of their work, and not just think us greedy . . .

Monday 20 August

. . . Passing several icebergs, we approached Cheapman Bay in visibility reduced by sleet which turned to snow. The coasts of the bay are mostly glacier faces and a long moraine barrier closes the inner part of the bay. We could see a large rock and a dead-straight line of kelp right across, so we approached it slowly and carefully, crossing where the kelp looked less dense. Soundings changed dramatically from 30 fathoms to six metres, and as we crossed the least depth we recorded was three metres . . .

Inside, the water was dead flat and icing over. Looking for maximum shelter we pushed on, but the pancake ice became heavier and more extensive. Although we found a good but narrow lead into a basin, not far from the glacier face, I decided that the risk of being iced in was too great and we came back out to a tiny cove with a small beach which looked inviting . . .

Walls of rock and ice rose sheer above us for several hundred metres, and the softly falling snow made it seem an incredible fairyland. Everywhere there were large lumps of floating ice to be avoided, but we anchored among them in a depth of only three metres and were immediately investigated by a big and handsome leopard seal, which swam around and under *Totorore*, frequently lifting her head out of the water no more than two metres away, to regard us with a big grin on her face.

Tuesday 21 August

. . . We motored over towards Price Glacier edge, but stayed inside the moraine barrier for an easier landing and anchored close off the boulder beach. Andreas and I went ashore in the dinghy, determined to find the hidden King penguin colony . . .

After carrying the dinghy well up the beach we strapped on our snowshoes, which we had borrowed from Bird Island. To begin with we felt clumsy, but soon learnt the advantage of using them over the deep snow. Going uphill was warm work as there was no wind, and we had to strip off some of our outer garments. The snow glare was fierce so I used my goggles. We had a few tumbles with the snowshoes, and found steep slopes difficult . . . Icy patches were very hard to manage, and in one place I found myself skiing down quite a steep slope and wondered how I was going to be able to stop.

When we topped a ridge behind a spur which separated the two glaciers, we were able to look down on to a frozen lagoon surrounded by tussock, just behind the raised beach. There we saw a group of King penguins, which pleased and encouraged us. Maintaining our height we traversed the slopes, searching for tracks which would lead us to the main colony . . . until we came to a hidden valley in the unvegetated moraine at the side of the great Price Glacier itself. At first we saw only a Giant petrel and a Sheathbill, and then a group of adult penguins. Horray!! We had found it! As we came closer we could see another group, and then another, but where were the chicks?

It was not until we were almost among the groups that we finally saw them huddled together, with a small number of adult guardians, tucked behind a steep snow hillock. It was a huge group! However could we count them? The last record in January 1971 had given a total of 183 adults and eighteen chicks, with 50 of the adults incubating eggs. Obviously there had been a phenomenal increase.

We ate a lunch of milk biscuits, trail bread and a piece of chocolate while observing a Giant petrel devouring a dead chick, watched by a Sheathbill, and then started our counting . . . The adults were in six main groups on slopes above and around the chicks and were easy to count, but the chicks were so tightly packed that one's eye could not follow the lines along or across. We eventually agreed on a figure of 2275, which is probably within a hundred or so . . .

Occasionally a chick would break out from the crowd and waddle about ten metres up a slope to be fed by a newly arrived adult. After receiving the regurgitated food direct from the beak of its parent, it would waddle back to rejoin the crowd . . .

Wednesday 22 August

Some larger bergy bits floated past us during the night and one or two scraped alongside, but otherwise it was peaceful enough, except for some terrified noises from Malcolm, dreaming that he was trapped under the dinghy and a Leopard seal was about to take a bite out of him . . .

While we were still crossing King Haakon Bay, motor-sailing at seven to eight knots, the wind freshened suddenly to gale force and shortly afterwards the engine overheated and we had to switch off. In view of the numerous rocks, islets, icebergs and other floating ice which pepper the area I decided to seek shelter in Queen Maud Bay, so we hardened in the jib sheet and tried to weather the island to north of the long Hammerstad

Reef. Icebergs got in the way so we couldn't make it, and paid off to pass to leeward of the reef. Violent squalls laid us well over, putting the cockpit coaming underwater and soaking us with freezing spray, but we gradually made it . . . I couldn't help thinking about my dear mother-in-law Maud, back home supporting us by making rugs to raffle to raise funds to keep the expedition going. If she could see us now she would probably say, 'It looks very uncomfortable.' She would be so right.

Friday 24 August

It was dull and murky when we left Horten after breakfast, dodging many rocks and shoals over which the swell broke heavily. Keeping close into the coast we searched for possible albatross nesting sites on the tussock headlands, and for King penguins on the beaches. Entering a large bay almost entirely surrounded by glacier face, south-east of Holmestrand, we all felt the weird sensation of sliding downhill. It must have been some sort of optical illusion caused by the heavy dark sky astern, and the glare from the snowfield high above the glacier ahead of us, but it was really strange . . .

Approaching Holmestrand we could see that the whole bay was filled with ice, from small icebergs to fruitcake-sized pieces with a rustling, jostling, overall cover of smaller pieces in between . . . we pushed our way gently through with much grinding and crackling and leaving a clear trail astern, which gradually closed in again. In spite of all the ice, we could see breakers on the black shingled beach, or rather against the huge blocks of ice pushed up against the beach, so we forged our way behind some large rocks into a comparatively clear sheltered corner and anchored.

Andreas and I rowed ashore to the quietest spot . . . it was about half a mile and very slow, in spite of some good leads through the ice. Rowing in ice is like trying to row along a boulder beach with the oars jarring on the rock-like lumps. When we neared the beach the problem was to get past the car-sized blocks of ice which barred the way, and it took a while to force a passage towards some rocks . . .

Launching the dinghy was difficult because of all the large moving blocks of ice, but we managed it safely . . . Malcolm prepared a good dinner with tasty dried mince and instant mashed potatoes, followed by stewed dried apples with instant pudding. When we had finished we were alarmed by the crunching, grumbling sound of ice on the move. The wind, though light, had changed and the whole field of loose ice surrounded us, heaving in the swell and grinding its way along the sides of *Totorore* . . .

We are anchored in the middle of an icefield. It is loose ice but there is no clear water to be seen between the pieces. Some are small, but some are the size of a table, and they're grinding their way past us. It's not very pleasant at all . . . There's a big berg not very far away. We're hoping that won't join the small bits and come down on us too . . . if we get frozen into this lot we might be here for quite a long time.

Saturday 25 August

As far as we could see we had suffered no damage, so we started to force our way out of the icefield. To deflect the larger growlers we left our main Bruce anchor awash, with the kedge on its six-metre chain hanging down from it to give it extra weight. As our anchor chain leads over a roller on the end of the bowsprit, the anchors were hanging well ahead of the bow . . . it took an hour and a half to get out and it was a great relief to be finally in clear water.

The wind was southerly and very cold but once north of Cape Rosa we felt the lee. Skirting the rocks we looked for the cove where Shackleton and his crew had landed in their seven-metre open boat *James Caird* after their epic journey from Elephant Island in 1916. The cove was there for us to see, with its shallow cave where those weary men had sheltered, but it was too small for *Totorore* to enter and we anchored in a similar cove farther along.

The cape is where Shackleton's men had taken Wandering albatross chicks to eat, and twice since then albatrosses have been observed there, although the last time, in 1976, only four pairs had been located. Our job is to see how many chicks are here now.

Having covered the whole cape area, we found a total of eight widely spaced nests with chicks. We passed Vincent Island, McCarthy Island and McNeish Island, each named after one of Shackleton's crew. We stopped and went ashore at Peggotty Bluff, where they had camped, and peered up into the mountains where Shackleton and two others had set out to reach the whaling station at Stromness. Everything must have looked exactly the same to them then as it did to us.

Gerry Clark, *The* Totorore *Voyage*, 1988

To the Chathams on Matai

J. EDWARD BROWN worked for the Union Steamship Company in the early 1950s, when he did his first trip as a young radio operator to the Chathams, followed by many trans-Tasman trips and work on ferries out of Wellington.

Later, employed by the Post Office as a radio operator, superintendent and inspector, he travelled all over the Pacific, spending time in Niue and Tonga and using his maritime experiences for two published novels, *Luck of the Islands* and *The Glass Arm*, and a children's novel, *Chatham's Spy Ship*.

Radio operators gave way to technology — GPS and ship's computers — in the 1990s, but previously they were indispensable members of a ship's crew.

The G.S. *Matai* nosed into the seas kicked up by an equinox gale screaming up from the Antarctic. Black clouds zoomed at express speeds. And I was sick aboard a thousand-ton heaving rolling steel ship. The New Zealand government steamer slowly rolled — and rolled. She steadied and started to come back. A cross-sea smashed on her deck and the outer teak cabin door streamed water. Salt seas dribbled down inside. The government carpet floated.

I was lying on my bunk, wishing I was dead, on my first trip to sea, one day out of Lyttelton towards the Chatham Islands. Was this why I had memorised the resistor colour code? I knew that a one megohm resistor had a brown body which meant the first figure was 1, the end was black which was a zero, and the green dot was 5 cyphers following the first two. The knowledge wasn't much use in this situation. I knew many other facts, how to decipher schematic circuit diagrams, discuss the Q of a circuit, and I knew the Q communications code. I knew about 813 transmitting valves, about rheostats and potentiometers, and how to solder. I knew the principal undersea telegraph cable routes, the major world shipping lanes. I knew that New York was one word in the address of a telegram, but was counted as two in the text.

The *Matai* rolled sickeningly in the opposite direction. The water inside the bottle on the shelf at the end of the bunk performed crazy gyrations. A dirty white World War II cork life-jacket hanging behind the door swung backwards and forwards.

The radio room, through the connecting door, was a shambles. Drawers had come out of the desk and a conglomeration of papers and manuals skidded madly around the deck as the seas belted the ship. An emergency lifeboat radio set in a wooden box, untethered, slid about, spilling acid from its motor-cycle type batteries. What did I care? Death would be a relief.

The passengers were similarly afflicted. But they didn't have to work. I did, flat on my back or not. I was the wireless operator. The loudspeaker in a varnished wooden cabinet at the foot of the bunk hissed. It was wired to the radio room's receiver tuned to 500 kilocycles, the international distress and calling frequency, just below the standard broadcast band.

The regular ship on this run, the *Port Waikato*, was under repair and the *Matai* had been chartered by the Holm Shipping Company which ran a fleet of coasters and also the service to the Chathams. This crew was a motley collection, including me, picked up on the beach.

The second engineer was Burmese, polite and well spoken. How he had arrived in New Zealand he never explained. The morose chief engineer, in his mid-thirties and unmarried, was not a happy man. During World War II, and for some time after, he had been employed on American ships, but he only worked when he needed money, then he'd go ashore and do nothing until he was broke. The fourth engineer had never been to sea. He was as sick as I was.

The second mate was a regular Holm Shipping man who normally had a coastal command, but he didn't have a captain's ticket for this tonnage vessel. He sat at the table and glowered at the first mate who had a new uniform, new gold braid and a new ticket, and a hyphenated name. He was English, told to stay out of England, banished to the colonies for his sins. He didn't look as if he was enjoying himself.

Captain Wylie and the second mate enjoyed each other's company and the captain didn't confide in the mate.

The second mate was a story teller and he'd sit at the saloon table and say, 'Have you heard this one?' And launch into another filthy yarn.

The mate had a sextant in a polished wooden box, but we didn't have sunsights at noon, or starsights at night under the leaden skies. We might miss the Chatham Islands and head on for South America, the only land to the east of us.

The cook was a pastry-maker with his own business, another pickup, a singer of songs from HMS *Pinafore*, that Gilbert and Sullivan nautical comic opera with such patriotic choruses as 'A British tar is a soaring soul' and 'He is an Englishman'.

This voyage began at Wellington's Queen's Wharf, after a hot midday dinner aboard ship: soup, roast mutton and baked potatoes, apple pie. At 1 p.m. men came from the Pier Hotel across the street to toss the lines from the bollards and we sailed, on a 15-minute trip to the Miramar oil wharf in Evans Bay to bunker this oil-fired steamer.

Three hours later we went astern from the wharf and headed for Lyttelton. Up went my stranded wire aerial slung between the two masts. I watched anxiously. It was lowered in port to accommodate cranes working into holds, but smashed insulators and snapped wire when rehoisting while heading down harbour were common.

The halyards were tightened so the lead-in wire was tight, and the ship was ready for communication with the nearest coast radio station.

Power on the transmitter. The half-kilowatt transmitter's single MT6B Marconi valve, sitting in its asbestos ring, glowed bright enough to read by. This was the original Marconi transmitter fitted when the ship was built in 1929. It was self-excited, which had nothing to do with masturbation, but meant that it was not crystal-controlled on a fixed frequency, but emitted a frequency generated by means of inductance and capacity.

Just another fact a radio operator had to learn. A 'sparks' needed seemingly sexy knowledge, of frequency multiplying techniques, synchronous vibrators — which of course has as much to do with sex as a knowledge of aerial coupling or electron-coupled oscillators, radio wave propagation, and how to make a married joint. And lots more.

I called Wellington Radio in Morse code and transmitted a voyage report, TR MATAI BND LYTTELTON QTO WELLINGTON QRU. TR was a movement report. QTO meant I have left port, QRU had the assigned meaning of no telegraph traffic.

After the war the *Matai* had been retro-fitted with a Collins brand radio-telephone transceiver, removed from a bomber, for push-to-talk communications with lighthouses, but this was the age of Morse at sea, and telegrams via the Post & Telegraph Department coast radio stations were ships' usual means of communication.

The bulkhead electric fan for cooling was switched off, the radio room was warm and lit by voltage-dropping carbon filament lamps for charging the batteries from the ship's main dynamo, the voltage controlled by large brass knife switches.

We steamed south at ten knots, close to flat out, pitching gently. The long thin blue line of the South Island coast slid by. A seaman was making a kennel out of an orange box. A sick dog dozed mournfully at the end of a length of rope.

We berthed in Lyttelton at 10 a.m. to load fence posts, a tractor, beer in barrels and bottles, mail, 44-gallon drums of petrol and oil, fishing lines, pot scourers, clothes pegs, tinned soup, baked beans and school exercise books.

I had groceries to buy for the Chatham Islands Radio staff, bananas, oranges and sausages, a delicacy in a place where the main diet was fish and mutton.

I interrupted the cook's singing of 'On the Road to Mandalay' (which was loud enough to make the Burmese second engineer homesick) to ask him to store the sausages in the freezer.

Passenger bunks had been made up in Wellington. During the weekend two stewards stripped the blankets and carried them in laundry bags to the Inter Island Steamer Express ship *Rangatira*, where they had friends. The stolen goods would be away on Monday night. A stupid theft, which had to be discovered quickly, and was, by the chief steward, who could have been indignant because he wasn't a part of the theft. Stealing ship's gear and cargo was common. The English stewards could have been deserters, which was common in those times. They were discharged and the police asked to prosecute.

We were alongside for a week, loaded by wharf crane, each box, case, drum, individually man-handled into place in the hold.

The long 1951 waterside strike was over. Earlier that year, waterside workers' unions were deregistered and many men would not return to work with scabs who took the jobs. My father had stood firm and hung up his cargo hook forever. But the government's attempt at making the wharfies work faster had failed, the new wharfies were as cantankerous and exasperating as the old gang.

We departed at 6.30 p.m. Loading was completed earlier in the day, but we couldn't sail before the 6 o'clock bar closings because we wouldn't have a crew. Ships' crews had gone out in sympathy with the wharfies in that 151-day strike, and they were as truculent as ever.

It was drizzling with rain as we slipped out through the heads into the open sea. Now there was no land between us and Antarctica. My aerial was hoisted again and adjusted so the lead-in didn't swing against deck fittings. A race horse in a box on the aft deck looked wet and miserable. The dog crouched in its kennel.

It wasn't calm. I copied the 9 p.m. weather forecast from Wellington Radio. Captain Wylie came into the radio cabin. I rolled the weather message out of my Royal portable typewriter. He stepped out and I was sick in the sleeping cabin's handbasin.

The G.S. *Matai* was the Governor-General's yacht before World War II. Like government ships before her, she had been used for supplying lighthouses and checking for castaways on the Auckland, Campbell and Bounty Islands, as she steamed towards Antarctica. She was a beautiful yacht-like ship with raked bow, masts and funnel painted white, a varnished wheelhouse.

During the war the vice-regal cabins had been stripped, the Navy used her for escort, minesweeping and general patrol work in the Pacific. Since then she had also been used for undersea telegraph cable laying and repairs.

In the *Matai*'s saloon were two long mahogany tables, a piano, a magnificent clock set in a golden sunburst. Perhaps here there had been witty conversations, port, cigars.

In Christchurch I had bought a copy of *Present Indicative*, an autobiography by Noel Coward, and so on a rolling heaving bunk I read of London drawing rooms. Incongruous, though the presumably sophisticated viceregals who once travelled on the *Matai* would have known the salons and theatres of London. They were all English imports.

Why I bought that Coward biography I don't know — prompted by the cook's singing? I'd already concluded that going to sea was somewhat like a musical comedy. I've long ago lost the book, but out of curiosity, decades later, I checked the Christchurch Public Library index, intending to reread it. They didn't have a copy.

Among the passengers were two stock and station agents travelling to sell fertiliser, gumboots, fencing wire, shearing combs and sheep dip, and to buy wool and sheep.

Another passenger was Gregory Hunt, from a family of land owners, a deep-voiced man with a strangely sunken face, who wore a thick roll-neck pullover. I didn't recognise him after we arrived back in Wellington. He appeared in a brown business suit, and his face was plump. He'd left his false teeth behind in New Zealand.

I copied weather forecasts at 9 a.m. and 9 p.m. and every six hours transmitted the weather observation prepared by the bridge officer of the watch.

On a dark Saturday night we approached Chatham Island without lighthouses or beacons, and no lights of human habitation to be seen. I asked the radio station to switch on the light atop their tall radio tower.

We saw it. We weren't going to South America.

We anchored at 8 p.m. off the wharf. Voices were heard. A rowing boat. Its oars kicked up phosphorescence. 'Ahoy!' It was directed around to the Jacob's-ladder slung over the side and the company's agent and the postmaster boarded. The passengers disembarked into the rowboat.

Unloading started Sunday morning. It was blowing strongly. The *Matai* overhung the short top stroke of the T wharf. We surged backwards and forwards against motor car tyre fenders over the side.

The horse was lifted off in its box and trucked away up the red clay road, banished to this place to enjoy a life of stud duties and to race once a year with a Maori boy as a jockey at a picnic meeting unrecognised by any New Zealand racing organisation. Was it a thoroughbred, rescued from a dog tucker factory, but good enough to beat farm horses?

The dog had also been exiled, to bring fresh blood and to chase sheep which might not have seen a real dog that knew its business. It was taken away on a length of rope. The kennel was thrown overboard and floated briefly before sinking.

Maurice, a telegraphist at the radio station, came aboard for his groceries. He was one of the Post & Telegraph staff serving time at Chatham Islands Radio, keeping a shore watch on 500 kilocycles for ships, maintaining a primitive crackles-and-static short-wave radiotelephone service and sending and receiving telegrams.

The staff lived in buildings erected near the start of the 20th century. The station provided communications for steamers coming and going to Europe via Cape Horn at a time when the range of a ship's spark transmitter was limited. ZLC, the callsign, was the first and last contact with New Zealand.

We stopped talking. The engine had started. I dived outside to see all the lines cast off and the *Matai* getting under way. The wind caught her and she surged in against the wharf. Maurice jumped. The *Matai* surged out and we moved into the bay.

The wind had freshened and we were unable to get back alongside for several days. We had to pull out of Waitangi Bay and run for shelter around the island, shifting as the wind altered. We anchored off the eastern side of the island, and fishing lines were dropped. Every line would come up with two or three hooked fish. Everybody fished, including the captain, but not the English mate. The only contact he wished with fish was fried and on a plate with chips.

The mate wanted to listen to the London News, which was the BBC, rebroadcast on 2YA at 6 a.m. and 6.30 p.m., as it had been since World War II days. A receiver was connected to loudspeakers in the accommodation. For a crewman to have a radio of his own was unusual. Some items of New Zealand news were broadcast at 9 p.m. from 2YA, but there was no real news-gathering service. You could say nothing much happened. 1951 was a time of trams, import restrictions on many goods from overseas, meat parcels for Britain, two-penny postage.

Take it from Here wasn't his idea of entertainment, but at 2 p.m. 2YA broadcast the *Classical Hour*, at 3.30 p.m. was *Music While You Work*, but daytime reception at a distance of 500 miles was not good. At night we received the *Lifebuoy Hit Parade*, *Dossier on Dumetrius*, *Dad and Dave*, *The Adventures of Charlie Chan*. The commentaries from the Wellington Racing Club and the trotting were heard with difficulty, as was the rugby, Auckland versus Hawke's Bay at Eden Park.

The cook's singing was entertaining and penetrated the saloon when we were eating his cakes and buns. 'Does your chewing gum lose its flavour on the bedpost overnight' was my favourite.

I copied Morsed news from ZLL5, one of the Wellington Radio transmitters. Britain was making noises about the Suez Canal, a war was being fought in Korea and items about Russian Migs and the Yalu River were mentioned. I kept radio watch from 8 a.m. to 10 a.m., noon to 2, 4 to 6 and 8 to 10 p.m. while we steamed and anchored in remote bays.

On the port bulkhead of the radio room was the 1920s technology automatic alarm, a Marconi receiver Type 332 using two three-electrode valves of the Marconi DER type and Marconi DE7 type four-electrode valves. They were silvered inside and stuck out horizontally. This receiver stood guard for calls of SOS during the 16 hours I wasn't on watch.

It was said that the alarm was invented by the Marconi Company because shipping companies didn't want to pay the wages of three radio operators to keep watch 24 hours a day, as was thought necessary in the wake of the *Titanic* disaster. Its radio receivers were permanently tuned to 500 kilocycles, which had to possess a sensitiveness equal to that of a crystal detector connected with the same aerial — in other words, equal to a crystal set. So stated the Radio Communications Convention.

Three loud bells were provided, one on the ship's bridge, one in the radio room and one in the operator's sleeping cabin. On the varnished wooden table, in an oak box, was the selector type 333 which was actuated by the alarm signal, consisting of 12 four-second dashes separated by one-second spaces. It was sent before the well-known three dots and three dashes and three dots of SOS. The selector had cogs, levers, cams, contacts, magnets and coils. The box had a glass top so it could be seen in operation. It looked like a mad horologist's nightmare when it was decoding an incoming signal and trying to decide if it should ring the bells. One section of a ship's radio operator's certificate examination was knowing what each cog and wheel, pawl and cam actually did. I practised drawing the complicated mechanical parts and memorised the sequence in case the examiner asked me to explain. He didn't.

Alarms became more sophisticated with time and eventually, with transistors, were electronic in operation. Later, on some ships, there was selective calling apparatus which responded to special tones, like a telephone number, enabling a coast station to call an individual ship, so starting the telex machine or summoning the operator to the radio room for telegraph traffic or radiotelephone calls. And then, of course, satellites and real telephone communication.

But that wasn't how it was in October of 1951. For the bridge I provided time signals from Wellington Radio, which broadcast pips relayed directly from the Carter Observatory using the call-sign ZMO. There was also WWV, the United States time signal stations, for checking the chronometer.

We returned to Waitangi. I gave Maurice a couple of Christchurch newspapers which would be useful for lighting fires under the free coal allowance the staff received. We unloaded bagged coal for their cooking and heating. Maurice loaned me his mud-splattered army Indian World War II vintage motor-cycle, a battered machine that had been available from the War Assets Realisation Board very cheap in the 1940s, ideal for the bad Chathams roads.

I kicked the starter. The engine roared but the kick starter didn't return to its rest. Maurice said, 'When you put it in gear it will come up.' I rode over sand and clay, mud and water, without helmet or goggles, as free as the wind, of which I'd really had enough. It was good to get away from the ship, but it was akin to riding in a cross-country rally. I went as far as the racecourse with its miniature public viewing stand, used only on New Year's Day. The rest of the year sheep ate the grass. There was no sign of the dog, but it wasn't mustering time. Nor did I see the racehorse.

The Chatham Islands, an outpost of New Zealand, was seldom thought about by mainland people, noticed only as an addition to the mainland weather forecast. For the Chathams this usually meant wind and rain.

Sheep farming and fishing were the main occupations, the lucrative crayfish industry was in the future, and so was an airstrip.

I didn't stop the engine. I was afraid the starter wouldn't kick it back into life and I'd be stranded. I revved the motor, skidded it around in despatch rider style and headed back to the main settlement. I arrived back at the pub and store on top of the headland. It sold horse collars and sticky fly-papers. The frozen stuff we had brought was already gone. Outside were cart-like horse-drawn joggers with rubber tyres, an old Bedford army truck.

A barrel of beer had been tapped and was being drunk by men in dungaree trousers, oilskin coats, gumboots and felt hats. The first mate was drinking with the resident commissioner, the government's representative, like a governor. There was a New Zealand police constable somewhere about. The mate looked at home. It figured. The second mate would be on the ship supervising the cargo. The mate had probably done an apprenticeship in one of the better English shipping companies, Blue Funnel or P & O, so how he had arrived on the *Matai*, I don't know. He probably thought he should be captain.

Captain Wylie was a dour older man, thin, a long-time employee of the company. Holm ships were small, with cramped accommodation. If he enjoyed the expansive quarters of the *Matai* he didn't show it. He wore a sports jacket and grey trousers, and on the bridge a grey felt fedora.

I didn't have a uniform, I was wearing my Harris-tweed sports jacket and grey woollen trousers. The mate was the only man in uniform. He didn't like to dirty his hands. When looking at cargo-handling operations he wore a white boiler suit, gloves, and looked helplessly at the sheep. The second mate was a rough and tumble seaman who had been an AB before getting a ticket.

The barman wandered off to serve store customers and Jack, the radio station superintendent, went behind the counter to pour. There were no pennies in circulation. A penny box of matches cost threepence, with all prices adjusted upwards to the nearest silver coin.

I rode back to the ship in the back of the resident commissioner's Land-Rover, the mate in the front.

We steamed across to Pitt Island, a few miles from Waitangi, anchored, but couldn't load the wool because it was too rough. We drifted for a day before the weather abated. A surf-boat for cargo work was carried on the for'ard hatch. Its engine refused to run. The ship's motor-boat was launched and towed the surf-boat between the wharf and the ship. Then the surf-boat was caught by a big sea while leaving the landing and swamped. The wool was thrown overboard and the crew beached the boat.

Dry wool was still to be loaded, but we had already lost considerable time, and we had to load fish at Port Hutt, so the captain decided to leave. She was well behind schedule, and if she was overtime the company would lose a substantial sum of money on the charter. We loaded fish at Port Hutt, 10 miles from Waitangi. The weather was still bad and we couldn't lie alongside the *Manuka* for direct transfer of fish.

The *Manuka* was a steam trawler, floating at permanent moorings, a mother ship for small launches day-fishing. Her main engine was derelict, planks were laid across the cylinder tops and a table and stools installed. The space so formed was used as a mess. Diesels to power the refrigeration machine were installed in cabins. She was noisy with diesels pounding. She was also cold and lonely. Their wireless for broadcast reception was not going. I took it back to Waitangi for repairs by the P & T radio technicians.

I went ashore with the fourth engineer and hunted for paua. The crew worked nonstop for 24 hours transferring frozen fish and then empty diesel oil drums. The surf-boat was hoisted up and swung inboard and went out of control. It crashed through the promenade deck, smashing glass and wooden frames. Captain Wylie groaned softly and stared at the open sea. The mate was in charge of that operation.

We returned to Waitangi to pick up passengers and load live sheep. They didn't want to go to sea but they wouldn't be unhappy for long — they were for the chop on arrival in Wellington, literally. Sometimes it was cheaper to drive sheep off a cliff into the sea than ship them to New Zealand. Only the wool could be stored indefinitely and then, as at Pitt Island, it could be dumped in the sea, although they did recover the lost bales to be dried and repacked for later shipment.

The open ocean was kinder, now placid. Sheep stank and shivered outside my external sleeping cabin door for the two-day voyage. What had been projected to be a 10-day trip stretched to a month.

In Wellington the sun was shining bright on calm harbour waters and cabbage leaves, potato peelings and the general sweepings thrown overboard from ships. The sheep were trucked away. I never saw the mate at the shipping office when I paid off, never saw him again. He probably left the colony for greener pastures, but paddocks without sheep. I did encounter the Burmese second who turned up on the *Tamahine* when I sailed on that ship. And the cook? I suppose he went back to his baking after his voyage afloat.

This was the life for me. I was off to sea permanently. I would ride the ocean wavelength. Three square meals a day, eight hours of simple watch-keeping. The radio room was squared away now, papers back in drawers, floor dried, seasickness gone. The emergency lifeboat radio set was tied down under the table ready for immediate use, not required. And really, that trip across to the Chathams had been no more than a rough day at the office, not a hurricane, nor even a simple storm, but an ordinary gale which the ship had ridden through, just as I had.

J. Edward Brown

PART FOUR

DRAMA AT SEA

Cross-Tides

The little lap-dogs of the ample-bosomed sea,
The waves that frisk and wag their tails and run,
How playfully they lick the unlovely legs
Of spinsters who coquette Minorca-like with
Neptune,
Paddling preposterously.

And how they buffet (blinding with their spray)
The slim bows of canoe boy-freighted
Whose dripping blades incise the swelling wave.
(The seaward-straining islander is there,
And the Viking with the shield
Swung outboard for the whale-path:
Both tamers of the tide.)

The sea opposes playfully the boy,
Lasciviously laves those luckless legs,
Considerably smoothes the sands
For earnest-minded men to write
That God is Love.
Man is the master
And the great waves lick his feet.

But there are places where the sea
Owes no such domination, where the gull
Wheeling and screaming in the venomed spume
Lives yet precarious, and the swirl of waters
Sucks at the snaggle teeth of death
And dares the rocks defy it.
Rarely man ventures there. His hold
Is too uncertain. Jagged sea and sky
Whip to his skin the salt that stings.

The daily ripple of the tides of thought
Runs in and out and round about,
Makes little sallies to explore
The rock-pool where the limpets live and love,
And likes to rattle sea-shells by the shore.
The little wavelets of the human mind
Are happily concerned with little things:
Their surface-play does not disturb
The swallowed men, and bones of broken ships.
All dormant lies the power that rives the sands,
Splinters the granite from the whelming cliff.

Denis Glover

'Written Primarily
for Dreamers'

JOHN WRAY'S classic *South Sea Vagabonds* was first published in England in 1939, and again in 1988 in the Mariner's Library, a series boasting such famous names as Joseph Conrad, Miles Smeeton and Bernard Moitessier. Not bad for a boy from Auckland who built his boat on his parents' front lawn.

Though he claims in his Preface that he is not a writer and never will be, John Wray is a storyteller through and through. The story begins with a 21-year-old dreamer, sacked from a tedious office job, resolving to design and build himself a boat. Around the shores of the Hauraki Gulf, he finds three stout logs of kauri, and in April 1932 starts building the 34ft *Ngataki*. The first move of the finished hull towards the water is a near-disaster: *Ngataki* gets out of control and ends up with her bow buried in a roadside wall. At her eventual launch, water gushes in through the hole for the propeller shaft, left unplugged in the excitement.

But soon Wray is to have his rewards — and his survival tests. Six glorious carefree and happy months after launching, he takes off with three mates for a Pacific island cruise. And later, with that voyage, a trans-Tasman ocean race, some months of island trading and a cruise to Tahiti behind him, Wray sets off in 1936 on a trip to Norfolk Island. On this passage he and his beloved *Ngataki* would be pushed to the very limit.

*A*s I sit down to pen these words, I have in my mind's eye a mental picture of you as you read what I have written. You are seated in a comfortable arm-chair, drawing at your favourite pipe and with your feet well up on the mantel-piece. You are still fairly well tanned from the sun and wind and salt water of last season's sailing. You are hard of eye and square of jaw. It is obviously useless to try to deceive you — utterly useless to trump up some story that during the few months which followed I did anything in the nature of work. I may as well admit straight off that I did — well, call it nothing. Nothing, that is, except sail my boat, cruise in my boat, eat, sleep and drink in my boat.

For me there will never be any pleasure in this world that will compare with those months of sailing round our beautiful coast in my own boat. They were days of perfect bliss.

I visited all the beaches where I had found kauri logs. I went ashore and looked at the places where I had found the different logs. When I was alone I talked to the beaches: 'There you are, Beach, just look what I've built out of those old logs, that you've been hiding all these years beneath your old grey stones.' And I would look at where that log had been, at the slight hole that was in some cases still visible between the rocks; and then I would look at my trim white vessel peacefully anchored in the calm waters out in the bay.

Some of the timber in that boat of mine had, but two years ago, been lying here amongst these rough rocks in the shape of a weathered kauri log!

It was all very wonderful; at least, I thought so.

The timber in my boat was more than just timber to me. Every solitary piece of wood in it I knew and I loved. The deck beam just above my head in my bunk had come out of the log with the beach on the outside of Waiheke Island. Long before it was ever built into the boat that beam and I were fast friends. It is a true friend still. Day after day, year in, year out, it cheerfully and steadily holds up that small portion of deck above my head, doing its duty nobly and well. It is the same with every other bit of wood in my ship.

You probably think me childish for harbouring such ideas, but to me it was all very wonderful.

It was summer time in New Zealand and the weather was ideal for cruising. For a couple of months I made an honest penny by taking pleasure parties out in the boat. Then I began to long for the blue water again. It is very funny. When one is at sea, one dreams of green fields and nice, solid land. One sets extra sails in order to make port as soon as possible. But after a week or two of harbour life one begins to dream of deep water and the free and easy life out at sea.

But it was really a meeting of the Ngataki Club that started off our next trip. The Club was still an active body and when we were in port 'meetings' were held every fortnight. On this occasion a selected group of members had gathered in the cabin and, over a keg, were discussing as usual boats in general and *Ngataki* in particular.

'Do you realize,' said my brother Geoff sternly, 'that you haven't been out to sea now for nearly three months?'

That, as I say, started it off. Within an hour details of a trip to Norfolk Island were finalised. Besides, there were some people there who wanted to return to New Zealand, so we would go and bring them back.

A couple of days later, on Monday, 23 March 1936, we waved farewell to a small group of friends and slowly sailed away from the Royal Akarana Yacht Club. Eddie Ansell, Don Alexander and myself were the crew and we were bound for Norfolk Island, 700 miles away. The breeze was light but fair and at a modest four knots we headed for the wide open spaces. At 6 p.m. we dropped into 'deep-sea' routine and set watches — three hours on and six hours off.

The first couple of days passed uneventfully as we slowly sailed up the New Zealand coastline. The second evening Cape Brett, the last of New Zealand, was passed and we set a course north-west by west for Norfolk Island.

That evening I got a time signal for our chronometer, and listened to the weather report: 'A severe tropical cyclone is centred west of Norfolk Island, moving south-eastwards. In the eastern Tasman Sea there will be strong easterly gales and rough to high seas.'

That didn't sound too good to us aboard *Ngataki*, but an east wind was a fair wind for us and a gale need not be too bad — a bit tricky on the steering, perhaps, but we would make good time. My boat was strong and could stand any storm. They didn't say how intense the cyclone was and, anyway, our glass showed no signs of it yet . . . And so we carried on.

Sometime during my watch a blaze of lights appeared on the horizon. It was the inter-colonial liner *Wanganella*. I signalled her with my torch: 'Yacht *Ngataki*. Please report us all OK.'

The next morning, Wednesday, it was blowing a hard easterly and we were swooping along before it at eight knots. As the morning drew on, the wind freshened, so that at 10 a.m. we were doing nine knots, which was a bit too much for our tubby craft. We pulled down a reef in the mainsail which made things a bit easier. At midday, even with the reef, we were driving the ship too hard. 'Are you there, Don?' I yelled. 'We'll have to double reef the mainsail. I can't hold her. It's starting to blow now.' We had carried on too long already and it took us over half an hour to put in the second reef. The heavy mainsail pulled and thrashed like a demon. But we did not mind. There is always something exhilarating in a clean fight with the elements — provided you are sure of winning.

So we hung on and pulled at the reefing points, until eventually the devil in the sail was subdued. Now the ship was much easier. I went down to rest while Don carried on at the tiller.

I was dozing when a sudden loud report brought me back to earth. 'Are you there, Johnny?' yelled Don. 'Shake it up; the mainsheet's parted!'

I scrambled up and attempted to capture the boom. I grabbed one end of the broken mainsheet and tried to get the sail in. But the pressure on it was altogether too much. I pulled with all my might, but could not get the boom in an inch.

'Look out!' yelled Don. There was a crash as a huge wave hit us and I was catapulted into the air. The next second I was in the water with the *Ngataki* fifteen yards ahead, sailing away from me at eight knots, running before the storm. I realised with a feeling of panic there was little hope of young Don gaining control of the ship or stopping her mad rush.

In rare moments such as these it is lucky that one has not time to dwell on the situation. I saw the log line streaming past and grabbed it, but immediately released my grip and let it slide through my hands. Just in time, I had remembered how slender was the screw that fastened the log to the deck. If I had hung on, the weight of my body would have pulled the whole outfit off the stern of the boat. 'Grab the log line!' I yelled frantically. With the greatest presence of mind, Don immediately let go the tiller, grabbed the line and took a turn round the horse. At the same instant I came to the end of the line and hung on to the log for my life.

It takes a long time to describe it, but it was little more than a second from the time I was thrown off the boat to the time I was hanging on to the log. In these circumstances one has to think and act pretty quickly.

Hampered by the heavy military overcoat I was wearing, I had to put everything I had into the supreme effort of getting back to the boat. The line was light and fairly old, and every moment I expected it to part. Hand over hand, inch by inch, that twenty yards seemed more like a mile. Eventually I reached the boat. Don helped me on board and I lay for a while on deck exhausted. Only those who have tried it can know how hard it is to haul oneself through the water at eight knots.

We at length rove a new mainsheet and I went down below. I crawled into my bunk again. I had had enough excitement for one day. But apparently Father Neptune decreed otherwise. An hour later I was awakened again by a terrific crash. The boat was thrown bodily to leeward midst a smother of foam and spume. Water poured through the main hatch and added to the general confusion down below. I was thrown out of my bunk and hastily scrambled on deck just in time to see Don, who had been washed overboard, climbing back on deck. He had luckily grabbed the mainsheet and was able to get back on board again. We had broached-to and it was quite clear that we had carried on too long. This was a bit too much for a joke. We would have to heave-to, even though it was a fair wind.

The staysail, now viciously kicking and thrashing, was lowered and lashed down and the mainsail was hauled hard inboard, as we hove-to. *Ngataki* came nearly head to wind and began to ride the waves easily, but she had a lot of water in her — six inches above the floor — and she was not too buoyant.

Eddie was down below pumping. Keeping a weather eye open to windward for breaking seas, I attempted to re-lash the dinghy which had broken adrift on deck. I was naked now, so was Don. It was no good wearing any clothes on deck under these conditions.

The wind gradually increased to full hurricane force and the mainsail was lowered, for no canvas, however strong, could have stood up to it. The seas were rapidly mounting higher and higher. Away to windward I saw a gigantic breaker advancing. From a slightly different direction another huge sea was coming towards us and it began to look as though those two hills of water would just about meet where our little ship lay. 'Look out, Don!' I yelled. I sprang into the rigging and climbed up the shrouds. I got twelve or fifteen feet above the deck, but there was no getting away from *that* sea.

I have a dim recollection of an enormous wall of white, seething water bearing down on us, a violent, sickening crash, and the next instant I was under water. There was a deafening, roaring noise in my ears, and all the forces of the world were pulling me away from the shroud to which I clung.

The wire shroud was torn from my grasp and I was in green water, somewhere below the surface. I swam to the surface and there, a few yards away, I saw the keel of my *Ngataki* sticking up in the air. A bit of the topside was also showing, but it seemed she was sinking fast. We were 100 miles off land; there was no hope of swimming *that* far through shark-infested waters.

This, then, was the end.

For something better to do, I swam over to poor *Ngataki*, and climbed up the topside. A moment later I saw Don climbing on to the stern. We looked at each other and grinned weakly. Then, wonder of wonders, the boat began to rotate and the mast appeared. It began to rise out of the water as the gallant *Ngataki* slowly righted herself.

It was the proudest moment of my life seeing my ship right herself; even relief at being saved from a watery grave gave place to pride at that moment. I actually grinned. 'How's that?' I yelled to Don. 'Wonderful!' he shouted. It was. That the ballast did not break loose and burst through the cabin-floor can be attributed only to a merciful Providence. Then Eddie's head popped out of the half-open hatch. He had been down below the whole time. Sitting on the cabin ceiling in the dark, Eddie had decided he was on his way to the bottom of the sea. Now he was intensely surprised and relieved to find the ship was still above water.

But she was only just floating. Water had poured through the partially closed main hatch and there were over three feet of water in the cabin. In calm water the *Ngataki* had a foot of freeboard, but now the decks were awash. We would have to work like maniacs if we were to keep the ship afloat. Our decks were swept clean. Our leeward bulwarks had been torn off and, together with lifebuoys, spars, dinghy, etc., were floating away down to leeward. But that mattered little. The main thing was to keep the boat afloat till we could get a bit closer to land. It was too far to swim from there!

'Go for it, lads, bail for your lives!' And we did, with pots and buckets and everything we could lay hands on. If we got another breaker now, we would never survive it. I groped in the water-filled lockers until I found our five-gallon drum of whale oil. Then I attempted to pour it overboard on the waters to windward of us. But, of course, it was a hopeless task. The shrieking wind blew the oil back over my naked body and over the ship. What happened next would have been funny at any other moment but at the time the humour of it was not apparent. Crouching on deck — with the wind at hurricane force it was impossible to stand up — I tried to get a grip on something to steady myself. But the ship was so slippery from being sprayed with the blighted whale oil that I could not get a hold on anything and the next thing I knew I was being blown — sliding on my seat — right down to the stern of the ship. There I luckily grabbed the horse, or I would have gone overboard for a third time.

With an axe I cut the boom, gaff and sail from the mast and on a couple of warps I let the whole affair out over the bow to act as a sea anchor. But it made no difference. I let out more gear on ropes but still she would not ride head to wind. Our only hope was to run before it. I pulled in all the gear from the bow and let it out over the stern. It sounds a simple operation but it took a couple of hours to do. I could not afford to get any help from the other two, for they were bailing incessantly.

All our sails, spars, anchors and oil drums were tied to ropes and let out over the stern until we had lines and ropes trailing behind. The move proved very effective and as long as we kept running dead before it the floating gear behind remained to windward of us.

It was now about 6 p.m. and getting dark. We carried on, I keeping the ship dead on in the ever-increasing seas, while Don and Eddie bailed for their lives. Down below was utter chaos. Everything that would float was swirling about on top of the water. Lockers, drawers and cupboards were all being smashed and burst open by the force of water surging below as the ship rolled and pitched. The floating debris considerably hampered Don and Eddie in their bailing, and every now and then a bit of board or a locker door would come flying out of the hatch as it got in the way of their buckets. They stuck to it like heroes, carrying on hour after hour. It was a case of life and death and we all knew it.

The wind blew harder than ever. I had never known anything like it. I think it was also raining, although I could not distinguish rain from spray or anything else. It was pitch dark and there was no light of any sort on board. I steered by the wind on the back of my neck.

Endless hours went by and the water below was, if anything, gaining on us. We had shipped no seas, thanks to the gear streamed out behind us, so we must have developed a bad leak somewhere. About midnight — we could only vaguely guess the time, our clocks and watches having become useless — I handed the tiller over to Don, while I crawled around the boat feeling if any of the ports had been smashed. But they were all sound. Then I remembered a little generating plant that I had recently fitted. Sure enough, the engine had come adrift and water was pouring in through the exhaust pipe. No wonder the bailers were making no headway! I plugged it up and resumed my steering.

Further endless hours dragged by. It was the longest night I had ever spent. So great was the force of the wind that we were doing about five knots under bare poles and dragging all the gear behind. I could not look back, for the rain or spray — whichever it was — hurt too much, but I could take a quick peep now and then by covering my face with my hands and looking through the slits between my fingers. But all I could see was, naturally enough, fairly harmless.

At long last day dawned — a grey, cheerless dawn, but infinitely better than the horrors of darkness. We carried on all day, taking it in turns to bail, bailing, bailing, always bailing.

About 3 p.m. the wind lightened as we got nearer the centre of the hurricane, but the seas seemed to get even higher and mounted and pitched upwards from all directions. But, with the wind losing strength, the seas lost some of their terrifying breaking-crests which are so dangerous to small craft. During the comparatively calm spell the water was bailed out nearly down to the floor. We had a good pump on board, but, with the mess that was now in the bilge, it continually got blocked and was useless. I took the opportunity of straightening out some of the rigging. A lot of the gear behind had broken away, but luckily the mainsail was still there. It was hauled in and fastened, with the boom and gaff, back in place on the mast. I climbed the gyrating mast and rove a couple of temporary halyards to haul the sail up if necessary, for we must be getting somewhere near the New Zealand coast and we might be wanting that sail soon.

It grew dark and soon after the wind started howling again, this time from the sou'west. But tonight it was not so bad. We had most of the water out and the ship was more buoyant. Again the night seemed endless. Towards morning I thought I heard the roar of distant breakers, but the night was pitch black and nothing could be seen. At the first sign of dawn I went on deck and looked around, and there, less than a mile down to leeward, was the rocky New Zealand coastline, with miles of merciless surf, clearly visible in the half-light, thundering in.

No time was to be lost if we were to avoid being wrecked. Luckily, the wind had now moderated and we could show a little sail. The staysail and double-reefed mainsail were hoisted; we had to try somehow to claw off that rocky shore against the high wind and mountainous sea. We plugged along, the ship being more underneath than above the water. The spray flew high over the masthead, but we were getting no farther from the rocks.

We shook out a reef in the mainsail and carried on under single reef. *Ngataki* knew what was wanted of her. She heeled right over and ploughed along. If anything carried away, we were done. But the gear stood up to it and I was grateful for the heavy mast and the stoutness of the shrouds and canvas. Our gallant little craft climbed up each wall of water, shattered the top of the sea and sank into the trough again. We were winning now — gradually drawing away from the hungry surf.

About 2 p.m., by the sun, Cape Maria Van Diemen was sighted through the haze. Once round there, we would be safe, but about five miles off the

Cape there is a shallow patch which breaks even in moderate weather. Now, as we drew closer, the seas became terribly confused and started to break in all directions. Suddenly a huge sea broke fifty yards away on our beam; then one broke on the other side of us. Our stern lifted high in the air and the bow went down so far I thought we were going to turn a complete somersault. With a roar we started to plane on the sea. The bow wave was colossal and there was a white stream of foaming water level with the deck from bow to stern as we rushed madly along at an unbelievable speed for nearly a minute. I threw every ounce of weight on the tiller to keep her dead before it. If we had swerved a fraction of a point we would have broached-to and all would have been lost. But we were lucky again and soon we were out of that ungodly sea. Darkness found us past the Cape in the relatively calmer waters of the East Coast.

There followed three days of uneventful sailing down the coast. Conditions were fairly comfortable, as comfortable as wringing-wet clothes, wet bunks and water sloshing round the floor would allow, for the weather was by no means fine and we could do no drying.

At long last we reached port. Good old Auckland! There never was a crew more pleased to see it. Without wasting any time we hurried ashore. Terra firma at last! There had been many times during the last few days when we thought we would never see land again.

Auckland had not suffered the full force of the storm, the centre of the cyclone passing about three hundred miles away. Nevertheless, the damage done around the water-front was very extensive. When we saw the wrecked boats, the smashed retaining walls and other obvious signs of storm damage, we considered ourselves very lucky to have escaped with our lives.

Ngataki was in a terrible mess and would have to be virtually rebuilt inside. There was no better place to do this than up the little Wairoa River. So, after a few days, we sailed inland. There was plenty of fresh water there with which to wash everything and plenty of peace and quietness to effect repairs.

Like all nasty experiences, that unhappy trip had taught me a few lessons. It had shown the remarkable effectiveness of running before a storm towing a mass of gear. We had survived a full hurricane, yet with no more than a bare foot of freeboard we had shipped very little water. Had the ship been free of water inside, we would have lived through it quite comfortably. The streaming of canvas out aft, with ropes from two corners of each sail so that they lie flat on top of the water, causes advancing breakers to break before they reach the ship. The more gear one has out aft, I decided, the safer will be the ship.

In my humble opinion, any small boat, if well-found and strong enough, can live through a hurricane if it does as we did — run before it, towing all spars, sails, drums, etc. behind. It is probably the only way of riding it out — unless the boat is a small one and has a sea-anchor big enough to hold it head to wind. And even then, riding head to wind, there is an enormous strain on the rudder (which must be lashed) when a breaking sea hits it. On a larger boat, say over thirty-five feet, the sea-anchor would have to be so large to keep the boat head to wind, that the strains would be too great. In a hurricane no canvas will stand up to the force of the wind, so it is, of course, impossible to heave-to. There are only two alternatives: riding to a sea-anchor, or running before it and towing gear, and, unless the boat is under thirty-five feet, the latter method, to my mind, is the best.

It also taught me another lesson: not to be too cocksure of myself. On the first couple of days of that trip I had thought no harm could befall us. I had been to sea several times before and I knew all about it. My ship was strong enough and could stand anything at all. I was so sure of myself that I had not bothered to stow the anchor and chain below. They were on deck all ready for our arrival at Norfolk Island. I had not even taken any special precautions in lashing the gear on deck and I had not troubled to see that the hatches were securely fastened. I came to grief. It was only the sheerest luck that we remained afloat and escaped with our lives.

Since that unhappy trip I have been very careful. Now I am a little afraid of the sea. Captain Slocum once said that a little fear at sea is a jolly good thing for safety. I believe him. For just a little fear will keep you up to the mark. It will make you keep everything shipshape and it will make you prepared for anything *all* the time. In a well-found boat, if you do this, no harm will befall you. But, if you do not treat Father Neptune with the respect he undoubtedly deserves, he will, sooner or later, creep up behind you with that lump of lead piping. And that will be that!

John Wray, *South Sea Vagabonds,* 1939

Fog at Sea — Silent as Death

'WOULD I DO IT AGAIN? The answer is no . . . the north Atlantic to my mind is the most horrible, cold, evil place to hold a race — which is conceivably the reason it is held there,' drily commented Dame Naomi James, in *Kriter Lady*. The only woman to finish the 1980 Observer Single-handed Trans-Atlantic Race (a creditable 24th of 88 starters), she also knocked three days off Claire Francis's women's record.

Two years earlier, James had sailed into nautical history as the first woman to circumnavigate the world non-stop, in the process setting a new record of 272 days, male or female. The largely inexperienced young New Zealander suddenly found herself a world celebrity, an author and a Dame.

Entering the OSTAR, she was no stranger to gales, capsizes, rigging problems, seasickness, icebergs and anxieties about her navigational skills. There was her famous seafaring husband, Rob James, to beat, if she could. Fog, though, freezing and impenetrable, silent as death over the Newfoundland Grand Banks — this was something you didn't encounter in the ferocious southern oceans . . .

*O*n the 22nd [June] my log records:

I'm crossing the Grand Bank of Newfoundland — I think. Feeling miserable and a little scared because I'm not sure of my navigation. It's very foggy and very cold. Despite the recent reasonably good weather, I've not been able to take accurate sights, so I've been on dead reckoning for the last couple of days. Knowing where I am starts to mean a lot now that land is getting closer. Most worrying is the echo sounder, which keeps flickering onto 15 or 20 fathoms, and for that to be true I must be very near the Virgin Rocks, which are unlit and not very high out of the water. On the other hand I can't pick up the radio DF bearing on Cape Race which is quite close to the rocks, so I must believe I'm not near them. I'd go south if I could, but the wind is WSW and I'm making a good course on this tack — only it's taking me always slightly north. Tacking would be ridiculous unless I'm really near the rocks. I'm in a dilemma. I wish I believed myself more.

I was also apprehensive about the icebergs which were reported to be lying about 100 miles north of my estimated position — which was fine, providing I was where I thought I was. The fleet was very lucky that year: the icebergs were well north. I'd not had to make the sweep round the Newfoundland Bank which had been necessary in other years. I had stuck to the Great Circle course as closely as possible. But it looked as if that had not been the course to choose. The leading boats had mostly followed the rhumb line.

The apprehension brought out my morbid tendencies. I was inclined to be too introspective and to dwell too much on the nasty things that could befall Rob and me. I was particularly obsessed about being hit by a ship, yet I didn't keep an adequate watch, which was paradoxical. The chance of avoiding the ship fated to hit me on the few occasions I looked out seemed so unlikely that there was no point in keeping watch at all. At least, not when I was feeling miserable. I spent gloomy hours going through the procedures for abandoning ship — if I hadn't been killed by the collision — and my imagination always stumbled on certain aspects of that dreadful necessity: getting into the life raft but being unable to cut the painter, or slipping on the edge of the raft and pushing the can-opener through the side so that the whole thing collapsed slowly under me. Such pleasant thoughts occupied me in moments of uncertainty. For all that, I was seldom really depressed. Many of those silly imaginings had the effect of making the dangers we all faced seem ludicrous. It didn't diminish them, but it brought home the fact that moaning about them did no good at all. I was well prepared in case of emergency and fairly confident that I wouldn't do any of those daft things.

On 23 June I blew the top out of the yankee, which left me with only one decent sail to set on the forestay. There was slightly too much wind for the big furler, but I had to put it up or sacrifice a lot of speed. It was an enormous sail to hoist successfully alone and caused me a great deal of trouble. At last, however, I'd more or less got it up, when it jammed on the forestay. Squinting up, I could see the top piece of the broken furler gear, which appeared to be jammed on the stay. Hoping to dislodge it with a good jerk on the halyard, I wound hard on the winch — and cursed myself for an idiot. About eighteen inches of luff tape ripped off the sail. I backed the sail and hauled it down to the deck again to assess the damage. It looked difficult to mend. However, before I tried to fix it, I had to get the broken piece down off the forestay, otherwise I couldn't use the luff groove at all. Armed with a broom and a harness, I climbed nearly to the top of the mast, anchored myself securely and swiped at the thing with the broom. It was too far away for me to reach it, and too far to land many accurate hits. After a lot of loud bashing, which didn't succeed in moving the fitting an inch, I came down again.

Out of breath and feeling very exasperated, I made a cup of tea while trying to work out the next step. 'How the devil am I going to make it to Newport with no decent headsails at all?' I asked myself angrily. I was really making a mess of things. Perversely, the wind had now gone lighter, too much for the big genoa loose luffed but not nearly enough for the storm jib. The storm jib it had to be, though, and with it set I was doing about 3½ knots. Terrific!

From sails I turned my mind to the next pressing problem: navigation. I was just picking up the bearing on Cape Race at an estimated distance of 130 miles. It was too weak for me to take a fix, but seemed to be in the right sector. It was raining incessantly and the fog pressed against the boat like a mire. I longed to tack, but would not. I just had to believe myself rather than the depth sounder, or my imagination, and tacking would lose me so many miles that I refused to give in to my fears. Instead I stayed for hours at the radio direction finder, looking for signals to confirm my position. There seemed nothing I could do about the mess on the forestay and it assumed a lower priority while I was unsure of my whereabouts.

Over the radio I heard that Phil Weld on *Moxie* was still 350 miles off Newport, his progress seriously hindered by light winds. At least I wasn't the only one thus afflicted.

On the 24th more wind arrived with a vengeance. I was forced to take down all but the storm jib for a few hours as a force 8 howled out of the west. It eased to a gusty force 7 after a while and *Kriter Lady* plodded on into the steep waves caused by the shallow water over the bank. In that amount of wind the storm jib was all the sail I needed forward of the mast, so the bad weather was helping me under the circumstances.

Despite the calm the day before I managed 100 miles from noon to noon, which brought me within 800 miles of Newport. I continued on dead reckoning as the sun and the horizon were persistently hidden by fog. Thankfully the wind shifted to the south, allowing me to make a course direct for Newport, passing close to Sable Island to get a position check. I was up a lot in the night and saw two ships. Another one passed quite close but I didn't see it; I just heard its engines thumping and an occasional blast on a fog-horn. I had a little gadget with me which was supposed to pick up ships' radar signals, but it never seemed to work.

In the morning as I was finishing my grilled mince on toast I was badly startled by a series of loud whistles. I leapt from my chair and stood for a second with my mouth open, listening, trying to make out which direction it came from and if it was a ship close at hand. I scrambled on deck in a panic, and then my heart jumped. Three large black pilot whales thrust their blunt noses out of a wave three feet from the cockpit, rose ponderously from the sea and splashed me in their wake. There were dozens of them swimming along with the boat, keeping very close but never touching the hull. I was nervous lest they should get too friendly. Without bothering to change into oilskins, I started filming them. By the time I'd used up a roll of film I was damp and frozen, and had to change into drier clothes. Changing didn't make much difference; I was damp again before long and had to stay that way as my heater refused to work. Nearly everything I had was wet. I couldn't dry any clothes but could warm the little chart room by turning on the cooker. The leaks over the bunk were the most trying: the only way to keep my duvet moderately dry was to spread a sheet of polythene over it, which generally had the effect of channelling the water down my neck or over my feet.

According to the BBC *Moxie* was due to finish within a few hours, followed by Phil Steigel, Wally Green, Mike Birch and Nick Kieg. I was very pleased at Phil Weld's success; he was a very popular man in single-handed sailing and did a lot to make the sport more acceptable to the public. I could have wished any of the front runners a win; they were all good friends and great people.

According to Rob's Argos reports from my father-in-law and my dead reckoning we were 100 miles apart. He was ahead and south of me, going fast. Over the next twenty-four hours (as I learned later) he had a fantastic run of 240 miles in a straight line to Newport, whereas I did only forty on a course towards the Arctic Circle. A small depression must have slipped between us, giving Rob following winds and me head winds.

My log on the 25th records:

The floor is clean — because I've swept it. Funny how little things like a grubby floor make you feel bad. Miserable night last night. Kept feeling I was going to be hit by a ship but didn't have the will-power to keep a watch more often. I went to my bunk as usual just before dark and shuddered at the feel of my cold damp duvet. I told myself it wasn't wet, just cold, and made myself lie still for half an hour till it warmed up. Warm, clammy cocoon, clinging to my chilly feet. Pillow smelt musty, so I put it under the slightly less wet one. I was up and down a dozen times during the night, just waking up suddenly as if something were wrong and getting out of my bunk quickly to peer through the windows before realising that nothing had in fact disturbed me. There was nothing to be seen all night except the moon and some stars, which appeared for the first time in weeks. Close reefed, with the storm jib giving some pull, we're plodding along on the wrong course. It's going to be a miserably poor run in miles made good to Newport.

I heard on the news that Phil Weld had finished early that morning. I was glad for him but felt frustrated at my own lack of progress. There were good aspects to the day though. The sun was out and the horizon clear, so I lost no time in getting sights. Unfortunately they put me thirty miles back along my track. I'd been counting on the current running at half a knot, but perhaps it wasn't at all. I got out all my wet clothes and bedding and festooned the deck with them. It was suddenly warmer, a sign that I was on the edge of the Gulf Stream coming up from the Gulf of Mexico. I had lived in my Javlin polar suits day and night since the start. It was good to find some summer weather and get rid of those . . . suits completely.

On the morning of the 26th I sorted out all the charts of the approach and the finish. They looked rather daunting. There were so many shoals and buoys and lights around the place. Why on earth should anyone want to finish a race in such a confused looking area? There was a nasty patch of shallow water called Georges Bank which lay pretty much in my path. I would have to go round it; there wasn't enough depth in parts for my keel and I couldn't be sure of missing the shallow spots unless I knew precisely where I was.

The fog came back by the afternoon, but the wind stayed a steady force 4 — delightful sailing weather, but without a suitable sail forward I lost a lot of speed. Fortunately the wind shifted enough to allow me to steer the right course, which was a great improvement.

Miraculously the wind held all that day and the next. I made a steady 5 ½ knots, trying all the while to swallow my irritation at not being able to do 7½. My annoyance showed all too clearly in the state of my fingernails, which I had bitten right down. When there were no fingernails left to chew, I started pulling at my eyelashes until I ended up with a bald spot. I didn't notice what I was doing until too late, and then was doubly annoyed at myself for my stupidity.

The fog remained, close and impenetrable, making navigation dependent on radio direction finding alone. RDF had never seemed to be very accurate in the past, but absolute accuracy hadn't been so important; it was usually sufficient to know where one was to the nearest ten miles. Ships occasionally sounded their foghorns out of the murk and I would try to call them up to get a position. On one occasion I was successful, but the position didn't tally with my dead reckoning. It was at least fifty miles farther north. I decided later that they had given me the wrong figures. It was worrying, but by that time I had a rough fix from two RDF stations which I trusted rather than the ship's position. I hope they didn't think they were where they told me, otherwise they might have been in for a few surprises.

Later that afternoon I noted in my log:

How the world changes when the fog clears. It's receded almost to the horizon and I can now see a couple of miles over a sea ruffled by a steady breeze. Small waves collide with each other making little plopping sounds and I keep thinking there are dolphins around. There were some earlier, but they didn't make their presence known by squeaking in the normal way. I only discovered them when I was fetching some water and one jumped right under my nose, making me nearly drop the bucket. The water seems quite chilly again. I hope this doesn't mean there are any icebergs about. I've plotted the reported ones on the chart and they are north of me . . .

The 27th turned into a horrible day. A headache I'd developed during the night would not be lulled with tablets and by afternoon was making me ill. And the wind played a nasty trick on me at midday by suddenly going light. I waited twenty minutes for it to return, and when it didn't I took out a couple of reefs from the main and hoisted the big genoa. As soon as I'd finished and the sails were setting nicely, the wind puffed up again and kept going. Several hours and a lot of hard work later, I finished with two reefs and the storm jib again. At last, feeling weak and shaky, I got below, made some toast and baked beans which I forced down. It didn't stay down for long, so I resorted to two paracetamol and two seasickness tablets and retired to my bunk. I tried to relax so the tablets could work, but the motion was becoming violent. Every now and then, just as I was dropping off to sleep, *Kriter Lady* would leap through a wave crest leaving my stomach suspended as she fell to the bottom. Putting in the last reef and winching it home finished me off completely; I was ill for a long time before I crawled shakily back to my bunk. I wondered if I had eaten something bad but couldn't think of anything out of the ordinary. From time to time I got up to glance around, but lacked the willpower to dress up and pull the yankee clear of the water which was slowly devouring it. It was tied to the lifelines and couldn't go completely, but was probably getting torn. In the squalls *Kriter Lady* was overcanvassed, tearing along through the waves, burying her bows in and tossing great sheets of water over her back; at other moments she didn't have enough sail up and was sluggish, slowing to 2 knots as the waves knocked into her. I just let her alone and lay in my bunk listening. The barometer had fallen, yet the weather didn't look too bad. Even so, when the wind lulled around midnight and I should have taken out a reef, I delayed until 3.30 for the forecast — which was force 7 in my area — and then only tacked to get a better course . . .

On the morning of the 29th I searched through my list of frequencies for Newport, eventually making contact with a station called Ocean Gate. The operator was very pleasant but seemed confounded at the name 'Kriter', asking me to spell it three times. Once we got over that difficulty, everything went smoothly and I was soon talking to race control at Goat Island marina. Rob had arrived at eight that morning and was now having breakfast. I called again later and he was waiting for me. I went through the same set of anxieties before talking to him as he had when I came back from my circumnavigation. Had being alone under difficult conditions changed him? Had he gone at all weird? I remembered how much he had hated his qualifying trip and that had only lasted three days. But the moment I heard his greeting and his laughter, I knew it hadn't made the slightest difference to him. He started to tell me about the crossing, how miserable he had been at times, but how well the boat had gone, then checked himself, remembering that I still had a couple of hundred miles to go. He had arranged to come out on a boat to meet me, no matter what the time, and suggested I call again in twelve hours to report progress.

Bearings from various RDF stations put me farther on than my dead reckoning, which cheered me up. The sun was making feeble attempts to penetrate the mist, so I grabbed the sextant and wedged myself on deck to shoot it when it appeared. Just then, out of the murk, I heard the soft mooing of a foghorn. My position should have been close to the Nantucket light vessel, and there indeed it was. I altered course to get closer, but the sound was farther away than I thought. After deviating a mile I still hadn't seen it, so I altered course again and continued on. It was definitely the light vessel; the signal corresponded to the one on the chart. Suddenly it stopped, which was odd as the fog hadn't cleared away altogether. I tried calling the vessel on VHF and to my delight they answered immediately. Yes, they had just 'secured the horn down', a singular choice of words I thought; I didn't like to ask them why.

I now had an excellent fix and put my sextant back in its box. A hundred miles to go! Doing 5 knots in a reasonable breeze I could expect to be in next day if it held. My efforts to make contact on VHF failed, but eventually I got hold of Rob on the distress frequency. I made myself understood that I would call again in twelve hours, and left off to concentrate on navigating.

Visibility was down to a few yards at times, so locating the buoys at the corners of the shoals was going to be a matter of good luck rather than good management. Five hours after leaving the light vessel, I stumbled across the next buoy and couldn't believe my luck. I now knew I was on the south-west corner of the Nantucket shoals. Buoy hopping, if I could continue to find them, was going to be the most accurate way of getting in. I headed towards the next lot, ten miles away south of the Buzzard's lighthouse. The breeze was holding up beautifully and I felt all fired up for the chase and prepared for the long vigil without sleep. I watched the course very carefully in order to keep to a strict line for the buoys which could easily be missed in the fog. Like magic, the next ones appeared on cue. I felt like the proverbial cat with the cream. There were twenty miles left to the finishing line. I marked a course of 320° magnetic for the buoys three miles south-east of the Brenton Reef tower, which marked the outer end of the line, and called Rob again. Reception was very bad, but I got my position through and said I'd call again at midnight. It was early evening and the wind was beginning to drop.

The fog remained as thick as ever. I spent the long hours in the cockpit, listening out for ships and watching the course. At midnight the wind suddenly dropped away and my heart sank a little. I was hoping not to have to spend the whole night on watch, but now it looked as though I might have to. Contact with Rob failed completely and I only just managed to get a message through to race control that I was by the buoys three miles from the line and nearly becalmed. To my relief I heard a faint hoot off to port and altered course towards it. A small buoy corresponding to the one on the chart flashed confidently out of the fog.

As I glided alongside it the wind failed completely and *Kriter Lady* stopped in the dead calm. Three miles to go and no wind at all, not even a cat's paw. Something had to be tried though, so I put up the big genoa and turned the boat towards the Brenton tower. Every now and then a tiny whisper of wind touched the water and I was waiting for it. *Kriter Lady* moved almost imperceptibly forward and in an hour I estimated that I had gone almost half a mile with the help of the tide. I could hear the deep boom of the Brenton tower on my port bow and I continued to take RDF bearings from it. Slowly we crept forward and another two hours passed. The boom got louder and higher up and then, to my utter astonishment, stopped.

I couldn't believe it. Zero visibility and the tower was no longer sending out a signal. How could that possibly be? I suddenly felt totally disorientated and confused. Had I heard the tower at all? Perhaps it was a ship that I had heard. If so, where was the tower?

There were muffled hoots, whistles and booms sounding in all directions. In desperation I grabbed the chart from down below to try to make sense of all the signals. I couldn't see which one the tower could be. It didn't occur to me that it might have broken down. I couldn't entertain the notion that such an important navigational mark should just cease in thick fog. Either I had just crossed the line, or I was somewhere else and likely to run into a rock at any minute. I hastily jotted down the time of twelve minutes past four, then dived on deck to take the sails down. If I hadn't crossed the line I obviously wasn't going to be able to find it in that murk as I couldn't find the tower anyway. I felt so lost and confused that I was almost weeping. Where was I?

It was deadly quiet except for the sounds from foghorns. I secured the sails and stood on deck for a while to calm down and think what to do next. If I kept away from all the sounds of bells and hoots and stayed more or less where I was, I must be all right as I hadn't hit anything coming in. After a little while and a cup of tea, I thought again about finding out where I was by slowly going up to one of the buoys and trying to identify it. I turned on the motor and moved cautiously towards the nearest. I kept

DRAMA AT SEA

turning off the engine to listen for the sound of breakers or disturbed water. The hoot I was heading for was getting very loud and quite high up, when I caught the clang of a bell just off to port of it. I swung *Kriter Lady* hurriedly around towards it and in a few seconds was upon it. I had to go within a few feet to identify the colour. My mouth went completely dry as I realised there was no bell near the Brenton Reef tower. I turned in a close circle around the bell and headed back onto a reciprocal course, my heart beating madly at the thought of the hazard the bell might be marking. When it was a little distance away again I stopped the motor and studied the chart. There was a bell close to the Beavertail Point tower, a mile away from Brenton Reef, with a rock between the bell and the tower. So I knew where Beavertail Point was, but where was Brenton Reef? I felt defeated. It must have been there somewhere, but I was too stupid to be able to find it.

With the engine off, *Kriter Lady* drifted in the quiet. I suddenly detected the sound of breaking water. But it wasn't very loud and didn't sound as if it was on a shore. I slowly crept towards it, moving this way and that with the engine, but always turning it off after a few yards to listen. The last time I came up on deck from turning off the engine I gasped and rushed to put the wheel hard over. Dead ahead, a couple of yards away, was an enormous steel leg. Another emerged, and there, towering above me, silent as death, was the Brenton Reef tower.

With the appearance of the tower the doubts and fears of the last few hours fled, to be replaced by relief and not a little annoyance at that wretched structure, which now lurked only a few yards away but out of sight in the fog. Keeping within hearing of the water lapping round its feet, I turned *Kriter Lady* in a wide circle and started to think about what to do now. It suddenly struck me that I *had* crossed the finishing line when I thought, and I had been right by the tower when it had stopped booming. The lines of my RDF bearings were evidence of that, although I lost confidence in them at the time. It will be difficult to prove my finishing time, I thought, as I surveyed the blank walls of dripping mist, but then I decided abruptly that as no one was about there was no way to dispute it.

What to do now, I wondered, having described a full circle around the tower and started on a second one. Shall I try to find my way to the marina in this fog, or will I get lost again? I had hardly handled a boat on my own in inshore waters before and the remembrance of going between that bell and the rock on the other side of the harbour decided me not to push my luck. Anyway, surely Rob will come out to find me sooner or later, I mused, and the place he'll head for is the line. That decision made, I put *Kriter Lady* up-tide of the tower so that she would drift slowly past it, while I made myself some breakfast.

It was six in the morning and voices were beginning to come alive on the VHF, which I had left on throughout the night, hoping someone might call me up. My repeated calls for attention went unanswered, so there was obviously something wrong with my transmitter. Several hours passed as I ate my breakfast and kept *Kriter Lady* by the tower. So far a dry throat and smarting eyes were the only effects of not having slept for a long time.

At about eight o'clock, to my delight, I heard Rob's voice over the VHF announcing that he was coming out to look for me. Immediately afterwards I was startled by a great booming horn right over my head — the tower was back in action. I waited on deck, listening intently to the various sounds about the harbour. Presently I heard the thin wail of a foghorn that sounded like a yacht approaching. I answered on my foghorn, and soon a yacht appeared — but not Rob, I was disappointed to learn. It was a boat called *Sleuth*, just returned from Bermuda. I asked if the crew would call up race control and tell them where I was, which they immediately did. To my great surprise the yacht *Great Britain II* answered; she too was on her way to find me. This was the yacht in which Rob had sailed around the world and she had subsequently been sold to a Swedish girl. It was beginning to look like I would have quite a welcome.

Sleuth kept me company while the crew had breakfast and we chatted. Although they were a distance away, talking to people impressed upon me the definite fact that the race had ended: there was to be no more cold, damp duvets, seasickness and apprehension — for a while at least. *Sleuth* eventually made off towards the harbour entrance, leaving me feeling drowsy and happy.

A couple more hours passed with vessels gliding by on either side towards the entrance, horns mooing all the while. At last I heard a dim commotion of foghorns and shouting — from two different directions! I blasted a tune in reply — not easy on a foghorn — and out of the fog came *Great Britain II* and a big motorboat swarming with people and cameras, and Rob grinning away on the foredeck. There was much confusion and shouting, and a good deal of laughter, before Rob was able to launch himself perilously off the motorboat and onto *Kriter Lady*. We were both wearing radio mikes — I'd had one with me all along and was requested to put it on as soon as the boat came into view — but that did not disturb our greeting.

Rob looked in excellent form, though rather pale in the lower half of his face; he'd grown a beard during the race but shaved it off the day he got back because it looked awful.

While I started to tell him all the marvellous things that had happened to me in the past few hours, he got *Kriter Lady* moving towards the marina, about an hour's distance away. I interrupted my narrative continually to wave and shout to the crew of *Great Britain II*, which bore along majestically beside us, looking about three times our size. My head was soon spinning and I was stuttering with tiredness by the time the marina came into view. Rob suggested I take over the wheel to guide her in while he handled the ropes. A crowd of people waited on the pontoon, among them André Boisseaux and his wife; they had looked out of their window over morning coffee and seen me go past the headland on the way to the marina. I was delighted I hadn't come in at 5 a.m. after all. David Stevens was there, beaming all over his face, and his wife Pat, and a lot of other friends. They were all tremendously pleased that I was the first woman in and had managed to break the woman's record.

When the interviews were over and the landing formalities completed, we took *Kriter Lady* round to the berth assigned to her for her stay in Newport. Once all was tidily stowed on board, Rob took me by car to a friend's flat, where we were made extremely welcome. Lisa had already prepared a lunch of nothing one would ever expect to find on a boat, had a bed ready with wonderfully clean, sweet-smelling sheets, and a bath with hot running water, without the merest hint of salt about it. The last thoughts of the afternoon dissolved in a sigh, face down in the softness of a still, dry pillow.

Naomi James, *At Sea on Land,* 1981

Castaways
on Disappointment Island

THE CASTAWAYS of Disappointment Island is something of a curiosity. It reads like a stirring first-person novel. Today it would probably
be published under the name of the narrator and survivor of the
Dundonald shipwreck, Charles Eyre, 'as told to the Rev. Herbert Escott-
Inman'. But from its first publication in 1907 to a third in 1980, this
survival story has endured under Escott-Inman's name, although his
Author's Note is at pains to reassure us that it is a true story all through
— 'everything is told just as it really happened . . . [this is] Charles
Eyre's story, just as he told it to me.'

The steel four-masted barque *Dundonald*, on passage from Sydney
to Falmouth with 32,700 bags of wheat, ran aground on one of the
remote Auckland Islands, 200 miles off the southern tip of New Zealand, on 7 March 1907. Among the twenty-eight crew on board was
the young seaman Charles Eyre, on only his second ship but already a
Cape Horner. After nearly five months on Disappointment Island battling for survival, Eyre and fourteen other survivors made it to food
depots on Auckland Island, about six miles away, in frail coracles constructed from wood and the salvaged sails. They were eventually found
there in November by the Government steamer *Hinemoa*.

*A*nd so the days passed, and Wednesday, the 6th of March, dawned —
the last day in the life of the *Dundonald*.

It was not very bad in the earlier part of the day, but it rained a good
deal, and was so overcast that the captain could not get the sun. It was my
trick at the wheel from eight until ten and then I was relieved by an A.B.
named Santiago Marino, who took my place and stayed there until 12.30,

when our watch — the second mate's starboard watch — was relieved by the mate's port watch.

We were to turn out again at four for a couple of hours. The four hours from four to eight in the evening are called the dog watch. From four to six is the first dog watch, and from six to eight second dog watch.

It was our second dog watch, and during those two hours the weather grew very dirty. Our mainsail and crossjack were already in; and during our watch below the crowd on deck took in the upper top-gallant sails.

The fore and mizzen were already made fast, but there were three fellows working aloft at the main top-gallant sail; and just as we came on deck they sent one of their number — James Cromarty, a lad of sixteen, rated as deck boy — for more help.

The ratings on a sailing-ship are, starting at the bottom: D.B., deck-boy; O.S., ordinary seaman; and A.B., able seaman.

Well, Cromarty came down from aloft, and went up to the second mate.

'Please, sir, we want another gasket up there, for we cannot get the weather-clew of the top-gallant sail in.'

Mr Maclaghlan looked up.

'Who is up there, my lad?' he asked.

'Ellis and Findlow, sir,' the answer came.

'Very well. Eyre' — and he turned to me — 'just take a gasket up and see what you can do. You had better take another hand with you, though.'

I took the gasket, and called to a young German, Herman Queerfelt, and up we went to relieve the other two fellows, Robert Ellis and Alf Findlow, and a hard job we had of it, what with the new canvas, all soaking wet, and the wind and rain.

It was now blowing great guns, and raining in torrents; and, to make matters worse, a dense mist came up on the wind, so that it was impossible to see a foot before you. And up there we toiled and tugged, and held on for dear life, until the job was done; and then we came down only to be met with another order.

'Clew up fore and mizzen lower top-gallant sails!'

Soaked with the rain and the spray, looming like ghosts in the mist, we obeyed the order; and after we had clewed them, it was away aloft again to make them fast. I remember that I was with Low and another fellow on the fore. Poor Low! He was a good shipmate and sailor. Little did we think, either of us, as we worked away there, of the fate which was to be his ere another day had dawned.

The gaff topsail and the inner and outer jibs had already been taken in during the dog watch, for the wind kept increasing in fury.

Down at last we came for the second time, all dog tired, sick of the weather, and soaked to the skin; and then we started to coil all the running gear and make it fast to the sheer poles to prevent the heavy seas from washing it all over the place, as they swept across the decks; and then, just about eleven o'clock, the captain gave the order to check her in a bit.

'Weather cro'jack brace!'

The order was passed along, and we checked her in a couple of points, and had all the ropes coiled just after seven bells (11.30).

I had a little oilstove on board, and in cold weather, in the middle of watches, if I had time, I used to make some tea for the second mate and myself, for he was a good fellow, and I was very friendly with him; and so now, having my hands free for the time, and being soaked through and chilled to the bone, I thought that a pannikin of good hot tea would not be half bad.

'What do you say to a drop?' I asked the mate; and he nodded appreciatively.

'Wouldn't come amiss, Eyre,' he said; and off I went.

I had the stove securely lashed up, and I soon had the water boiling, and the tea under way. My word, how good it was! I carried some out to Mr Maclaghlan, who was quite as much in want of it as I was, and we stood sipping it side by side, and growling at the weather; but little did either of us so much as dream that it would be the last tea which we were to taste for many a long, long month.

'Don't show any signs of clearing,' he observed, as he stood there screening his pannikin with his hands, for the wind was strong enough to blow the tea clean out of it. 'There is one comfort, it can't last for ever.'

Whew! screamed the blast through the cordage with a shrill sound.

Smash, splash! the seas came dashing against our sides, sending showers of spray stinging into our faces.

'That puts a little warmth into one!' Mr Maclaghlan gave a sigh of satisfaction as he handed me back the empty pannikin.

Ding, dong! One bell — a quarter to twelve — gave the watch below notice that they would have to turn out and relieve us in a quarter of an hour's time; and I can honestly say that I wasn't a bit sorry to hear the signal given, for in all my voyaging I had never had a more miserable watch on deck.

Day after day we had not had a glimpse of the sun to cheer us up; it was leaden sky above and leaden sea below, and a grey mist around, until the greyness and gloom of it seemed to get right into one's body and weigh on one's spirits.

'Won't I just be glad to get my wet gear off and turn in!' I reflected, as I stood there waiting until the watch below came up. They were only a quarter of an hour after one bell, but that quarter of an hour seemed as long as a whole watch when a fellow felt dog tired and perished with the cold; and all the time the *Dundonald* was forging her way through the waves, and reeling from their great thundering blows.

Ah, at last the watch below tumbled up, and they didn't seem to move too quickly as if they enjoyed it. They mustered aft, and the mate coming on duty took the second mate's report, and sent the relief to the forecastle and the wheel.

It did not take me long to change my wet clothes; but I think that I must have been very unlucky, for though I had plenty of good, warm vests in my chest, I picked up the first that came to hand, and it was an old one — the very oldest indeed that I possessed.

But on it went, and I lit my pipe and turned in, whilst outside the wind howled, and I could hear the wash of the water on the deck.

Now, it was always a habit of mine after turning in during the night watches to read for half an hour some book on seamanship, as I was working up for my second mate's examination, and that night I made no exception, tired out though I was.

There was another fellow berthed with me, a deck boy named George Ivimey. Poor fellow, it was his first voyage, and he was having a rough time of it. Well, I read for half an hour, according to custom, and then I laid aside my book and prepared for a snug three and a half hours' sleep, when all of a sudden came the cry, above the roar of the storm:

'All hands on deck.'

Ivimey looked over at me. I thought that they wanted help to get the topsails in, and we neither of us liked the idea of turning out from our warm bunks. But turn out we did soon after, for I heard a cry again:

'Land on the weather bow, sir!'

Land! I was out of my bunk like one thing. I made a grab at the first thing that came to hand, a pair of thin dungaree trousers, a big pair of seaboots, a coat, an oilskin and sou'wester, and last of all my knife. That is a thing a sailor never forgets at such times, if he thinks at all. A knife may stand between him and death. A man may make clothes, as we made them, or he may go without clothes, but he can't make a knife or do without one.

Well, I grabbed these things — first come first taken. I did not stop to get them all on, but with an armful I raced out on to the deck to see what all this was about.

And then as I got outside the half-deck door I witnessed a sight such as I have never seen before, and which I pray I may never see again — a sight which has burnt itself into my memory, and will never be forgotten by me whilst I live.

'Land ahead!'

What may not that cry mean to the sailor? It may tell of the end of the voyage and the drawing near to the 'desired haven', or it may be the note of danger, or distress — perhaps of death itself!

Land, where no land was expected! — In such a storm, on such a night, there was something ominous in the cry which had brought me, half-dressed, to the *Dundonald*'s deck.

And what a sight was that which greeted my eyes!

There are moments which seem to have a lifetime of experience crowded into them; moments when the memories of years pass through the brain; moments when the eye takes in with one glance scenes, even to minute details, which may afterwards take hours to describe. And so it was upon this occasion. A single glance served to take the scene in, and the next moment I was racing back to warn my companion of the danger. But to tell you of what I saw will be an entirely different business.

Still, I must attempt it to the best of my ability. 'Land!' was the cry which I had heard as I lay snug in my bunk, and land was what my startled eyes saw as I rushed on deck. Land, terribly near; but what land? No artist who desired to paint a picture of desolation could have conceived a more terrible scene than that which now met my gaze.

Land! Land so close that the most inexperienced eye could have detected the peril we were in — a land of black, frowning, threatening cliffs, which seemed to tower up to eternity.

If you have been out in a thick fog, you will know how strangely objects spring into view as you walk along. One moment nothing but the veiling mist, then a strange, blurred image, and then, before you know it, you are right up to it — tree, wall, man, animal, or whatever it may be.

So it had been now. Driving through the dense mist, battling with rain-filled winds, staggering beneath the blows of the waves, the brave ship had gone, like some strong man battling patiently against many oppressing obstacles; and then suddenly, out of the mist, that vision of rocky headland that burst upon the astonished eyes of the watch on deck.

Land! We seemed to be running head on, into a narrow bay — no pretty bay with shelving beach and shell-strewn sand, but a bay of upleaping, volcanic rock, black, sheer, forbidding. From two or three points on the port bow, and right round on the starboard side, as far as the quarter, those cliffs, the sentinels of that lonely land, stood, their summits lost in the overhead mist — the mist that pressed down so low that even our own tops seemed indistinct in its wreathing veil. They rose from deep water, too; it needed but a glance at the waves to tell that. The seas came running in from the waste beyond — great, unbroken monsters — until they met the rocks at the cliffs' foot, when they broke with a roaring which filled the very air, and sent mighty columns of spray high upwards.

And in the smother of foam below, strange objects like long, writhing, black snakes could be seen — snakes which darted out towards the *Dundonald*, as if welcoming her to the grave which she was so soon to find. Not snakes really, but great masses of seaweed as thick as a man's wrist, and night on twenty feet long.

That was the picture. Long as it takes to describe it, a single glance seemed to take it all in, and I rushed back, shouting to George Ivimey to get a move on him, and I hastily finished getting into my clothes.

'Hurry, man! Hurry up!'

And with my warning to Ivimey there came the mate's call from the deck:

'Weather fore braces!'

I raced out on to the deck again almost as the command was given. The moment that land had been sighted they had braced the yards sharp up, hoping that they might weather the cliffs; but now, as it became apparent that any such hope was vain, they were going to try and wear her short round — an almost impossible task in that confined space, and yet the only chance that we had left. It was that, or rushing bow foremost into those terrible cliffs. A desperate chance, but still a chance which, if missed, would never return.

Had we continued our present course, in less than five minutes the *Dundonald* would have struck, her jibboom would have snapped like a carrot, the head-stays would have gone, and down the masts would have crashed, with the result that no one would have lived to tell the tale.

The captain knew it, and he gave the order. It was wonderful to see how calm and collected he was as he stood there. His very calmness seemed to infuse itself into the crew. A chance — a dog's chance only — but he took it, and gave the order to wear her round.

I rushed to the fore-braces with several others — who were working with me, and who were the after ones, I cannot say — and we strained and hauled with all our might to get the heavy yards round. It was a race against time, and who could say which would win? Round the yards came, but nearer and nearer drew the shore. It would be a terribly near thing if the *Dundonald* cleared it.

Crash!

A shivering shock seemed to run through the vessel. It was as though she were a living thing, knowing her danger, and trembling at it. She had struck a sunken reef with terrific force, but the next moment she was over it, and afloat again, though that rude shock must have sorely damaged her plates.

'There, she feels it!'

The words were shouted into my ear just as the ship struck the reef, and I turned, to see Low beside me.

We did not stop working, though. Our orders were to swing the yards, and swing them we would, so long as they were there to swing, until we were told to belay.

'What is the name of the island, anyhow?' I shouted back. And his answer came:

'Stewart Island.'

Poor Low! He was sadly out of his reckoning there, for Stewart Island is just south of New Zealand; and we, as we afterwards found out, were far south of that.

'Stewart Island,' he said, and then, just as we got the yards round, the mate came rushing along the deck, shouting at the top of his voice: 'Let go the topsail halyards!'

Away we rushed, and I never saw Low again. What his subsequent fate was, and how he met that fate in a brave attempt to scale those cliffs, I shall tell you later. He was separated from me in the rush across the deck, and I never saw him again.

But I remember just as the order came that Lee, the carpenter, who was standing close to us, turned and asked us whether we thought we could weather the land, and I answered that I did not think anything of the kind.

I knew that the captain was doing the only thing that could be done; but I knew, too, and so did many another there, that we would never get out of a hole like that, for there was not room to wear the ship.

Well, with the mate's order, we rushed to the halyards — some to the fore and others to the main and mizzen. In less than a second the falls were cast off the belaying-pins, and down came the three heavy yards with a run; and then came another order — a terribly significant one:

'Clear the boats, lads!'

Clear the boats! Desert our brave old ship in her hour of need, and trust our lives to those frail craft! Alas! it was not a case of deserting. All that skilled seamanship could do had been done, and the doom of the barque *Dundonald* was fixed.

But the order was given, and life itself might depend upon prompt obedience.

We were away, and upon the skids in half a second, some working at the port lifeboat, and some at the starboard.

Crouching there, the wind driving by, and stinging like a whip lash, almost numbed to the bone with the cold, with clouds of spray drenching us, we worked like madmen; and yet as calmly as if there were no peril. We moved quickly, but every man knew just what he was doing; there was no trace of that worst of perils — panic — at least not with the crowd at my boat.

I can see that scene now. I had my sheath knife, and was cutting the canvas cover away for all I was worth, when I happened to glance over to the other boat, and there I saw Sam Watson — the black who had killed the shark, you know — and I think that the fear of it all had got hold of him. He was standing erect, the whites of his eyes showing strangely, and he had an oar in his hands, which were raised high above his head.

'Too late! Too late!' I heard him scream in an eldritch tone. 'Too late!'

It might be too late, but the order was given, and it had to be obeyed. We got the cover and gripes off, and I was dipping the fall round the after tackle, as there was no turn in it, when I became aware of the startling fact that I was alone.

Alone! What had happened? Had my shipmates deserted me, or had some monster wave swept them away, and yet spared me?

Alone! No; I saw a dim form disappear and make aft. And, as I glanced after it, I saw other forms just dimly outlined in the mist. Well, it was no use staying there, for I certainly could not do anything with the lifeboat by myself.

I jumped out of the boat, quick as a flash, and raced along the bridge from the skids to the poop; that, as most people know, is captain's ground, where only the officers are permitted, together with such men as are ordered there for duty. But there was no time for ceremony now; poop and forecastle, stem and stern, the *Dundonald* was doomed; and, from first to last we knew it.

There stood the captain, his son Jimmy by his side — a poor, scared little lad, struggling bravely to hide the fears which were surely no disgrace, as he stood by his father. There were the mates, and around them clustered the hands, waiting for the captain's orders, and still, in spite of their peril, showing that they had confidence in him. And there, too, sticking to his post, was the man at the wheel.

You may talk of this hero, and that; but, to my mind, I looked at a hero then. He was only a common seaman, a Swede named Andersen, but standing there at the wheel, as though he were out in mid-ocean, with no peril nigh.

The air was full of strange noises now — wind voices, and sea voices, moaning, sobbing voices, as of storm spirits, singing the dirge of the fated ship, which now had swung round, and was running stern first into a small sort of bay. She ran it slowly; for you must understand that when we hauled the foreyards aback it stopped her headway, and she did not gather sternway very quickly.

How awful those cliffs looked as we got close to them! How the foam churned and hissed, and that long waving sea-weed seemed to stretch out, as if eager to claim us for its prey.

The captain gave the order that all hands were to get lifebelts on, and the sailmaker went to get them. These lifebelts were kept in the sail locker, which was next to my berth; and despite the sea which now swept the decks, he went and got them out, passing them along to the second mate, who in turn handed them up to the rest of us. As quick as lightning, but as calmly and methodically as if nothing were wrong was everything done; and the captain, his son by his side, stood there superintending it all, and seeing that every man had one of those precious life-belts, so that he might have a chance in the last fight that was to come.

And then Andersen, never leaving go of the wheel, revealed of what sort he was; for he called over and asked for orders — and what orders do you think? He asked whether he should leave the wheel 'when the vessel struck' stern first on those frowning cliffs!

Think of it! I have read of the skeleton of the Roman soldier found at Pompeii, and have heard the story of how he stood there on guard forgotten by all in their terror-filled flight, and waiting for death because he had not received permission to desert his post; but what of Andersen, who asked for permission to leave the wheel 'when the ship struck?' Well, I have got my own opinion as to which of those two is the greater hero.

'Leave it at once, my man,' said the captain. 'You can do no more good there,' and Andersen obeyed; but scarcely had he relinquished his hold of the spokes, when a tremendous sea caught the rudder, and the wheel went round at an awful pace; then the rudder itself must have struck a rock, and the sudden jerk of stopping it sent the wheel into a hundred pieces.

If we had any chance before, that would have killed it; our ship, unmanageable, drifted in; and we waited for the crash which was to end her.

And as we drew nearer to those terrible cliffs, their dreadful aspect only increased. Many a glance was cast towards them, in the hope of discovering any pathway to their summit, in case we managed to escape the fury of the waves and reach their base; but they seemed to forbid the faintest hope. Straight as the side of a house they appeared from where we were. A sailor can generally manage to find a foothold; but not even a sailor can walk up a perpendicular wall; and that was what those cliffs most resembled to our despairing eyes, as we looked upon them from the deck of the *Dundonald*.

As we looked, we noticed on our port side, just abaft the beam, there was a big tunnel of cave in the cliff face, which ran right through to the other side, and through this a big sea was running with tremendous force. From where I stood this tunnel appeared to be about fourteen feet wide, and its top was about thirty feet above the sea.

I have heard many storm sounds during my voyaging; but I do not think that I ever heard such a dismal noise as the waves made rushing through that great, yawning tunnel. It was a weird, hollow sound, which seemed to shiver on the air; and in spite of everything that we could call up of nerve and pluck, it found a way into our hearts.

It was enough to make any man afraid. There was the cave with the waves rushing through; there the tall cliff with the hissing foam and the lashing weed; there were the great, madly leaping waves bearing down upon us, as though they knew that our end had come, and were rejoicing at our plight. The night was as black as ink, and the icy blasts were full of slanting rain and drifting mist. The earlier part of the night had been bad enough, but this was far and away the worst.

And now the poor ship seemed as if she had run aground upon some great shelf of sunken rock; for she got no nearer to the face of the cliffs, but lay heeling over towards the land, whilst the seas broke in relentless fury over her decks.

We knew that she was not on a beach, for we could tell by the run of the waves that deep water was there, so she must be resting upon some outjutting crag; off which, if she had rolled, she would have sunk in deep water . . .

We did not quite know what to make of our position — that is, the crew did not; but I think the captain knew. I looked into his face several times — it was as calm and unmoved as ever, and yet there was something there which I had not seen before. From the moment when the *Dundonald* started going down he had known what was before us, and he was a brave man, who saw death ahead, and prepared to meet it fearlessly. Only when now and again he looked down at his son I saw his lip tremble. Perhaps he was thinking more of those at home, who would watch, and wait, and pray for their safe return, and yet never see them more, until they shall meet before that sea which is like unto a sea of glass, in the kingdom where no night is, nor pain, nor sorrow, parting, nor death . . .

'We shall have to get out of this, mister,' said the captain to the first mate, as another big sea came rushing over. And, indeed, it didn't take much to tell us that if we didn't clear we might get caught like rats in a trap and drown without a chance of making a fight for it.

'I think so, sir,' the mate answered; and so a general move was made, and we managed to get up on the forecastle head.

And not a bit too soon, for scarcely had we got clear, when she began to ship seas on her main deck, one after another.

We had not got much doubt by this time as to what was before us. From point to point we had been driven by the waves, and if they reached us here, there was nothing left but the rigging, where we might hang until it was all washed away from the poor, dying barque.

And so we all stood waiting, whilst wind and sea sang the *Dundonald*'s dirge, and the mist drifted like a winding sheet above us.

And there came a picture of a far-away home in dear old England, and of the loved ones who would never greet me again, and I wondered how they would grieve, when, after long days of waiting, the story of the wreck became known. The father, the mother, and all the dear ones — what were they doing now, and were they thinking about me?

Poor Jimmy Thorburne was crying softly to himself, and no wonder. Poor little fellow, it was a sad ending to the voyage which he had taken to make him well. The captain looked at him, and turned his head away, and I heard him mutter huskily to the mate:

'Take care of him, mister.'

It was the last thing I heard him say. Out of the darkness a monster of a wave sprang. It rose, it came clear over the forecastle head from the port side. I was facing aft when it came, by the after-rail of the forecastle head;

the captain, the mates, and Jimmy were with me. The sea burst upon us, and we clung on like grim death. Some were on the forestay, others were on the jibboom, others, like myself, on the deck.

Out parallel we were dragged by the wave, then it was gone, and the ship seemed to have slipped down into a great hollow, with a solid wall of water rising above her on either hand. It was as though she were in a grave; and indeed she was in her own grave. I saw not a single one of my companions. I was alone — buried with the ship, the water rising higher and higher above me.

Then it seemed to stop. It bent, it curved over on either hand, and then down, down it came, thousands and thousands of tons. That watery grave was filling in — the brave *Dundonald* was buried.

H. Escott-Inman,
The Castaways of Disappointment Island, 1911

Evangaline's
Delivery Trip

DELIVERY TRIPS are supposed to be routine. The people who do them are usually professionals or highly experienced yachties. But around New Zealand's challenging coast, with its unpredictable weather patterns, every now and again one goes badly wrong.

One such was the trip to bring a sturdy 55ft workboat, the *Evangaline*, from Picton to Auckland in September 1987.

The skipper, Ian Walker, an Auckland marine broker, had sailed the Hauraki Gulf since a teenager and owned a Whiting 29 called *Tailgunner*. His blue-water experience included the 1986 two-man Round North Island race. Crew Bill Subritsky and Joe Henry were part Maori, experienced fishermen and mechanics. Both worked for the tow truck and panel repair business run by *Evangaline*'s new owner, Evan Watson. There was no shortage of experience or skill on board.

Everything was routine until Gisborne. There was nothing in the forecast to delay departure for East Cape . . .

*W*e cast off from Picton in our vessel *Evangaline* at 0600 hours on Sunday 13 September 1987, on a fine, beautiful morning. We had approximately 1600 litres of diesel on board with 640 litres on the aft deck in four drums, lashed securely.

The forecast was for west to northwesterly winds, 20 to 25 knots, dropping in the evening. Tory Channel, 1000 hours, was typical; a 12 to 15ft swell on entering Cook Strait. Running the two 8L3 Gardner diesels, at 750 revs (8.5 to 9 knots) they were quietly waffling along, a beautiful sound, low key and rhythmical.

The first excitement was as we approached Karori Light. A different

339

sea, confused and agitated. We headed south to get a better motion as the vessel's motion had become violent. The wind was 20 knots but there was a very confused sea. One fuel drum came loose but eventually Joe and I managed to re-secure it.

We settled down to a watch system of one hour on, two hours off. I called Wellington radio on VHF, advised of our intentions and ETA Gisborne about 45 hours away (the last time I used the radio).

At about 1800 hours on Sunday we rounded Cape Palliser; the wind a 20-knot northwesterly, with confused seas and lots of crayfish pot buoys around. We settled down to dusk with cups of tea and a 'snack attack' created by Bill. Every three or four hours Joe checked header tanks in the engine room and pumped fuel from the stern tanks. It took 20 to 30 minutes in very uncomfortable conditions — the rolling engine room, diesel smells and engine room noise.

Sunday night we were approaching Cape Turnagain and the sea was 'like porridge' as Joe put it. Lumpy, rolling, with a good moon and no boats about.

Dawn off Castlepoint, with much of the same — wind still 20 knots west to northwest and Bill stoking up for morning snack attack. He managed to smoke out the bridge deck so we all had tears and a laugh, darkness and smoke.

Monday, noon, off Cape Kidnappers. The wind had increased to 30 knots, overcast, with rain threatening. Bill was on watch and I advised of the course for Portland Island, approximately 70 miles east/northeast of Napier. I went below for a shut eye. Bill called after an hour or so to say he could see nothing due to the rain and had 'lost the bloody island'. After a worried consultation with the full crew we established that we were in fact on course. Rounded Portland Island at 1800 hours with 'happy hour' cups of tea. Set course for Gisborne, ETA, midnight. I had a set of headphones which were well patronised and I often saw a Maori dancing to the music (soundless to the others) and driving on. They were good company.

Our problems started with conflict on the charts as to the leading lights for entering Gisborne Harbour. Were they 'fixed' or Quick Flashing? If you haven't done this entrance at night before, don't. We spent an anxious two to three hours around too many crayfish pots at two to three knots speed under Tuahine Point. Finally we saw a fishing boat coming out so we went back and went in. The run is about three miles out from the inner harbours and the lights are fixed green. Joe was below and Bill and I anxiously monitored the printout depth sounder. At times we stopped as we were in real shallow water (the vessel draws 6ft 8in). Finally tied up in the inner harbour at 0255 hours beside the fishing boats.

Bill and I were greatly relieved, had a couple of rums and turned in at 0330 hours. We had taken 45 hours from Picton . . . I phoned Ross (at Hauraki Yachts and Launches) from a local garage at 0630 hours, told him we were OK, and asked him to phone my son Yogi and dad (my wife Jane was in Rarotonga). Ross said they had had a gale over in the last day or so, 50 knots, and said to take care. I also rang Keith, my godfather, who came down to check us out.

We took on 750 litres of fuel and discussed the forecast with local fishermen. Bill went to the police station and filled in the 10-minute form. Our ETA was Tauranga, 30 hours, by approximately 1700 hours Wednesday. (In fact I should have filled out the 10-minute form myself; Bill, unaware of exactly what equipment we had aboard, said that we did not have a EPIRB on board, an omission which would later cause confusion.) The forecast was 20 to 30 knots west to northwest — similar to what we had been experiencing.

We departed at about 1100 hours. It was sunny, windy with lumpy seas but this presented us with no problem. We made good progress up the coast past Tolaga Bay and Tokomaru Bay, to East Cape. We saw the light a long way off, about four hours before we arrived. The local radio forecast was still the same. I came up from shuteye at midnight and we were half a mile from East Cape and between East Island. Conditions were okay so I thought it was okay to proceed. The swell was increasing quickly but there wasn't much wind, say 15 knots. The swell was about 15 to 20 feet.

As we passed East Cape light by about two miles, the swell was very big. Bill had the starboard door open, Joe was steering and I was watching the depth — shallow becoming deeper. Soon after we were past the island and the swell was very big, maybe 30ft — it was hard to estimate. There was no moon and it was pitch black except in the arc of East Cape light.

Then all hell broke loose.

A monster wave broke right on the bow. We picked ourselves up off the floor. Glass had exploded everywhere. Joe was screaming he was cut, his face streaming with blood. Bill wrapped a towel around his face to stem the blood. I grabbed the wheel and Bill ran down to check the lower cabin. Not much was said. We were drenched and the bridge cabin was in total chaos. Two smaller waves came through — I am not sure of this, but water poured through the broken windows. Those windows were half inch thick armour plate glass, and there was one to go.

The engines never faltered and we were going over enormous waves; up and down like a rocking horse. I said to Joe, towel tied to his head, 'Why is there no wind?'

Soon after it came, a full gale, even more enormous seas, waves breaking. I quartered the seas to avoid the water pouring through the broken windows. I kept on heading out to sea. The wind had veered to southwest and I estimated it at 40 to 50 knots, very confused, with whitecaps all around. Bill said the bilge pumps were coping but there was a lot of water in the vessel and she was sluggish and frightening to handle.

It was now around 0200 to 0300 hours, Hicks Bay lights disappearing to the south. We were very concerned about how much more the vessel could take. Bill put a lifejacket over my head — it was like I was getting the last rites. We got the flares, bleeper and raft ready and discussed our predicament. We thought it unwise to turn around as the seas might roll us over. The wind was westerly now and Hicks Bay was considered a lee shore. It was best to keep heading out to sea.

We fired four or six parachute flares from inside the bridge cabin. Because of the violent motion some of the flares went low and a few went up in the sky. We reckoned no one was coming to help us anyway. We were on our own.

Joe called port or starboard as I was flat out keeping the boat from being bowled over. No lights, all the electrics had sparked, fizzled and ceased to exist, except for the masthead light which kept flickering. We prepared the raft for a quick launch and set about keeping the vessel afloat in the raging seas.

By dawn, the water was gaining in the bilge from the regular flow pouring in the two broken windows. Everything was soaked. The cabin was in turmoil with everything being thrown about, including the new fridge. The table was upside down. The wind continued to howl and the seas were enormous and breaking in many directions. We activated the EPIRB bleeper during the early morning and settled down to fighting the steering wheel. Joe had stopped bleeding. We had no first aid box on board.

Sometime before dawn I was smacked in the mouth with the wheel spokes, breaking a tooth. Dawn, Wednesday, the seas were the same, much of the same all day. I was still on the wheel, Joe and Bill bailing on the hour as the bilge pumps had given up. The water pump on the starboard engine gave up so Joe by-passed the salt water intake and sent the bilge water pumping through both engines to keep them cool. This was a fantastic effort by Joe. While he did it the vessel was being thrown all over the ocean. Joe was also in the engine room, pumping fuel every four hours from the aft tanks to the engineroom tanks. Land was away south, barely visible. We kept heading northwest in enormous seas and howling winds.

By midnight on Wednesday I said to a very tired crew that I had to have 10 minutes' sleep. My eyes were open but my brain was dreaming. I had been 24 hours on the wheel and working hard, backing the throttle on one engine, powering on the other, to climb the seas. Frequently I called 'hang on' as we climbed the side of a wall of water. I estimate that some seas were as high as five times the boat's beam of 15ft 6in — 75ft.

I lashed the wheel with electrical wire to the manual gearbox levers about midnight and we all cuddled together to get warm for a nap in the wet mess. All the bedding was wet and we braced ourselves among the debris on the floor of the main cabin. We catnapped and bailed until first light Thursday, checking our course regularly.

The seas had continued the same all night. I was wearing my hand-held sighting compass around my neck. This was constantly being used to check our heading as the torch batteries were flat and we had no other means of monitoring our heading, although when the wind blew on my face, I knew that I was steering too high, so I would untie the steering and drop down a bit. Generally our course was northeast.

The kero lamp was swinging from the cabin beams, on its last tank of fuel. During the night we had had turns at getting into the exhaust pipe cupboard and hugging the twin pipes to get warm. We were all suffering from cramp through dampness. Joe told me he was worried about Bill, who just wanted to go to sleep and in his mind was 'going to die'.

We tried to keep him involved but he didn't want to know. Thursday, day three, daylight. Bailing 100 buckets every hour, huge seas, wind and blue sky. We woke Bill and said we needed help to syphon fuel from the remaining three 44-gallon drums. We had lost one, it bowled out the starboard bulwark! This was completed some hours later with all the fuel now in the boat tanks. We cast the remaining drums adrift as they were charging about doing more damage. We had nothing to eat as it was sodden and the water had turned rusty with all the motion. Joe and I kept busy — I steering, he pumping fuel from the aft tanks to the engine tanks and keeping an eye on the circulating bilge water. Both of us were bailing. Joe has a great saying — 'in for a grin', the 101st bucket was his always for a grin.

Sometime in the day we boarded up three quarters of the two broken windows which helped cut down the cold and water intake but we still received our regular rogue waves. We cast our EPIRB adrift as we didn't think it was working so anything was worth trying.

The day turned to night and Joe and I had a deep discussion. I thought we might make land on the eastern side of Great Barrier or similar. I thought something would happen Friday. It had to, we had fuel until dusk Friday, then that was it. The wonderful Gardners never missed a beat, except on one occasion during fuel syphoning, but Joe nursed them along. Some-time after midnight Thursday Joe and I were taking turns at one hour watch, then bailing 100 buckets. The bailing took 30 minutes. We sat along the sink bench and noticed that the seas were definitely becoming smaller and the wind had dropped. We kept the lamp going with three bottles of Blue Stratos aftershave and engine oil.

About 0200 hours I saw a distinctive flash, 1-2-3, then nothing for 13 seconds, then another three flashes. I called to Joe — we timed it and double checked, then woke Bill. We were ecstatic! We gathered our sod-den charts from the exhaust cupboard and looked for the light. Slipper Island on the Aldermans. We became very much alive.

As dawn was approaching I could sometimes see the shore lights of Whangamata on top of the big swell. When we were sure of our position, I slowed the boat down to avoid running into rocks. After coming this far, I didn't want to destroy what we had achieved. Suddenly we saw Mayor Island away to port, and this pleased us. Daybreak, Friday, we found the rum and drank it with boiled rusty water. We also became bold enough to cook a concoction Joe found. By this stage we were prepared to eat and drink anything.

The seas rolled back, it still blew but we were alive and heading for Whitianga, party time. Bill — balaclava and Swandri, bearded, red eyed. Joe — scarface and dried blood. I — cut under the nose, congealed blood and broken tooth. What a team we were, limping into Whitianga. Steering to port was difficult so we had to run the starboard engine at fewer revs to keep a straight line. We talked about what we would do when we tied up.

We finally tied up at Whitianga wharf at about noon on Friday 72 hours after becoming a submarine off East Cape and being overdue in Tauranga by 36 hours. We saw no planes or anyone looking for us. Joe and Bill kissed the wharf and instantly befriended the local wahines on the wharf. Joe and I phoned Auckland and the locals came to our assistance, with a four-inch pump from the Ministry of Works to pump the bilge, a local glass merchant effected temporary repairs, etc. The pump took 45 minutes to pump us dry!

The vessel was repaired sufficiently to motor to Auckland a week later.

She underwent 2½ months of repairs at McMullen and Wing's hardstanding at Mt Wellington.

Footnote: From Thursday morning until Friday noon, Ross Barnett from Hauraki Yachts was in constant touch with Search and Rescue, phoning fishermen and motels around the East Cape area asking them to check if they knew of *Evangaline* sheltering in any of the bays. Without fail these people checked and phoned back. An Orion aircraft was sent to look for us as the EPIRB was activated. The plane found a yacht holed at Hicks Bay and thought the bleeper had come from the yacht, so stopped searching until it was established the bleeper was from *Evangaline*. Unfortunately I did not fill in the 10-minute form at Gisborne and Bill had not been aware of our safety equipment. On Wednesday at 9.26 a.m. Don Corlett of Hicks Bay reported no sign of *Evangaline*, 50 to 60 knot winds and 30ft waves at Hicks Bay.

Search notes by Ross Barnett: The report I got from Search and Rescue seemed wrong to me. I had sailed in the two-man Round North Island race with Ian so I knew how he would react. Our saying is 'if in doubt, head out' so when Search and Rescue said the boat was at Hicks Bay undergoing repairs I knew Ian would have phoned and told us. That's why I phoned all the towns around the East Cape and asked locals if they had seen *Evangaline* or heard from her. All negative. I told Search and Rescue that Ian would not leave the boat until the last possible minute. We had the fishing boats out of Tauranga check around during the sched time. I spoke to George Mason's daughter at Great Barrier Radio who was very helpful. All the people I spoke to were most helpful, going out of their way to help.

Ian Walker,
'Evangaline's *terrifying delivery trip*', 1990

Rescuing Crumpy

JACK CROOKS has worked, in New Zealand and overseas, as a carpenter, construction worker, wool-presser, wharfie, commercial fisherman and boat-builder. He began sailing on the Invercargill estuary in Idle Alongs and 14-footers. In 1954, as an apprentice panel-beater, he began building a 38ft cruising yacht in which to sail around the world.

Tuarangi, with masts stepped and sails made in Stewart Island and her fit-out done in Auckland, was launched in 1961. Jack was 29. By 1965, with three or four crew, he had completed his circumnavigation — the east Australian coast (where this encounter with Barry Crump took place), across the Indian Ocean to Durban, Cape Town and into the Atlantic, West Indies, Panama, and back home across the Pacific. He was later awarded the Royal Akarana Yacht Club's Blue-water medal.

These days, having sold *Tuarangi* in 1977, he sails on a friend's boat, often to Stewart Island and in the annual Foveaux Strait race.

'*H*ey Jack, I think you'd better come on deck. We're coming up on this island and I can see something moving about the beach.'

Owen was on the helm and there was a note of urgency in his voice, which had me swinging quickly out of my bunk and heading for the companionway. I paused at the chart table to glance at the chart. Cairns to Princess Charlotte Bay. I looked at my watch. It was nearly midday. We had sailed from Cooktown at 0830 and had been doing a good six knots in the fresh south-east trade wind. This meant we must have covered about twenty-four miles which would put us roughly ten miles south of Cape Flattery. I peered at the chart again. We must be approaching Three Isles.

'Is it the one with the light tower on it?' I bellowed.

'Yes.' shouted Owen. 'There's definitely something moving.

'Can't be,' I said confidently as I climbed on deck. 'These islands are just specks of sand. Nothing can live on them.' I glanced over at a typical cartoonist's desert island with one coconut palm. This one also had a steel light tower mounting a flashing navigation light. Something, though, was crawling around the beach.

I reached below and snatched the binoculars from the chart table. 'Must be a dog or something. Wonder how it got there?' Bracing myself against the motion of the boat I levelled the glasses. It was a man! He was stamping out a huge SOS on the sand.

We were coming up on the island fast now. A red flag was being waved, smoke went up, people were running up and down the beach waving frantically.

'Bloody hell,' I shouted. 'There's people everywhere.' *Tuarangi* had the bit in her teeth, hissing along, rail down, on a broad reach. We were almost abeam of the island, in a few minutes we'd be passed and would have to beat back. No easy task in a gaff ketch against wind and sea. I shouted down the hatch for the rest of the crew, then pounded along the deck to let go the main halyards.

The *Tuarangi* was a 12-metre double-ended, Norwegian-type gaff ketch, a William Atkin Ingrid design. I built her over a period of six years in my mother's back yard in Invercargill, with a little help from my friends.

The object was always a voyage around the world. I wanted to sail as far as it was possible to go and you can't go further than around the world. As I had only sailed small boats on the Invercargill estuary I didn't say too much about this.

Six years is a long time to spend building a boat, but apart from the necessity to earn money to pay for materials, I wasted a lot of time perched on the hedge or the roof of the house, admiring the sweep of her sheer or the rake of her sternpost. I guess it takes longer to build a beautiful boat.

By the time the boat was finished the sea was calling and two of my friends who had helped with the building were free to join me. Peter Baxter was recovering from a broken romance and Jack Hargraves had been personally invited by the university authorities not to return next year. What the hell, we were away.

We fitted the boat out over at Stewart Island, where Micky Squires, a fisherman friend, sewed the sails and spliced the rigging for us. While over there, I read a best-selling book called *A Good Keen Man* written by someone called Barry Crump. It was a great yarn and I passed it around.

Every one reckoned Crump must be a bit of a hard case.

A frigid voyage up the New Zealand coast in the middle of winter took us to Auckland. We encountered our first storm off Napier but were so green we weren't sure if it was a real storm or not. Years later I met the first mate of a big freighter that had been through the same blow. 'How bad was it?' I asked him. He raised his eyebrows. 'Well we were worried.' Seemed they'd had their bridge washed out.

Auckland was a great spot to earn money and do jobs on the boat which the voyage up the coast had shown to be necessary. At the beginning of 1963 we were ready to cross the Tasman. We were joined by a friend, Johnny Morton, who was to come as far as Sydney, and completed the crossing in the very respectable time of seven days.

One of the highlights of the voyage was to be the passage up the Queensland coast inside the Barrier Reef. This would also be one of the most dangerous legs of the world voyage. We mostly relied on charts past their 'use by' date that had been presented to us by friendly ships officers. For the reef however, I bought a full set of up-to-date charts, light lists and pilot books. Many cruising yachts had left their bones on the reef and I was determined this would not happen to *Tuarangi*.

The best time to sail up the Barrier Reef is June, July, August when the south-east trades are blowing. This would also enable us to arrive in South Africa before the hurricane season started in the Indian Ocean in November.

In Brisbane we were joined by Englishman Owen Jones who was coming as far as Durban. Older than us, he had somehow survived the war flying terrible old Swordfish aircraft against the Japanese. He had worked at many things since, including, incredibly to us, a stint as a gentleman's gentleman. He was immediately nicknamed Jeeves.

Sometimes Owen would make a batch of scones for afternoon tea. As we sat down to them he would say in a posh accent. 'What a pity the vicar can't be here.' We would all take it from there and carry on a crazy conversation in what we imagined to be upper-class English accents while we ate hot buttered scones and sipped our tea.

By the time we reached Gladstone at the beginning of the Barrier Reef we were having serious engine trouble. New parts were necessary, but it was a foreign engine and the nearest agent was in Melbourne. Jack volunteered to hitch-hike south.

Two weeks later he returned with the parts and the news that Ned Kelly was alive and well and selling engine parts in Melbourne.

We sailed from Gladstone, with the engine purring but our finances much depleted. Worse, we were two weeks behind schedule in our appointment with the Indian Ocean. Wending our way northwards, along the seemingly never-ending Australian coastline, we heard on the grapevine that Barry Crump and his brother Bill were operating a charter boat out of Cooktown. When we finally sailed into the Endeavour river we wondered if they would be about.

We tied up at the public wharf and went ashore. As usual I was carrying the ship's papers. One of the bugbears of cruising the Australian coast was the requirement to enter and clear customs at each port of call. Worse, at that time no differentiation was made between large ships and small yachts, which meant, if we put in to some small town for a loaf of bread and a bottle of milk I would struggle with a mountain of paperwork in the customhouse while the rest of the crew lounged in the pub.

In a small place like Cooktown with no resident customs officer, the local policeman would do the honours and I duly presented myself at the police station. The cop was sitting on the verandah, feet up on the rail, chair tipped back, wide brimmed hat over his eyes. 'Gidday,' I said. 'We've just sailed in. We're from New Zealand.'

His eyes opened. 'I can tell that. You heading north?'

I nodded. 'Thursday Island.'

'Well watch yourselves. She's a no man's land up there. People often just disappear.' He yarned to me for a while about his hobby of looking for World War II aircraft that had come down on flights from Brisbane to New Guinea during the war.

'A whole flight of Kittyhawks was lost once. They're still up there somewhere. None of the pilots made it back.'

I said we'd be careful and raised the packet of papers. 'You want to check these?'

'Won't bother, mate.' He nodded his head. 'Pub's down the road.'

The Half Sovereign Hotel, we were told, used to be the Sovereign, until half of it was blown down by a cyclone and never rebuilt. We found the Crumps, Barry and brother Bill, propping up the bar.

They seemed quite pleased to see us, especially when I put a pound on the bar and invited them to have a beer. 'Service is terrible here,' grumbled Barry. 'The other day, Bill had to go over the road to the Post Office and send a telegram to the barman asking him to serve us.'

Half a dozen Aussies at the other end of the bar regarded us in that deadpan way Aussies have. They traded a few desultory insults with Bill and went back to gazing morosely into their beer from under the wide brims of their hats.

'Heat affects their brains up here,' said Barry.

We gathered trans-Tasman relations weren't exactly cordial.

Barry spun some great yarns about crocodile shooting in the northern swamps and creeks. Later, we went back with him and Bill to the old boat-house they were living in, near the spot where Captain Cook came ashore.

Barry's girlfriend, Jean, cooked a feed and there were more yarns, more beer. They told us they were heading up the reef in the morning in their launch *Waterwitch* with paying customers, two couples from South Australia. I said we'd stay another day and sail north on Monday morning. None of us realised how vital this information was to be to them.

Early on Sunday morning we were woken by the tooting of a fog-horn and shouts of, 'Get out of bed, ya lazy sods.'

The *Waterwitch*! We stuck our heads out the hatch, waved, and returned yawning to our bunks, pleased we weren't moving until tomorrow.

At 0830 the following morning we pulled away from the Cooktown wharf and were soon bowling along under full sail in the trade wind.

'I bet it's Crump,' said Jack, as we let go the anchor and furled the sails. The castaways had gathered in a group on the beach but were too far away for us to recognise.

We rigged the main halyard and put our large leaky old clinker dinghy in the water. We decided Jack would row in alone. If he rowed fast he should make it to the beach before the dinghy sank. 'Better take some water,' I said, 'they might be thirsty.'

He returned with Barry and Bill Crump. They were thirstier than any-one I had ever seen before. No mere mugs of water would suffice, we filled large bowls and watched in astonishment as they drank greedily.

While Jack returned for the others they told us their story. They had landed on the island the previous afternoon to collect shells. Clad only in bathing suits and expecting to be away for only half an hour or so, they took neither food nor water with them.

While they were ashore, Alan, a man of about sixty, decided to go back to the boat to get his shirt as he was getting sunburnt. Not saying anything, he took the dinghy and rowed out to the boat. While he was below, the anchor dragged off the reef into deep water and the boat was away. The others came running down to the beach to find the boat drifting fast as the wind caught her. They shouted to Alan to start the engine but, with no experience of diesel engines, he nearly killed himself cranking against the compression. If he had lifted the compression levers the engine would have started at once, but he didn't know that.

On the island, watching their boat drift away and disappear in the distance, the situation of the castaways was desperate. They were lightly clad, had no shade from the sun and no water. In northern Queensland you don't last long without water. There were nine small bitter coconuts on the island's one tree and that was all they had.

After dark, they saw the lights of several ships but were unable to attract their attention. They buried themselves in the sand and spent a miserable night. Morning bought the return of the sun and the agony of thirst and sunburn. The one hope they clung to was that the *Tuarangi* was sailing from Cooktown first thing in the morning.

It must have been a long anxious wait for them. What if we had decided to stay another day? What if we passed by without seeing them? Knowing this could be their only chance they prepared as best they could, scratching an SOS in the sand and readying a flag and a fire.

Just before midday they sighted our sails. We were going to pass close but were approaching fast. They lit their fire and waved the flag frantically. Bill decided to stamp out another SOS in the sand and it was his doing this that first attracted Owen's attention.

We got them all aboard, six of them. Jean, the two Crumps, Alan's wife and the other couple, Doug and his wife. With them fed, watered and made as comfortable as possible we faced the problem of what to do about the missing boat and the old man. We put out an emergency call on the radio but got no response. Obviously it was going to be up to us.

The mainland, ten miles away, was a long curving surf beach that swept north to Cape Flattery. The *Waterwitch* would most likely have ended up on this beach somewhere south of the cape. We got underway, headed across to the beach and sailed north outside the line of breakers. We could see nothing at first, then a column of smoke went up. As this coast was uninhabited it was almost certainly Alan. At least he was alive, a great relief to his poor wife. It was impossible to anchor off the beach, so we ran up a flag to let him know we'd seen him and made for the nearest anchorage around Cape Flattery. We would have to go overland to reach the wreck.

After a meal, Barry, Bill, Doug, Jack and I set out for the wreck. We took water bottles, a little food and a couple of rifles in case we met wild cattle. Barry was to be in charge. He told us it would be hard going. That was an understatement. I remember scrub, thick bush, swamp and sand hills but foremost in my memory is a huge muddy lagoon. Impossible to go around, we had to wade through its waist-deep waters. We were in the middle, when Barry stopped, looked around and said in a conversational tone to Bill: 'I think the way the wind's blowing, all the crocodiles will be at the other end.'

Crocodiles! If we could have risen vertically and run along the top of the water we would have done so. As it was, we had a pretty good go at it. If Barry was trying to hurry us along, he certainly succeeded.

Four and a half hours after leaving, we arrived at the wreck. It had long since been dark, and for want of a nicer word we were buggered. Old Alan had done a good job. He'd salvaged everything movable from the *Waterwitch* and built a humpy out of spars and sails. He made us cups of tea and fussed around like a mother hen. We were a bit annoyed at this, as *we* were supposed to be the rescuers.

The next morning, we were up at first light. The *Waterwitch* was doomed. Badly sprung on the starboard side, there was no hope of salvaging her without the right gear. Using an axe and a pry bar we stripped her of everything, even removing the engine. It was a sad job wrecking the beautiful little boat. When Barry first raised the axe he said, 'This is breaking my heart.' I knew he meant it.

The engine was filled with oil, wrapped in a sail and stored behind the sand hills with the rest of the gear. We had a cup of tea and prepared for the return journey.

No one was keen to go back through the lagoon, so it was decided to walk along the beach then cut inland across the top of the cape. It was a long way but we reckoned it couldn't be worse than the way we'd come. In this, we were wrong. It was worse. Much worse.

Barry said we could have anything we wanted from the wreck, but we'd have to carry it ourselves. I decided to take the dinghy oars. We badly needed a new pair. Alan had salvaged all his and his wife's personal belongings from the boat and though we tried to talk him out of it, was determined to take them back. Barry was adamant. No one must help him. 'It might seem hard but we're going to have enough trouble getting ourselves back without loading up with junk. He'll soon realise he can't carry it and get rid of it.'

The beach was covered in an amazing collection of flotsam. There were thousands of Japanese glass fishing floats, millions of jandals, no doubt also from fishing boats. We found a perfect little dinghy, a sailor's hat and a message in a bottle. We left it all and pressed on.

Climbing the sand hills to the top of Cape Flattery was a hell trip. We didn't have enough water, would never be able to carry enough water. No matter how much you drank, the heat, reflected back from the sand, sucked it out of you. I remembered the cop in Cooktown saying how people just disappeared up here. I could well believe it. Become exhausted and dehydrated, sink down in the sand and you wouldn't get up again.

Alan had been jettisoning belongings for some time. The last thing to go was a magnificent brass chamber pot. It was left in lonely splendour on top of Cape Flattery, perhaps one day to be found by a wandering Aboriginal. What would he make of it? Perhaps it's still being used as a cooking pot in some lonely camp.

I was tempted to get rid of the oars many times, I was also carrying a rifle and it was hard going but I somehow managed to stagger on.

Five hours after leaving the wreck we broke out of the sand hills on to the beach. We ran for the sea, stripping off our clothes as we went. 'Could be sharks,' warned someone. 'Bother the sharks,' we shouted as we plunged into the glorious sea. Well, that wasn't actually what we shouted, but you get the drift.

We now had eleven people on our boat, which was designed for a crew of four. The problem was, how to get them back to Cooktown, a hard slog to windward against a rough sea and strong wind. Gaff ketches have many virtues but they are not renowned for being close-winded and our small engine was useful only in a calm. A southbound fishing boat would solve the problem if one came along.

We had finished a meal on deck when one did appear, heading south. It was too good a chance to miss and we fired off a couple of flares to attract their attention. They altered course towards us. So did a small freighter which had appeared unnoticed around Cape Flattery. Talk about feast or famine. I was worried the freighter might run aground as we were in quite shallow water and we ran around the deck frantically waving it away while encouraging the fishing boat to come on. Sort of like directing traffic.

At last, to our relief the freighter turned away and resumed her voyage, no doubt with much muttering on the bridge about stupid boaties. The fishing boat anchored nearby. Jack rowed over and spoke to the crew. He returned with the news that they were only interested in money and would take the castaways south for three pounds a head, a lot of money in 1963.

We were outraged. One of the reasons help is freely given at sea (in our part of the world anyway) is that next time, it might be you in trouble.

Barry had a rant about mercenary Australians, which was a bit embarrassing as we had four Aussies onboard. Then Jack mentioned the fishermen were actually new Australians (foreigners newly settled in Australia), so we all had a good rant about them and felt a bit better.

Our castaways went into a huddle and announced they would pay the money to avoid putting us to more trouble and holding us up even longer. This was nice of them, but I didn't see why the greedy fishermen should benefit from other people's misfortunes so told them we'd sail for Cooktown first thing in the morning.

It took us nearly fourteen hours to beat back, making long tacks out to the reef and back to the mainland. The *Tuarangi*'s old log says 'Berthed at Cooktown wharf at 2000. Landed passengers and their gear and retired to the pub.'

While we were in Thursday Island, I wrote up the story of our adventure and thinking people might be interested, posted it off to a local newspaper. I heard no more about it.

A couple of years later, back in the old home town, I happened to be passing the offices of the evening paper. Curious, I walked in 'Did you ever get that story about rescuing Crump?'

'Oh yes,' said the bloke behind the desk, 'but we couldn't publish it.'

'Why not?' I asked.

'We decided it was a put-up job.'

'A put-up job?'

'Well, famous New Zealand author is wrecked on a remote Australian island. Then, along comes a New Zealand yacht and rescues him. Crump had a new book out about that time. It was obviously a publicity stunt. Well, that was our assessment anyway.' His eyes strayed back to the papers on his desk and I turned away.

I wonder what Crumpy would have said to him?

Jack Crooks

Rogue Wave

GORDON MANN and owner Brian Murray were highly experienced yachtsmen when they agreed to enter *Green Hornet* in the 1999 Melbourne to Osaka two-handed yacht race.

Gordon, then 51, had learnt to sail as a child in Auckland, graduating from centreboarders to coastal racing keelboats, then to offshore racing in the 1993 inaugural Auckland to Fukuoka yacht race. He had four trans-Tasman crossings, a yacht delivery from Osaka to San Francisco and some 30,000 blue water miles under his belt. Brian, six years older, an Auckland businessman, had clocked up similar mileage, much of it in *Green Hornet* which he'd owned for ten years.

The race had started normally enough with twenty entries sailing out through the Port Philip heads. *Green Hornet* was one of two New Zealand boats, and meticulously prepared. After two or three days the weather began to worsen; by the sixth, they'd been three days riding out a storm off the New South Wales coast, due east of Sydney. They thought the worst of it was over.

*A*fter an uncomfortable night spent laying-a-hull riding out the force 10 storm, we finally got under way again at about 0800 hours. Brian took the first two-hour watch while I went below and, despite the violent motion, fell asleep on the saloon floor still dressed in wet weather gear, sea boots and safety harness.

The previous evening the wind had gusted to 55 knots. Even with only the storm trysail up *Green Hornet* was over canvassed, so we decided to lash the helm and lay ahull with no sail to ride out the storm till daylight, when conditions should ease.

Time passed slowly. We lay below listening to the crests of the breaking swells around us as they thundered past in the darkness. From time to time a big wave struck, rolling *Green Hornet* around, bursting open lockers to throw their contents horizontally across the cabin. A bottle of olive oil emptied itself, turning the galley floor into a skating rink. What should have been a five-minute task cleaning up took half an hour.

Dawn slowly relieved the darkness of the night. The wind eased to 30 knots, though the swells were a good ten metres high as they endlessly marched northwards generated by the low weather system parked to the south-east. The radio told of the rough night the other competitors had also endured. Four yachts had pulled out of the race and were seeking shelter on the eastern seaboard; damage included smashed windows, wrecked steering. One yacht had been rolled.

We'd also suffered some damage. Some time during the night we'd lost a spinnaker sheet overboard and it had caught around our folding propeller. From the banging on the hull after recovering the sheet, some repair to one of the folding propeller blades or the shaft support strut was going to be necessary. Brian and I decided to head towards the nearest sheltered water: Sydney about 120 miles to the west. There we could ascertain the damage and hopefully jury-rig a repair without losing too much time.

We hoisted the trysail as a steadying sail and Brian took the first two-hour watch. I went below and dropped asleep on a stack of sails on the cabin floor as Brian nursed *Green Hornet* towards Sydney.

Out of nowhere the rogue wave hit.

The 70-foot vertical wall of water lifted *Green Hornet* up higher and higher, then violently threw her down its face. The *Hornet* crashed to a shuddering halt as she hit the trough on her beam-ends. With a splintering of timber and fibreglass, the starboard side of the cabin was torn from the deck, along with half the cockpit bulkhead.

I was hurled, still asleep, across the cabin, breaking an arm, dislocating a wrist and splitting my head open.

I struggled to my feet dazed, trying to make sense of what had happened. In the cabin the water level was up to my knees; every item in the cabin seemed to be afloat in the rising water. What had happened — shit, we must've been rolled, get a bucket, bale her out, she feels so sluggish, where's Brian? My head was roaring, but the noise of the storm seemed muted and time had slowed down. I looked out of the companionway into the cockpit. Brian was there, sprawled against the lifelines at the transom, still attached to the boat by his safety harness. He looked stunned. When the wave had hurled the boat down its face, he'd flown through the air on the end of his safety harness. When she hit the trough, Brian slammed into the boom, breaking three ribs and gouging his shin on the starboard headsail winch.

'Send out a mayday!' he shouted.

I turned to where the radio should be on the starboard side of the cabin above the navigation station. It wasn't there. I realised we had suffered major structural damage. The side of the cabin top was pushed inwards about half a metre, torn from the side deck. I could see the radio through the cabin window sitting under the deck, with the sea steadily pouring over the gunwale straight into the boat.

I started to reach for the radio to see if we could get out a mayday, then realised with dismay that something was wrong with my right hand. I wasn't aware of any pain but my hand was dislocated from my wrist. I pulled on my fingers to try and realign my hand, but the wrist was so swollen I couldn't move it. There were also strange protrusions of bone.

It seemed to me that things couldn't get much worse. The sea was flooding in with every swell. There was no way we could save *Green Hornet*. The only hope was to take to the liferaft before we sank and take our chances on others rescuing us.

Unless we could get the liferaft launched in the next five minutes, we were going swimming. And swimming in the Tasman Sea in these conditions was not an attractive proposition.

Brian and I had struck up a friendship in March 1995 as we sailed across the Tasman during the delivery trip of the Greg Elliott racer *Elliott Marine* for the 1995 Melbourne to Osaka race.

We both expressed the desire, one day, to compete in the two-handed Melbourne–Osaka race. The idea was filed away, forgotten. I didn't have a yacht or the time and was unlikely to have either in the foreseeable future. From time to time I crewed on Brian's *Green Hornet*, an 11m Whiting design racing out of Westhaven, Auckland.

Late in October 1998, over a quiet rum after a race, Brian said to me, 'You know you promised way back that if I ever wanted to do the Melbourne to Osaka race you'd do it with me? Well, I've decided to do it, in the *Hornet*. Are you coming?'

I replied that this wasn't quite the way I remembered the conversation, but the challenge had been floating around in my mind as a 'must do, one day'. I agreed on the spot.

In some ten years, Brian had developed *Green Hornet* into a very competitive yacht. We'd raced her to Fiji and back, and put in some 5000 offshore miles together. I respected Brian's seamanship and the seagoing ability of *Green Hornet*. Our decision triggered a great deal of planning and preparation: a new mast, radar, weather fax and chart plotter to bring her up to Category Zero standard (the same level of seaworthiness required for the Volvo Round-the-World racers.) It was a measure of our preparations that *Green Hornet* was the first yacht to get through the pre-race safety inspection in Melbourne.

Standing amidst the chaos in the cabin, I realised, in a detached sort of way, that all of our preparations were meaningless and inadequate to cope with the calamity that had hit us. I'd often mentally rehearsed the steps to cope with likely disasters at sea. Never in my worst nightmares had I imagined structural damage of the kind we were facing, plus nursing a broken arm. *Green Hornet* was going to founder and there was absolutely nothing we could do to delay this or save her.

I turned back towards Brian. He was untangling himself from the lifelines at the rear of the cockpit.

'The radio's underwater,' I shouted. 'I can't send a Mayday. Get the EPIRB and liferaft.'

Brian moved to the portable Argos beacon lashed to the port stanchions at the rear of the cockpit. While he struggled to free it from its pouch, I had another look at my hand. It was grotesquely angled from my arm and I could see the fracture stretching my skin, almost penetrating it with the pressure. Brian thrust the beacon at me and I grabbed it with my left hand, wrapping the safety line several times around my wrist. This was our only link with the rest of the world, our only means to indicate to Search and Rescue where to look in the vastness of the Tasman. No way would I let it go.

'Get the 406 EPIRB and the emergency grab bag!'

'I can't, look at my arm.'

Brian looked at me aghast. There was (I later heard) a lump the size of a tennis ball on my forehead and a steady stream of blood running from the gash in my scalp. He stared at me, saying nothing but thinking, how could I still be standing when he was sure he could see my skull and what could be brain tissue.

'Stay there. I'll launch the liferaft.' Brian hefted the valise from the pipe berth into the cockpit and gave a grunt of pain. 'I think I've hurt my ribs,' he said.

I watched helplessly as he tied the liferaft tether to the eyebolt we'd especially mounted in the sill of the companionway into the cockpit. In what seemed like slow motion Brian threw the liferaft to leeward over the bent and twisted stanchions on the starboard side of the cockpit.

I watched the orange liferaft valise bobbing in the white foam and steel blue water. Brian pulled on the tether. Nothing happened! Fear gripped me. Our immediate survival depended on the triggering of the CO_2 cartridge to inflate the liferaft. Just how fail-safe was the system?

'Pull really hard, Brian — pull bloody hard,' I yelled, recalling from earlier safety demonstrations that some force was required to pull all the tether out and start the inflation sequence.

There was a loud pop and the liferaft started to inflate. It seemed to take forever and a plastic shroud was preventing it from inflating fully. With the emergency knife attached to the tiller, Brian gingerly sliced into the plastic. As the shroud split, the liferaft quickly deployed, floating right way up, with the wind trying to tear it away.

The water level in the hull was now up to my waist. The stern of the cockpit was at water level. Brian pulled the liferaft up to the transom and told me to get in. He steadied me as I went aft and half rolled, shielding my arm, through the entranceway of the liferaft on to the floor.

I struggled to my knees. We had improved our means of survival now that we had a liferaft to shelter in. I awkwardly tied the Argos beacon to a fabric loop in the liferaft; if we were capsized, it couldn't be lost. All we had to do was stay with the liferaft and wait for the distress alert to be picked up.

Looking through the entranceway, I could see Brian on his hands and knees seeking to recover the more powerful 406 EPIRB and our canister of emergency supplies. The cockpit was now awash and the raft straining at its tether some fifteen metres from the *Hornet*. The mast surprisingly seemed to be intact but as *Hornet* steadily sank by the stern the mast leaned menacingly over the liferaft threatening to snag the canopy as we rode up and down on the swells. Brian stepped into the sea and pulled himself by the tether hand over hand toward the liferaft. I helped him in. *Hornet* had now settled so far by the stern that with every swell that roared past the mast was hitting the raft threatening to capsize or puncture us.

We realised we were still attached to *Hornet*. It looked like the liferaft was going to be dragged under as she sank.

Desperately, we searched the interior of the liferaft for a knife. The consequences of being thrown out of the liferaft as it was dragged down would be disastrous. But Brian was sure that the tether had a weak link designed to ensure the liferaft broke free. The question was, how much force was required?

The answer came seconds later. With a jerk we came free from *Hornet* as the tether parted from the eyebolt. My final view of her was the last metre or so of the bow pointing skyward.

Strangely, now that we were free of our stricken yacht, I felt a sense of calm. We'd come through the immediate crisis of the sinking, and now had a small measure of control over our fate. I didn't fear the physical ordeal that might face us. I was positive the will to survive was going to get me through until we were rescued, no matter how long that might take.

Brian and I looked at each other. 'Turn the EPIRB on,' he said.

I read the instructions and activated the emergency switch. The reassuring blink of the L.E.D. indicated that the beacon was transmitting its distress signal to the circling satellite overhead.

Things could only improve now, I said to myself. There is a hell of a lot to survive for. I've got too much living ahead to die yet.

We took stock of our new 'home.' Although a four-person liferaft, there was barely room for the two of us. Brian closed the canopy entrance with the tie strung round its perimeter. Soon the temperature built up till it was too hot, so we reopened the entranceway to regulate the temperature. The liferaft lay to its sea anchor with the entranceway facing downwind, keeping us sheltered from spray and rain squalls. Fortunately we both had our harnesses on, so we attached them to the liferaft.

We looked over the 'assets' stashed in the liferaft: a heaving line attached to a throwing quoit, a rope-boarding ladder that we threw out the entranceway, a large plastic survival bag containing eight flares (four smoke and four parachute), plastic bags of water, blocks of food concentrate, fabric bags for bailing. Other odds and ends included a small penlight torch with half-flat batteries.

Both thirsty, we opened one sachet of water each, agreeing that we should have nothing to drink for the next 24 hours in order to shut down our kidneys. If we were not found for some time, our craving for water would not be so strong.

The liferaft canopy flapped and thrummed as the wind tore at it. The continuous roaring of the waves breaking on the crests of the swells reminded me of the surf at Muriwai beach on the west coast where I used to be a lifeguard. As each swell raced past the liferaft, its breaking crest threatened to capsize us.

Inevitably, a breaking wave hit hard, turning us upside down.

Brian tumbled out through the entranceway while I managed to stay inside lying on the canopy that had now become the floor. Brian was trapped outside while I was trapped inside. He tried to pull the liferaft over, while

I moved my weight around attempting to change the centre of gravity. It was impossible.

'Try and swim the liferaft around so that the wind and waves help roll it over,' I yelled. Brian swam the liferaft around and pulled himself up onto the downwind edge. Gripping the stabilizing pockets attached to the underside, he pulled on the liferaft. Slowly it started to roll upright. Inside I threw my weight against the now vertical floor and with a crash the wind did the rest.

Brian's head appeared at the entranceway, coughing up water and gasping for air. When the liferaft rolled upright it had fallen on top of him, the attached lines momentarily trapping him underneath.

'Help me!' Brian gasped. 'I've swallowed half the ocean.'

With my one good arm I helped pull Brian into the liferaft. He lay there coughing. 'God, I'm cold,' he said. 'I don't think I could do that again.'

We sorted out the tangle of tethers, throwing line, rope ladder, drogue, supply bag. I checked the EPIRB. It was steadily blinking out its reassuring alert to the rescue authorities. I imagined the resources being mobilised to rescue us.

'Hold on!' I said to Brian. 'Search and Rescue will be doing everything they can.'

We had activated the Argos beacon at 0945. The prime purpose of the beacon was to track the progress of the competitors for the race committee. The beacon sent a position to a satellite, which downloaded the information when it was in range of the French receiving station. The information received was typically about four to six hours after the beacon's position report.

There was also no homing capability to the beacon. For mayday alerts our intention had been to rely on triggering our 406 beacon, guaranteeing detection within twenty minutes at the nearest Land User Terminal (located in Wellington). The transmitted information included the name of the vessel, crew names and numbers, and most importantly, a homing signal for Search and Rescue aircraft.

Unfortunately this beacon was now lying on the bottom of the Tasman Sea along with *Hornet*. I knew that even without the 406 EPIRB our situation was not hopeless. The positions transmitted by our beacon would give Search and Rescue our drift. By dead reckoning, a fairly tight search area could be determined. Our rescue would only take a bit longer.

Sorting out the tangle after the liferaft capsize, we realised that about half of our emergency supplies had been lost. This included half of the flares, which we'd been examining when the breaking wave had hit. I found one jammed in the canopy but four had disappeared: a severe blow. With nowhere to stow them safely, I stuffed the remaining four flares inside my wet weather top.

The waves generated by the storm were still thundering past our liferaft. At the top of the passing swells, we could see an unending seascape of crescent-shaped waves remarkably reminiscent of sand dunes being pushed before the wind.

With the approaching roar of another huge wave, we braced ourselves. It flipped us easily as a cockleshell. We both swam the liferaft around to face downwind, and using the wind and waves, this time righted the liferaft with relative ease. Climbing back in, I discovered that all of the flares, bar one, had disappeared from inside my jacket. *What else could go wrong?*

With the small sponges provided, we bailed desperately. I gave Brian the last flare, which he put in his jacket pocket. Leaning our weight against the impact of each wave that hit us, we were managing to stay upright.

By early afternoon we'd not yet heard any sign of searching aircraft. Optimistically I'd hoped rescue by helicopter was possible, as we were only about one hour's flying time from the Australian coast. We constantly checked the EPIRB. The steadily blinking light showed us that it was still transmitting a signal. It was hard not to let a seed of doubt start to cloud one's resolve.

At about 1400 hours the crest of a large wave broke directly on to the canopy. The impact collapsed the canopy and filled the raft with water, all but tipping us into the water again; the wave's force split the canopy in half, exposing us to the elements.

Surely fate had no more misfortune to deal us? Exposure had now become a serious threat. We bailed the raft out yet again. The wind was *cold*. Brian made holes in the fabric of the canopy. Salvaging cord from the entranceway door, we threaded half of the torn fabric to the inflatable ridgepole to form a crude but effective bivouac. This gave us immediate protection from the direct effect of the wind. The other half of the canopy we pulled over our legs to try and trap some body heat.

The afternoon wore on. Still no sign of an aircraft searching for us. Surely any moment now we would hear the drone of engine noise as an aircraft flew its search pattern?

Dusk was approaching. Again a large breaking wave capsized us. In what now seemed a well-practised routine we soon had the liferaft upright and both of us back inside. Each swim, however, sapped body heat. Brian was shivering violently as we huddled together, trying to conserve body heat. It looked as if we were going to spend a cold night adrift unless Search and Rescue found us soon. The possibility of more capsizes through the night was not something I was looking forward to.

·Perhaps it was wishful thinking but the wind did seem to be dropping. If correct, we would probably survive the night without getting tipped over again. My fear was that if the weather conditions deteriorated, how would Brian cope with the cold, and how would I handle getting him back into the liferaft with only one effective arm?

While I sat there thinking about the long night ahead, we were startled by the appearance of a large black petrel. It hovered right in front of us, then deftly landed on the buoyancy chamber of the raft, right at our feet. Using its wings to maintain balance, it tried to move into the raft and let out a squawk when we waved it away. I'm sure the bird was only seeking rest for a while but Brian voiced both our thoughts. 'I'm buggered if I'm becoming its meal tonight.'

Darkness fell. We were not being hit so hard by waves and when they did they only partially filled the raft. We were kept busy continuously bailing with the two sponges.

At about 2030 hours we heard the faint drone of an aircraft to the west. It faded, then returned, each time coming closer, confirming that our distress beacon had been picked up. Our spirits soared. All we had to do was hang on till daylight.

Closer and closer the searching aircraft came. We marshalled our resources: one flare, and one penlight torch with a weak battery. We determined not to send off the flare until the pilot was flying straight at us. We would only get one shot at attracting his attention.

The aircraft flew its search pattern exasperatingly back and forth down wind from us. We could see navigation lights, but it was too far away to risk our only flare. Finally the searching aircraft moved towards us. This was it.

I waved the torch that looked about as bright as a glow-worm, while Brian readied the flare. 'Now,' I cried.

Nothing happened. Brian yelled in frustration, 'The metal trigger's come off. I can't get it back on.'

The plane disappeared behind us. Our spirits sank to rock bottom. How could the crew find us in the darkness, in these conditions? The aircraft flew past us again. Brian waved the torch. I held up a crumpled piece of tinfoil as a crude radar reflector.

Twice more the plane flew very close to our position as if it could see something, but was not absolutely certain of what it could see. Finally they flew directly at us, very low. They turned on their landing lights and waggled their wings. It seemed as if they were trying to provoke some signal from us, but all we had was the feeble glow from the torch. They then circled some distance down wind and for the rest of the night we could hear it. Sometimes close, other times in the far distance. We learnt later that the pilot had seen the faint glow and thought it was a masthead light.

Brian and I speculated on our situation. It seemed we had been located, judging by the action of the aircraft. But why did they not return to our position from time to time? We bailed and talked about everything and anything throughout the night, trying to keep warm by keeping as much water out as possible.

At Search and Rescue headquarters in Canberra, the first notification of our distress was advice from the French at about 1400 hours that an emergency signal had been activated. The Australian Search and Rescue (AusSAR) contacted race headquarters in Melbourne, who advised that a radio sked was scheduled for 1630 hrs. Depending on the outcome of the radio sked, a decision to proceed with a full alert would be made.

After unsuccessfully trying to raise us by SSB and requesting other yachts to try and raise us on VHF, a mayday alert was declared. Local pilots were given our latest beacon positions and calculation of our drift. Any vessel within six hours steaming was asked to respond. The coastal patrol boat HMAS *Warrnambool* responded, advising they could be in our area within twelve hours. The Search and Rescue machine had been set in motion.

All of this was unknown to us, of course. But we believed that all possible efforts would be made. All we had to do was hang on. After a long sleepless night, at about 0515 hours, the faintest lightening of the darkness showed dawn on its way. No sunrise was anticipated more eagerly.

We realised that we could no longer hear the aircraft that had kept our hopes alive all night. God, they have lost us! Surely they must know our position? The hopes of a quick rescue faded away. We felt very lonely, powerless to do anything to help our rescuers. Spontaneously bursting into song, we sang every piece of classical opera we knew to try and warm ourselves up. We settled in for a long wait.

At 0700 hours we saw an Australian Aerial Patrol SAR aircraft heading for us. They were still looking. The Partenavia flew slightly to the west of us, and then we lost sight of it. Suddenly its engine note changed as it banked and returned. They had spotted us. As they flew into sight they let off a siren, turned their landing lights on and waggled their wings.

Now we could truly believe that we would make it home alive. We both screamed and waved at the plane. We could be in Sydney in the next couple of hours. Surely a rescue chopper was already on its way?

About thirty minutes later, I said to Brian 'I'm sure I just heard voices.'

'Don't be bloody stupid,' he replied.

I pulled down one corner of the makeshift cover we'd erected and there, about 500 metres upwind, rolling wildly in the seas, was the coastal patrol boat HMAS *Warrnambool*. Commander Mark Shelvey had pushed the *Warrnambool* to the limit throughout the night. In the mad dash two crew members had been injured and the boat had also suffered damage. Eventually he was forced to reduce speed to twenty knots. The vessel was well outside her operational limits and in extreme danger.

On deck the crew were preparing a scramble net over the port side. There were two remaining problems. How were they going to get alongside without running us over? Second, how was I going to get up the side of the ship with only one arm?

I didn't have much time to dwell on the danger. With perfect judgement HMAS *Warnambool* drifted beam on. We drifted towards the stern but with a roar of engines in reverse *Warnambool* positioned herself with us amidships. A crew member threw a heaving line. Brian caught it while I fended off with my good arm. *Warnambool* was rolling so much that one minute we were at her guardrail, the next, her bilge strake would rise past, threatening to tip us over.

'Climb up,' a rating shouted.

'I can't, I've injured my arm,' I shouted back.

'O.K. slip this over yourself.' A rescue strop was lowered to me. As I knelt with my arms raised, I remembered to release my lifeline from the raft. I worked the strop over my arms and under clenched armpits. 'Go,' I screamed and fairly flew up the side as four seamen hauled me up to grab the guardrail. Willing hands held me and helped me over the rail, on to the deck. I looked back down at Brian still in the liferaft. 'We must get him up. Don't leave him, we must save him.' I was sobbing with relief and worried about Brian not making it aboard after all we had been through together.

'Get below, we'll get him. You're in the way here,' someone said brusquely.

They were right, of course. With a seaman helping, I soon reached the comfort of the wardroom and sat down heavily on a settee. The medic prepared to cut off my wet weather gear.

Then the door opened and Brian appeared.

'My God, were we pleased to see you guys,' he said to the medic.

That's putting it mildly, I thought.

Gordon Mann